Memory:

Systems, Process, or Function?

DEBATES IN PSYCHOLOGY

Series editor Dianne C. Berry
Series advisor Lawrence Weiskrantz

Martin Conway (ed.) Recovered Memories and False Memories

Dianne C. Berry (ed.) How Implicit Is Implicit Learning?

Jonathan K. Foster and Marko Jelicic (ed.) Memory: Systems, Process, or Function?

Memory: Systems, Process, or Function?

Edited by

JONATHAN K. FOSTER

and

MARKO JELICIC

OXFORD
UNIVERSITY PRESS
1999

OXFORD
UNIVERSITY PRESS

Great Clarendon Street, Oxford OX2 6DP
Oxford University Press is a department of the University of Oxford
and furthers the University's aim of excellence in research, scholarship,
and education by publishing worldwide in

Oxford New York
Athens Auckland Bangkok Bogotá Buenos Aires Calcutta
Cape Town Chennai Dar es Salaam Delhi Florence Hong Kong Istanbul
Karachi Kuala Lumpur Madrid Melbourne Mexico City Mumbai
Nairobi Paris São Paulo Singapore Taipei Tokyo Toronto Warsaw
and associated companies in Berlin Ibadan

Oxford is a trade mark of Oxford University Press

Published in the United States
by Oxford University Press Inc., New York

© Oxford University Press 1999

The moral rights of the author have been asserted

First published 1999

All rights reserved. No part of this publication may be
reproduced, stored in a retrieval system, or transmitted, in any
form or by any means, without the prior permission in writing of Oxford
University Press. Within the UK, exceptions are allowed in respect of any
fair dealing for the purpose of research or private study, or criticism or
review, as permitted under the Copyright, Designs and Patents Act, 1988, or
in the case of reprographic reproduction in accordance with the terms of
licences issued by the Copyright Licensing Agency. Enquiries concerning
reproduction outside these terms and in other countries should be sent to
the Rights Department, Oxford University Press, at the address above.

This book is sold subject to the condition that it shall not,
by way of trade or otherwise, be lent, re-sold, hired out, or otherwise
circulated without the publisher's prior consent in any form of binding
or cover other than that in which it is published and without a similar
condition including this condition being imposed
on the subsequent purchaser.

British Library Cataloguing Publication Data
Data available

Library of Congress Cataloging in Publication Data
Memory: systems, process, or fuction? / edited by
Jonathan K. Foster and Marko Jelicic.
(Debates in psychology)
Includes bibliographical references and index.
1. Memory. 2. Cognitive neuroscience. I. Foster, Jonathan K.
II. Jelicic, M. (Marko) III. Series.
QP406.M47   1999   612.8'2—dc21   98-34162

ISBN 0 19 852407 2 (Hbk)
0 19 852406 4 (Pbk)

1 3 5 7 9 10 8 6 4 2

Typeset in Times New Roman
by Alliance Phototypesetters, Pondicherry
Printed in Great Britain
on acid-free paper by
Biddles Ltd, Guilford and King's Lynn

For Nick, George, Ruby, and Hal

Preface

It is ironic (or perhaps appropriate) that a book about memory should have begun with an act of forgetting. When JKF paid a return visit to the Rotman Research Institute (RRI) in Toronto in March 1994 in order to attend the Institute's annual conference, he tried to make the most of the time away from the stresses of modern British academic life by catching up on a little research within the intellectual oasis of the RRI. During this time, he spent a few days sharing an office with fellow displaced European MJ.

Unfortunately, when JKF returned to the UK, he not very cleverly left his cheque book and sundry other valuables behind in Toronto. Fortunately, MJ was there to alert JKF to this fact via e-mail, before JKF's relationship with his bank manager deteriorated yet further. Thus began a friendship which has survived the ramifications of the Maastricht treaty, the Common Agricultural Policy and the coming of the Euro, not to mention a number of fiercely contested England–Holland encounters on the football (i.e. soccer, to our North American readers) pitch.

As we exchanged e-mail messages through 1994 and 1995, the idea of this book germinated and grew. In summer 1995, we approached potential chapter authors. As for our brief, we decided to issue authors with general guidelines rather than Stalinist directives, in order that a broad range of freely expressed academic opinions were presented. Finally, by the end of 1997, all the 'target chapters' were in. Alan Parkin then proceeded to put the rest of us to shame by turning around his summary chapter, which concludes the book, in under six weeks.

What, then, was the motivation for this book? As we approach the millennium, some of the central, albeit very ambitious, theoretical questions which we were interested in addressing were as follows. How is the organization and functioning of long-term memory currently conceptualized by leading theoreticians in the field? Where differences in outlook exist, is any form of synthesis possible between diverging viewpoints, especially between those researchers embracing what may be broadly regarded as 'memory as systems' and 'memory as processing' frameworks? If not, is a resolution to these questions feasible, or will it never be achieved?

Given the vast quantity and range of knowledge which is represented within the long-term memory store, it may seem counter-intuitive to suggest that all information is stored in the same way. On the other hand, applying Occam's razor, is a unitary, processing, or functional memory framework not preferable to the leporine fecundity of memory systems (just how many memory systems are there in 1999)? However, if we embrace such a viewpoint, how do we account for anecdotal observations and scientific reports that certain individuals have better memories for some types of information (short-term, long-term; names, faces; auditory, visual) than for others, implying distinct memory capacities, or modules, within individuals?

We hope that in compiling this book, we have provided a useful forum for debate, and that the material presented may contribute towards a satisfactory resolution of at least some of these questions (notwithstanding, of course, the fact that the lifeblood of every science is a reasonable quota of disagreement and controversy!). It is our belief that book chapters are especially valuable as a medium for theoretical discussion, because they offer researchers more opportunity than is available in empirically driven papers to advance new theoretical ideas, models, and speculations. At a time when there is increasing pressure to publish in high-impact, peer-reviewed journals over almost all other forms of scholarly output, and when the only other acceptable form of academic activity appears to be the submitting of grant applications, we also hope that the book will serve as a catalyst for future thinking, and will act as a framework around which researchers may be able to structure their theorizing about the organization and functioning of long-term memory. We would like to thank all the distinguished contributors to this volume for helping us to try to meet these goals.

We would also like to express our gratitude to Professor Don Stuss, Director of the Rotman Research Institute, for providing the fertile intellectual and congenial social atmosphere in which we first met, and which subsequently permitted the idea of this book to ferment. The environment provided by the Institute is reflected not only by the coming together of the two Editors, but also by the fact that four of the contributors (Anne-Marie Ergis, Jeff Toth, Endel Tulving, and Gordon Winocur) are also present or past members of the Institute.

We would also like to thank the editorial, production, and marketing team at Oxford University Press, for helping to bring the original idea of this book to fruition. Without OUP's willingness to back two unknown editorial quantities, this book would never have appeared. We also thank Martin Conway, who initially suggested that a new Oxford University Press book series would present a suitable medium for our proposed volume. We are grateful to Peter Meudell and anonymous referees for their feedback on the introductory chapter, and on the original book proposal, respectively. We are indebted to Katharine Reeve and Jane Hammond Foster for editorial help and advice. Finally, we would like to thank our families for tolerating our neglect of them during the preparation of this volume.

Jonathan Foster was the Rotman Research Institute Postdoctoral Fellow 1990–92. He was also funded by an Royal Society/NATO Postdoctoral Fellowship in Biological Sciences. He is now Lecturer in Neuropsychology at the University of Manchester. Marko Jelicic was the Baycrest Women's Auxiliary Alzheimer Research Fellow 1993–95. He is now Lecturer in the Department of Psychiatry and Neuropsychology, University of Maastricht.

J. K. F.
M. J.

February 1998

Contents

List of contributors	xi
1 Memory structures, procedures, and processes JONATHAN K. FOSTER AND MARKO JELICIC	1
2 Study of memory: processes and systems ENDEL TULVING	11
3 Components of processing HENRY L. ROEDIGER III, RANDY L. BUCKNER, AND KATHLEEN B. MCDERMOTT	31
4 Functional dissociation of brain regions in learning and memory: evidence for multiple systems ROBERT M. MCDONALD, ANNE-MARIE ERGIS, AND GORDON WINOCUR	66
5 Combining disruption and activation techniques to map conceptual and perceptual memory processes in the human brain TERESA A. BLAXTON	104
6 How does the brain mediate our ability to remember? ANDREW R. MAYES	130
7 The memory chop shop: issues in the search for memory systems MARY SUSAN WELDON	162
8 The architecture of human memory JOHN D. E. GABRIELI	205
9 Not one versus many, but zero versus any: structure and function in the context of the multiple memory systems debate JEFFREY P. TOTH AND R. REED HUNT	232
10 Component processes versus systems: is there really an important difference? ALAN J. PARKIN	273
Index	289

Contributors

Teresa A. Blaxton National Institutes of Health, Building 10 (Room 5C205), Bethesda, Maryland 20892, USA.

Randy L. Buckner Department of Psychology, Box 1125, Washington University, One Brookings Drive, St Louis, MO 63130-4899, USA.

Anne-Marie Ergis Rotman Research Institute, Baycrest Centre for Geriatric Care, 3560 Bathurst Street, Toronto, Ontario, Canada M6C 2J4. (Also at the Centre Paul Broca, Institut de la Sante et de la Recherche Medicale, Paris, France.)

Jonathan K. Foster Department of Psychology, University of Manchester, Oxford Road, Manchester M13 9PL.

John D. E. Gabrieli Department of Psychology, Stanford University, Stanford, CA 94305, USA.

R. Reed Hunt Department of Psychology, University of North Carolina, Greensboro, North Carolina 27412, USA.

Marko Jelicic Department of Psychiatry and Neuropsychology, University of Maastricht, Maastrich, The Netherlands.

Andrew R. Mayes Department of Clinical Neurology, Royal Hallamshire Hospital, Glossop Road, University of Sheffield, Sheffield S10 2JF, UK.

Kathleen B. McDermott Department of Psychology, Box 1125, Washington University, One Brookings Drive, St Louis, MO 63130-4899, USA.

Robert M. McDonald Department of Psychology, University of Toronto, Toronto, Ontario M55 1A1, Canada.

Alan J. Parkin Laboratory of Experimental Psychology, University of Sussex, Brighton BN1 9QG, UK.

Henry L. Roediger III Department of Psychology, Box 1125, Washington University, One Brookings Drive, St Louis, MO 63130-4899, USA.

Jeffrey P. Toth School of Psychology, Georgia Institute of Technology, Atlanta, GA 30332, USA.

Endel Tulving Rotman Research Institute, Baycrest Centre for Geriatric Care, 3560 Bathurst Street, Toronto, Ontario, M6A 2E1, Canada. (Also at Department of Psychology, Box 1125, Washington University, St Louis, MO 63130-4899, USA.)

Mary Susan Weldon Department of Psychology, Social Sciences II, University of California, Santa Cruz, California 95064, USA.

Gordon Winocur Rotman Research Institute, Baycrest Centre for Geriatric Care, 3560 Bathurst Street, Toronto, Ontario, M6A 2E1, Canada.

1
Memory structures, procedures, and processes

JONATHAN K. FOSTER AND MARKO JELICIC

Memory represents a key psychological process. It allows us to recall things from the past which may have taken place hours, days, months, or even many years ago. Our memories are intrinsically personal, subjective, and internal, yet without the primary capacity of memory, other important activities such as speech, perception, concept formation, and reasoning would be impossible. The range of different aspects of memory is large, extending from our vocabulary and knowledge about language and the world to our personal histories, skills such as walking and talking, and the more simple memory capacities (such as habituation and sensitization) found in lower animals. Amongst the diversity of memory processes, the principal focus in this volume is the long-term representation of complex associative human memory. This refers to the permanently stored representation of individual items and events. We present here a debate about the cognitive architecture of the human long-term memory system. The individual chapter authors represent some of the leading researchers and theorists in the field. Each chapter concentrates upon the central theoretical question of how long-term memory can best be conceptualized. In particular, is long-term memory best regarded as comprising multiple independent systems (each with distinct properties and attributes), as a processing framework which can be tapped via different levels of processing, or as a complex function which can be used in a flexible and task-appropriate manner? The authors of each chapter present their answers to this and related research questions. The book concludes with a synopsis and appraisal of the different facets of this intriguing debate.

THEORETICAL VIEWS OF MEMORY: A BRIEF HISTORY

Over the past two or three millennia, several different views of how memory is represented and organized have been proposed. Plato regarded memory as being like a wax tablet, in which impressions would be encoded, stored, and later retrieved. This trichotomy between registration, retention, and retrieval was also discussed in classical times by likening memories to birds in an aviary or books in a library. These classical metaphors all underlined the distinction between inaccessibility and unavailability of long-term memories, the former referring to information which is held in memory but which cannot be accessed, while the latter refers to information which is not held in memory at all. In the Middle Ages, it was thought that memories were subserved by the cerebrospinal fluid of the brain's ventricular system. Later, Descartes postulated that memory, together with other psychological capacities, was subserved by the pineal gland (the source of the 'animal spirits'). More recently, the empirical approach to memory was initiated by Hermann Ebbinghaus (1885), who wrote an influential monograph which marked the beginning of modern-day research into complex human memory. Ebbinghaus adopted the position that human memory could not be examined scientifically unless extraneous individual factors were first eliminated. He therefore developed a methodology in which repeated nonsense syllables were used as target stimuli. Later, Frederick Bartlett (1932), using more naturalistic materials, placed greater emphasis on the significance of meaning and different learning strategies in the functioning of memory than upon the kind of rigorous methodological control which was central to the Ebbinghaus tradition. Bartlett believed that effort after meaning was crucial for the registration and retrieval of real-world information into and from long-term memory, and focused upon memory for more ecologically valid materials. From a neurobiological perspective, Karl Lashley (1950) investigated the effects of surgical lesions of the brain on memory in non-human animals. Lashley observed a gross correlation between the total amount of brain tissue destroyed and the degree of memory impairment. His findings indicated the neural representation of memory (the 'engram') was highly distributed, and no one particular brain site could be identified as the locus of a specific memory.

Since the pioneering work of Ebbinghaus, many researchers have been exercised by the question of how many different memory systems exist. Indeed, the debate between the multiple systems and processing frameworks presented in this volume is foreshadowed by several previous debates in the empirical memory literature. Thus, many psychological models of memory make a distinction between short-term (or primary) and long-term (or secondary) memory stores or systems (for example James 1890; Atkinson and Shiffrin 1968). Short-term memory is related to the transient contents of conscious mental activity (with one influential view specifying the limit of this store as 7±2 items), while long-term memory is conceived as a larger memory store containing items which have already faded from consciousness. Evidence for this distinction comes from both the study of neurologically intact experimental subjects and the investigation of individuals rendered amnesic following the occurrence of brain damage. Other researchers have argued for the existence of more than these two stores (see Baddeley (1997) for a recent review). By contrast, some memory theorists have argued for the abandonment of the concept of short-term and long-term memory stores in favour of a more operationally based perspective (Craik and Lockhart 1972). Nevertheless, the distinction between short- and long-term memory stores continues to have many uses and adherents.

LONG-TERM MEMORY AND AMNESIA

As already noted, the term 'memory' can refer to numerous different kinds of remembering and types of knowledge. In this book, we will be dealing with information which is retained in long-term or secondary memory, also referred to by some authors as the permanent memory store. This memory store spans a period from a few minutes to a lifetime. It includes such activities as remembering which film you saw at the cinema the previous evening, the last time you saw a particular relative or friend, or the name of the world's tallest mountain. Within this system, evidence from amnesic subjects has proven particularly informative in determining the organization and operating principles of memory. Thus, amnesic individuals, such as the patient HM (Milner 1954), have profound memory loss for events which occurred after their brain damage (i.e. they manifest a severe *anterograde amnesia*), but relatively better preserved memory for events which took place before the occurrence of the brain damage (i.e. their *retrograde amnesia* is typically less severe). Amnesics also typically have preserved functions in other psychological domains; for example intelligence, perception, language, and motor functions. Importantly for theoretical views of long-term memory organization, amnesics continue to be able to learn specific types of new information, such as perceptual and motor skills. For present purposes, the central questions concern the detailed nature of the memory impairment manifested by amnesics, and the implications which the pattern of preserved and impaired performance has for theoretical accounts of long-term memory.

LONG-TERM MEMORY: SYSTEMS VERSUS PROCESSES

Over the past two decades, the field of memory research has grown tremendously. This rapid expansion has been reflected in an increasing number of views of the organization of human long-term memory. Although undoubtedly numerous, these varied viewpoints may be divided into two broad camps: the first characterizing memory structurally, i.e. as comprising multiple, different, empirically separable components or systems, and the second conceptualizing memory more in functional terms, as a common, and, some would argue, unitary and indivisible processing framework.

Most neuropsychologists studying individuals with (more or less) circumscribed brain lesions tend to think (sometimes overtly, but more often tacitly) in terms of memory being organized into distinct 'systems'. One corollary of this viewpoint is the characterization of amnesia in terms of intact versus impaired long-term memory systems. By contrast, most cognitive psychologists tend to embrace a 'processing' view of the operating characteristics of human memory, in which memory is conceptualized holistically. According to this viewpoint, the important dimensions of memory cross the boundaries proposed by systems theorists. Thus, while the systems view emphasizes separate neural systems mediating different aspects of mnemonic functioning (e.g. implicit/explicit, episodic/semantic, procedural/ declarative), the processing perspective focuses upon the differential mental operations in which individuals engage when confronted by a specific memory task (e.g. deep/shallow processing, conceptual/perceptual processing).

Systems-oriented neuropsychologists have tended to use dissociations between intact versus impaired memory systems following brain damage in order to characterize the organization of long-term memory. Amnesia is therefore viewed by systems theorists as a condition in which one is capable of performing certain memory tasks while failing in others, according to the precise characteristics of the structural memory impairment incurred. Over the past three or four decades, a wealth of putative explanatory dichotomies have been presented by neuropsychologists studying memory and amnesia. Specific distinctions in the memory and amnesia literatures have evolved from being temporally based (short-term versus long-term memory) to being based upon the information requirement of the task in question (semantic versus episodic memory), or on the ability to verbalize task requirements (procedural versus declarative memory). According to another dichotomy, the performance of amnesic patients on implicit (or indirect) memory tasks is considered to be preserved, but their performance on explicit (or direct) memory tasks is judged to be impaired.

Cognitive psychologists, the majority of whom tend to subscribe to the processing framework, have instead emphasized the common functional characteristics which may underlie putatively distinct memory systems. These researchers have argued that the categories proposed by systems theorists do not meet the criteria for separable memory systems. Rather, they argue that memory for an event depends upon the degree of overlap between those encoding operations engaged in during learning and the retrieval processes induced at test. Applying this approach to disordered memory, it has been suggested that not all the preserved and impaired abilities of amnesic individuals can be compartmentalized according to memory systems frameworks. Processing theorists argue that, even within paradigms which were thought by systems theorists to be mediated by one isolated system, amnesic abilities may show both preserved and impaired components. According to the processing framework, amnesics show preserved data-driven or automatic processing, but impaired conceptually driven or controlled processing, irrespective of the proposed memory system being tapped. In other words, processing theorists argue that not all procedural (or implicit, or semantic) elements of memory are intact, nor all declarative (or explicit, or episodic) elements impaired in amnesia. Rather, the strong processing view regards the nature of the cognitive processing (i.e. data-driven versus conceptually driven, automatic versus controlled) as the critical, orthogonal factor underlying the constellation of findings obtained in memory experiments. However, the polar dimensions of the processing framework have, in turn, been investigated and challenged by neuropsychologists subscribing to the memory systems framework.

THE DEBATE

Theoretical offensives and counter-offensives have been mounted by proponents of both the systems and processing frameworks. However, researchers subscribing to these opposing viewpoints have generally published in separate journals and attended (more or less) distinct sets of academic meetings. There has, historically, been relatively little opportunity for a frank exchange of views on this and related theoretical issues. In editing this book, we have aimed to present a range of opinions on how best to characterize memory function and dysfunction, and have taken as our starting point the historical disagreements between systems and processing theorists. We here present contributions from a cross section of memory theorists, half of whom fall broadly into the 'systems' school of memory theorists (Tulving; McDonald, Ergis, and Winocur; Mayes; Gabrieli), the other half of whom have in the past broadly aligned themselves with the 'processing' framework (Roediger, Buckner, and McDermott; Weldon; Blaxton; Toth and Hunt). Finally, a chapter appraising the pros and cons of the different authors' theoretical positions is presented by Alan Parkin.

'SYSTEMS' THEORISTS

In his chapter, Endel Tulving first presents the view that there is no logical conflict between the processing and systems frameworks, but, rather, that the two are complementary. He argues that the real controversy concerns the existence of unitary versus multiple long-term memory systems. Tulving proceeds with a contrasting account of what he refers to as the cognitive (i.e. process oriented) and neurocognitive (i.e. systems oriented) approaches to the study of memory. He presents a brief description of the unitary and multiple memory systems frameworks, and contrasts remembered events with acquired knowledge. Tulving briefly discusses different memory systems, before concluding with a personal, historical account of how he was 'converted' from an ardent belief in memory as a unitary system to his current thinking in terms of separate, dissociable memory systems. Tulving concludes that the conflict between the unitary and multiple systems perspectives is a passing fad, with the future belonging to the multiple systems framework. He invites all cognitive theorists to renounce their unitarian faith and instead engage upon the quest for a fuller understanding of multiple memory systems.

In their chapter, Robert McDonald, Anne-Marie Ergis, and Gordon Winocur present an account of multiple memory systems in terms of functional dissociations within brain systems. Data from both the human and non-human literatures are considered. The framework which these authors adopt is one of diverse associative and memory functions mediated by separate structures (including the hippocampus, amygdala, prefrontal cortex, thalamus, and basal ganglia). Together, it is argued that these regions comprise an array of integrated yet functionally dissociable neural circuits. Drawing predominantly on findings using the lesion methodology, McDonald *et al.* argue that memory should not be regarded as a unitary process. By contrast, they present evidence that, within the brain's complex organization, differentiated structures can be implicated in subserving specific components of learning and memory, and that these functions can be dissociated using sensitive behavioural paradigms. In the opinion of the authors, the empirical evidence suggests a hierarchical organization, with certain structures (dorsomedial thalamus, prefrontal cortex) being involved in the mediation of broadly based functions which are necessary for many different types of learning and memory, whereas other structures, such as the hippocampus, amygdala, and caudate nucleus, are identified with more specialized functions. They conclude by specifying some of the challenges which remain; for example, in specifying the functional significance of other brain regions which are known to be involved in learning and memory, in considering the functional relationships within important brain regions, and in exploring the relationships between different brain regions and the component processes of memory which they mediate.

Andrew Mayes argues that different types of memory, which are dependent upon brain regions with very different anatomical organizations, are likely to rely upon different kinds of encoding, storage, and retrieval processes. Methods of distinguishing between different memory systems and processes are considered. These criteria are then used by Mayes to interpret the ways in which different kinds of memory are mediated. He argues that the brain is a plastic system, and as it processes information it also stores that information by modifying the connectivity of at least some of the same neurons which originally represent the processed information. As different types of information are represented by different brain regions, memory for those kinds of information should also be mediated by those brain regions. Functional, neuropsychological and other kinds of double dissociation should, therefore, be found between tests of memory for different kinds of information. Mayes argues that, by focusing on the goal of locating the brain regions which represent stored representations for qualitatively different kinds of memory information, and on quantifying the number of different memory systems, we run the risk of neglecting other important questions, such as whether any processes are optionally used to retrieve the same kinds of memory, and whether physiological storage processes (used by neurons to hold information for different periods of time) are different for different kinds of information. Mayes highlights the importance of identifying the kinds of processes (probably through clarifying the concept of process) which mediate memory for different kinds of mnemonic information. This may enable us to develop tight criteria, rather than simply loose guidelines, for distinguishing between different kinds of memory processes. He presents a framework of four kinds of process or mechanism underlying long-term memory which, he argues, offers a processing approach to questions about putatively different kinds of memory system.

In his chapter, John Gabrieli reviews recent empirical evidence which bears upon the opposition between the multiple systems and single system (i.e. 'processing') frameworks. He concludes that (1) the systems view provides a more accurate account of memory failure in amnesia, and can account for the perceptual/ conceptual dissociations central to the 'processing' account; and (2) more useful than either dichotomous approach is one that defines a memory system as a specific neural network which mediates a particular mnemonic process. He argues that there are now many points of theoretical consensus and convergence among processing and systems researchers. However, there may be a remaining intellectual tension concerning the important issue of how human memory should best be investigated: whereas most cognitive psychologists investigate human memory through behavioural experiments on healthy, young subjects, neuropsychological sources of evidence instead focus on the study of brain-damaged individuals or upon brain imaging studies. Gabrieli argues that neuropsychological investigations of this type offer valuable sources of constraining data for cognitive psychologists continuing to perform their traditional forms of behavioural investigation. He contends that memory research has entered a new era, in which equal weight should be given to the neuropsychological and cognitive perspectives in seeking to comprehend more fully the workings of human long-term memory.

'PROCESSING' THEORISTS

Henry Roediger (a pioneer of the systems approach) and his co-authors Randy Buckner and Kathleen McDermott take an historical look at the systems/process debate, from around 1980 onwards. These authors traces the evolution of both approaches from their pre- 1980 precursors, and examine how each approach has developed since. Roediger *et al.* reflect upon the critical issues of logic and terminology, and consider the extent to which the systems and processing frameworks have blended and converged over the years, and the degree to which they have remained truly distinct. The authors argue that, by applying stringent criteria for the definition of distinct memory systems, most of the proposed systems are found wanting. Conversely, if one focuses on the methodology of converging dissociations in order to define distinct memory systems, then there is evidence for a plethora of such systems. On the other hand, examined historically, the processing theories have fared little better, as specific predictions of the processing frameworks have been found wanting. Roediger *et al.* conclude by championing a component processing framework to explain the workings of human memory. They argue that this approach takes the best from both the systems and processing frameworks, by emphasizing both the intricacies of the different cognitive processes which underlie performance on any given memory task, and the neural underpinnings of these processes.

Teresa Blaxton proposes a framework for mapping conceptual and perceptual processing onto neurological substrates. She argues that the field of functional brain mapping offers great promise for researchers interested in probing the organization of long-term memory, and for mapping memory functions onto brain structures. However, she urges researchers to establish high methodological standards when using each of the available array of modern brain imaging tools, and emphasizes the importance of converging data obtained from a variety of experimental techniques. Blaxton contends that in verbal memory paradigms conceptual processing is subserved by left mesial and temporal lobe structures, together with left inferior frontal cortex. She further argues that perceptual processes are subserved by the sensory regions engaged during the initial perception of the stimuli at encoding. Experimental findings from brain activation and stimulation studies are presented, together with data obtained from experiments testing memory-impaired patients with unilateral temporal lobe lesions. Blaxton concludes by acknowledging the irony that someone who regards herself as a processing theorist should be so concerned with the question of brain structures subserving memory. She argues that both the conceptual/perceptual distinction made by processing theorists and the implicit/explicit distinction made by systems theorists are valid, and that both frameworks are needed in order to account for the totality of findings in the memory literature.

Mary Sue Weldon first examines the issue of what exactly constitutes a system. She argues that without an operational definition of a system, it is problematic to decide whether memory comprises different subsystems, much less their precise number. In confronting the question of definition, Weldon also reflects upon the concept of a system in other sciences and academic disciplines. She raises the question of whether it is appropriate to extrapolate from studies of impaired memory to theories of normal memory, and the extent to which one's definition of a system bear upon the validity of this approach. She also consider the pros and cons of two methodological approaches beloved of systems-oriented researchers, namely lesion-based studies and neuroimaging experiments. Weldon challenges the view that the best alternative to a unitary view of long-term memory is represented by the notion that memory comprises multiple anatomically and functionally distinct systems. Further, she argues that, in the fevered search for more memory systems, several fundamental issues are being overlooked; for example, the issues of how best to define a system, whether functional categories of description will necessarily map isomorphically onto anatomical structures, and whether anatomy presents the most appropriate neurobiological characteristic through which to map specific memory mechanisms. She concludes by considering the possibility that, while some forms of memory may be mediated via dedicated neural hardware, other forms may be subserved via neural apparatus which is shared with other mental or physical functions. Again, the final emphasis is on determining the psychological component processes underlying the performance of specific memory tasks.

In their chapter, Jeffrey Toth and Reed Hunt present a 'neofunctional' account of memory. Toth and Hunt view memory as a mental function which takes place in the broad context of environmental demands and subject-determined goals, and argue that incorporation of contextual factors should form a central component of any complete account of memory. The authors accuse multiple systems theorists of participating in a form of neural Cartesianism by 'neuralizing' what are essentially psychological and behavioural events. They further argue that memory systems theorists present an account which is biologically meaningful but not psychologically meaningful. By contrast, Toth and Hunt state that the appropriate emphasis should be on mind rather than brain, arguing that every interesting memory 'system' was first identified and then elucidated at the psychological, behavioural, or functional level before its neural mediation could be investigated. They further argue that this will always be the case. These authors accept that there are important differences between the different forms of memory identified by memory systems theorists, and that at some level these different forms of memory reflect the operation of different brain processes. However, these authors challenge the notion that these different forms of memory must be considered as entirely separate and independent memory systems. Toth and Hunt's focus is, rather, on investigating how memory is integrated with other cognitive processes such as perception, attention, reasoning, and action. They advocate a complementary approach to that of the memory systems-oriented researcher, in which the similarities (rather than the differences) between different memory tasks are considered.

SYNTHESIS

The area which this book attempts to cover is controversial, and one in which a variety of viewpoints have hitherto existed. The multidisciplinary nature of memory research, together with recent research developments, offers an opportunity for a fruitful exchange of ideas between researchers who have, in the past, adopted quite different theoretical perspectives. In bringing together this collection of authors, we have sought to delineate their differences in greater detail, and to attempt to determine whether there is any potential for convergence or common ground between current theoretical viewpoints.

In the final chapter of the book, Alan Parkin draws together the various threads of the preceding discussion. In particular, he considers the degree to which each of the previous chapters considers the criteria of functional independence, stochastic independence, differing neural substrates, and functional incompatibility. These criteria are regarded as lying at the cornerstone of memory systems theory. Parkin then considers the different theoretical alternatives to memory systems which are presented in the book. Finally, he presents his opinion of the current status of the debate, and offers a considered evaluation of the range of theoretical positions put forward in the preceding chapters.

REFERENCES

Atkinson, R. C. and Shiffrin, R. M. (1968). Human memory: a proposed system and its control processes. In *The psychology of learning and motivation: advances in research and theory* (ed. K. W. Spence), Vol. II. Academic, New York.

Baddeley, A. D. (1997). *Human memory: theory and practice*. Erlbaum, Hove.
Bartlett, F. C. (1932). *Remembering*. Cambridge University Press.
Craik, F. I. M. and Lockhart, R. S. (1972). Levels of processing: a framework for memory research. *Journal of Verbal Learning and Verbal Behavior*, **11**, 671–84.
Ebbinghaus, H. (1885). *Über das Gedächtnis*. Dunker, Leipzig.
James, W. (1890). *Principles of Psychology*. Holt, New York.
Lashley, K. (1950). In search of the engram. *Society of Experimental Biology Symposium*, **4**, 454–82.
Milner, B. (1954). Intellectual function of the temporal lobes. *Psychological Bulletin*, **51**, 42–62.

2
Study of memory: processes and systems

ENDEL TULVING

A dozen or so years ago I wrote a paper under the title, 'How many memory systems are there?' It consisted of three sections. In the first I presented some pretheoretical reasons for hypothesizing the existence of multiple memory systems, in the second I described a ternary classification scheme of memory, and in the third I discussed the nature and logic of evidence for multiple systems (Tulving 1985*a*, p.385).

In the final section of the paper I observed that, 'The puzzle of memory systems is not and will not be an easy one to solve. Many difficulties have to be overcome before we can expect more rapid progress' (Tulving 1985*a*, p.395). I mentioned some of the sources of frustration there and then, and have discussed others elsewhere (Tulving 1986, 1993). One difficulty that I did not anticipate was the longlasting vehement opposition to the simple idea of multiple memory systems. Had anyone predicted at the time that ten or fifteen years later we would still be arguing about the issue, or assembling opposite views under the heading of 'single versus multiple systems of memory', as witnessed by the present volume, I would not have believed it. I too know, of course, that we scientists love to hate new ideas (Barber 1961), and that we routinely resist facts that do not fit into whatever comfortable framework we have managed to adopt or to construct. But time and time again the history of science shows that eventually all relevant facts and worthwhile ideas do get accepted. So, what is holding up the advent of multiple memory systems?

Progress, of course, has occurred. More and more cognitive students of memory seem to be willing to go as far as to accept the idea that perhaps there are indeed *two* different 'kinds' of memory. Then, faced with a number of differently labelled dichotomies—declarative versus procedural, episodic versus semantic, controlled versus automatic, conscious versus unconscious, intentional versus unintentional, explicit versus implicit, hippocampally based versus non-hippocampally based, and several others—many of them get cold feet and immediately seek safety again, this time in a dichotomy. They do it in one of two ways. Some try to figure out which of the many dichotomies is the 'right' one, on the interesting assumption that if one dichotomy is valid then all others are invalid. Others use the good old levelling treatment and force all the existing dichotomies into a single overarching dichotomy, and try to be happy with that.

Going from a unitary system to two is progress, of course, but far too timid. Even if we did not have all the facts that point to more than two memory systems we should eagerly explore the possibility that the real number is larger. Although it is true that scientists frequently begin their efforts at classification by taking a whole and dividing into just two parts, everyone knows that Nature herself abhors dichotomies as much as she abhors a vacuum.

In this chapter, the term 'multiple' in the expression 'multiple memory systems' means 'an as yet unknown number that is probably larger than four', because we already have reasons to distinguish between at least four long-term systems (Schacter and Tulving 1994). Here I explain what I mean by the expression, how the view it represents differs from the 'unitarian' view of memory, and why I think it makes a better description of nature than the single-system view.

First, however, we have to be very clear about what it is that we are debating in this volume. There happen to be two rather closely related issues, easy to confuse with each other. One of these is under scrutiny here whereas the other is not. The issue that is being discussed here has to do with single versus multiple memory systems. The related issue that is *not* being discussed has to do with memory processes versus memory systems. Unless we clearly distinguish between the two, we will be wasting a lot of time on an irrelevancy, perhaps even without realizing that we are doing so.

The idea of the opposition between 'processes' and 'systems' is a false belief. It probably came about because process-oriented students of memory have tended to line up under the banner of unitary memory and the distinction between two different issues became blurred. Thus the process-oriented unitary view of memory came to be contrasted with the multiple systems view, leading some observers into thinking that there exists a conflict of 'processes versus systems (Foster and Jelicic, Chapter 1 this volume; Masson and Graf 1993, p.5). The idea was that there are two opposing camps: (i) one whose members explain phenomena of memory in terms of processes and their interactions within the general framework of unitary memory, and (ii) another whose members eschew process-based explanations and explain phenomena of memory in terms of the operations of multiple systems. I argue in this chapter that there is no controversy between process views and systems views of memory. The controversy is about unitary versus multiple memory systems.

The remainder of this chapter is organized into three main parts. The first one spells out the differences between process-oriented versus systems-oriented approaches to the study of memory, and explains why these approaches are not, and cannot be, in conflict. The second describes and illustrates the differences between unitary versus multiple memory theories, and shows why they necessarily must be in conflict. The third describes some critical empirical findings that converted me from being a faithful unitarian to a believer in multiple memory systems. The essay concludes with the prediction that the future belongs to multiple memory systems.

COGNITIVE AND NEUROCOGNITIVE APPROACHES TO THE STUDY OF MEMORY

For a long time there was only one general orientation to the study of learning and memory in psychology. Beginning with Ebbinghaus it went through various changes, some more substantial and some less so, but its essence stayed more or less the same for almost a hundred years. Gradually, however, the study of memory expanded beyond its original boundaries, and today it is possible to think of at least two somewhat different approaches, or orientations, to the study of memory. I refer to them as 'cognitive' and 'neurocognitive.' This section of the chapter describes the two, beginning with their working definitions.

The *cognitive approach* is a psychologically inspired approach to the epistemological explanation of the mechanisms underlying cognitive processes involved in a wide variety of memory tasks, on the basis of empirical evidence obtained from controlled experiments with normal human subjects interpreted in mentalistic (information processing) terms, all aimed at the construction of theories and models of memory. Researchers within the cognitive tradition tend to stay aloof from, and frequently do not approve of, the kinds of pursuits conducted under the neurocognitive orientation.

The *neurocognitive approach* is a biologically inspired approach to the determination of the ontology and organization of functioning neurocognitive structures that comprise memory, on the basis of a wide range of empirical evidence, including studies of cognitive consequences of brain damage interpreted in reductionist terms, all aimed at a natural classification of memory. The neurocognitive approach embraces the fact of different memory processes. It also allows, and approves of, the kinds of pursuits conducted under the cognitive orientation.

These working definitions are presented in the form of two check lists in Table 2.1. The key words in the table should not be taken terribly seriously, but they do convey the general flavour of the two approaches.

Scientists who study memory from the cognitive perspective get their inspiration from watching people behave and from reading psychological accounts of behaviour, whereas those who study memory from the neurocognitive perspective get their ideas from psychology and other branches of biology. Cognitive researchers typically begin with individual observations of effects of variables and their interrelations on memory performance and then proceed to more comprehensive theories; neurocognitive researchers frequently begin with broad ideas about the

Table 2.1 Two approaches to the study of memory

Cognitive	Neurocognitive
Psychological	Biological
Epistemological	Ontological
Models; causes	Organization; classification
Explanatory	Descriptive
Predictions	No predictions
Human adults	'Higher' animals
Memory tasks	Memory systems
Mentalistic	Reductionistic
Cognitive processes	Brain/mind correlations
Behaviour	Brain lesions; neuroimaging

nature of memory and then check the validity of these ideas empirically. Cognitive research is epistemological in spirit: it seeks to understand the causes of the phenomena of interest. Conversely, neurocognitive research is ontological in spirit: it seeks to find out what memory is and how it functions. Cognitive researchers strive after explanation of phenomena in terms of mechanisms, and thrive on what are called 'predictions'; neurocognitive researchers attempt to describe what there is in nature and how it is organized, they are less keen on predictions. Like cognitive researchers, neurocognitive researchers are interested in the memory of healthy human adults, but they cast their nets much wider. In the activities of cognitive theorists memory tasks play a pivotal role; in the activities of neurocognitive theorists tasks are also important, but so are the origins, development, and the nature of the general brain/mind capability that we call memory. The orientation of the cognitive research is largely mentalistic, and its practitioners want to understand their subject matter in terms of cognitive processes; the orientation of neurocognitive research goes beyond mentalism to reductionism, and its practitioners are equally interested in understanding their subject matter in terms of the relation between cognitive and brain processes†. While cognitive theorists are perfectly happy considering only behavioural indices of memory performance, neurocognitive theorists add to behavioural indices those of neural happenings, measures derived from electrophysiological recording and functional neuroimaging.

Although the two orientations as described necessarily have fuzzy boundaries, it is not especially difficult to classify particular theorists or theories, and particular research programmes, either over historical time or at present, in terms of the two orientations. Thus, a nice prototypical illustration of the cognitive approach is that taken by Bower (1996), who describes an extension of a 'traditional memory theory' (p.27) that explains a variety of explicit and implicit memory phenomena, as well as global amnesia, without invoking multiple memory systems. A fine example of the neurocognitive approach is provided by Schacter (1992) who looks at many of the same issues as does Bower (1996). And an excellent example of an approach that fits somewhere between the two extremes is Johnson's (1993) MEM model.

Embeddedness and complementarity

The relationship between the two orientations is one of 'embeddedness': the neurocognitive approach includes but transcends the cognitive approach. It accepts the tenets and practices of the cognitive approach, and then reaches out farther. Thus, neurocognitive researchers accept the idea that memory phenomena can be explained in terms of psychologically conceived mechanisms or processes, and that

† Because of the explosive reaction that the term 'reductionism' frequently causes in the souls of many cognitive psychologists, let me hasten to say here that the 'reductionism' in the present context is benign. It is best thought of as what Bunge and Ardila (1987, p.52) refer to as 'ontological reductionism,' that is, an acknowledgement of the fact that the mind exists by virtue of emergent properties of the brain. 'Mentalistic' in Table 2.1 may also look suspicious, but should be taken in the sense of 'scientific mentalism' (Bunge and Ardila 1987, p.52).

it is possible to construct purely psychological theories of memory. Neurocognitive researchers make a great deal use of the data collected by cognitive researchers, even if they sometimes use the data for different purposes. But neurocognitive 'types' also believe that there is more to the study of memory than what the cognitive researchers are interested in. They take for granted that memory phenomena can be explained in a number of ways—cognitively, developmentally, in light of the evolution, and in terms of underlying physiological mechanisms—and that these different accounts are complementary rather than competing. They take it as a self-evident truth that useful lessons for understanding memory can be learned from work with children, or non-human animals, or brain-damaged neurological patients, or people under the influence of psychoactive drugs. Finally they believe that it is possible and worthwhile to construct theories, although they also ask whether the theories are true.

The points I have made illustrate what I mean by the relation of embeddedness between the two approaches. In terms of the listing of the properties of the two in Table 2.1, we can say that whereas the cognitive approach can be sketched in terms of the key words in the left-hand column, the neurocognitive approach is characterized by the entries in *both* columns.

Considering objectively the relationship between the two approaches, one should find it easy to conclude that they are complementary (Hayman and Tulving 1989; Schacter 1992). Either approach would be impoverished without the other, each adds value to the other, and the two orientations together point to a more powerful and more promising direction in which to seek understanding of memory than either one could accomplish alone. This is why eventually the two orientations can be expected to merge into one (Kelley and Lindsay 1996; Roediger and McDermott 1993).

If one accepts the idea that the two approaches complement each other, the conclusion naturally follows that there is no necessary conflict between them. If so, there is no room in the ongoing debates about memory, or at least there should not be, for expressions such as 'systems versus processes'. Earlier slips can be written off as simply reflecting the growing pains of our young discipline.

UNITARY VERSUS MULTIPLE MEMORY SYSTEMS

There does exist a real conflict, and a real controversy, and it has to do with unitary versus multiple systems. We turn to this side of the story next.

Memory's unitarianism

Memory's unitarianism (hence simply 'unitarianism') refers to a pretheoretical framework or orientation that holds memory to be an indivisible complex entity. It is one faculty, or capacity, or capability, or mode of information processing, or system.

Unitarianism has had a long and illustrious history, having ruled unopposed from the very beginnings of the experimental study of learning and memory to the recent past. It evolved out of a perfectly reasonable and justifiable framework for the psychological study of learning, including verbal learning. The framework was initially created and shaped by the fact that in most languages there exists only a single term for a concept such as learning, and only a single term for memory. It was easy enough for early philosophers to raise questions about, and for early psychologists to do experiments on, something that has a label, such as 'memory', but difficult, or even impossible, to do so with unnamed and therefore non-existent entities.

Whatever the reasons for the dogma of unitary learning, or unitary memory, the tacit assumption was so prevalent that it was seldom articulated, and, as is always the case with undifferentiated ubiquities, it had no name. It was smoothly passed from generation to generation of psychological students of memory by mental osmosis.

Only seldom was the credo of unitary learning expressed, but whenever it was done, the assertion was succinct:

All learning is essentially of a kind—the modification of behavior as the result of repeated stimulation under specified conditions. (Hunter 1934, p.497).

The central tenet of unitarianism was widely accepted, seldom discussed, and almost never questioned. (For occasional, failed attempts at rebellion, see Schacter and Tulving (1994).) When it was put under 'official scrutiny', as happened on the rare occasion of a conference in 1962 that Arthur Melton had organized to consider the taxonomy of learning, unitarianism was reaffirmed in ringing terms:

Are we to accept a conclusion that we will have different principles of learning for different species? Most of us would not accept this any more than we would accept the idea that we will have fundamentally different principles for different forms of human learning. (Underwood 1964, p.74).

When the field of verbal learning, under the impact of the 'cognitive revolution', was transmuted into the field of memory, many practices, procedures, and assumptions changed, but the pretheoretical orientation of unitarianism did not. (For an eyewitness account of that transition see Tulving and Madigan (1970).) The reason for its survival presumably was simple: no good grounds existed for questioning the unity of (long-term) memory. Under these conditions it was difficult to even think of the idea of non-unitary memory in the abstract.

Multiple systems

The idea of multiple systems emerged slowly and initially imperceptibly. It is possible to trace the idea as such back to the nineteenth century, although the apparently unstoppable onslaught of the current ideas had its origins in the recent past (Schacter and Tulving 1994.)

What does 'multiple systems' mean? How does it differ from the view of a unitary system? Not surprisingly, there is as yet no perfect agreement among neurocognitive theorists as to the best way of characterizing systems. Tentative suggestions have been offered by a number of authors (Cohen 1984; Eichenbaum 1994; Nadel 1994; Schacter and Tulving 1994; Sherry and Schacter 1987; Tulving 1985*a*; Weiskrantz 1987), but the search for a generally acceptable conceptualization of systems continues.

Here I can only express my own understanding of the idea of multiple memory systems. It is closely related to what Bunge and Ardila (1987) have discussed under the label of the brain/mind 'identity hypothesis'. The hypothesis comprises a positive assertion—all mental events are brain events, or brain activities—and a negative one—mental events are not 'represented' in the brain. Expressions such as 'representation', or 'memory trace', or 'neural substrate', may be used, as long as we realize that they are metaphorical only. This basic 'psychobiological perspective'—today Bunge and Ardila might have said 'neurocognitive perspective'—leads easily to the question of how the brain/mind is organized, and to the idea that it is organized in the form of interacting systems.

The brain is a supersystem composed of numerous subsystems, every one of which is coupled to some other subsystems, but none of which is directly coupled with all the other brain subsystems. Every brain subsystem has its specific function, or peculiar activity, in addition to performing general 'household' functions. But it cannot discharge its function in a normal way without the support of a number of other systems. . . Given the postulated identity of mental function and specific brain function, the consequence of all that for psychology is obvious. The mind is neither a single homogeneous block nor a collection of independent modules à la Gall or Fodor (1983). Instead, the mind is a functional system . . . that is, a collection of distinct but interlocked brain processes. (Bunge and Ardila 1987, p.164)

Bunge and Ardila speak of the brain/mind system in general, but their vision is equally appropriate with respect to divisions of the mind, such as memory. We could readily adopt a statement such as, 'Memory is a collection of distinct but interlocked brain processes', as a credo of both cognitive and neurocognitive perspectives of the study of memory.

Remembered events and acquired knowledge

Let us contrast the multiple systems view with that of unitary memory, and do so in terms of a concrete laboratory analogue of a real-world happening.

Imagine an intelligent, healthy, highly motivated test person participating in a laboratory experiment on memory. The experimenter shows the test person a printed sentence on the computer screen that says: 'AARDVARKS EAT ANTS', perhaps in a list of other similar kinds of statements, and later tests the test person's 'memory' for the 'target' sentence, using different kinds of tests. The test person performs successfully on all the tests. (For the purpose of the exercise here we assume that one test does not change the outcome of any other.)

The question we wish to ask is this: how do we conceptualize what happened? A generalized, theoretically neutral description of what happened is this: the test person witnessed an event, that is, a particular appearance of a particular set of printed words in a particular place at a particular time. The information about the event was encoded and 'stored', and subsequently used, in conjunction with relevant retrieval information, to perform the 'memory test' given by the experimenter.

Most students of memory would accept this description of what happened and would not worry too much about the particular metaphors or the particular language used. They would probably also agree that such an initial description leads to obvious questions. Can we say anything more specific about the 'information encoded'? What is this 'information about the event'? Even a simple event, such as the appearance of a printed statement about the dietary habits of certain four-footed animals with long necks comprises many components. What was the statement (what were the words, what does each word refer to, what does the sentence mean)? What was the appearance of the statement (typefont, colours of the type, background)? Why was it presented (how does it fit into what I know about the world)? Where did it appear (what part of the world, what continent, what country, what city, what building, what room, what display device, what part of the monitor screen)?† When did it appear (how old was I at the time, what day of the week was the experiment, what list did the event appear in, how early or late in the list)? These kinds of questions can go on and on. Immediately after the occurrence of the AARDVARK event, the test person can answer all these questions, plus many more. This means that she has information available and accessible about a large number of different aspects of the event. Much of this information, presumably, is encoded and stored, making it possible for the test person to answer the same questions about the event even after a delay, relying on her secondary or long-term memory.

So far the description of the event and its ramifications are presumably non-controversial. Apart from possible squabbling about the exact terms used, it should be acceptable to most students of memory. The controversy materializes when we pose the next apparently innocent question: where is this information about the AARDVARK event stored?

Unitarians would say, 'The information was stored as a representation of the event in the memory store', or something equivalent. Again, the actual terms used are less important here than is the singular form of the noun designating the mental aftereffects of the experienced episode. It is this assumed singularity that plays a pivotal role in unitarian thinking, and that leads to the quarrel with multiple systems theorists. To understand its implications, we have to consider what happens at the time of retrieval.

Retrieval of information about the event, for the unitarians, can take many different forms, depending upon particular retrieval queries and retrieval instructions.

† The concern with the world, continent, country, and city may seem a bit far-fetched, but these aspects of one's experience are exceedingly real, even if both the test person and the experimenter are unaware of them.

Different instructions set off different processes that produce, as output from the memory store, different kinds of information about the event. The test person could consciously recollect the event of seeing the AARDVARK sentence on the monitor screen, she could recall a part of the sentence, she could recognize it as familiar, she could answer the question 'What do aardvarks eat?' (even if she did not know it before the experiment), she could include 'aardvark' as one of the responses on a test in which she was asked to name animals, she could complete the word fragment A—D-AR- with 'aardvark' (even if she could not have done it before the experiment), or she could show a galvanic skin response to the word aardvark (even in the absence of any awareness of recollection or familiarity). All of these different 'measures of memory' would reflect 'memory for' the episode of seeing the AARDVARK sentence.†

Here comes a simple test for the reader. Please read the last sentence of the previous paragraph and make sure to fully process its meaning. (If you wish, you may re-read the whole paragraph.) After you have done so, answer the question: Does that last sentence ('All of these . . .') look reasonable to you? If you respond 'yes', and especially if you think that it looks perfectly reasonable, and if you cannot imagine how anyone could find something basically wrong with the statement, then you are a unitarian. Unitarians are people who talk about retrieval of (the information about) the event or the episode. They frequently would make claims such as, 'Although effects of perceptual identification can be independent of recognition memory, performance on both types of tests can apparently rely on *memory for particular prior episodes*' (Jacoby 1984, p.149, emphasis added), or such as, 'On an indirect test . . . *memory for the target episode* is inferred from its effect on task performance (e.g., facilitated fragment completion for previously studied words)' (Toth *et al.* 1992, p.46, emphasis added). Multiple memory theorists would never say anything like it, as we will see presently.

In brief, then, unitarians postulate a single (even if complex) representation of the event, in one (large) memory system, and talk about different aspects of that representation being retrieved in different tasks, all such retrieval implying 'memory for' the event. In the unitarian approach, dissociations in performance on different tests come about because different retrieval cues, or different retrieval instructions, serve to provide access to different features of one and the same representation of the event in the memory store. Unitarians believe that even when the event cannot be retrieved explicitly, it may be quite possible to retrieve it implicitly. People with memory impairment, too, may demonstrate their 'memory for' the experienced event through enhanced performance on tasks such as lexical decision, perceptual identification, or fragment completion. Because the source of such enhanced

---

† The term 'memory for an event', or 'memory for' whatever, is widely used. I put it in quotation marks, because I try to avoid using it wherever possible. I think of 'memory' as a general capacity to acquire, retain, and use information, and 'memory for' an event would therefore mean 'general capacity to acquire, retain, and use information for an event'. This, of course, is not what is intended. Instead of using the colloquial expression, 'memory for an event', one could use more precise expressions, such as 'recollection of an event', 'remembering an event', or 'retrieval of information about an event', depending upon the desired intention.

performance is the original study episode (an undisputed fact, of course), some writers have even referred to the retrieval manifested in such situations as 'episodic memory' (Light and La Voie 1993, p.220), a statement totally at odds with the meaning of episodic memory in the multiple-memory theory (Wheeler *et al.* 1997).

Different memory systems

How would a multiple-memory theorist answer the question, 'Where is the information about the AARDVARK event stored?' The answer is 'It depends entirely on what aspect of the event you are talking about.' This answer means that there is no 'single' engram, or single memory trace, or single representation of the event. (By 'single' I do not mean 'localized'. A 'single' representation may be 'distributed', either abstractly or neuroanatomically, yet act as a common unit.) The perceived event is 'assembled' by many interacting brain systems, many of which are changed in the process. As a result, different kinds of information, representing the many different aspects of the event, are stored at different independent 'storage sites'. These sites correspond to memory systems and their subsystems, although different systems and subsystems also vary in ways other than just the storage sites (Schacter and Tulving 1994). There is nothing resembling a 'single representation' (single trace, single engram) of the AARDVARK event anywhere in the brain.

Different memory systems have evolved to serve special functions that cannot be readily duplicated by other systems (Sherry and Schacter 1987). For example, one of the functions of primary memory, or working memory (Baddeley 1986), is to make a neurocognitive 'sketch' of the perceived event. The properties of the sketch depend on the event, its context, the nature of attentional processing of the input, and other variables. Parts of the sketch are accessible to the rememberer in the form of immediate conscious awareness, and the information it contains can be used in ongoing mental activity. While working memory operates on the incoming information in this manner, other memory systems in the complex, massively parallel computational machine that is the brain are also involved, separately from the processes of working memory (Pashler and Carrier 1996; Shallice and Warrington 1970, Tulving and Patterson 1968). Thus PRS, the perceptual representation system (Schacter 1990; Tulving and Schacter 1990), encodes and stores information about the features of the visual objects represented by the letter strings AARDVARKS EAT ANTS. The semantic memory system, or a set of its (presumably) numerous subsystems, encodes and stores propositional information about the feeding habits of animals named aardvarks. The episodic system integrates, registers, temporally dates, and spatially localizes the rememberer's experience of the experience of being present and witnessing the sentence appearing on and disappearing from the screen.

For a multiple systems theorist there is no such thing as 'implicit retrieval' of the information about an event. Nor does any kind of implicit retrieval of information laid down at the time of the event constitute a 'memory for the event'. Information about an experienced event can be retrieved only explicitly, that is, with conscious awareness of the earlier experience. Such explicit retrieval is called 're-membering', or 'conscious recollection'. It is important to note, lest confusion reign, that what is remembered, or consciously recollected, is not the event, but the event as experienced (Perner and Ruffman 1995; Wheeler *et al.* 1997).

A person serving as a subject in an experiment in which the AARDVARKS EAT ANTS display is presented for inspection can, later on, implicitly (that is, without conscious awareness of the source of the information) retrieve (that is, make use of) other kinds of information that were encoded and stored at the time when the original event occurred. Such implicit retrieval may be manifested in perceptual priming: the subject could demonstrate enhanced ability to identify and name any of the three presented letter strings. In the multiple systems view, such enhancement would be regarded as an 'expression' of the perceptual representation system, PRS.

Implicit retrieval may also be manifested in the subject's improved ability to answer questions such as 'Can you tell me something about the feeding habits of the animal whose name appears first in the dictionary?' In the multiple systems view, such an improvement in memory performance would be regarded as an unknown mixture of expression of semantic and episodic memory. When the subject no longer remembers the experienced AARDVARK event, but still knows the answer to the question, or when the subject is amnesic and cannot consciously recollect the study episode but knows the learned fact (Hayman *et al.* 1993; Markowitsch *et al.* 1993), we can conclude that the expressed knowledge represents an output of the semantic memory system. In theory, one could expect perfectly normal perceptual or conceptual priming even if the respondent's episodic memory system were totally dysfunctional, or even if there were nothing left of the originally stored information about the event in the episodic memory system.

Thus, the multiple systems view of basic differences between the remembered experience, knowledge of a fact, and enhanced ability to identify an object, even if all of them originate in the 'same event', leads to the expectation that different areas of the brain are involved in these different achievements. We return to this issue later in the chapter.

Implicit memory versus episodic remembering

It also follows from what has been said that people who have suffered the kind of brain damage that causes amnesia do not and cannot demonstrate their 'memory for' the experienced event through enhanced performance on tasks such as lexical decision, perceptual identification, or fragment completion, because these tests do not address any questions about the remembering of the experienced event. The tests address the person's ability to perform a current task that need not, in any way, depend on information stored about the experienced event as such. Also, amnesics do not demonstrate their 'memory for' the event by being able to answer the question, 'What do aardvarks eat?' There is no reason, in the multiple systems world, why anyone, whether amnesic or not, cannot make use of information stored in semantic memory without invoking one's episodic-memory capacities (Tulving 1995).

A person's enhanced ability to name the objects that the experimenter gives them credit for, on a priming test (e.g. complete the word fragment A—D-AR- with 'aardvark') or the semantic memory test ('What do aardvarks eat?'), may have, and in experiments does have, its origin in a specific episode, but the enhancement is independent not only of the remembering of the episode, but also of the episode itself. It is independent of the *remembering of the episode*, as demonstrated by various dissociations between priming and explicit recognition (Tulving *et al.* 1982; Hayman and Tulving 1989; Nyberg and Tulving 1996). It is independent of the *episode itself* in the sense that no particular episode is necessary for the enhancement. Exactly the same effect-enhanced performance on the priming task and the semantic question-answering task could have come about as a consequence of a large variety of rather different episodes. A particular event may be sufficient to create the neural basis for an enhanced skill or added knowledge, but it is not necessary.

A stark contrast to such a state of affairs in implicit memory—a given event is sufficient but not necessary for subsequent enhancement of performance—is episodic remembering. What a person consciously recollects of the event depends very much on the event and the person's original experience of it. The appearance of the AARDVARK sentence in a particular place at a given time in a given place is absolutely necessary for the person's remembering of the experience of that particular event. There is no way that a different event could be substituted for the one actually experienced without changing the 'memory for' the event.†

In sum, then, according to multiple systems theory, there is no single representation of an originally encountered event anywhere in the brain. Different kinds of information about the event are 'stored' in different memory systems and subsystems, and used as needed. Dissociations in performance on different tests of retrieval come about because the relevant information is independently accessible from these different 'storage sites' in the brain. The kinds of information that support perceptual priming and the operations of semantic memory exist, and can be used, independently of the information that is necessary for conscious recollection of previously experienced events.

CONVERSION OF A UNITARIAN: A PERSONAL CONFESSION

I said earlier that psychological students of learning and memory who lived and worked before the 1970s were unitarians, even though they did not realize it at the

† It is well known that recollections of past events are not always veridical and that sometimes people can remember events that never happened (Roediger and McDermott 1995; Schacter *et al* 1996). Such 'false remembering' is not yet understood and is being vigorously studied. More complete understanding no doubt will come with further research. The lack of complete veridicality of remembered events, however, does not change the basic nature of episodic memory, or its differences from PRS and semantic memory.

Study of memory: processes and systems 23

time. I was one of them. I collected my first data in a learning experiment in 1957. If someone had asked me at that time how many different kinds of learning there were, I would not have understood the question. (The term 'memory' was still taboo at the time, and young beginners in the field did not dare to use it any more than they would dare to question what passes for political correctness in our more enlightened age.) How many different kinds of air are there? How many different kinds of water? Kinds of learning? What silly questions!

I was a unitarian, not only because I did not know any better, but also because I too had been imprinted on Occam's razor and had learned about the inestimable virtues of parsimony. Science was a search for the general principles and universal concepts governing phenomena we were interested in, and splitting up what one was going to study was obviously not the way to begin. Therefore, for me learning was learning, and memory was memory. In my zeal I wielded Occam's razor wherever and whenever I thought I saw a chance. Thus, organization was organization, information was information, items were items, cues were cues, retrieval was retrieval, and to top it all off I wrote several papers passionately defending the 'fact' that there is no difference between recall and recognition. At the time I had not yet heard of Einstein's dictum that it is the duty of scientists to simplify nature as much as possible but not more, and if I had, I might have thought that even Einstein had his limitations.

Now that I have come to my senses I am a bit embarrassed about some of the things I said and wrote in my ardour for parsimony, even if I can rationalize it by attributing it to idealistic ignorance of the youth. Besides, I am glad that I experienced the faith, because I feel that it makes me more tolerant now of the views of those who have not yet seen the light. I am even more glad that I myself was lucky enough to realize the errors of my early ways before it was too late to do anything about them. I now think of unitarianism as something like measles, or puberty: an inevitable and necessary, but relatively painless and transitory, stage in one's life that most people get over in the normal course of maturation and development.

What brought about my 'conversion'? Like all historical questions, this one too does not have an objective answer. About the best I can do is to imagine that my original faith was shaken by facts that kept piling up that were at variance with the theme of unity. In addition I can put my finger on specific instances that greatly helped me to shape my new convictions and, later, to keep them. In the last part of this chapter, which is even more personal than the rest of it, I mention four 'critical incidents', although their actual number is considerably larger.

Stochastic independence

The first incident was an experiment we did in the summer of 1980 and published two years later (Tulving *et al*. 1982). Subjects were shown long lists of individual words and later tested for (i) their ability to recognize the words (old or new?), and (ii) their ability to complete the graphemic fragment of the word (e.g. say ASSASSIN when shown the fragment A—AS—N). The words that the subjects had studied were, of course, recognized much more readily than non-studied words, and, not surprisingly, also more readily identified in the fragment completion test.

What was totally unexpected was the fact that whether or not a subject remembered having seen a particular word in the study list, as judged by the recognition test, had no bearing whatsoever on whether or not the subject could complete or not complete the fragment of the same word. The two performances were stochastically independent. The finding was unexpected and novel, because no such independence between different measures of mnemonic consequences of study of a single set of items had ever been reported before. All previous experiments, in which different measures of memory of individual items had been subjected to a contingency analysis of the sort we used, had always shown at least positive even if not perfect association between the measures (e.g. Flexser and Tulving 1978; Ogilvie *et al*. 1980; Postman *et al*. 1948; Rabinowitz *et al*. 1977, 1979; Tulving and Wiseman 1975; Wallace 1978; Watkins and Tulving 1975).

What was going on? A reasonable idea, fortified by the findings from amnesic patients (Warrington and Weiskrantz 1968, 1974) was that we had bumped into a new kind of memory, one obeying different principles than those involved in the memory supporting old/new recognition. Hence we surmised that 'priming effects in word-fragment completion may be mediated by a cognitive system other than episodic and semantic memory' (Tulving *et al*. 1982, p.336).

Man without episodic memory

A second eye-opening experience consisted in my meeting and studying a man (KC) who, as a result of traumatic brain damage that he had suffered in a motorcycle accident in 1980, has completely lost the ability to remember any personally experienced events although in most other respects he is quite normal (Tulving 1985*b*; Tulving *et al*. 1988*b*). Especially interesting to me was the fact that he had retained a great deal of the knowledge that he had acquired during the years before the critical injury. His language is intact, he can read and write and solve problems, he knows mathematics, geometry, history, and how to play chess and the organ. He knows who he is, where he lives, where he went to school, and has no difficulty locating the family summer cottage on the map of Ontario, where has spent a lot of time. He can even learn new factual information, albeit slowly, and shows more perceptual priming than an average college student (Hayman *et al*. 1993; Tulving *et al*. 1988*b*, 1991). He has good manners, has a quiet sense of humour, and never confabulates. Also important is the fact that as long as he stays inside the house, and goes for walks only in the immediate neighbourhood, which he knows, he is perfectly capable of looking after himself in every respect; he requires no supervision or caretaking of any kind.

KC accomplishes all that, and much more, without being able to consciously recollect any experience he has ever had. His anterograde amnesia, especially for autobiographical events, is as dense as that of any other amnesic ever described in the literature, including HM (Corkin 1984), although, unlike HM, he can learn, slowly and laboriously, new factual verbally expressed information (Hayman *et al.* 1993; Tulving *et al.* 1991). His retrograde amnesia for personal happenings extends back to the earliest days of his life. Regardless of how precisely or specifically he is prompted and reminded of happenings in his past, and regardless of how hard he tries, he cannot remember, that is consciously bring to mind, any events, single or repeated, from any period of his life. Cases resembling that of KC have now been described by others (Hodges and McCarthy 1993; Markowitsch *et al.* 1993; Calabrese *et al.* 1996; Van Der Linden *et al.* 1996).

The striking dissociation between KC's totally dysfunctional episodic memory and his relatively functional semantic memory, as well as his excellent perceptual priming, suggests a separation of the corresponding processes at the neural level. His case represents an extreme illustration of the conclusion arrived at in an extensive clinical neurological investigations of memory and amnesia almost half a century earlier (one that I did not know about at the time when I was spending time with KC):

A study of pathways of memory formation has revealed a basic fact not suspected when this study began—there are two separate pathways for two kinds of memories. The one is memories of life experiences centering around the person himself and basically involving the element of time. The other is memories of intellectually acquired knowledge not experienced but learned by study and not personal. (Nielsen 1958, p.25)

Brain imaging

The third critical event supporting my growing convictions about multiple memory systems occurred in 1987 in Lund, Sweden. David Ingvar and Jarl Risberg, two well-known pioneers in the development of the technique of measuring regional cerebral blood flow (rCBF) in awake, alert people, kindly agreed to collaborate with me in doing a pilot study comparing episodic and semantic memory retrieval. In this study we measured changes in cortical blood flow that signalled changes in neural activity. During some brain scans in our study, subjects were silently reminiscing about past personal happenings; during other scans, they were thinking of the facts they knew in a given category. We found three subjects who consistently produced strikingly uniform results: episodic remembering of past events was accompanied by relatively higher levels of blood flow in anterior cortical regions, whereas retrieval of semantic knowledge was associated with relatively higher activations of posterior cortical regions (Tulving *et al.* 1988*a*; Tulving 1989).

Thus, as a result of our little study we had visible evidence that living brains distinguish between thoughts involving 'self-in-the-past' and thoughts about less personal happenings of the world. Although the finer grain of the blood flow data was uninformative, and although we could not rule out alternative interpretations, I found the data most encouraging: they fit surprisingly well into the developing pattern.

A fourth incident, or rather a series of incidents—I think of them as 'clinchers'—consisted in the confirmation, extension, and refinement of our Lund findings. In 1993 we gained access to the newly established positron emission tomography (PET) facility at the Clarke Institute of Psychiatry at the University of Toronto, and could begin serious brain imaging studies of episodic and semantic memory. The results of the Toronto studies (Kapur et al. 1994; Moscovitch et al. 1995; Nyberg et al. 1996b, 1997; Tulving et al. 1994) as well as those reported by other laboratories (Andreasen et al. 1995; Fletcher et al. 1995a,b; Shallice et al. 1994) showed striking differences in the neuroanatomical sites that are involved in episodic and semantic retrieval. One of the most consistent findings is that retrieval of semantic (general knowledge) information engages left prefrontal cortex more than right prefrontal cortex, whereas retrieval of episodic information engages right prefrontal cortex more than the left. This pattern of brain activation, labelled hemispheric encoding/retrieval asymmetry, or HERA, was unexpected in terms of existing knowledge, but it has turned out to be remarkably robust (Buckner 1996; Haxby et al. 1996; Cabeza and Nyberg 1997; Nyberg et al. 1996a, 1997). Other regions of the brain have been identified that show differential activation in episodic versus semantic retrieval (Buckner and Tulving 1995; Shallice et al. 1994; Fletcher et al. 1995a,b; Cabeza and Nyberg 1997), and more will undoubtedly be found in the future. But the data already available have added powerful support to the biological reality of separate memory systems.

With these kinds of experiences, it is easy, and fun, to be converted, even if it means that I have ambivalent feelings about the non-believers. Those students of memory who have not met people such as KC, and who have not done any PET or fMRI studies of memory, and who therefore can afford to think that 'perhaps there is something wrong there, somehow', may get away with thinking unitarian thoughts, but I suspect that it will not be for long. The whole *Zeitgeist* in our field is changing, rapidly.

CONCLUSION

The title of this chapter is 'Study of memory: processes and systems'. The crucial word in it is 'and'. Both processes and systems constitute the warp and the woof of the fabric of memory: we cannot have one without the other any more than we can have continents without oceans or heredity without environment. One can, and people usually do, approach the study of memory either from a cognitive (process oriented) or a neurocognitive (systems oriented) perspective, but on logical and rational grounds there is no conflict between them. The two approaches are complementary, and both are necessary for a fuller understanding of memory. Because all memory systems operate in terms of processes—some shared with other systems, some unique—the issue of processes versus systems is a non-issue. There can be no conflict between process and systems orientations, and no controversy.

There still exists what appears to be a real disagreement today between those who believe in a single system and those who believe in multiple systems. This disagreement, however, is more a tiff than a serious rift. Moreover, there is every reason to believe that the tiff is a passing phenomenon that will soon be behind us. The weight of evidence is relentlessly shifting in favour of multiple memory systems, and there is no sign that the trend is going to stop or to reverse. This is why the future will belong to the idea of multiple memory systems.

Because the eventual general acceptance of multiple memory views is no longer in doubt, it would be appropriate to invite all cognitive theorists to renounce their unitarian faith and to join the effort to contribute constructively to the solving of the many daunting problems that lie on our way to a fuller understanding of memory with its multiple processes and multiple systems!

ACKNOWLEDGEMENTS

I thank Kathleen McDermott and Martin Lepage for constructive criticisms of this chapter. My research is supported by a foundation by Anne and Max Tanenbaum in support of research in cognitive neuroscience, and by the Natural and Engineering Research Council of Canada (grant A8632).

REFERENCES

Andreasen, N. C., O'Leary, D. S., Arndt, S., Cizadlo, T., Hurtig, R., Rezai, K., *et al.* (1995). Short-term and long-term verbal memory: a positron emission tomography study. *Proceedings of the National Academy of Sciences of the USA*, **92**, 5111–15.

Baddeley, A. D. (1986). *Working memory*. Oxford University Press.

Barber, B. (1961). Resistance of scientists to scientific discovery. *Science*, **134**, 596–602.

Bower, G. H. (1996). Reactivating a reactivation theory of implicit memory. *Consciousness and Cognition*, **5**, 27–72.

Buckner, R. (1996). Beyond HERA: contributions of specific prefrontal brain areas to long-term memory. *Psychonomic Bulletin and Review*, **3**, 149–58.

Buckner, R. and Tulving, E. (1995). Neuroimaging studies of memory: theory and recent PET results. In *Handbook of Neuropsychology*, Vol. 10 (ed. F. Boller and J. Grafman), pp.439–66. Elsevier, Amsterdam.

Bunge, M. and Ardila, R. (1987). *Philosophy of psychology*. Springer, New York.

Cabeza, R. and Nyberg, L. (1997). Imaging cognition: an empirical review of PET studies with normal subjects. *Journal of Cognitive Neuroscience*, **9**, 1–26.

Cabeza, R., Kapur, S., Craik, F. I. M., McIntosh, A. R., Houle, S., and Tulving, E. (1997). Functional neuroanatomy of recall and recognition: a PET study of episodic memory. *Journal of Cognitive Neuroscience*, **9**, 254–65.

Calabrese, P., Markowitsch, H. J., Durwen, H. F., Widlitzek, H., Haupts, M., Holika, B., *et al.* (1996). Right temporofrontal cortex as critical locus for the ecphory of old episodic memories. *Journal of Neurology, Neurosurgery and Psychiatry*, **61**, 304–10.

Cohen, N. J. (1984). Preserved learning capacity in amnesia: evidence for multiple memory systems. In *The neuropsychology of memory*, (ed. L. R. Squire and N. Butters), pp.83–103. Guilford Press, New York.

Corkin, S. (1984). Lasting consequences of bilateral medial temporal lobectomy: clinical course and experimental findings. In *H. M. Seminars in Nuerology*, **4**, 249–59.

Eichenbaum, H. (1994). The hippocampal system and declarative memory in humans and animals: Experimental analysis and historical origins. In *Memory systems 1994*, (ed. D. L. Schacter and E. Tulving), pp. 147–201. MIT Press, Cambridge, MA.

Fletcher, P. C., Dolan, R. J., and Frith, C. D. (1995a). The functional anatomy of memory. *Experientia*, **51**, 1197–207.

Fletcher, P. C., Frith, C. D., Grasby, P. M., Shallice, T., Frackowiak, R. S. J., and Dolan, R. J. (1995b). Brain systems for encoding and retrieval of auditory-verbal memory: an *in vivo* study in humans. *Brain*, **118**, 401–16.

Flexser, A. J. and Tulving, E. (1978). Retrieval independence in recognition and recall. *Psychological Review*, **85**, 153–71.

Fodor, J. G. (1983). *The modularity of mind*. MIT Press, Cambridge, MA.

Haxby, J. V., Ungerleider, L. G., Horwitz, B., Maisog, J. M., Rapoport, S. L., and Grady, C. L. (1996). Face encoding and recognition in the human brain. *Proceedings of the National Academy of Sciences of the USA*, **93**, 922–7.

Hayman, C. A. G. and Tulving, E. (1989). Contingent dissociation between recognition and fragment completion: the method of triangulation. *Journal of Experimental Psychology: Learning, Memory, and Cognition*, **15**, 228–40.

Hayman, C. A. G., Macdonald, C. A., and Tulving, E. (1993). The role of repetition and associative interference in new semantic learning in amnesia. *Journal of Cognitive Neuroscience*, **5**, 375–89.

Hodges, J. R. and McCarthy, R. A. (1993) Autobiographical amnesia resulting from bilateral paramedian thalamic infarction. *Brain*, **116**, 921–40.

Hunter, W. S. (1934). Experimental studies of learning. In *Handbook of general experimental psychology*, (ed. C. Murchison), pp.497–570. Clark University Press, Worcester, MA.

Jacoby, L. L. (1984). Incidental versus intentional retrieval: remembering and awareness as separate issues. In *Neuropsychology of memory*, (ed. L. R. Squire and N. Butters), pp. 145–56. Guilford Press, New York.

Johnson, M. K. (1993). MEM: memory subsystems as processes. In *Theories of memory*, (ed. A. F. Collins, S. E. Gathercole, M. A. Conway, and P. E. Morris), pp.241–86. Erlbaum, Hove.

Kapur, S., Craik, F. I. M., Tulving, E., Wilson, A. A., Houle, S., and Brown, G. M. (1994). Neuroanatomical correlates of encoding in episodic memory: levels of processing effect. *Proceedings of the National Academy of Sciences of the U.S.A.*, **91**, 2008–11.

Kelley, C. M. and Lindsay, D. S. (1996). Conscious and unconscious forms of memory. In *Memory*, (ed. E. L. Bjork and R. A. Bjork), pp.31–63. Academic, San Diego.

Light, L. L. and La Voie, D. (1993). Direct and indirect measures of memory in old age. In *Implicit memory: new directions in cognition, development, and neuropsychology*, (ed. M. E. H. Masson and P. Graf), pp.207–30). Erlbaum, Hillsdale, NJ.

Markowitsch, H. J., Calabrese, P., Liess, J., Haupts, M., Durwen, H. F., and Gehlen, W. (1993). Retrograde amnesia after traumatic injury of the fronto-temporal cortex. *Journal of Neurology, Neurosurgery and Psychiatry*, **56**, 988–92.

Masson, M. E. J. and Graf, P. (1993). Introduction: looking back and into the future. In *Implicit memory: new directions in cognition, development, and neuropsychology*, (ed. M. E. H. Masson and P. Graf), pp.1–11. Erlbaum, Hillsdale, NJ.

Moscovitch M., Kapur S., Köhler S., and Houle S. (1995). Distinct neural correlates of visual long-term memory for spatial location and object identity: a positron emission tomography (PET) study in humans. *Proceedings of the National Academy of Sciences of the USA*, **92**, 3721–5.

Nadel, L. (1994). Multiple memory systems: what and why, an update. In *Memory systems 1994*, (ed. D. L. Schacter and E. Tulving), pp.39–63. MIT Press, Cambridge, MA.

Nielsen, J. M. (1958). *Memory and amnesia*. San Lucas Press, Los Angeles.

Nyberg, L. and Tulving, E. (1996). Classifying human long-term memory: evidence from converging dissociations. *European Journal of Cognitive Psychology*, **8**, 163–83.

Nyberg, L., Cabeza, R. and Tulving, E. (1996a). PET studies of encoding and retrieval: the HERA model. *Psychonomic Bulletin and Review*, **3**, 135–48.

Nyberg, L., McIntosh, A. R., Cabeza, R. Habib, R, Houle, S., and Tulving, E. (1996b). General and specific brain regions involved in encoding and retrieval of events: what, where, and when. *Proceedings of the National Academy of Sciences of the USA*, **93**, 11280–5.

Nyberg, L., McIntosh, A. R., and Tulving, E. (1997). Functional brain imaging of episodic and semantic memory. *Journal of Molecular Medicine*, **19**, 863–70.

Ogilvie, J. C., Tulving, E., Paskowitz, S., and Jones, G. V. (1980). Three-dimensional memory traces: a model and its application to forgetting. *Journal of Verbal Learning and Verbal Behavior*, **19**, 405–15.

Pashler, H. and Carrier, M. (1996). Structures, processes, and the flow of information. In *Memory*, (ed. E. L. Bjork and R. A. Bjork), pp.3–29. Academic, San Diego.

Perner J. and Ruffman T. (1995). Episodic memory an autonoetic consciousness: developmental evidence and a theory of childhood amnesia. *Journal of Experimental Child Psychology*, **59**, 516–48.

Postman, L., Jenkins, W. O., and Postman, D. L. (1948). *American Journal of Psychology*, **61**, 511–19.

Rabinowitz, J. C., Mandler, G., and Patterson, K. E. (1977). Determinants of recognition and recall: accessibility and generation. *Journal of Experimental Psychology: General*, **106**, 302–29.

Rabinowitz, J. C., Mandler, G., and Barsalou, L. W. (1979). Generation-recognition as an auxiliary retrieval strategy. *Journal of Verbal Learning and Verbal Behavior*, **18**, 57–72.

Roediger, H. L. III and McDermott, K. B. (1993). Implicit memory in normal human subjects. In *Handbook of neuropsychology*, Vol. 8 (ed F. Boller and J. Grafman), pp.63–131. Elsevier, Amsterdam.

Roediger, H. L. III and McDermott, K. B. (1995). Creating false memories: remembering words not presented in lists. *Journal of Experimental Psychology: Learning, Memory, and Cognition*, **21**, 803–14.

Schacter, D. L. (1990). Perceptual representation systems and implicit memory: toward a resolution of the multiple memory systems debate. In *Development and neural bases of higher cognitive functions*, Annals of the New York Academy of Sciences, Vol. 608, (ed. A. Diamond), pp.543–71.

Schacter, D. L. (1992). Understanding implicit memory: a cognitive neuroscience approach. *American Psychologist*, **47**, 559–69.

Schacter, D. L. and Tulving, E. (1994). What are the memory systems of 1994? In *Memory systems 1994*, (ed. D. L. Schacter and E. Tulving, E.), pp.1–38. MIT Press, Cambridge, MA.

Schacter, D. L., Reiman, E., Curran, T., Yun, L. S., Bandy, D., McDermott, K. B., *et al.* (1996). Neuroanatomical correlates of veridical and illusory recognition memory: evidence from positron emission tomography. *Neuron*, **17**, 267–74.

Shallice, T. and Warrington, E. K. (1970). Independent functioning of the verbal memory stores: a neuropsychological study. *Quarterly Journal of Experimental Psychology*, **22**, 261–73.

Shallice, T., Fletcher, P., Frith, C. D., Grasby, P., Frackowiak, R. S. J., and Dolan, R. J. (1994). Brain regions associated with acquisition and retrieval of verbal episodic memory. *Nature*, **368**, 633–5.

Sherry, D. F. and Schacter, D. L. (1987). The evolution of multiple memory systems. *Psychological Review*, **94**, 439–54.

Toth, J. P., Lindsay, D., and Jacoby, L. L. (1992). Awareness, automaticity, and memory dissociations. In *The neuropsychology of memory*, (2nd edn), (ed. L. R. Squire and N. Butters), pp.46–57. Guilford Press, New York.

Tulving, E. (1983). *Elements of episodic memory*. Clarendon, Oxford.
Tulving, E. (1985a). How many memory systems are there? *American Psychologist*, **40**, 385–98.
Tulving, E. (1985b). Memory and consciousness. *Canadian Psychology*, **26**, 1–12.
Tulving, E. (1986). What kind of a hypothesis is the distinction between episodic and semantic memory? *Journal of Experimental Psychology: Learning, Memory, and Cognition*, **12**, 307–11.
Tulving, E. (1989). Memory: performance, knowledge, and experience. *European Journal of Cognitive Psychology*, **1**, 3–26.
Tulving, E. (1993). What is episodic memory? *Current Perspectives in Psychological Science*, **2**, 67–70.
Tulving, E. (1995). Organization of memory: quo vadis? In *The cognitive neurosciences*, (ed. M. S. Gazzaniga), pp.839–47. MIT Press, Cambridge, MA.
Tulving, E. and Madigan, S. A. (1970). Memory and verbal learning. *Annual Review of Psychology*, **21**, 437–84.
Tulving, E. and Patterson, R. D. (1968). Functional units and retrieval processes in free recall. *Journal of Experimental Psychology*, **77**, 239–48.
Tulving, E. and Schacter, D. L. (1990). Priming and human memory systems. *Science*, **247**, 301–6.
Tulving, E. and Wiseman, S. (1975). Relation between recognition and recognition failure of recallable words. *Bulletin of the Psychonomic Society*, **6**, 79–82.
Tulving, E., Schacter, D. L., and Stark, H. A. (1982). Priming effects in word-fragment completion are independent of recognition memory. *Journal of Experimental Psychology: Learning, Memory, and Cognition*, **8**, 336–42.
Tulving, E., Risberg, J., and Ingvar, D. H. (1988a). Regional cerebral blood flow and episodic memory retrieval. *Bulletin of the Psychonomic Society*, **26**, 522.
Tulving, E., Schacter, D. L., McLachlan, D. R., and Moscovitch, M. (1988b). Priming of semantic autobiographical knowledge: a case study of retrograde amnesia. *Brain and Cognition*, **8**, 3–20.
Tulving, E., Hayman, C. A. G., and Macdonald, C. A. (1991). Long-lasting perceptual priming and semantic learning in amnesia: a case experiment. *Journal of Experimental Psychology: Learning, Memory and Cognition*, **17**, 595–617.
Tulving, E., Kapur, S., Craik, F. I. M., Moscovitsch, M., and Houle, S. (1994) Hemispheric encoding/retrieval asymmetry in episodic memory: Positron emission tomography findings. *Proceedings of the National Academy of Sciences of the USA*, **91**, 2016–20.
Underwood, B. J. (1964). In *Categories of human learning*, (ed. A. W. Melton) pp. 47–78. Academic Press, New York.
Van Der Linden, M., Bredart, S., Depoorter, N., and Coyette, F. (1996). Semantic memory and amnesia: a case study. *Cognitive Neuropsychology*, **13**, 391–413.
Wallace, W. P. (1978). Recognition failure of recallable words and recognizable words. *Journal of Experimental Psychology: Human Learning and Memory*, **4**, 441–52.
Warrington, E. K., and Weiskrantz, L. (1968). New method of testing long-term retention with special reference to amnesic patients. *Nature*, **217**, 972–4.
Warrington, E. K. and Weiskrantz, L. (1974). The effect of prior learning on subsequent retention in amnesic patients. *Neuropsychologia*, **12**, 419–28.
Watkins, M. J. and Tulving, E. (1975). Episodic memory: when recognition fails. *Journal of Experimental Psychology: General*, **104**, 5–29.
Weiskrantz, L. (1987). Neuroanatomy of memory and amnesia: a case for multiple memory systems. *Human Neurobiology*, **6**, 93–105.
Wheeler, M., Stuss, D. T., and Tulving, E. Episodic memory, autonoetic consciousness, and the frontal lobes. (1997). *Psychological Bulletin*, **121**, 331–54.

3
Components of processing

HENRY L. ROEDIGER III, RANDY L. BUCKNER, AND
KATHLEEN B. McDERMOTT

COMPONENTS OF PROCESSING

The debate about how to explain differences among measures of memory is often framed as being between proponents of unitary versus proponents of multiple memory systems. However, in our opinion, this way of characterizing the issue is misleading. No one involved in this debate argues that memory is 'unitary' or monolithic, in the sense that all memory processes are alike. The argument is (or has been) over how to characterize the manifold differences found between measures and forms of memory.

The contribution of this chapter will be to place the debate in historical context, to summarize some persuasive points made by each side, and to suggest that more recent discoveries may have left the debate of the 1980s in the dust of the past—both points of view have validity (and drawbacks), and rapprochement is in order. However, as Santayana's famous dictum reminds us, we should be mindful of this past history or else be condemned to repeat it. We suspect that the future will see repetitions of the systems/processes debate in many forms, for the issues raised are enduring ones, and the solutions to these thorny problems are often not straightforward.

The systems/processes debate occupied many researchers during the 1980s. However, several proponents on both sides of the debate had declared it largely resolved by the early 1990s. For example, on the systems side, Schacter (1990) subtitled his chapter on perceptual representation in implicit memory as 'Toward a resolution of the multiple memory systems debate.' A few years later, from the processing side, Roediger and McDermott (1993) endorsed the 'components of processing view' championed by Moscovitch, among others (Moscovitch 1992; 1994; Moscovitch *et al.* 1993). In addition, Blaxton (1995) and Gabrieli (1995) have also voiced support for similar resolutions to the debate. We continue to endorse this component processes solution in our present chapter, but first we set the stage with a brief review of the history of the debate.

STRUCTURE AND FUNCTION

The debate between structural and dynamic approaches to exploring psychological phenomena is an old one and has occupied centre stage in various eras during the history of psychology (ably reviewed by Boring (1950) among others). The early influence of the phrenologists led to discussion of localization of function—could discrete parts of the brain be isolated as the seat of perceiving, remembering, or thinking? (Of course, the phrenologists also hoped to find a seat for a moral sense, a sense of humour, and many other traits.) From a different direction, structural psychologists led by Wundt and Titchener tried to dissect mental experience by describing the sensations, images, and affections called up by environmental stimuli. The aim, in the attempts of both the phrenologists and the structuralists, was to explain psychological phenomena in terms of either neural or psychological structures. The question they tried to answer was: what structures explain psychological phenomena?

At least three groups of scholars argued against these structural approaches (Roediger 1990*a*). The Act psychologists of the Würzburg school declared that psychological phenomena were dynamic and therefore could not usefully be stopped and dissected. Later, the Gestalt psychologists produced many perceptual phenomena (such as demonstrations of apparent motion) that provided serious challenges to structural explanations of perception. Similarly, the functional tradition in American psychology, which emanated from scholars at the University of Chicago and Columbia University, provided functional explanations of phenomena and argued that structural accounts were at best incomplete and at worst wrong. They emphasized that behaviour and psychological experience were dynamic and could not be stopped and analysed, as the structuralists attempted to do.

The predecessors of the structure/processing debate noted in the previous paragraph were primarily concerned with conscious experience of an individual while perceiving. In fact, the early structural/functional debate centred around perception as its content area.

Problems and phenomena of memory rarely played a major role in the controversy, perhaps because many experimental psychologists of this century who studied memory were raised in the intellectual environment of functional and behavioural approaches, which favoured study of dynamics unfolding over time. From time to time scholars worried about structural questions (do memory traces decay? where is new learning encoded in the brain?), but for the most part a functional approach was adopted by memory researchers.

The primary structural question raised about memory in the first half of the century in mainstream experimental psychology was the 'search for the engram' (or location of memory traces in the brain) made famous in Lashley's (1950) paper. Lashley (1929) had reported an extensive series of experiments in which he made lesions of various sizes (and in diverse locations) in the brains of rats; he then tested the rats on mazes, which varied in difficulty. Lashley's findings surprised him: the location of the lesion did not seem to affect learning ability in rats, but the size of the lesion did. He developed his famous principles of equipotentiality of structures (all seemed important in learning) and mass action (the size of the lesion is critical).

In reflecting on this work in his 1950 paper, Lashley wrote 'The series of experiments has yielded a good bit of information about what and where the memory trace is not. It has discovered nothing directly of the real nature of the memory trace. I sometimes feel, in reviewing the evidence of the localization of the memory trace, that the necessary conclusion is that learning is just not possible. It is difficult to conceive of a mechanism that can satisfy the conditions set for it. Nevertheless, in spite of such evidence against it, learning sometimes does occur' (pp. 477–8). Structural approaches to learning and memory were perhaps at a low point in 1950, but the second half of the century would see their return.

MEMORY SYSTEMS

In the 1960s the situation changed, when researchers, picking up on the early suggestion of William James, distinguished between primary (short term) and secondary (long term) memory (Waugh and Norman 1965). Although cast in terms of a metaphorical model of various memory 'stores' holding information of one type or another, the theories of memory postulating different storage systems became quite popular for several reasons. First, they were easy to understand and captured the layperson's vocabulary of describing memory: memories are stored in various places, and the process of retrieval was thought to be one of searching the various stores in an attempt to find the information (Roediger 1979, 1980). Second, the models could be cast in mathematical form and could therefore potentially render more precise predictions than models and theories stated verbally. Third, the models suggested numerous experimental tests and therefore became grist for the empirical mill (e.g. Glanzer 1972). And fourth, if one took seriously the idea that there really were different memory stores, one store holding information over the short term and the other over longer periods, then different neural underpinnings of the two memory systems would be expected. This prediction was borne out in the seminal work on the amnesic patient HM, who had intact short-term memory but severe impairment of certain forms of long-term memory (Scoville and Milner 1957; Corkin 1968). For all these reasons and perhaps others, the late 1960s and early 1970s saw experimental psychologists collecting evidence to bear on the two-store (and then later, multistore) models of memory.

Of course, not everyone was enamored of this new approach. Tulving and Patterson (1968) produced data that were difficult to explain in terms of storage systems and went on to comment that 'In the long run, nothing much can be gained by postulating a homunculus searching through one or more types of memory store for desired mnemonic information' (p.247). Many others debated whether the evidence really required postulation of different storage systems that obeyed different laws (e.g. Wickelgren 1973).

In 1972 Tulving first proposed the terms episodic and semantic memory for retention of personal episodes or events (in which recollection of time and place of occurrence were crucial for their retrieval) and for retention of general information that was ahistorical, respectively. Although the information in semantic memory may have been learned at a particular time and in a particular place, these qualities did not need to be retrieved when the general knowledge was accessed from semantic memory. The standard laboratory tasks of recall and recognition for recently studied events were then deemed measures of episodic memory. Tests tapping general knowledge or semantic memory were generally less prevalent in 1972 (or even now), but Tulving (1972, p.395) mentioned four laboratory paradigms as qualifying as experiments on retrieval from semantic memory: retrieving a word from a fragmented presentation, such as naming *ASSASSIN* from A__A__IN (Horowitz *et al.* 1970); retrieving a word when given its definition, as in studies of the tip-of-the-tongue effect (Brown and McNeill 1966); identifying words from brief, tachistoscopic presentations (e.g. Winnick and Daniel 1970); and the lexical decision task, in which subjects make decisions about whether or not letter strings form English words (Rubenstein *et al.* 1970). Because all these tasks became quite popular after 1972, albeit for many purposes in addition to the study of semantic memory, Tulving's singling them out for special attention in 1972 was prescient.

In his 1972 essay, Tulving waffled a bit on whether episodic and semantic memory were to be treated as two different stores or systems. Was the distinction a useful heuristic, or was it a fundamental distinction between two information-processing systems? He seemed to be proposing two separate systems, but he wrote that he distinguished between the two types of memory 'primarily for the convenience of communication, rather than as an expression of any profound belief about functional structural separation of the two' (p.384).

Using Kolers' (e.g. 1975) paradigm involving reading of inverted text, Cohen and Squire (1980) obtained data that they interpreted as providing evidence for the two different types of memory proposed by the philosopher Gilbert Ryle (1949): declarative memory (the kind used in knowing that something happened) and procedural memory (knowing how to do something). The notion that these two represent fundamentally different systems for retaining information has received increasing evidence over the years (for example as summarized in Squire (1987)). In Squire's (e.g. 1994) typology, declarative memory is subdivided into two systems: episodic and semantic memory.† Non-declarative systems include skills and habits, priming, classical conditioning, and non-associative learning. These latter types of memory will be discussed in a later section.

Since 1980 a tremendous volume of material has been published about memory systems, including several book-length treatises (e.g. Schacter and Tulving 1994*a*),

---

† Curiously, short-term memory or working memory (Baddeley 1986) is left out of many modern schemes for memory systems, including Squire's (1987, 1994) typical representation. Tulving (1985) wrote a paper addressing the question that formed the title of his paper: 'How many memory systems are there?' His tentative answer there was 'three', but curiously he made no mention of short-term or working memory in the paper. A few years later, Tulving and Schacter (1990) wrote about memory systems again and now short-term/working memory was included as one of five main memory systems. Apparently, Tulving finally overcame his earlier misgivings (see Tulving and Patterson (1968) and included short-term memory.

and now the current tome joins the mix. There is no easy way to summarize the current debate. The number of putative systems has grown rapidly over the years and, in our opinion, the criteria for postulating systems have never been pinned down. That is, many authors use different criteria and there seems little general agreement emerging on what are the critical systems comprising human memory. For example, the systems identified by the various writers in the Schacter and Tulving (1994*a*) volume employ different criteria, different names, and have different approaches to the whole issue—yet all writers were writing in support of their view of memory systems. With this cacophony of opinion from supporters, one hardly needs critics.

Here we consider a set of criteria that we think are clearly defensible and see how far we can get by rigorously applying them. In an important paper that attempted such a specification, Sherry and Schacter (1987) postulated four criteria that must be satisfied in order to postulate a difference between two memory systems: (1) functional dissociations between tests tapping different systems; (2) stochastic independence between these tests; (3) different neural pathways for the memory systems; and (4) functional incompatibility between tests tapping the two systems. In general, the 'laws of memory' should be different for different memory systems. These are fine criteria, and we would be happy to see them rigorously applied. However, we suspect that most of the systems currently under discussion would fail to meet them (Roediger *et al.* 1990).

Functional independence

Consider just the most typical form of dissociation, which has been shown repeatedly in both normal and pathological populations: an independent (or subject) variable affects performance on an explicit memory test such as recall or recognition and yet has no effect (or even an opposite effect) on primed word fragment or word stem completion. Obviously, Sherry and Schacter's (1987) first criterion, functional independence, is met. Prior to 1990, the observed dissociation would have been interpreted as evidence for a distinction between episodic and semantic memory in Tulving's (1972, 1983) typology. Within Squire's (e.g. 1987) organization, the dissociation would have supported the contrast between the episodic subsystem of declarative memory and the priming subsystem of procedural memory. Functional dissociations are a necessary criterion for any postulation of separate systems (or separate processes) and have been rightly emphasized.

However, dissociations between two measures of memory can be interpreted in many different ways. They are the grist for every theorist's mill. Interpreting an interaction between performance on any given explicit memory test and any particular implicit memory test as evidence for putative systems underlying the tests is premature, in the absence of considerable supporting evidence (although this inferential leap is made in many articles). With only two tests—one alleged to measure episodic memory and one to measure a priming subsystem of procedural memory—the constraints are few. The information-processing requirements of the two tests may differ in many other ways. Roediger (1984) suggested that at a bare minimum researchers postulating a difference between systems or processes should include at least four memory measures in their experimental designs; such an approach would help tighten the inferential net around the constructs of interest. That is, one should have two measures of episodic memory (e.g. a recall measure and a recognition measure) and two implicit memory measures (e.g. priming on word stem completion and on the lexical decision task). This strategy is rarely followed, even today, because theorists would have the discomfort of finding dissociations that are awkward to explain by prevailing theory. What happens when recall and recognition are dissociated by an independent or subject variable? Do we then declare that separate memory systems underlie the two types of test? We return to these questions below.

Stochastic independence

Stochastic independence refers to the relation between performance on two tests, as aggregated across subjects and items. The assumption is that if performance is uncorrelated across the two tests, then the tests are tapping different memory systems. For example, Tulving *et al.* (1982) obtained stochastic independence between recognition and primed completion of fragmented words. Whether one succeeds in recognizing an item on a recognition test does not predict priming on a later word completion test. Similar results were obtained by others with different implicit tests (e.g. Jacoby and Witherspoon 1982). Some have had trouble replicating this effect (e.g. Hintzman and Hartry 1990), and numerous methodological objections have been raised about measures of stochastic independence (in Hintzman and Hartry (1990) and numerous other papers). We will not consider those criticisms here but will assume that the method is relatively free of the various artifacts of which critics have complained.

Our question is different: if two tests are stochastically independent, can this evidence be used to postulate different memory systems? We take a detour before trying to answer this question. Interestingly, the criterion of stochastic independence is rarely applied by most researchers postulating distinct memory systems. We ask why, if it is supposed to be so critical to the enterprise, as Tulving (1985) and Sherry and Schacter (1987) maintained. Has anyone ever shown (or sought to show) that short- and long-term memory are stochastically independent?

Testing for stochastic independence is only possible in a particular method of conducting memory tests. The standard method uses an episodic recognition test followed by an implicit test of word completion. Although much useful information about the relation between tests might be gained by the method of testing for stochastic independence (especially when used in its more sophisticated forms such as Hayman and Tulving's (1989*a*) method of triangulation), we suspect that the method is not general enough to be useful across widely disparate types of test reflecting different memory systems. Could one establish stochastic independence between pursuit rotor tracking (tapping procedural memory) and some task tapping episodic memory? How would one approach this question? For these reasons, experiments seeking to establish stochastic independence are rarely employed by researchers trying to establish separate memory systems.

We suspect that most researchers working within a memory systems perspective now see the criterion of stochastic independence as irrelevant. For example, only one set of contributors in Schacter and Tulving's (1994a) volume on memory systems bothered to consider issues of stochastic independence; the one group that did (Metcalfe et al. 1994) was interested primarily in testing the CHARM model's account of independence and how binding operations may differ between explicit and implicit tests. In fact, in that same volume, in Schacter and Tulving's (1994b) initial chapter discussing the criteria for memory systems, stochastic independence was not mentioned!

Why was a criterion that was once accorded a place of special importance in postulation of memory systems (Tulving 1985; Sherry and Schacter 1987) later dropped altogether (Schacter and Tulving 1994b)? No one has ever said, but we can speculate that the incoming data simply showed the criterion would not work, even in those special cases when it can be applied. Hayman and Tulving (1989b) performed experiments in which, following study of a list of words (e.g. AARDVARK), subjects took successive tests with either the same fragments on the two occasions (A _ _ D _ _ RK, A _ _ D _ _ RK) or different and complementary fragments (A _ _ D _ _ RK, _ A R _ V A _ _). When subjects received implicit memory test instructions, successive testing with the same fragments revealed strong dependence on the two tests, indicating that the same system was being tapped (according to the standard logic). However, with the same implicit test orientation, successive testing with different fragments revealed striking independence!

Are we really to imagine that testing the same target item (AARDVARK) with different fragments recruits different memory systems? No, of course not. Hayman and Tulving (1989b) argued that their results showed hyperspecificity of perceptual operations within a data-driven, perceptual priming system of implicit memory. We believe this is a valid conclusion; specificity of perceptual operations plays a critical role in priming in data-driven implicit memory tests (Roediger and Srinivas 1993; Srinivas 1993). However, our point here is that Hayman and Tulving's (1989b) results clearly show that stochastic independence cannot be used to distinguish between memory systems because independence can occur within a memory system. No criteria have been proposed to distinguish when stochastic independence between two tests indicates different memory systems and when it indicates 'hyperspecificity' of operations within a single system. Thus, one criterion proposed by Tulving (1985) and endorsed by others (e.g. Sherry and Schacter, 1987) simply seems irrelevant at this point.

Different neural pathways

Another criterion necessary for distinguishing between memory systems is that tests must rely on different neural pathways. This criterion may be satisfied in distinguishing between explicit and implicit tests, but how much or how little similarity must there be between the neural pathways to qualify as 'different'? Consider study of a word (ASSASSIN) and then two later tests, one involving implicit word fragment completion (thought to tap a priming subsystem of non-declarative memory or a perceptual representation system) and the other an explicit test of word fragment cued recall (thought to tap episodic memory). In these two tests, subjects produce the same word to the same cue (e.g. A _ _ A _ _ IN). Surely some processes and some neural systems used in producing the word in these two different tests will be the same; others will be different. How different must they be to qualify as 'different systems'? If only one process distinguishes the two, do we deem the two tests as relying on different memory systems?

We make the assumption that different neural processes must be used whenever a dissociation is obtained between memory tests within an experiment. That is, if we observe a difference in behaviour on two tests as a function of an independent variable, and if we make the assumption that all behaviour is caused by neural processes, then any dissociation in behaviour must be caused by different neural processes. If we call these neural processes a 'system', then the interaction is caused by different neural systems. So, in some sense, any interaction between tests as a function of an independent variable implicates two different memory systems, in this rather narrow sense of the term *system*. Indeed, we believe that the criterion is a valid one, but if it is systematically applied, the number of 'memory systems' would be quite large. Roediger (1990a) counted about 25 systems that would meet this criterion, and that was years ago. The number would probably be larger now. The criterion that different neural pathways must exist is a necessary one for postulating memory systems, but it has not yet been specified in a compelling way. Any two tasks that can be dissociated must rely on different neural systems. Are they then said to rely on different memory systems?

Functional incompatibility

The criterion of functional incompatibility as specified by Sherry and Schacter (1987) requires 'memory systems to be specialized to such a degree that the functional problems each system handles cannot be handled by the other system' (Sherry and Schacter 1987, p.439). This criterion is quite compelling in some cases (e.g. in their application of different systems that birds have evolved to retain songs and to find food). However, the criterion is less obvious when applied to standard paradigms of human memory under consideration here: when given a fragmented word as a cue, why should recollecting that the corresponding word was on the study list necessarily be 'functionally incompatible' with producing the same word when given instructions to say the first word that comes to mind? Why couldn't the two systems cooperate in producing the word? To our knowledge, no one has ever answered this question in a compelling way. Similarly, why would retrieving the fact that someone recently said 'Stan Musial was a great baseball player' be functionally incompatible with retrieving this fact from semantic memory?

Sherry and Schacter (1987) argued that the criterion of functional incompatibility was critical to establishing different memory systems, but it has rarely been applied to the study of human memory systems. Applying evolutionary arguments to memory for written words may be stretching matters a bit, anyway. Western writing systems were only invented by the Phoenicians a few thousand years ago. Because no one thinks the brain has significantly evolved over this time frame, whatever neural systems underlie word priming and word recall presumably evolved for other reasons and are now being used for these purposes. Therefore, although the criterion of functional incompatibility seems perfectly plausible, it has never been rigorously applied to the delineation of differences between forms of human memory. We suspect that many distinctions between memory systems that are now endorsed would not withstand scrutiny on grounds of functional incompatibility.

In concluding this section, we again note that the primary criterion that has been used to distinguish memory systems is the logic of functional dissociation and, less often, converging dissociation; the secondary criterion is demonstration of different neural pathways, implied by the first. If we primarily use these two criteria, then the number of systems uncovered will be quite large—as indeed seems to be borne out by recent history. Numerous systems have been postulated and many more will be, including another possibility listed below. And most of the discoveries have been about memory systems using traditional psychological paradigms. Rarely have theorists considered other biological memory systems, to which we now turn, albeit briefly.

THE BIOLOGY OF MEMORY: OTHER NON-DECLARATIVE SYSTEMS

A typology of memory systems such as Squire's (1987, 1994) scheme leads to the interesting question as to what set of phenomena should qualify as reflecting 'learning and memory'. The way people ordinarily think about remembering is probably reflected prototypically in episodic memory: remembering the personal experiences of one's life. The general knowledge reflected by the concept of semantic memory also seems to fall comfortably under a broad definition of memory. It seems reasonable to say that we remember (or know) that Abraham Lincoln was the sixteenth president of the United States. But the non-declarative memory systems begin stretching our usual notion of memory. If you get up from your chair to leave the room, do you 'remember' how to walk? When you reach down to tie your shoelaces, do you have to remember how? When you streak across the court to execute a forehand volley, do you have to remember how to do so? Using the word 'remember' seems strange in these contexts and, of course, that is just the point that Tulving (1983, 1985) and many others have made. These 'non-declarative' memory systems (Squire 1994) seem to share only one feature in common: they are not declarative systems. How far do we extend the word memory to include other biological systems that seem to fit? Why aren't these other biological systems considered non-declarative memory systems? Let us pursue this question with some examples.

A standard definition of learning is change in behaviour as a function of experience (excluding changes due to maturation, fatigue, and other states). An interesting feature of this definition is that many different biological systems show 'learning and memory'. Neurobiologists study long-term potentiation (LTP), seen as a basic learning mechanism throughout the nervous system. This name refers to processes of change at the level of the synapse; a brief burst of activation of presynaptic fibres leads to enhancement of efficiency in the synapse that can last many hours, even weeks. LTP is observed in many brain structures and seems to serve as a general learning mechanism.

Many other systems besides neural ones reveal phenomena that satisfy the behavioural definition of learning and memory. For example, immunologists study learning and memory in the immune system: the experience of inoculation of a vaccine causes a change in the immune system's behaviour (producing antibodies) that will ward off invasions of antigens that would normally produce the disease. Immunologists refer to the immune system as having a memory and in fact refer to memory cells in the immune system. The abstract of a recent paper in *Science* by Ahmed and Gray (1996) begins 'The immune system can remember, sometimes for a lifetime, the identity of a pathogen' (p.54). The concept of immunological memory is well established. It is worth quoting some passages about the memory of the immune system from a standard biology textbook by Chiras (1993):

> The first time an antigen enters the body, it elicits an immune response, but the initial reaction—or *primary response*—is relatively slow and of small magnitude... During the primary response antibody levels in the blood do not begin to rise until approximately the second week *after* the intruder has been detected.... If the same antigen enters the body at a later date, however, the immune system acts much more quickly and forcefully... This greatly fortified reaction constitutes the *secondary response*... [and] during a secondary response antibody levels increase rather quickly, only a few days after the antigen has entered the body. The amount of antibody produced also greatly exceeds quantities generated during the primary response. Consequently, the antigen is quickly destroyed, and a recurrence of the illness is prevented. (p.360)

Psychologists of memory will quickly recognize the general class of phenomena known as *priming* in the previous passage. The introduction of an antigen into the immune system the first time (eliciting the primary response) produces priming on the second occasion. Indeed, the immune system shows enhancement in the two primary measures that psychologists have collected on implicit memory tests: magnitude of response (greater amount of antibody production) and speed of response (the immune response occurs much more quickly). The mechanism by which priming of the immune response occurs is through the creation of what are called memory cells. We quote Chiras (1993, p.360) again:

> During the primary response, some lymphocytes divide to produce memory cells. Memory cells are immunologically competent B cells that do not transform into plasma cells. Instead, they remain in the body awaiting the antigen's reentry. These cells therefore create a relatively large reserve force of antigen-specific B-cells. When the antigen reappears, memory cells proliferate rapidly, producing numerous plasma cells that quickly crank out anti-

bodies to combat the foreign invaders... during the secondary response, the memory cells also generate additional memory cells that remain in the body in case the antigen should appear at some later date.

Immune protection afforded by memory cells can last 20 years or longer and explains why once a person has had a childhood disease, such as mumps or chicken pox, it is unlikely that he or she will contract it again. Resistance to disease that is provided by the immune system is known as immunity. From an evolutionary standpoint, this adaptation serves us extremely well, greatly reducing the incidence of infectious disease. Without it, humans would probably not be able to survive.

Clearly, the immune system is a memory system, although it never seems to be referred to as another non-declarative memory system. Ahmed and Gray (1996) note that matters are not quite so well understood as the previous textbook rendition would have one believe, and that many mysteries exist in immunological memory to tantalize researchers. They argue that one needs to consider T-cell memory and B-cell memory separately, and to distinguish between effector cells and memory cells, to gain a more complete understanding and to provide for more effective vaccines. We need not worry about the details of their proposal, but only point to the fact that scientists in other fields study non-declarative memory systems that somehow never make it into psychologists' schemes.

Other biological systems besides the immune system exhibit memory, including the female reproductive system. Roediger (1993) pointed out that the female reproductive system (the FRS) shows priming from a single prior episode, just like other non-declarative memory systems. Women having their first baby take on average 9.5 hours in labour, whereas for second and later children, the average is only 6.6 hours. The data show savings in both the latent phase of labour (dilation of the cervix, 1.6 hours) and the active phase of labour (the rapid finish of dilation and descent of the fetus, 1.3 hours), for a total of 2.9 hours. (Because most cognitive psychologists are more accustomed to measuring priming in milliseconds, it is worth pointing out that this priming effect is substantial: 21 600 000 milliseconds.) This huge savings shows that the female reproductive system functions as an implicit memory system: the first act of labour creates processes that transfer efficiently to facilitate the speed of response execution when the same situation arises again. The mechanisms are not completely understood, but this phenomenon gives new meaning to Rozin's (1976) hot tubes theory of priming.

The point here is that there are many non-declarative memory systems besides those proposed in the current literature. Their omission seems curious. What qualifies some non-declarative systems as memory and not others?

PROCESSING THEORIES

Processing theorists retain the legacy of Bartlett (1932) and Neisser (1967). Cognitive processes are difficult to isolate and study. We might speak of sensation, perception, memory, and thinking as if they represent different entities, but in actuality, they are intertwined. Perceptual recognition of common objects can only be achieved if one has knowledge of them from prior experience; events must be perceived to be remembered later; and thinking doubtless involves complex operations that draw on perception of the problem and what aspects of similar problems can be retrieved, and so on. Isolating processes such as 'memory' or even 'episodic memory' and treating them as quite different and unrelated to other cognitive processes is not profitable. Bartlett (1932, p.15) pointed out that '... in order to understand how and what we remember, we must set in relation to this how and what we perceive'. Neisser (1967, especially Chapter 11) emphasized the same point. All cognition is constructive—perceiving, remembering, and thinking—and these processes cannot be cleanly separated one from another. In fact, processing approaches frequently look to perceiving (as in the Bartlett quote) as a touchstone for understanding remembering. Neisser (1967, p.285) wrote against the concept of memory traces being stored in some fixed way and then being called up to the footlights of consciousness in recall or recognition. Rather, remembering, like perceiving, is best construed as an achievement or construction: 'The analogy being offered asserts... that the role which stored information plays in recall is like the role which stimulus information plays in perception. In neither case does it enter awareness directly, and in neither case can it be literally reproduced in behavior, except after rather special training... One does not see objects simply "because they are there" but after an elaborate process of construction (which usually is designed to make use of relevant stimulus information). Similarly, one does not recall objects or responses simply because traces of them exist in mind, but after an elaborate process of *re*construction, (which usually makes use of relevant stored information)'. Principles of perceiving and remembering are similar, and remembering can be understood by analogy to perceiving.

More recently, Craik and Lockhart (1972) gave new impetus to processing theories of cognition and to the intimate relation between perceiving and remembering by their levels of processing framework. Memory was conceived as a byproduct of perceiving, broadly conceived, and perceiving could be considered as passing through various stages, from 'shallow' processing that emphasized surface features of words or objects to 'deep' processing that invoked meaning. The levels of processing framework generated a mammoth amount of research in the 1970s and attracted some critics. However, for present purposes the levels of processing framework put emphasis on processing operations as critical to understanding of memory.

At about the same time, Paul Kolers argued in a series of papers for an approach to memory in terms of mental operations. The hallmark of the procedural approach, harking back to Bartlett (1932) and Neisser (1967), was that performance on memory tasks could be described as skilled performance and that one should look to the procedures of mind to explain cognitive performances (e.g. Kolers 1975; Kolers and Smythe 1979; Kolers and Roediger 1984). Many experiments can be interpreted as supporting such a procedural approach, including several revealing dissociations in performance on tasks that all measured recognition of words (e.g. Kolers and Perkins 1975). In particular, Kolers' experiments showed that transfer from one task to another benefited to the degree that the procedures underlying performance on the two tasks were similar (see Kolers and Roediger (1984) for a review).

Coincident with these observations, Bransford *et al.* (1979) (see also Morris *et al.* 1978) introduced the notion of transfer appropriate processing as a complement or alternative to the levels of processing approach. Their experimental work showed that meaningful processing does not always produce superior retention to processing that focuses on surface features. If the test were one that drew on surface properties of the material (Did a word rhyming with *eagle* appear in the list?), then initial processing during encoding that drew attention to these phonemic or sound properties could produce retention superior to 'deep' semantic processing. The critical determinant of performance, according to proponents of transfer appropriate processing, is the interaction of mental procedures engaged between encoding and retrieval; this approach is similar in many ways to the idea in the encoding specificity hypothesis (Tulving 1983). By matching or mismatching conditions between study and test, various groups of researchers showed that shallow processing of encoded information could produce recall or recognition equivalent to deep, meaningful encodings (e.g. Fisher and Craik 1979; McDaniel *et al.* 1978) or even lead to memory superior to deep processing (e.g. Morris *et al.* 1978; Stein 1978).

All the experiments reported in the papers just cited produced strong interactions: performance on one test often reversed when compared with that on another test. However, all the tests were of explicit, or episodic, or declarative memory. As Kolers and Roediger (1984) noted 'If dissociations are found among tests tapping the same memory system, then the discovery of dissociations between tasks cannot be taken as evidence for different memory systems' (p.438). On the procedural view, 'dissociation is the natural state of affairs, not what needs explaining' (ibid.).

As we have seen in the previous sections, converging dissociations are the primary evidence used to justify postulation of memory systems, but a wider view of the cognitive literature shows that such findings are commonplace and can often be given other interpretations. Although it may make sense to say that reading one version of rotated text (in Kolers' inverted reading paradigm) relies on a 'different cognitive system' than does reading a different version of inverted text (see Kolers and Perkins 1975), no one has seriously proposed that performance in the two cases relies on different memory systems. But why not? The evidence is as compelling in this case as it is elsewhere.

Proponents of memory systems views have sometimes been accused of not being very precise and specific (e.g. Neely 1989; McKoon *et al.* 1986). That might be true on occasion, but probably processing theorists are guilty of being just as fuzzy. Defining precisely what a mental process or procedure is has eluded all writers. Even distinguishing between classes of processes is difficult. We review here, briefly, one attempt to distinguish between data-driven and conceptually driven processes, a broad distinction that ties into perceptual theory and that might provide a bit more specificity to the rather wooly notions of the procedural approaches.

Following Jacoby's (1983) lead, Blaxton (1989), Roediger and Blaxton (1987) and Roediger *et al.* (1989) argued that a critical distinction that cut through tests used to measure explicit recollection and those that assessed priming on implicit memory tests was between data-driven (bottom-up or perceptual) processing and conceptually driven (or top-down) processing. Briefly, many implicit memory tests challenge the perceptual system by presenting brief displays, or fragmented forms, of pictures or words. The standard method is to present these randomly, with no meaningful context. The subjects' task is to guess the identity of the item seen under these impoverished conditions. According to the logic of transfer appropriate processing, performance on such priming tests should benefit to the extent that the study phase provides appropriate practice for the later test. Therefore, reading the word in the first phase would be expected to lead to greater priming than generating it from a conceptual clue. Because the transfer test involves reading from an impoverished display, then prior practice reading the word should lead to greater transfer than would generating the word from conceptually related information. Most (but not all) implicit memory tests in common use are data-driven or perceptual tests, a point to which we return below. Conversely, conceptual tests are those that draw on meaningful concepts, and such tests will benefit from study experiences that augment conceptual processing, such as generating information. Therefore, on these tests, there should be better performance when people generate a concept during a study phase rather than read the word naming the concept. Most explicit memory tests qualify as conceptual tests, but again there are exceptions (see tests used by Blaxton (1989), Morris *et al* (1978), and Stein (1978), among others).

Roediger *et al.* (1989) specified converging operations to determine whether a test was to be classified as a perceptual or conceptual test. For example, conceptual tests should show a generation effect (generating would lead to a benefit relative to reading on these tests) and a level of processing effect (with deeper, meaningful encoding leading to better performance than shallow, perceptual encoding). On implicit tests that require visual processing, reading should lead to greater priming than generating (because of practice at perceiving the word), and there should be little or no level of processing effect. (Perceptual processing of the word is assumed to be roughly the same in shallow and deep encoding conditions; however, see Bergman (1998) for doubts concerning this point.)

In principle, explicit and implicit tests could be either perceptual or conceptual. However, there has generally been a correlation such that explicit (or episodic) tests are conceptual, and implicit tests are perceptual (Roediger and Blaxton 1987). It is perfectly possible to have implicit conceptual tests (e.g. Blaxton 1989; Srinivas and Roediger 1990), but they usually show relatively small priming effects (for reasons that remain poorly understood). Constructing perceptual explicit tests is more difficult, although as noted above, they do exist (e.g. Blaxton, 1989;

Stein 1978). (The reason it is difficult to construct such tasks is that the very instruction to 'remember one's past' seems to call up meaningful processing in the effort to comply.) When subjects are given word fragment cues on an explicit test (i.e. with instructions to recall words from a recently studied list that match the cue words), recall is guided partly by perceptual processes (to determine the identity of the word) and partly by conceptual processes (presumably to decide if it were one of the words presented). Many studies (e.g. Challis and Sidhu 1993; Challis *et al.* 1993; McDermott and Roediger 1996; Weldon *et al.* 1989, 1995) provide research consistent with this point.

The guiding idea of transfer appropriate processing, combined with the distinction between perceptual and conceptual tests, goes a great distance towards accounting for the voluminous literature comparing explicit and implicit memory tests (see Roediger and McDermott (1993) for a review). However, some problems exist, too, and their nature is similar to those arising for the systems theorists. For example, several embarrassing interactions crop up. Toth and Hunt (1990) manipulated words varying in orthography; some were regular and others were quite distinctive (YACHT, for example). This would seem to be a perceptual manipulation —common or bizarre orthography—and yet it affected free recall, a conceptual test according to Roediger *et al.*'s (1989) classification. The orthographic manipulation also affected primed word fragment completion, with greater priming on words with distinctive as compared to regular orthography. Therefore, a perceptual variable affected performance on both a perceptual implicit test and a conceptual explicit test, a pattern not predicted by the theory.

Another outcome that provides a similar problem was reported by McDermott and Roediger (1996), who found dissociations occurring between conceptual tests. They manipulated conceptual repetition, in which a concept is repeated but the token representing the concept is not. For example, the word *elephant* might be followed by a picture of an elephant or it might be followed by an associate, such as *tusk*. McDermott and Roediger (1996) showed that such conceptual repetition strongly affected free recall of the target concept (*elephant*), but this manipulation had no effect on primed word fragment completion for the target (E _ EP _ A _ T). This outcome replicated a finding of Roediger and Challis (1992) and is completely in line with the predictions of Roediger *et al.*'s (1989) framework: the conceptual variable affected the conceptual but not the perceptual test. The problems arose on the other two conceptual tests included: category cued recall (an explicit test) and category instance generation (an implicit test). Both of these are conceptual tests, so we would expect the patterns to be like those in free recall, but they were not. In the category instance generation test, priming was unaffected by conceptual repetition, unlike free recall. In addition, pictures did not produce more priming than words, although the free recall test showed the usual picture superiority effect. Weldon and Coyote (1996) also reported in several experiments that pictures and words produce equivalent priming on the conceptual implicit tests of category generation and word association. The results from category cued recall test in McDermott and Roediger's (1996) experiments were also problematic from the transfer appropriate processing view. Although a picture superiority effect was obtained, conceptual repetition did not have an effect on this test. Thus, the three conceptual tests used by McDermott and Roediger (1996) produced three different patterns of outcome, inconsistent with predictions from the theory. Of course, some of these results are also inconsistent with all memory systems theories. After all, free recall and category cued recall both tap episodic memory, and yet they can be dissociated. Similarly, as we discuss in more detail below, free or cued recall is also frequently dissociated from episodic recognition. By the logic of functional dissociation discussed above, free recall, category cued recall, and recognition are then supported by different systems.

All these results show that the distinction between perceptual and conceptual processing is only a start; other types of processing must be introduced. McDermott and Roediger (1996) suggested that different types of semantic information might be postulated and pointed to Cabeza's (1994) research, which dissociated two different conceptual implicit memory tests. Just as more memory systems are added to account for unpredicted dissociations, so must more processing distinctions be added to account for a different set of awkward dissociations.

THE DEBATE

The remarks above give a sketchy version of the debate between memory systems and memory processes points of view in the 1980s, leaving out many details and several important considerations. Now, as we remarked at the beginning of the chapter, the debate seems over, or at least has temporarily subsided. In a sense, both sets of theories have become so cumbersome and diffuse that testing between them is difficult or impossible. An historian looking back might wonder if this were not always so—the theories could not really be compared at any point in a fair test.

We believe that this hypothetical claim is untrue. Rather than pitting general amorphous frameworks against one another, which probably is impossible, one can instead test relatively specific forms of the theories in which one might make relatively specific predictions. Blaxton (1989) did just that. She observed that the dissociations usually used as evidence for the separation of episodic and semantic memory (such as between free recall and recognition on the one hand and primed word fragment or word stem completion on the other) could be due to either (or both) of two factors. Tulving (1983) had interpreted the dissociations between these tests as evidence for the distinction between episodic memory (the system responsible for recognition and recall) and semantic memory (the system originally thought responsible for primed word fragment and word stem completion). Blaxton (1989) noted that free recall and recognition were conceptual tests and that word stem and word fragment completion were probably perceptual tests. She carried out several experiments to try to determine whether it was the difference in the memory system tapped that accounted for the dissociations, or whether it was the type of information processing required (perceptual or conceptual) that provided the better explanation. Thus, the theories could be pitted against one another and were specific enough to make precise predictions.

Partial results of one of her experiments are shown here in Fig. 3.1. Briefly, subjects either read or generated items during a study phase and then took one of five tests (although we consider only four here): free recall (an episodic memory test and a conceptual test), answering general knowledge questions (a semantic memory test that is a conceptual test), graphemic cued recall (an episodic memory test that is based on perceptual clues, so is therefore thought to be data-driven or perceptual), and word fragment completion (a semantic memory test by Tulving's (1972) classification but, Blaxton assumed, largely a perceptual or data-driven test). The critical question was whether the dissociations between tests would work out to be those predicted by the specific memory systems account (the distinction between episodic and semantic memory) or according to the transfer appropriate processing logic (distinguishing between perceptual and conceptual tests). According to Tulving's episodic/semantic distinction, the two episodic memory tests should show parallel patterns and be dissociated from the two semantic tests, since they tap a different system obeying by different laws. According to Blaxton's (1989) transfer appropriate processing approach, the two perceptual tests should show the same pattern of effect and be dissociated from the two conceptual tests.

As the results in Fig. 3.1 show, the two perceptual or data-driven tasks behaved the same way: more priming occurred on the word fragment completion task after reading the words during the study phase than after generating them, and there was similarly greater recall from reading than generating on the graphemic cued recall test. On the other hand, generating produced greater free recall and more priming

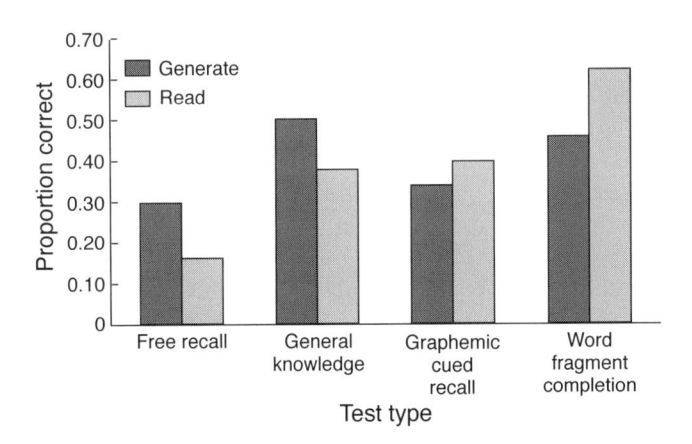

Fig. 3.1. Selected data from Blaxton (1989). The finding that generating words from conceptual cues leads to better memory performance than simply reading the word does not generalize to all types of memory tests: on perceptually based tests, the reverse pattern is observed.

on the general knowledge test than did reading. Two episodic memory tests (graphemic cued recall and free recall) were dissociated, as were two semantic memory tests (answering general knowledge questions and completing word fragments).

If psychologists practiced the logic of strong inference (Platt 1964), in which a critical result rules out an entire class of theories, Blaxton's (1989) experiments (and many others like them, e.g. Srinivas and Roediger (1990) and Tajika and Neuman (1992)) would have put an end to claims that dissociation experiments provide a firm foundation for the distinction between episodic and semantic memory. But of course that did not happen; theories in psychology are flexible. Spurred partly by Blaxton's (1989) data and partly by other considerations from neuropsychological data, Tulving and Schacter (1990) announced the discovery of another memory system, the perceptual representation system (PRS). The PRS was essentially the systems-language response to data-driven or perceptual processing in transfer appropriate processing terms. In the new theory, Tulving and Schacter (1990) argued that tasks such as word fragment completion, word stem completion, lexical decision, and word identification from brief displays all depended on the word form system, a subsystem of PRS. Further, PRS was believed to be pre-semantic, or to operate at a level in the cognitive system before meaning was attached to words. Semantic memory was still included in the new proposal, still believed to be used to access general knowledge as in answering general knowledge questions (but excluding those about forms of words). To account for the finding that non-linguistic three-dimensional objects could show priming, yet another subsystem was proposed—the structural description system (Tulving and Schacter 1990).

All these developments are fine—there is always room for more memory systems and subsystems, of course. In fact, on the basis of the current understanding of the primate visual system, we anticipate there will be dozens of dissociations across perceptual tasks and, as a result, the postulation of numerous perceptual memory subsystems. An examination of the most recent anatomic roadmap of the visual system shown in Fig. 3.2, which is an update of work by Van Essen *et al.* (1992), points us toward this prediction. Dozens of visual areas have been identified; these areas are believed to segregate into multiple, but highly interdependent, processing streams. If these processing streams, or points along these streams, can be biased via priming, we expect a similar roadmap to evolve to characterize perceptual memory subsystems.

While applauding advances in our knowledge of memory systems, it is worth pausing here to note that three of the four tasks listed by Tulving (1972) as quintessential semantic memory tasks (word identification, lexical decision, and word fragment completion) are now believed to have nothing whatsoever to do with semantic memory! Indeed, a real difficulty for testing memory systems proposals is that no behavioural tests seem to rely on any single memory system for their execution, and so no tests can be firmly pinned to the operation of a single memory system. Even free recall—seemingly the quintessential test reflecting episodic memory—is believed to have a component of semantic memory involved. Tulving

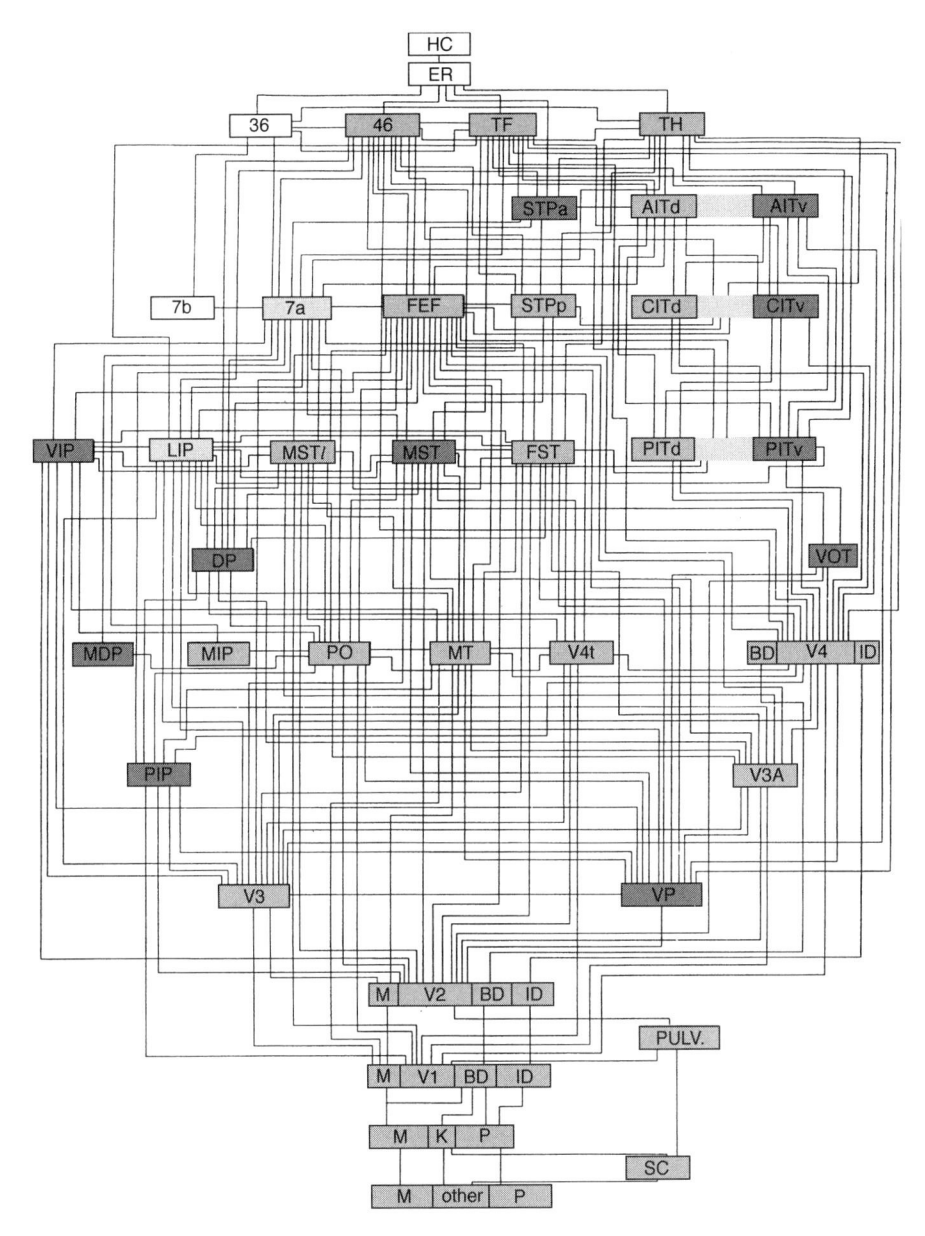

Fig. 3.2. A map of visual areas and their connectivity as tentatively proposed by Van Essen *et al.* (1992; reprinted with permission). The many areas are interconnected and are presumed to segregate into parallel, but highly interdependent, processing pathways. Notions of memory subsystems such as the visual word-form and structural description system (Schacter and Tulving 1994*b*) are probably heuristics that capture priming phenomenon manifested by facilitated processing within portions of this highly complex, and interdependent, set of visual areas.

(1985) developed his remember/know procedure to reflect, respectively, contributions of episodic and semantic memory (or remembering and knowing) on performance of ostensibly episodic memory tests. His data showed that cued recall tests and recognition tests seem to have larger contributions of semantic memory (manifested in a larger proportion of *know* responses) than did free recall; however, sometimes subjects use the *know* response even in free recall tests. The remember/know technique has been used by many researchers (for reviews see Gardiner and Java 1993; Rajaram and Roediger 1997), and most experiments show relatively high proportions of know responses on explicit memory tests; this pattern, according to Tulving (1985) reflects semantic memory contributions.

Tulving and Schacter (1990) proposed various specialized memory subsystems of the perceptual system. In the same year, Roediger (1990a) pointed out that evidence could be adduced for many other memory systems besides the handful that had achieved popularity at that point. For example, neuropsychologists interested in language have found evidence for separate input and output phonological stores for speech (Kolk *et al.* 1985; Berndt 1987), and similar input and output stores are believed to exist for writing (Bub and Kertsez 1982; Ellis *et al.* 1983). Similarly, Paivio (1969, 1986), Kosslyn (1980) and many others have documented differences between distinct long-term memory systems for handling visual and verbal information, yet these systems are rarely represented in the available catalogues of memory systems. One is left with the impression that the collection of memory systems included in any particular scheme is driven only in small part by the extant data, because some obvious entries (such as visual and verbal stores) are often overlooked.

Even more interesting are plausible candidates for memory systems for which no one has ever made a case. We would like to propose here that recall and recognition memory tests represent different memory systems. After all, the systems that these two tests must draw on meet most of the criteria that Sherry and Schacter (1987) discussed. First, neuropsychological evidence reveals dissociations between recognition and recall in comparisons of brain-damaged patients and control subjects. Hirst *et al.* (1986, 1988) equated recognition in memory-impaired patients with that of control patients by confounding some factor such as presentation time or retention interval, to bring the patients up to the level of normal subjects. However, even when patients were equated with control subjects in recognition, they still performed disproportionately worse in recall. This striking dissociation in patients is akin to those between explicit and implicit measures that supported other distinctions between memory systems. Patients can be relatively intact on one measure as compared with normal subjects and still disproportionately worse on the other measure.

A second, quite large, body of evidence also reveals functional dissociations between recall and recognition. One is the well-known word frequency effect in recall and recognition: high-frequency words produce greater recall than low-frequency words, but low-frequency words are better recognized than high-frequency words (e.g. Balota and Neely 1980; Gregg 1976). This differing effect of word frequency on recall and recognition has long been noted, but the finding has never been injected into the discussion of memory systems.

Of course, word frequency is not the only variable that dissociates recall and recognition, (see Tulving (1976) for a review of other data relevant to this issue). To mention just one more example, Eich (1985) had subjects study words in one of two different rooms, using one of two strategies. One group of subjects used interactive imagery in which they imagined the referent of each presented word interacting with an object in the room. The other group of subjects imagined the referent of each word floating in space. Eich's primary interest was whether subjects would show better retention if they were tested in the same room as at study than if they were tested in a different room. He gave them a free recall test 48 hours later and this was followed by a recognition test. The predicted pattern of testing in the same room leading to greater free recall than testing in a different room did hold, but only for subjects who used interactive imagery (imaging the object interacting with something in the room) during study. The room in which the test occurred did not matter for subjects who had used the isolated imagery instruction. For present purposes, the more interesting pattern arose in comparing the recall and recognition performance: the integrated imagery instruction led to greater recall than did the isolated imagery instruction (0.38 versus 0.25 of the 24 words), but the isolated imagery condition led to greater recognition of the words (0.94 to 0.90). This last outcome was statistically significant, despite the probable ceiling effect and despite the fact that the recognition test followed the recall test. Many other functional dissociations between recognition and recall have also been reported, so there seems little doubt about their reality.

Finally, although we have previously argued that stochastic independence between tests is not a telling measure for identifying different memory systems, it is worth pointing out that many studies have shown a remarkable (if still incomplete) independence between recall and recognition, too, when they are directly compared in the recognition/cued recall paradigm used by Tulving and Thomson (1973). Tulving and Wiseman (1978) first reported the (near) independence of recognition and recall and, although some exceptions do occur, later research has largely confirmed their original observations (Nilsson and Gardiner 1993).

These three lines of evidence all support the proposition that different memory systems underlie recognition and recall. The dissociations strongly imply that different neural systems (in the sense defined above; systems differing in at least one component) must exist. The evidence we have cited has long been known. Indeed, the word frequency effect in recall and recognition pre-dates most of the more recent evidence about dissociations between tests. Why is it that no one has ever proposed that recall and recognition are tests that represent different memory systems? The probable reason is that the evidence does not fit comfortably with any current theories. Recall and recognition are believed to be tests that draw on episodic memory and, as yet, no one has proposed that there exist subsystems of episodic memory. But on the same grounds as there exists evidence for other systems and subsystems, there is ample reason to believe that recall and recognition reflect the operation of 'different memory systems'. Not to belabour the obvious, but if we use these same criteria for distinguishing memory systems, soon today's 25 to 30 will seem a quaint relic of the past.

WHERE ARE WE NOW?

To summarize our argument thus far, both the memory systems and the processing views of the 1980s appear far too simple in the late 1990s. Both views have become more complex, of course, as theorists added new wrinkles (new systems, new processing considerations) to account for findings inconsistent with current theory. However, we believe some resolution has been achieved, and in particular we think that a new approach, one that might be called *the components of processing framework*, represents the appropriate way to conceptualize the issues. These ideas have been put forward in most complete form by Moscovitch and his colleagues (e.g. Moscovitch 1994; Moscovitch *et al.* 1993; Witherspoon and Moscovitch 1989), although others have made similar points (e.g. Hintzman 1990; Shimamura 1993; Tenpenny and Shoben 1992). This approach, as Witherspoon and Moscovitch (1989, p.29) put it, is 'based on the assumption that performance on each task requires the operation of many components, some of which are common to tasks and some of which are not. Performances on each task may be independent from each other to the extent that their components differ (or the information they use is different), leaving open the possibility that some components (or types of information) may be more critical in this regard than others.' Any two tasks that are dissociated must differ in at least one component task.

Moscovitch's (1994) theory involves more assumptions and is more complex than the above quote would imply, but for current purposes we use the guiding idea captured in the quote above. Some pairs of tasks may involve only a single difference in components; comparisons between other pairs of tasks may involve many differences. The only critical point for the remaining exposition is that any two tasks that are dissociated must have at least one component process that differs between them (Hintzman 1990).

Let us consider a thought experiment with three groups of subjects. Each group is given a series of word stems (the first three letters of words) as a cue for their task, so the perceptual display at test (e.g. COU_____) is the same for each of the three groups. One group is simply instructed to say the first word that comes to mind that fits each stem. A second group studies a list of words and then performs the same task as the first group: they see word stems and try to generate the first word that comes to mind that completes each stem. However, now some of the stems represent words that had been previously studied (e.g. COURAGE). The third group of subjects studies the same list of words as the second group and they receive the same word stems at test. However, they are instructed to use each stem to think back to an item in the list and to produce words to fit the stems only if the words had occurred in the list. The procedure given the second group above conforms to the usual task instantiating an implicit memory test, whereas the third group represents a typical explicit memory test. The first group represents a baseline measure against which priming is calculated in the implicit memory test.

What 'systems' are used for these three tasks? According to current thought (e.g. Schacter 1994; Tulving and Schacter 1990), different memory systems underlie performance for at least the second and third groups of subjects, and perhaps for all three. The first group of subjects (given the simple word completion test) must rely on lexical memory to produce words from the internal lexicon. The second group (given a primed word completion test) relies on the visual word form system, a subsystem of the perceptual representation system, which will create priming for the recently studied words. The third group (given a cued recall test with word stem cues) is supposed to rely on a different system, the episodic memory system. One justification for this theory is that the latter two tasks can be readily dissociated. For example, manipulating the level of processing has great effects on explicit word stem cued recall (like group 3), but little or no effect on implicit word stem completion (group 2) (Graf and Mandler, 1984; Roediger *et al.* 1992).

From the point of view of Moscovitch's components of processing theory, however, we might analyse the situation somewhat differently. The first condition above—completing word stems—relies on a complicated set of processing components. That set of components represents a cognitive system achieving the task—producing words from three letters. When subjects have studied some of the words prior to completing stems, components of that system responsible for completing the word stems might change—some might be added, others might drop out. But these are changes in components of the system, not the engagement of an independent system. When the third groups of subjects is tested, the system might change yet again—different components involved in remembering must be brought into play. We can refer to these final differences in the components as a 'memory system' perhaps, but little is gained by doing so. Rather, new processing components are brought into play that can create differences between tests. (We elaborate on this point below.)

How can we find out what components of the various tasks are and what do these components tell us about the notion of a 'memory system'? Recently developed functional neuroimaging techniques such a positron emission tomography (PET) and functional magnetic resonance imaging (fMRI) can help delineate them (Posner and Raichle 1994).

In a series of studies conducted by the Washington University Neuroimaging Group and Schacter and his colleagues (Squire *et al.* 1992; Buckner *et al.* 1995*a,b*, 1997; Schacter *et al.* 1996), brain pathways activated during word stem completion were explored. Important to our discussion of memory systems, the focus of these studies was how brain pathways changed in relation to different memory demands. Each of three variants of the word stem tasks described above were imaged using PET.

In the first variant, subjects were imaged while completing word stems to form the first words that came to mind (e.g. they saw COU, and were to say 'courage').

No related study words were presented prior to this test, so this task represented a baseline, or a 'non-primed' variant of word stem completion. Such a task has many processing components: subjects must visually process the stems, retrieve words that complete the stems, and use the retrieved words to guide speech production. Not surprisingly, when brain activation during this task was compared with a low-level reference task that did not contain any of these components, a large number of brain regions were activated (Fig. 3.3A). These regions included multiple areas within visual cortex, presumably activated by the perceptual demands of the task, as well as motor/premotor areas that were activated by the speech production and articulatory demands of the task. Several higher-order brain regions including areas within left prefrontal cortex were also activated—perhaps due to the lexical retrieval demands of the task (see Buckner *et al.* (1995*b*) for discussion). This complex anatomy, although expected considering the task analysis, falls against the backdrop of the tendency to treat 'non-primed' word stem completion as a control task for memory effects without consideration of its inherent processing demands. We will come back to this point later.

The second variant of the word stem completion task studied was a primed version of the task: up to half of the word stems could be completed using words that had been presented a few minutes prior to the PET scan. This variant represents the manipulation that has gained word stem completion its fame (e.g. Graf *et al.* 1982). When the functional anatomy of this second primed variant of word stem completion was explored, it was found to be nearly identical to that of non-primed word stem completion (Fig. 3.3B). Visual, motor, and left prefrontal areas are all activated. If one were examining the task in a different world, one which had not stumbled upon the importance of priming effects, we would probably be writing this chapter and saying the two variants (primed and non-primed word stem completion) activated the same complex anatomy in response to roughly similar sets of task demands. However, because focus was on the correlates of priming, the two variants were compared directly. Primed word stem completion showed less activation of bilateral visual regions compared with non-primed word stem completion (Fig. 3.3B). Such a finding, we believe, shows a correlate of incidental memory retrieval on implicit tests. Prior exposure to words increased the efficiency of generating the word stem completions, as reflected by the tendency to generate study words above baseline levels and to decrease voice onset latencies. At a functional anatomic level, these performance effects correlated with reduced neural activity in perceptual brain areas. These areas were activated by the task in its non-primed form, but did so to a lesser degree after word stem completion was primed. Does such an effect represent a memory system?

Within Schacter and Tulving's (1994*b*) explication, such an effect would reside within the perceptual representation system; to be more specific, within the visual word form subsystem. Here is where we find difficulty: if that is the case, then where does non-primed word stem completion fit? It seems more intuitive that both primed and non-primed word stem completion would be conceptualized as tasks with highly similar cognitive demands. In this instance, the implicit memory

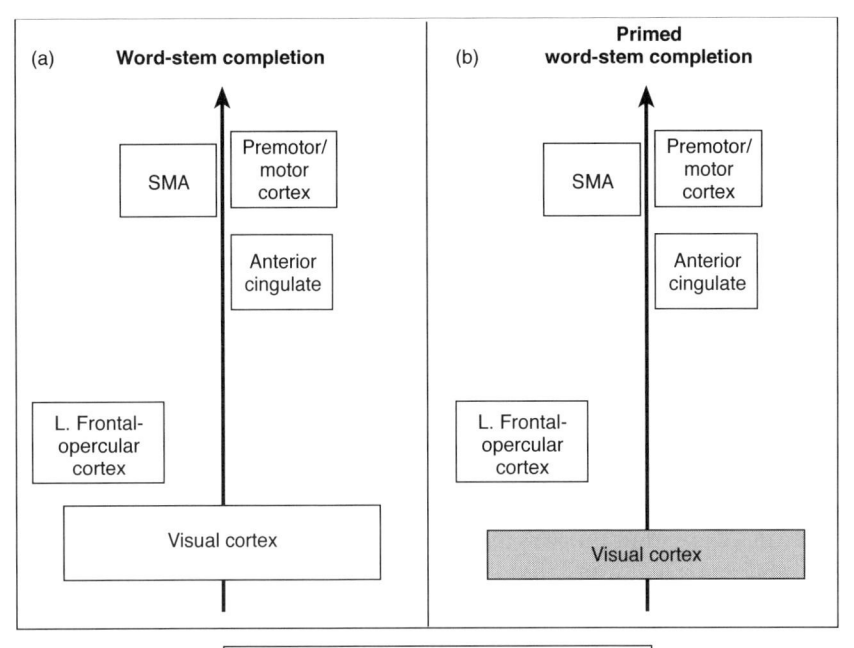

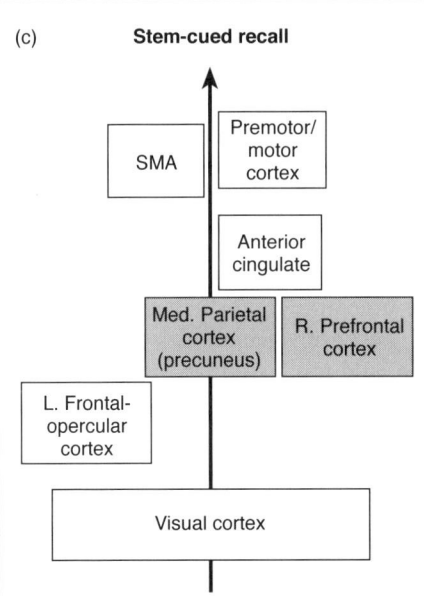

Fig. 3.3. Heuristic diagrams show some of the brain areas believed to be activated during three variants of word stem completion including (A) unprimed word stem completion, (B) primed word stem completion, and (C) an episodic retrieval variant involving stem cued recall. Brain areas are displayed hierarchically, as indicated by the arrows. The three variants overlap considerably. Primed word stem completion appears to show activation reductions in certain areas (for example visual cortex, as shown by the reduced size of the box representing the multiple visual areas). Stem cued recall activated additional areas including medial parietal cortex and right prefrontal cortex.

effect does not reside within a distinct memory system but rather is a processing modification of a existing system: the processing pathway is facilitated, and behavioral and neural correlates of this facilitation are observed. Blaxton and her colleagues (Blaxton et al. 1996) have generalized this finding to word fragment completion. Related facilitation effects have been observed using fMRI during object naming (Wiggs Martin, in press), object decisions (Buckner et al. 1998), categorical decisions (Demb et al. 1995), and during direct repetition with word stem completion (Buckner et al. 1997). These facilitation effects, which were observed during a primed variant of the word stem completion task, can be contrasted with findings from the third variant.

The third variant of the task demanded explicit memory retrieval, thought to involve the episodic memory system. Subjects were shown study words prior to the PET scan and then, during the scans, explicitly instructed to use the stem cues to intentionally recall the study words. (This variant is often referred to as stem cued recall.) Depending on one's theoretical view, such a procedural change could either represent a major task modification, switching in a different memory system to engage in word stem cued recall, or it could be considered a rather straightforward addition to the other variants of word stem completion. In support of the latter view, the task is roughly similar in its organization to non-primed and primed word stem completion variants: subjects view word stem cues, retrieve words from memory, and produce those words. Thus, demands related to perceptual processing, lexical retrieval, and speech production (or writing, depending on the output mode) seem roughly comparable. On the other hand, the requirement with respect to the class of words to be retrieved had changed dramatically. Subjects were no longer instructed to retrieve just any word that completed the stems, but rather were asked to access words associated with the specific study lists. This last demand reflects the essence of episodic retrieval, because information had to be recalled from a specific time and context. Behavioural performance did reflect a change in processing, because voice onset latencies increased over non-primed word stem completion, and more study list words were generated in cued recall than in word stem completion (Buckner et al. 1995a).

When the functional anatomy of stem cued recall was explored, two findings were obtained. First, all of the areas activated during non-primed and primed word stem completion were again present, including visual, motor, and left prefrontal areas. How do we account for such a finding? Within a memory systems perspective there appears to be little room to discuss the similarities between non-primed and primed stem completion (a task that has traditionally been thought to tap semantic memory, or perhaps word form and lexical systems) and stem cued recall (a task that taps episodic memory). We believe the conclusion generated from the data is that all of these variants of word stem completion share highly similar processing demands and functional anatomy. They all tap many of the same systems.

However, this point should not be taken too far. The second finding was that, in addition to the areas activated in common across all of the variants of word stem completion, stem cued recall selectively activated bilateral anterior prefrontal cortex (right > left) and posterior medial parietal cortex (precuneus) (Squire *et al.* 1992; Buckner *et al.* 1995*a*). One or both of these two additional areas have now been shown to activate across a wide range of additional episodic retrieval tasks involving both recognition (Haxby *et al.* 1996; Kapur *et al.* 1995; Rugg *et al.* 1997) and recall (Andreasen *et al.* 1995; Buckner *et al.* 1996*a*; Schacter *et al.* 1996). Tulving *et al.* (1994), in an influential paper, drew attention to the preferential involvement of right prefrontal areas during episodic retrieval within the hemispheric encoding/retrieval asymmetry (HERA) model. Although there has been disagreement regarding the details and exactly where emphasis should be placed, there has been a wide range of support for Tulving's perspective and the general idea that episodic retrieval preferentially activates certain brain areas (Buckner 1996; Fletcher *et al.* 1997). In fact, the emphasis in the field has shifted from simply identifying these brain areas to determining their specific processing contributions (e.g. Kapur *et al.* 1995; Schacter *et al.* 1996; Rugg *et al.* 1997).

Thus the findings of both broad similarities and key differences observed across the variants of the word stem completion tasks challenge us with the need to build a framework, such as Moscovitch's (1994) components of processing view, that can both incorporate these similarities as well as the differences. Our point is that a memory systems perspective pushes one to dwell on the differences rather than the similarities, yet the latter may be equally or more important (see Buckner 1996). If characterization is focused on the similarities and differences as themselves the data of interest, a powerful experimental leverage point is gained. We are able to describe the processing structures and the memory-related changes that modify them.

Such data, which we believe support the utility of a components of processing framework, do not in anyway undermine the findings that certain brain areas or pathways provide critical processing functions for sets of memory tasks. A wealth of data has supported the idea that medial temporal lobe structures provide a critical processing function for 'declarative' memory (Squire 1992; Cohen and Eichenbaum 1993). However, such a finding does not necessitate that all tasks impaired after medial temporal lobe damage are the same, or even highly similar— so why should they be said to reflect a 'memory system', if great differences exist between the tasks alleged to be supported by the 'same system'? They appear to share in common the reliance on one or more critical sets of functions accomplished by medial temporal lobe structures. The logical extension of this argument is to explore the processing contributions of medial temporal lobe structures. Current research along such lines suggests that certain medial temporal lobe structures may facilitate the binding of certain perceptual and conceptual contents of a processing event—a necessary step towards forming many memories (Cohen and Eichenbaum 1993; Squire *et al.* 1992). One might even name the class of memories that cannot form after medial temporal lobe damage 'declarative memories' or 'medial temporal lobe dependent memories'.

Our difficulty starts when the dependency on a critical processing function leads to the hypothesis of a separate memory system. The tendency then is to concentrate on the similarities of tasks thought to be represented by the same system (and to ignore their differences). In the same vein, tasks thought to represent different systems are contrasted; their differences are emphasized, and any similarities that might exist between the tests are de-emphasized. An extreme instance of this problem occurs in the domain of 'declarative' memory research, in which the actual processing demands of the tasks engaged during encoding and retrieval are often forgotten. Consider an example. Let us start with word stem cued recall, a task thought to involve episodic/declarative memory. If subjects process words in terms of their meaning (e.g. by making pleasantness ratings) during a study phase, recall is better on this task than if prior study involved more superficial judgments (e.g. judging whether the word contained an *e*). In addition, priming on implicit memory tests using word stems is largely unaffected by this study manipulation (Graf and Mandler 1984; Roediger *et al.* 1992). The separation between performance on an explicit test (word stem cued recall, presumably supported by an episodic/declarative memory system) and performance on an implicit test (primed word stem completion, underlain by a non-declarative priming system) seems clean. However, there is a problem: the same encoding tasks (shallow or deep processing) that have no effect on implicit word stem completion do have effects on other implicit tests, those involving conceptual tests. Greater priming occurs on conceptual tests such as producing category instances after deep than after shallow processing (e.g. Srinivas and Roediger 1990; Hamann 1990), just as with word stem cued recall. How does the distinction between declarative and non-declarative memory systems help us to understand this similarity in performance across tests? We suggest it does not, but instead deflects attention from such issues. Squire (1994) has alluded to this point when referring to declarative and non-declarative knowledge: 'The two kinds of knowledge can arise independently. Some tasks tap primarily what has been acquired declaratively; some tap nondeclarative knowledge; still other tasks measure the contribution of both declarative and non-declarative knowledge' (p.205).

In our opinion, Moscovitch's (1994) components of processing view provides a clearer way of conceptualizing these matters: the processes engaged by each test can be compared and contrasted within his approach. Both the overlap and differences in brain pathways activated by different tasks can be examined and each are considered important. Within such a framework, functional anatomical exploration progresses by asking the questions: (1) What are the relevant brain structures/pathways that are activated when we administer memory tests to subjects? and (2) How are these processes/structures modulated across memory tasks and stages of memory? Those distinctions that provide useful heuristics across wide ranges of tasks are amenable to study as well as those that account for fairly circumscribed memory processes. The component processes framework permits us to ask both more general questions (how both similar and different effects might be manifested across many tests) and more precise questions (about involvement of specific processes and structures on particular tests). The components of processing approach points the way toward future conceptualization and the empirical study of processes and structures underlying memory.

CONCLUSIONS

In the early 1980s, proponents of systems theories believed that a handful of memory systems—two at first, maybe five or six later—were sufficient to explain the workings of human memory. As we have documented here, those ideas fail for both logical and empirical reasons. If one postulates stringent, interlocking criteria for memory systems such as those suggested by Sherry and Schacter (1987), then most of the proposed systems fail to meet them. However, if one accepts the criteria currently in use, essentially converging dissociations, then there is evidence for dozens of systems, and there would seem little use in even producing a catalogue of the different names, essentially a botany of memory.

The processing theories have faired little better, in a sense. Although capturing in a general way the dissociations that have been found between memory tests, specific predictions of various processing theories have also been found wanting. It is easy to dissociate two conceptual tests, for example, which, according to Roediger (1990*b*), should not happen under some conditions, but it does (e.g. McDermott and Roediger 1996).

The components of processing approach, championed primarily by Moscovitch (1994) and his colleagues, represents a melding of the best of the processing theories (emphasizing the varied and complicated cognitive processes underlying performance on any particular task) and the systems theories (emphasizing the neural underpinnings of those processes). The components of processing view is more sophisticated and more complex, but captures much better the reality of the mind/brain processes and systems that researchers seek to understand. The new tools permitting imaging of the brain (PET, fMRI, MEG, and others) will lead to a greater understanding of the components of processing that underlie memory.

REFERENCES

Ahmed, R. and Gray, D. (1996). Immunological memory and protective immunity: understanding their relation, *Science*, **272**, 54–60.

Andreasen, N. C., O'Leary, D. S., Arndt, S., Cizadlo, T., Hurtig, R., Rezai, K, Watkins, G. L., Boles Ponto, L. L., and Hichwa, R. D. (1995). Short-term and long-term verbal memory: A positron emission tomography study. *Proceedings of the National Academy of Sciences of the USA*, **92**, 5111–15.

Baddeley, A. (1986). *Working memory*. Oxford University Press.

Balota, D. A. and Neely, J. H. (1980). Test-expectancy and word-frequency effects in recall and recognition. *Journal of Experimental Psychology: Human Learning and Memory*, **6**, 576–87.

Bartlett, F. C. (1932). *Remembering: a study in experimental and social psychology*. Cambridge University Press.

Bergman, E. T. (1998). The levels of processing effect on an implicit memory task: Analysis of a perceptual processing factor. Unpublished manuscript.

Berndt, R. S. (1987). Symptom co-occurrence and dissociation in the interpretation of agrammatism. In *The cognitive neuropsychology of language*, (ed. M. Coltheart, G. Sartori, and R. Job), pp.221–33. Erlbaum, London.

Blaxton, T. A. (1989). Investigating dissociations among memory measures: Support for a transfer appropriate processing framework. *Journal of Experimental Psychology: Learning, Memory, and Cognition*, **15**, 657–68.

Blaxton, T. A. (1995). A process-based view of memory. *Journal of the International Neuropsychological Society*, **1**, 112–114.

Blaxton, T. A., Bookheimer, S., Zeffiro, T. A., Figlozzi, C. M., Gaillard, W. D., and Theodore, W. H. (1996). Functional mapping of human memory using PET: Comparisons of conceptual and perceptual tasks. *Canadian Journal of Experimental Psychology*, **50**, 42–56.

Boring, E. G. (1950). *A history of experimental psychology*. Appleton-Century-Crofts, New York.

Bransford, J. D. Franks, J. J. Morris, C. D., and Stein, B. S. (1979). Some general constraints on learning and memory research. In *Levels of processing in human memory*, (ed. L. S. Cermak and F. I. M. Craik), pp.331–54. Hillsdale, NJ, Erlbaum.

Brown, R. and McNeill, D. (1966). The tip-of-the-tongue phenomenon. *Journal of Verbal Learning and Verbal Behavior*, **5**, 325–37.

Bub, D. and Kertesz, A. (1982). Evidence for lexicographic processing in a patient with preserved written over oral single word naming. *Brain*, **105**, 697–717.

Buckner, R. L. (1996). Beyond HERA: contributions of specific prefrontal brain areas to long-term memory retrieval. *Psychonomic Bulletin & Review*, **3**, 149–58.

Buckner, R. L., Petersen, S. E., Ojemann, J. G., Miezin, F. M., Squire, L. R., and Raichle, M. E. (1995a). Functional anatomical studies of explicit and implicit memory retrieval tasks. *Journal of Neuroscience*, **15**, 12–29.

Buckner, R. L., Raichle, M. E., and Petersen, S. E. (1995b). Dissociation of human prefrontal cortical areas across different speech production tasks and gender groups. *Journal of Neurophysiology*, **74**, 2163–73.

Buckner, R. L., Goodman, J., Burock, M., Rotte, M., Koustaal, W., Schacter, D., Rosen, B., and Dale, A.M. (1998). Functional-anatomic correlates of object priming in humans revealed by rapid presentation event-related fMRI. *Neuron*, **4**, 68.

Buckner, R. L., Raichle, M. E., Miezin, F. M., and Petersen, S. E. (1996) Functional-anatomic studies of the recall of pictures and words from memory. *Journal of Neuroscience*, **16**, 6219–35.

Buckner, R. L., Koutstaal, W. M., Schacter, D. L., Petersen, S. E., Raichle, M. E., and Rosen, B. R. (1997). fMRI studies of item repetition during word generation. *Abstracts of the 3rd Annual Meeting of the Cognitive Neuroscience Society*.

Cabeza, R. (1994). A dissociation between two implicit conceptual tests supports the distinction between types of conceptual processing. *Psychonomic Bulletin and Review*, **1**, 505–8.

Challis, B. H. and Sidhu, R. (1993). Massed repetition has a dissociative effect on implicit and explicit measures of memory. *Journal of Experimental Psychology: Learning, Memory, and Cognition*, **19**, 115–27.

Challis, B. H., Chiu, C-Y., Kerr, S. A., Law, J., Schneider, L., Yonelinas, A., and Tulving, E. (1993). Perceptual and conceptual cueing in implicit and explicit retrieval. *Memory*, **1**, 127–51.

Chiras, D. D. (1993). *Biology: the web of life*. West Publishing, St Paul.

Cohen, N. J. and Eichenbaum, H. (1993). *Memory, amnesia, and the hippocampal system*. MIT Press, Cambridge, MA.

Cohen, N. J. and Squire, L. R. (1980). Preserved learning and retention of pattern analyzing skill in amnesia: dissociation of knowing how and knowing that. *Science*, **210**, 207–9.

Corkin, S. (1968). Acquisition of motor skill after bilateral medial temporal-lobe excision. *Neuropsychology*, **6**, 255–65.

Craik, F. I. M. and Lockhart, R. S. (1972). Levels of processing: a framework for memory research. *Journal of Verbal Learning and Verbal Behavior*, **11**, 671–84.

Crowder, R. G. (1982). The demise of short-term memory. *Acta Psychologia*, **50**, 291–323.
Demb, J. B., Desmond, J. E., Wagner, A. D., Vaidya, C. J., Glover, G. H., and Gabrieli, J. D. E. (1995). Semantic encoding and retrieval in the left inferior prefrontal cortex: a functional MRI study of task difficulty and process specificity. *Journal of Neuroscience*, **15**, 5870–8.
Eich, E. (1985). Context, memory, and integrated item/context imagery. *Journal of Experimental Psychology: Learning, Memory, and Cognition*, **11**, 764–70.
Eichenbaum, H., Cohen N. J., Otto, T., and Wible, C. (1991). Memory representations in the hippocampus: functional domain and functional organisation. In *Memory: organization and locus of change*, (ed. L. R. Squire, N. M. Weinberger, G. Lynch, and J. L. McGaugh), pp. 163–204. Oxford University Press, New York.
Ellis, A. W., Miller, D., and Sin, G. (1983). Wernicke's aphasia and normal language processing: A case study in cognitive neuropsychology. *Cognition*, **15**, 111–44.
Felleman, D. J. and Van Essen, D. C. (1991). Distributed hierarchical processing in the primate cerebral contex. *Cerebral Cortex*, **1**, 1–47.
Fisher, R. P. and Craik, F. I. M. (1979). Interaction between encoding and retrieval operations in cued recall. *Journal of Experimental Psychology: Human Learning and Memory*, **3**, 701–11.
Fletcher, P. C., Frith, C. D., and Rugg, M. D. (1997). The functional neuroanatomy of episodic memory. *Trends in Neuroscience*, **20**, 213–23.
Gabrieli, J. D. E. (1995). A systematic view of human memory processes. *Journal of the International Neuropsychological Society*, **1**, 115–18.
Gabrieli, J. D. E., Stone, M., Vaidya, C. J., Askari, N., Zabinski, M. F., and Rabin, L. (1996). Neuropsychological and behavioral evidence for the role of attention in implicit memory. *37th Annual Meeting of the Psychonomic Society, Chicago*.
Gardiner, J. M. and Java, R. (1993). Recognising and remembering. In *Theories of memory*, (ed. A. Collins, S. Gathercole, M. Conway, and P. Morris), pp. 163–88. Erlbaum, Hillsdale, NJ.
Glanzer, M. (1972). Storage mechanisms in recall. In *The psychology of learning and motivation*, Vol. 5, (ed. G. H. Bower and J. T. Spence) pp. 129–93. Academic, New York.
Graf, P. and Mandler, G. (1984). Activation makes words more accessible, but not necessarily more retrievable. *Journal of Verbal Learning and Verbal Behavior*, **23**, 553–68.
Graf, P., Mandler, G., and Haden, P. (1982). Simulating amnesic symptoms in normal subjects. *Science*, **218**, 1243–4.
Gregg, V. H. (1976). Word frequency, recognition, and recall. In *Recall and recognition*, (ed. J. Brown), pp. 183–216. Wiley, London.
Hamann, S. B. (1990). Level-of-processing effects in conceptually-driven implicit tasks. *Journal of Experimental Psychology: Learning, Memory, and Cognition*, **16**, 970–7.
Haxby, J., Ungerleider, L. G., Horwitz, B., Maisog, J. M., Rapoport, S. L., and Grady, C. L. (1996). Face encoding and recognition in the human brain. *Proceedings of the National Academy of Sciences of the USA*, **93**, 922–7.
Hayman, C. A. G. and Tulving, E. (1989*a*). Contingent dissociation between recognition and fragment completion: the method of triangulation. *Journal of Experimental Psychology: Learning, Memory, and Cognition*, **15**, 228–40.
Hayman, C. A. G. and Tulving, E. (1989*b*). Is priming in fragment completion based on a 'traceless' memory system? *Journal of Experimental Psychology: Learning, Memory, and Cognition*, **14**, 941–56.
Hintzman, D. L. (1990). Human learning and memory: connections and dissociations. *Annual Review of Psychology*, **41**, 109–39.
Hintzman, D. L. and Hartry, A. L. (1990). Item effects in recognition and fragment completion: contingency relations vary for different subsets of words. *Journal of Experimental Psychology: Learning, Memory, and Cognition*, **16**, 955–69.

Hirst, W., Johnson, M. K., Kim, J. K., Phelps, E. A., and Volpe, B. T. (1986). Recognition and recall in amnesics. *Journal of Experimental Psychology: Learning, memory, and Cognition*, 12, 445–551.

Hirst, W., Johnson, M. K., Phelps, E. A., and Volpe, B. T. (1988). More on recognition and recall in amnesics. *Journal of Experimental Psychology: Learning, Memory, and Cognition*, 14, 758–63.

Horowitz, L. M., White, M. A., and Atwood, D. W. (1970). Word fragments as aids to recall: the organization of a word. *Journal of Experimental Psychology*, 76, 219–26.

Hunt, R. R. and Einstein, G. O. (1981). Relational and item-specific information in memory. *Journal of Verbal Learning and Verbal Behavior*, 20, 497–514.

Hunt, R. R. and Toth, J. P. (1990). Perceptual identification, fragment completion, and free recall: concepts and data. *Journal of Experimental Psychology: Learning, Memory, and Cognition*, 16, 282–90.

Jacoby, L. L. (1983). Remembering the data: analyzing interactive processes in reading. *Journal of Verbal Learning and Verbal Behavior*, 22, 485–508.

Jacoby, L. L. and Witherspoon, D. (1982). Remembering without awareness. *Canadian Journal of Psychology*, 36, 300–24.

Kapur, S., Craik, F. I. M., Jones, C., Brown, G. H., Houles, S., Tulving, E. (1995). Functional roles of prefrontal cortex in retrieval of memories: a PET study. *NeuroReport*, 6, 1880–4.

Kolers, P. A. (1975). Specificity of operations in sentence recognition. *Cognitive Psychology*, 7, 289–306.

Kolers, P. A. and Perkins, D. N. (1975). Spatial and ordinal components of form perception and literacy. *Cognitive Psychology*, 7, 228–67.

Kolers, P. A. and Roediger, H. L. (1984). Procedures of mind. *Journal of Verbal Learning and Verbal Behavior*, 23, 425–49.

Kolers, P. A. and Smythe, W. E. (1979). Images, symbols, and skills. *Canadian Journal of Psychology*, 33, 158–84.

Kolk, H. H. J., Van Grunsven, M. J. F., and Keyser, A. (1985). On parallelism between production and comprehension in agrammatism. In *Agrammatism* (ed. M. L. Kean). Academic Press, Orlando.

Kosslyn, S. M. (1980). *Image and mind*. Harvard University Press, Cambridge.

Lashley, K. S. (1929). *Brain mechanisms and intelligence*. University of Chicago Press.

Lashley, K. S. (1950). In search of the engram. In *Symposia of the Society for Experimental Biology*, No. 4, pp. 454–82. Cambridge University Press, London.

McClelland, J. L. (1995). Constructive memory and memory distortions: a parallel-distributed processing approach. In *Memory distortion*, (ed. D. L. Schactor), pp. 69–90. Harvard University Press, Cambridge, MA.

McDaniel, M. A., Freedman, A., and Bourne, L. E. (1978). Remembering the levels of information in words. *Memory & Cognition*, 6, 156–64.

McDermott, K. B. and Roediger, H. L. (1996). Exact and conceptual repetition dissociate conceptual memory tests: problems for transfer appropriate processing theory. *Canadian Journal of Experimental Psychology*, 50, 57–71.

McKoon, G., Ratcliff, R., and Dell, G. S. (1986). A critical evaluation of the semantic-episodic distinction. *Journal of Experimental Psychology: Learning, Memory, and Cognition*, 12, 295–306.

Metcalfe, J., Mencl, W. E., and Cottrell, G. W. (1994). Cognitive binding. In *Memory systems 1994*, (ed. D. L. Schacter and E. Tulving), pp.369–94. MIT Press, Cambridge, MA.

Morris, C. D., Bransford, J. P., and Franks, J. J. (1978). Levels of processing versus transfer appropriate processing. *Journal of Verbal Learning and Verbal Behavior*, 16, 519–33.

Moscovitch, M. (1992). Memory and working-with-memory: a component process model based on modules and central systems. *Journal of Cognitive Neuroscience*, 4, 257–67.

Moscovitch, M. (1994). Memory and working with memory: evaluation of a component process model and comparisons with other models. In *Memory systems 1994*, (ed. D. L. Schacter and E. Tulving), pp. 269–310. MIT Press, Cambridge, MA.

Moscovitch, M., Vriezen, E. and Goshen-Gottstein, Y. (1993). Implicit tests of memory in patients with focal lesions or degenerative brain disorders. In *Handbook of neuropsychology*, (ed. F. Boller and J. Grafman), pp.133–73. Elsevier, Amsterdam.

Neely, J. H. (1989). Experimental dissociations and the episodic/semantic memory distinction. In *Varieties of memory and consciousness: essays in honour of Endel Tulving*, (ed. H. L. Roediger and F. I. M. Craik), pp.229–70. Erlbaum, Hillsdale, NJ.

Neisser, U. (1967). *Cognitive psychology*. Appleton-Century-Crofts, New York.

Nilsson, L.-G. and Gardiner, J. (1993). Identifying exceptions in a database of recognition failure studies from 1973 to 1992. *Memory & Cognition*, **21**, 397–410.

Paivio, A. (1969). Mental imagery in associative learning and memory. *Psychological Review*, **76**, 241–63.

Paivio, A. (1986). *Mental representations: a dual coding approach*. Oxford University Press, New York.

Platt, J. R. (1964). Strong inference. *Science*, **146**, 347–53.

Posner, M. I. and Raichle, M. E. (1994). *Images of mind*. Scientific American Library, New York.

Rajaram, S. and Roediger, H. L. (1997). Remembering and knowing as states of consciousness during retrieval. In *Scientific approaches to consciousness*, (ed. J. D. Cohen and J. W. Schooler), pp.213–40. Erlbaum, Mahwah, NJ.

Roediger, H. L. (1979). Implicit and explicit memory models. *Bulletin of the Psychonomic Society*, **13**, 339–42.

Roediger, H. L. (1980). Memory metaphors in cognitive psychology. *Memory & Cognition*, **8**, 231–46.

Roediger, H. L. (1984). Does current evidence from dissociation experiments favor the episodic/semantic distinction? *Behavioral and Brain Sciences*, **7**, 252–4.

Roediger, H. L. (1990*a*). Implicit memory: a commentary. *Bulletin of the Psychonomic Society*, **28**, 373–80.

Roediger, H. L. (1990*b*). Implicit memory: retention without remembering. *American Psychologist*, **45**, 1043–56.

Roediger, H. L. (1993). Learning and memory: Progress and challenge. In *Attention and performance XIV*, (ed. D. E. Meyer and S. Kornblum), pp.510–28. MIT Press, Cambridge, MA.

Roediger, H. L. and Blaxton, T. A. (1987). Effects of varying modality, surface features, and retention interval on priming in word fragment completion. *Memory & Cognition*, **15**, 379–88.

Roediger, H. L. and Challis, B. H. (1992). Effects of exact repetition and conceptual repetition on free recall and primed word fragment completion. *Journal of Experimental Psychology: Learning, Memory, and Cognition*, **18**, 3–14.

Roediger, H. L. and McDermott, K. B. (1993). Implicit memory in normal human subjects. In *Handbook of neuropsychology*, Vol. 8, (ed. F. Boller and J. Grafman), pp.63–131. Elsevier, Amsterdam.

Roediger, H. L. and Srinivas, K. (1993). Specificity of operations in perceptual priming. In *Implicit memory: new directions in cognition, development and neuropsychology*, (ed. P. Graf and M. E. J. Masson), pp.17–48. Erlbaum, Hillsdale, NJ.

Roediger, H. L., Weldon, M. S., and Challis, B. H. (1989). Explaining dissociations between implicit and explicit measures of retention: a processing account. In *Varieties of memory and consciousness: essays in honour of Endel Tulving*, (ed. H. L. Roediger and F. I. M. Craik), pp.3–14. Erlbaum, Hillsdale, NJ.

Roediger, H. L., Rajaram, S., and Srinivas, K. (1990). Specifying criteria for postulating memory systems. In *The development and neural bases of higher cognitive functions*, (ed. A. Diamond), pp.572–95. New York Academy of Sciences, New York.

Roediger, H. L., Weldon, M. S., Stadler, M. L., and Riegler, G. L. (1992). Direct comparison of two implicit memory tests: word fragment and word stem completion. *Journal of Experimental Psychology: Learning, Memory, and Cognition*, **18**, 1251–69.

Rozin, P. (1976). The psychobiological approach to human memory. In *Neural mechanisms of learning and memory*, (ed. M. R. Rozenzweig and E. L. Bennet), pp.3–48 MIT Press, Cambridge, MA.

Rubenstein, H., Garfield, L., and Millikan, J. A. (1970). Homographic entries in the internal lexicon. *Journal of Verbal Learning and Verbal Behavior*, **9**, 487–94.

Rugg, M. D., Fletcher, P. C., Frith, C. D., Frackowiak, R. S. J., and Dolan, R. J. (1997). Differential response of the prefrontal cortex in successful and unsuccessful memory retrieval. *Brain*, **119**, 2073–83.

Ryle, G. (1949). *The concept of mind*. Hutchinson, London.

Schacter, D. L. (1990). Perceptual representation systems and implicit memory: toward a resolution of the multiple memory systems debate. In *Development and neural bases of higher cognition*, (ed. A. Diamond), pp.543–71. New York Academy of Sciences, New York.

Schacter, D. L. (1994). Priming and multiple memory systems: Perceptual mechanisms of implicit memory. In *Memory systems 1994* (ed. D. L. Schacter and E. Tulving), pp. 233–68. MIT Press, Cambridge, MA.

Schacter, D. L. and Buckner, R. L. (1998). Priming and the Brain. *Neuron*, **20**, 185–95.

Schacter, D. L. and Tulving, E. (ed.) (1994a). *Memory systems 1994*. MIT Press, Cambridge, MA.

Schacter, D. L. and Tulving, E. (1994b). What are the memory systems of 1994? In *Memory systems 1994*, (ed. D. L. Schacter and E. Tulving), pp.1–38. MIT Press, Cambridge, MA.

Schacter, D. L., Alpert, N. M., Savage, C. R., Rauch, S. L., and Albert, M. S. (1996). Conscious recollection and the human hippocampal formation: evidence from positron emission tomography. *Proceedings of the National Academy of Sciences of the USA*, **93**, 321–5.

Scoville, W. B. and Milner, B. (1957). Loss of recent memory after bilateral hippocampal lesions. *Journal of Neurology, Neurosurgery, and Psychiatry*, **20**, 11–21.

Sherry, D. F. and Schacter, D. L. (1987). The evolution of multiple memory systems. *Psychological Review*, **94**, 439–54.

Shimamura, A. P. (1993). Neuropsychological analyses of implicit memory: Recent progress and theoretical interpretations. In *Implicit Memory: New Directions in Cognition, Development, and Neuropsychology*, (ed. P. Graf and M. E. Masson) pp. 265–85. Erlbaum Associates Press, Hillsdale, NJ.

Squire, L. R. (1987). *Memory and brain*. Oxford University Press, New York.

Squire, L. R. (1992). Memory and the hippocampus: a synthesis from findings with rats, monkeys, and humans. *Psychological Review*, **99**, 195–231.

Squire, L. R. (1994). Declarative and nondeclarative memory: multiple brain systems supporting learning and memory. In *Memory systems 1994*, (ed. D. L. Schacter and E. Tulving), pp.203–31. MIT Press, Cambridge, MA.

Squire, L. R., Ojemann, J. G., Miezen, F. M., Petersen, S. E., Videen, T. O., and Raichle, M. E. (1992). Activation of the hippocampus in normal humans: a functional anatomical study of memory. *Proceedings of the National Academy of Sciences of the USA*, **89**, 1837–41.

Srinivas, K. (1993). Perceptual specificity in nonverbal priming. *Journal of Experimental Psychology: Learning, Memory, and Cognition*, **19**, 582–602.

Srinivas, K. and Roediger, H. L. (1990). Classifying implicit memory tests: category association and anagram solution. *Journal of Memory and Language*, **29**, 389–412.

Stein, B. S. (1978). Depth of processing reexamined: the effects of the precision of encoding and test appropriateness. *Journal of Verbal Learning and Verbal Behavior*, **17**, 165–74.
Tajika, H. and Neuman, E. (1992). Effects of memory test instructions on dissociations between explicit and implicit measures of retention. *Psychologia—An International Journal of Psychology in the Orient*, **35**, 76–83.
Tenpenny, P. and Shoben, E. J. (1992). Component processes and the utility of the conceptually-driven/data-driven distinction. *Journal of Experimental Psychology: Learning, Memory, and Cognition*, **18**, 25–42.
Toth, J. P., and Hunt R. R. (1990). Effect of generation on a word-identification task. *Journal of Experimental Psychology: Learning, Memory, and Cognition*, **16**, 993–1003.
Tulving, E. (1972). Episodic and semantic memory. In *Organization of memory*, (ed. E. Tulving and W. Donaldson), pp.381–403. Academic, New York.
Tulving, E. (1976). Ecphoric processes in recall and recognition. In *Recall and recognition*, (ed. J. Brown), pp.37–73. Wiley, New York.
Tulving, E. (1983). *Elements of episodic memory*. Oxford University Press, New York.
Tulving, E. (1985). How many memory systems are there? *American Psychologist*, **40**, 385–98.
Tulving, E. and Patterson, R. D. (1968). Functional units and retrieval processes in free recall. *Journal of Experimental Psychology*, **77**, 239–48.
Tulving, E. and Schacter, D. L. (1990). Priming and human memory systems. *Science*, **247**, 301–6.
Tulving, E. and Thomson, D. M. (1973). Encoding specificity and retrieval processes in episodic memory. *Psychological Review*, **80**, 352–73.
Tulving, E. and Wiseman, S. (1978). Relation between recognition and recognition failure of recallable words. *Bulletin of the Psychonomic Society*, **6**, 79–82.
Tulving, E. Schacter, D. L., and Stark, H. A. (1982). Priming effects in word fragment completion are independent of recognition memory. *Journal of Experimental Psychology: Learning, Memory, and Cognition*, **8**, 336–42.
Tulving, E., Kapur, S., Craik, F. I. M., Moscovitch, M., and Houle, S. (1994). Hemispheric encoding/retrieval asymmetry in episodic memory: positron emission tomography findings. *Proceedings of the National Academy of Sciences of the USA*, **91**, 2016–20.
Van Essen, D. C., Anderson, C. H., and Felleman, D. J. (1992). Information processing in the primate visual system: an integrated systems perspective. *Science*, **255**, 419–423.
Waugh, N. C. and Norman, D. A. (1965). Primary memory. *Psychological Review*, **72**, 89–104.
Weldon, M. S., and Coyote, K. C. (1996). The failure to find the picture superiority effect in conceptual implicit memory tests. *Journal of Experimental Psychology: Learning, Memory, and Cognition*.
Weldon, M. S., Roediger, H. L., and Challis, B. H. (1989). The properties of retrieval cues constrain the picture superiority effect. *Memory & Cognition*, **17**, 95–105.
Weldon, M. S., Roediger, H. L., Beitel, D. A., and Johnston, T. R. (1995). Perceptual and conceptual processes in implicit and explicit tests with picture fragment and word fragment cues. *Journal of Memory and Language*, **34**, 268–85.
Wickelgren, W. A. (1973). The long and short of memory. *Psychological Bulletin*, **80**, 425–38.
Wiggs, C. L., and Martin, A. (in press). Properties and mechanisms of visual priming. *Current Opinion in Neurobiology*.
Winnick, W. A. and Daniel, S. A. (1970). Two kinds of response priming in tachistoscopic word recognition. *Journal of Experimental Psychology*, **84**, 837–51.
Witherspoon, D. and Moscovitch, M. (1989). Stochastic independence between two implicit memory tasks. *Journal of Experimental Psychology: Learning, Memory, and Cognition*, **15**, 22–30.

4
Functional dissociation of brain regions in learning and memory: evidence for multiple systems

ROBERT M. McDONALD, ANNE-MARIE ERGIS, AND GORDON WINOCUR

> The discovery of the highly differentiated structure of the cerebral cortex and of the possibility of strict differentiation of function between its various parts may be counted among the great achievements of science (Luria 1966, p.13).

The ability to demonstrate that the entire brain, not just the neocortex, is anatomically and functionally dissociable has created a unique opportunity for understanding complex brain/behaviour relationships. One technique has been esspecially useful: the study of the effects of lesions on behaviour. Despite criticism, this technique continues to be a cornerstone of functional neuroscience and this is particularly true in the study of the neural basis of learning and memory. Theories and experiments directed at understanding the contributions of specific brain structures to learning and memory are driven largely by functional changes that have been associated with selective damage to these areas.

Understanding the complexities of how the mammalian nervous system acquires information and how it transforms this information into appropriate behaviour is fundamentally important to our understanding of both animal and human behaviour. Interestingly, early attempts to address this issue were not at all promising. In what are considered classic studies, Lashley (1929) produced localized brain lesions in rats and assessed learning and memory performance on a variety of tasks. Despite extensive experimentation, Lashley was unable to interfere with specific memories and concluded that memories are distributed throughout the brain in a non-specific fashion. As will become clear throughout this chapter, subsequent research has forced a drastic reformulation of views regarding localization of brain function in learning and memory.

During Lashley's time, there was a theoretical division that dominated animal-based psychological learning theory. The division was based on a distinction between stimulus–response (S–R) theories of associative learning (e.g. Hull 1943) and Tolman's (1932) notion that emphasized stimulus–stimulus (S–S) learning. The S–R theories suggested that learned behaviour is based on the acquisition and retention of chains of S–R associations. Tolman's idea was that learning consists of forming associations between external stimuli and constructing cognitive maps of the environment that can be used to navigate to various goals in the environment. In a provocative paper, Tolman (1948) suggested that animals might have the ability to learn about a particular experience in more than one way. In other words, both S–R and S–S, learning abilities could be available to the animal. This insight inspired the now widely accepted notion that there are multiple forms of memory and that the underlying systems are distributed throughout the brain (Schacter and Tulving 1994).

The concept of multiple systems in the mammalian brain represents an important advance in terms of understanding the organization of learning and memory. An important implication of this approach is that these systems interact synergistically or competitively to produce behaviour. We believe that the latter notion has important explanatory power and forms the basis of a conceptual framework for describing the functional relationship between specific brain regions in the intact organism, as well as in the compensatory process of adapting cognitively to effects of brain damage.

In this chapter, we focus on five brain regions—hippocampus, amygdala, thalamus, prefrontal cortex, basal ganglia—that have been reliably identified with learning and memory processes. Our aim is to show that, notwithstanding specialization within subfields, each region mediates a unique and critical aspect of learning and memory. The distinctiveness of each structure's contribution is an important point that is often lost when selective lesions produce similar looking deficits on the same task. A significant development in biopsychological research is the emergence of sensitive paradigms capable of separating the contributions of the various regions to learning and memory. Functional dissociation studies have also shown that the different brain regions work together in an integrated fashion in solving even relatively simple tasks, a fact that must be taken into account in describing multiple systems and the relationship of specific structures to these systems. As we pursue this objective, we will draw on convergent evidence from animal and clinical neuropsychological research that supports the parsimonious conclusion that functions mediated by the various brain regions are relatively invariant across species.

HIPPOCAMPUS

Initial support for the idea that the mammalian nervous system contains independent learning and memory systems came from Scoville and Milner's (1957) discovery that patients with medial temporal lobe damage that extended to hippocampus were selectively impaired in acquiring certain types of information. Such patients were unable to remember contextually bound experiences beyond a short period of time. They were similarly impaired on formal tests of learning that required formation of new associations (e.g. paired-associate learning, visually guided complex maze learning). By comparison, these patients performed normally on other tests of learning and memory. For example, they had no difficulty on 'indirect' or 'implicit' tests of memory in which a prior experience influences subsequent behaviour without the patient having conscious recollection of the initial experience, or in acquiring perceptual-motor skills that, similarly, do not require conscious memory for a specific event. This discovery suggested that one type of learning and memory was subserved by the hippocampus and related structures, while other types are not dependent on this region.

The discovery of the medial temporal lobe amnesic syndrome inspired research directed at obtaining a fuller understanding of the neural substrate of learning and memory and at describing the respective contributions of precise structures. This work led to a variety of dual-memory theories that focused especially on the hippocampus and emphasized its dominant role in complex mnemonic processes. Of these early theories, two in particular have had a lasting impact—O'Keefe and Nadel's (1978) cognitive map theory and Hirsh's (1974) contextual retrieval theory. These theories are important for at least three reasons: (1) they provided plausible explanations for apparently contradictory findings in animals and humans with hippocampal damage; (2) they provided the basis for the idea of multiple memory systems; (3) they suggested that the type of learning attributed to the hippocampus enabled a particular cue or event to have more than one meaning based on the presence of another cue. The latter notion underscores the role of the hippocampus in the flexible use of stimulus cues for associative learning and provides the basis for subsequent theories that emphasize relational (Eichenbaum et al. 1992) and configural (Sutherland and Rudy 1989) learning processes.

O'Keefe and Nadel's (1978) highly influential cognitive map theory differentiated between a 'locale' system and a 'taxon' system. The locale system is a mapping system that utilizes the circuitry of the hippocampus to create a spatially organized map of the environment. The taxon system is an S–R system, independent of the hippocampus, which represents inflexible relationships between specific stimuli and associated responses. According to O'Keefe and Nadel, the hippocampus, as part of the locale system, is critical to forming associations between spatially displaced environmental cues, thereby providing the basis for relating events to precise locations. O'Keefe and Nadel were primarily concerned with the involvement of the hippocampus in processes that are fundamental to the development of spatial memory in animals but they also argued that similar processes mediate the laying down of memory traces for episodic events in higher species. Their theory was a powerful influence on current thinking that emphasizes the structure's function in forming associations between unrelated stimuli or in linking personal experiences to their spatial–temporal context. Other (unspecified) structures comprise the taxon system, which mediates the representation of non-episodic information that forms the basis of skill and procedural learning.

Hirsh's (1974) theory is similar in the sense that it assigns a critical role to the hippocampus in forming associations between environmental stimuli which, in many cases, involve contextual information. The integrity of these associations and their representations were viewed as particularly important since accurate long-term memory is related to their reinstatement at the time of retrieval. Although implicit in O'Keefe and Nadel's theory, Hirsh emphasized the importance of the hippocampus for re-creating the necessary spatial–temporal events that facilitate long-term recall. (Although the subject of some controversy, the role of the hippocampus in using contextual information for this purpose is well established (e.g. Penick and Solomon 1991; Kim and Fanselow 1992; Winocur and Olds 1978).) In one important sense Hirsh's theory departed from that of O'Keefe and Nadel. Hirsh maintained that the hippocampus mediated spatial and non-spatial relationships and, in doing so, set the stage for subsequent models that take a broader view of hippocampal function (e.g. Solomon 1979; Winocur 1980; Sutherland and Rudy 1989; Eichenbaum *et al.* 1992).

Other lines of evidence support the idea that the hippocampus is essential for learning and remembering specific relationships. Anatomical analysis has shown that the hippocampus receives polymodal sensory information and has a vertical and horizontal organization (Amaral and Witter 1989). As an online recipient of polymodal sensory information, the hippocampus is in a position to form accurate representations of complex external environments. The hippocampus' intrinsic organization allows the structure to acquire and store complex relationships by distributing sensory information throughout its structure, thereby creating a mechanism for the integration of previously unrelated stimuli. Consistent with the neuroanatomical evidence, electrophysiological analyses have shown that neurons intrinsic to the hippocampus have unique firing characteristics that reveal direct relationships between firing rates and the location of rats (O'Keefe and Dostrovsky 1971; Ranck 1973). The existence of place units in the hippocampus of behaving animals is consistent with the structure's involvement in acquiring and storing complex relationships among external events in the environment. In addition to providing direct support for O'Keefe and Nadel's (1978) theory, this discovery has implications for the hippocampus' involvement in other forms of associative learning.

The hippocampus is a critical locus of damage in the medial temporal lobe amnesic syndrome and must be intact for non-human animals to perform a variety of spatial and non-spatial relational tasks. The importance of the hippocampus in spatial learning and memory has been demonstrated reliably in Olton's radial arm maze (Olton *et al.* 1979) as well as in other spatial tasks (e.g. Morris *et al.* 1982). In the standard version of the radial arm maze, rats are placed on a central platform with eight arms radiating from it in all directions. The animal's task is to obtain food which is located at the end of each arm. The most efficient way of accomplishing this is to adapt a 'win-shift' strategy in which the rat must remember where it has been and enter each arm only once. Rats with hippocampal lesions perform poorly on this task, a deficit that clearly implies a failure of spatial memory.

The adverse effects of hippocampal lesions on non-spatial tests of learning and memory have been well documented in a wide range of tasks. In recent years, considerable interest has centred on the use of matching and non-matching to sample tasks, partly because of their usefulness in modelling certain aspects of the amnesic syndrome in humans. In an enlightening study, Zola-Morgan and Squire (1986) tested monkeys with damage to hippocampus on a non-spatial test of non-matching to sample. An important feature of the results was that hippocampus-damaged monkeys performed normally when the delay between the sample and test trials was relatively short, but the performance declined at longer intervals. Similar observations have been recorded in hippocampus-damaged rats tested on a non-spatial matching to sample task (Winocur 1992), and other non-spatial tasks that involve high levels of interference (Winocur 1979) or the requirement that specific information be retained beyond a critical duration (e.g. Winocur 1985, 1991; but see Aggleton et al. 1986).

The latter findings are consistent with clinical evidence that medial temporal lobe damage, involving large parts of the hippocampus, produce severe disruptions of long-term memory without affecting memory for events at short intervals (Squire et al. 1993). This pattern gave rise to the notion that the hippocampus is critical for the transfer of temporarily held information to long-term storage in cortical networks where it can be readily accessed at later times.

Whereas medial temporal lobe amnesics suffer profound memory loss for events subsequent to brain damage (anterograde amnesia), there is also evidence of retrograde amnesia in such patients. The classic patient, HM, for example, is reported to have temporally graded memory loss for premorbid events (Marslen-Wilson and Teuber 1975; Corkin 1984) that date back several years before his surgery. To varying degrees, similar results have been observed in other patients with hippocampal damage (Rempel-Clower et al. 1996). There is also evidence that the same pattern is found in rats (Winocur 1990; Cho et al. 1995) and monkeys (Zola-Morgan and Squire 1990), although temporal parameters vary widely with the task and perhaps with the amount of hippocampal tissue destroyed (Nadel and Moscovitch 1997). The failure of hippocampus-damaged animals and humans to remember more recent premorbid events has been interpreted as consistent with the idea that the hippocampus is involved in the process of transferring memories into a more permanent representation. Applying this notion to the retrograde amnesia effect raises the interesting question of temporal characteristics of the process. The observation that hippocampal patients can suffer memory loss for events that date back several years would seem to imply that, for certain types of information at least, the process can indeed take a very long time.

In general, there is good correspondence between the patterns of memory loss reported in hippocampus-damaged animals and those observed in humans. Milner and her colleagues (Smith and Milner 1981; Pigott and Milner 1993) have shown that medial temporal lobe amnesics are impaired on tests of spatial learning and memory, with the effect most reliably identified with right-hemisphere damage. One study assessed the ability of medial temporal lobe patients to learn and remember spatial relationships between objects in an array, and between stimulus elements of complex visual scenes. Patients with right medial temporal lobe damage were impaired on both tasks and the deficit was correlated positively with the amount of damage to the hippocampus.

As is well known, medial temporal lobe amnesia extends to non-spatial material and numerous studies have demonstrated HM's impaired abilities in paired-associate learning, tests of free and cued recall, as well as recognition memory for lists of words. In line with the animal data showing a time-dependent effect in anterograde amnesia, several authors report normal short-term memory in HM (Wickelgren 1968) and in other medial-temporal lobe amnesics (Zola-Morgan *et al*. 1986; Muramoto *et al*. 1979), but poor long-term memory. One study, in particular, is interesting because it utilized a matching to sample task and produced results that map on nicely to the animal findings. Sidman *et al*. (1968) administered verbal and non-verbal versions of this task to HM and consistently found normal performance at very short delays but progressively deteriorating performance as the interval between sample and test trials increased.

Having suggested that hippocampal involvement in memory function is broader than that envisaged by a narrow interpretation of O'Keefe and Nadel's cognitive map theory, it is important to add a qualifier. There is controversy over the structure's role in recognition memory. Until recently, it was believed that the hippocampus combined with the amygdala to control this form of memory. This view derived largely from work with monkeys in which combined lesions to amygdala and hippocampus disrupted performance on non-matching to sample tasks involving trial-unique objects (Murray and Mishkin 1984). However, subsequent work has shown that this impairment may have been due to damage to the perirhinal cortex (Murray and Mishkin 1989; Zola-Morgan *et al*. 1989).

Mumby and colleagues (Mumby *et al*. 1992: Mumby and Pinel 1994) obtained similar results with rats. These investigators found that lesions to the perirhinal cortex severely impaired performance on a delayed non-matching to sample task with non-recurring items. Separate or combined lesions to the amygdala and hippocampus had no effect on performance at any delay. Work from other labs has shown that the disruptive effect of perirhinal cortex lesions on object memory does not extend to other learning and memory tasks that are sensitive to hippocampal dysfunction. For example, Kolb *et al*. (1994) confirmed that perirhinal lesions disrupted performance on Mumby's delayed non-matching to sample task but did not affect spatial navigation on the Morris water maze. Similarly, Ennaceur *et al*. (1996) compared groups of rats with perirhinal or fornix lesions on a series of spatial learning and memory tasks and two tests of object recognition memory. They found a clear dissociation in that fornix-damaged rats were impaired on the spatial but not the object-recognition task, whereas the opposite was observed in the perirhinal group. Interestingly, the same dissociation was reported by Gaffan (1994) who tested monkeys with lesions to perirhinal cortex or fornix on a matching to sample, object recognition problem and a spatial discrimination task. The perirhinal-lesioned monkeys were selectively impaired on the recognition task, whereas the fornix group exhibited the opposite pattern.

Notwithstanding the relative consistency of the animal findings, the issue is not yet resolved. Recently, Reed and Squire (1997) administered a range of recognition memory tests to six amnesic patients with lesions restricted mainly to the hippocampal formation. All patients exhibited significant impairment, indicating that recognition memory impairment may indeed be part of the medial temporal lobe amnesic syndrome.

Finally, there is consistency regarding the effect of hippocampal damage on rule or procedural learning, and on tests of semantic memory where successful performance does not require recollection of a specific (spatial or non-spatial) event. HM and other medial temporal lobe amnesics can acquire motor skills (e.g. rotary pursuit, tower of Hanoi, mirror drawing) and retain semantic information that is well established in their knowledge base (Corkin 1965; Gabrieli *et al.* 1988). Furthermore, to the extent that such patients have been tested on repetition priming tests of implicit memory (e.g. Milner *et al.* 1968; Gabrieli *et al.* 1990) the typical finding is normal performance. Similarly, experimental animals have been administered a wide range of discrimination, operant conditioning, and avoidance tasks that assess rule learning, but not episodic memory, and the consistent finding is that hippocampal damage does not interfere with performance on these tasks.

In summary, there is considerable agreement that hippocampal damage produces a profound memory loss for specific events in animals and humans. In rodents, this loss has been demonstrated most often on tests of spatial memory but there is also compelling evidence that the loss extends to non-spatial memory. Current interpretations of hippocampal function vary widely but most theories agree that the structure is critical to (1) the process of forming new associations between unrelated stimulus events, (2) consolidating these associations when they are deemed necessary for later conscious recall, and (3) to reinstating contextual cues during conscious retrieval. On the other hand, the evidence indicates that the hippocampus is not needed for non-episodic rule or procedural learning and memory.

An important question that emerges from the review of the hippocampal literature is the extent to which this structure is exclusively involved in conscious, episodic memory function. Our brief reference to perirhinal involvement in object recognition is a clear signal that other structures are implicated in some aspects of this complex process. As the putative contributions of other structures are reviewed in subsequent sections, an attempt will be made to compare and contrast their roles in learning and memory. As differences between the respective roles of various brain regions become apparent, attention will be directed to experiments that permit functional dissociations and a more precise description of each structure's contribution.

AMYGDALA

There is widespread agreement that the amygdala is involved in the process of attaching positive and negative valences to experienced events, and in the organization of appropriate emotional behaviour. This general view derives from Kluver and Bucy's (1939) classic description of behavioural abnormalities in monkeys with large lesions to the medial temporal lobe area. Their symptoms included hypersexuality that was often directed at inappropriate objects, hyperorality, perceptual deficits (psychic blindness), and lack of emotional responsiveness. Because the lesions affected most structures in the medial temporal lobes, subsequent investigators sought to determine if the various behavioural changes could be related more precisely to specific structures. This work pointed to the amygdala as a critical component of the neurobiological substrate of emotion.

Early animal studies focused mainly on the effects of amygdala lesions on the expression of aggressive, defensive, and fearful behaviour, all of which, of course, have a substantial emotional component. The consistent finding was that amygdalectomized animals of various species showed a decrease in these behaviours in response to stimuli that naturally evoke them (see LeDoux (1995) for a comprehensive review). The animal research proved to have clinical implications in that it prompted the use of amygdalectomy in the treatment of patients displaying uncontrollable violent tendencies. Although clinical reports often lack empirical documentation and the evidence regarding the treatment's utility is controversial, it seems clear that most patients experience reduced affect after amygdala surgery (Valenstein 1973).

Important insight into the nature of the amygdala's role in emotionality was provided by observations of the effects of lesions to the structure on social behaviour. In a widely cited study, Rosvold *et al.* (1954) produced amygdala lesions in two aggressive monkeys (Dave, Zeke) in a colony of eight monkeys. The lesion caused the previously dominant monkeys to fall to the bottom of the social hierarchy. In contrast to their pre-operative assertive behaviour in relation to other monkeys, Dave and Zeke became extremely submissive and cringed in the presence of threatening signals. While there are different interpretations of their behaviour, one view is that, following amygdalectomy, Dave and Zeke were no longer able to interpret emotionally charged events. This is an important contribution to the debate because, in addition to whatever hard-wired role the amygdala may play in the production of an emotional response, it suggests that the structure is involved in the cognitive process of deciding on the emotional nature and significance of a particular event. Other authors have also emphasized the adverse effects of amygdalectomy on higher-order processing of environmentally based information that results in inappropriate affective responses (e.g. Sarter and Markowitsch 1985; Rolls 1990).

The anatomical organization of the amygdala suggests that it is a convergence site of polymodal sensory input that signifies the presence of negative (e.g. painful stimuli, temperature extremes, threatening events) or positive (e.g. food, water, sexual partners, social contact) events in the environment. In addition, electrophysiological studies, using extracellular single-unit recording methods, have provided evidence for a variety of evoked responses in neurons intrinsic to the amygdala. Neurons within the amygdala respond to sensory stimuli from all modalities (Ben-Ari *et al.* 1974; Bordi and LeDoux 1992), and to biologically significant stimuli with positive or negative valence (Bordi and LeDoux 1992). The amygdala also responds to stimuli that do not have a significant emotional component but, interestingly, evoked responses to such stimuli habituate quickly (Pascoe and Kapp 1985).

Against this background is the interesting observation that humans who have undergone amygdalectomy are impaired in recognizing and processing information about faces (Jacobson 1986; Aggleton 1992). The selectivity of this impairment rules out a generalized memory disturbance and raises the possibility that such patients have difficulty understanding the information conveyed by facial expressions. This issue has been addressed in patients with Urbach–Wiethe disease, a rare condition that produces bilateral damage that is restricted mainly to the amygdaloid complex. In separate studies, Adolphs et al. (1994) and Young et al. (1995) found that face recognition, in itself, was normal in such patients. However, both patients were impaired at identifying emotions that were signalled through facial expressions. In addition, Young et al.'s patient, DR, had difficulty recognizing faces presented in an emotional context and in matching faces on the basis of their emotional expressions.

Cahill et al. (1995) reported similar deficits in a Urbach–Wiethe patient, BP, who was asked to recall events of a story that contained some emotionally salient elements. In contrast to controls who typically exhibited superior memory for the emotional parts of the story, BP displayed equal recall for neutral and emotionally arousing components. Taken together, the evidence indicates strongly that poor processing of emotional information is a primary effect of amygdala damage.

Considerable evidence in the animal literature supports the hypothesis that the amygdala performs an associative function in linking biologically significant events to related environmental stimuli. In one of the earliest behavioural studies to make this point, Weiskrantz (1956) attributed the poor performance of amygdalectomized monkeys on food-reinforced visual discrimination problems to an inability to attach appropriate value to non-reinforcing stimuli. Corroborative evidence comes from studies of aversive conditioning in which amygdalectomized cats and rats were impaired in learning conditioned fear responses in tasks requiring active or inhibitory avoidance of shock-associated stimuli (Ursin 1965; Cahill and McGaugh 1990). In addition, studies, utlizing classical conditioning paradigms, have shown that amygdalectomized monkeys are impaired at acquiring a conditioned fear response, as measured by galvanic skin responses (Bagshaw and Coppock 1968). These findings are generally consistent with Goddard's (1964) conclusion that a critical function of the amygdala is related to the process of associating neutral stimuli and emotional experiences.

Analogous deficits have been observed in humans with amygdala damage although there are very few patients with damage to this region that does not extend to other medial temporal lobe structures. A recent experiment by La Bar et al. (1995) studied classical fear conditioning in a group of unilateral temporal lobectomy patients who sustained damage to amygdala and hippocampus. Significantly, these patients displayed little of the declarative memory deficit associated with medial temporal lobe amnesia. However, they were impaired on several measures of emotional responsiveness, including the ability to form associations between neutral (tone) and aversive (white noise) stimuli, as well as in learning conditional discrimination involving different stimulus–response pairings. The authors note the similarities between these results and those obtained in parallel studies of fear conditioning in animals with restricted lesions to the amygdala or hippocampus. Studies of this nature provide the best available evidence that the amygdala's role in attaching appropriate emotional responses to sensory stimuli is similar in animals and humans.

The range of emotionally charged behaviour that can be identified with amygdala function has been broadened to include a variety of natural behaviours. In a particularly interesting paradigm, Everitt *et al.* (1987) studied the effects of basolateral amygdala lesions on the motivation of rats to perform an operant response to gain sexual reward. Initially, the males were allowed to interact with a female in heat in the presence of a light. The males were then transferred to an operant task and trained to press a lever to produce the light. If the male observed the response schedule and maintained the light (which served as a secondary reinforcer) for a fixed duration, it gained direct access to the female in heat. Whereas normal male rats were motivated and learned the response pattern, the amygdala-lesioned rats did not. The lesioned rats did not differ from normal rats in their responses to the presence of a female. All rats displayed normal sexual responses but the ability of a conditioned reinforcer to maintain sexually motivated behaviour was disrupted by amygdala lesions. In line with other work that emphasizes the amygdala's involvement in emotional conditioning, this result directly implicates the amygdala in an associative function that relates biologically significant and emotional events to relevant stimuli.

A similar conclusion was drawn by Gaffan (1992) on the basis of a different line of inquiry. Gaffan found that the amygdala is selectively involved in the process of associating stimuli with a task-related primary reward and not in associations between discriminative stimuli or between stimuli and responses. In an elegant study, Gaffan and Harrison (1987) pre-operatively trained monkeys on a series of visual discrimination problems in which the discriminanda were also associated with auditory stimuli that served as secondary reinforcers or non-reinforcers. The animals' task was to respond to visual stimuli which produced auditory secondary reinforcers that had been associated with food reward. As expected, bilateral amygdalectomy severely impaired performance on this task but, to determine the precise nature of the deficit, Gaffan and Harrison made use of an asymmetrical lesion technique. Two groups of monkeys sustained a unilateral lesion to the amygdala and a contralateral lesion to the visual or auditory association cortex. Given that auditory, not visual, stimuli were associated directly with primary reinforcement, if the amygdala participated selectively in associations involving biologically relevant information, then only the disconnection from the auditory system should affect performance. This indeed was the case. The failure of the visual disconnection to affect performance indicated that the amygdala was not involved in the process of forming associations between environmental stimuli and other stimuli that do not have primary reward value. These results provide compelling evidence that 'the amygdala is important for associating sensory stimuli with the intrinsic incentive value of . . . (reward), and not with . . . other attributes (Gaffan and Harrison 1987, p. 291), as well as making the important point that the processes reflect dissociable neural systems.

Similar conclusions may be drawn from studies with rats. For example, Kesner and Andrus (1982) found that the amygdala's role in processing affect-related information extends to making decisions based on magnitude of reinforcement. Rats with lesions to the amygdala behave abnormally on a variety of tasks in which the preferred response is determined by the amount of reinforcement associated with it. In another study, Kesner and Williams (1995) showed that amygdala lesions disrupted rats' performance on a conditional learning task in which sweetened or non-sweetened food predicted the presence of reward on a subsequent test trial. The deficit was independent of the length of the interval between study and test trials, which varied between 1 and 20 seconds. Significantly, hippocampal lesions did not affect performance on this task. Of particular interest was the finding that rats with hippocampal lesions were no different than controls even at the longest delay, although the enduring effects of the sweet flavour after the study trial may have been a factor here.

Numerous examples in the rat literature provide evidence that the amygdala's unique role in emotional conditioning can be dissociated from that of the hippocampus in learning and memory. There has been considerable interest, for example, in the neural basis of contextual fear conditioning as measured by a freezing response to contextual stimuli that were paired with foot shock. There is some controversy here, but the general consensus is that the amygdala and hippocampus are both involved (Kim *et al.* 1993; Phillips and LeDoux 1992), but in different ways. Damage to the hippocampus selectively impairs conditioning of contextual stimuli to foot shock, but has little effect on fear conditioning in a classical paradigm. In contrast, lesions to the amygdala block expression of the conditioned fear response to both conditional and background contextual stimuli. The hippocampal deficit probably reflects a failure to integrate contextual stimuli with conditional stimuli (Winocur, 1997), whereas the amygdala deficit is clearly a function of a failure to process emotion-laden information.

Similar results were obtained by McDonald and White (1993) with a different paradigm. In that study, they demonstrated a triple dissociation in which the differential effects of amygdala and hippocampal lesions were also distinguished from the effects of lesions to the caudate nucleus. Three adaptations of the eight-arm radial arm maze were developed—a standard (win-shift) version, a win-stay version in which rats learned to re-enter arms for food, and a conditioned cue preference task in which food was paired with a lit or darkened arm. Rats with hippocampal lesions were impaired only in the standard version of a task, reflecting their difficulty on tests of spatial memory. The caudate group was impaired on the win-stay task, suggesting a deficit in stimulus–response learning (see section on caudate nucleus). The amygdala group performed normally on the above tasks, but were impaired on the condition-cue preference task, confirming the importance of this structure in learning about reinforcement. Interestingly, McDonald and White's results suggest that the amygdala is needed for first-order associations between environmental stimuli and reinforcement. This finding contrasts with Gaffan and Harrison's (1987) view that the amygdala is part of the neural substrate for *second*-order conditioning in which a neutral stimulus, because of its association with reinforcement, acquires secondary reward value. While this apparent discrepancy does not argue against the amygdala's role in forming emotional memories, it does highlight the need to consider potentially confounding variables related, for example, to differences in species studied, lesion locations, and task demands.

Recently, Bechara *et al.* (1995) demonstrated a similar dissociation in patients with selective damage to the amygdala or hippocampus. Subjects were administered a classical conditioning task in which visual or auditory conditioned stimuli (CSs) were paired with loud noises and conditioned fear was measured by skin conductance activity. SM, a patient with restricted damage to the amygdala, failed to acquire the conditioned fear response, despite being able to produce the appropriate skin conductance response as an unconditioned response (UCR) to the loud noises. On the other hand, SM had excellent memory for relevant facts associated with the conditioning situation. A patient with bilateral damage to the hippocampus, WC, displayed the opposite pattern—normal fear conditioning but poor episodic recall. Finally, a third patient with bilateral damage to hippocampus and amygdala, RH, was impaired on both fear conditioning and episodic memory tasks.

In summary, research involving animals and humans, yields a consistent pattern with regard to the functional significance of the amygdala. There is little doubt that the amygdala participates in emotional behaviour and especially in the process of attaching emotional significance to environmental events. Its role in producing emotional behaviour is less certain, although there is evidence that the structure is also involved in this aspect of emotionality. Research suggests that the central nucleus of the amygdala may be important for both functions. Several studies have shown that selective damage to the central nucleus impairs the conditioning of emotional behaviour without necessarily affecting the unconditioned responses (Davis 1992). On the other hand, lesions to regions of the lateral hypothalamus that receive projections from the central nucleus of the amygdala interfere with the production of autonomic and freezing responses associated with emotionality (LeDoux *et al.* 1988).

With respect to the amygdala's associative function, the favoured inteterpretation is that the structure contributes to the process of integrating external and internal events with emotional correlates of those events to facilitate new learning or accurate memory processes. It is important to distinguish the amygdala's role in learning and memory from that of other structures, such as the hippocampus, that have a more generic involvement in such functions. The recent demonstration that the respective contributions of the amygdala and the hippocampus to learning and memory can be experimentally dissociated (LeDoux 1995), offer strong support for a division of function along these lines.

THALAMUS

The importance of the thalamus for normal memory function came into focus with the publication of Victor et al.'s (1971) classic monograph on Korsakoff's syndrome. This condition, associated with a prolonged history of alcohol abuse and nutritional deficiencies, is characterized most prominently by profound anterograde and retrograde amnesia that is disproportionate to other changes in intellectual or psychological processes. The neuropathology of Korsakoff's syndrome is extensive and variable but Victor et al.'s anatomical analyses indicated that damage to specific (anterior and dorsomedial) thalamic nuclei is common to most cases. Because of the widespread brain damage, Korsakoff patients are of limited value in terms of localizing memory function, but Victor et al.'s discovery directed attention to the memory capabilities of patients with restricted thalamic damage resulting from stroke or tumour.

Not surprisingly, patients with lesions restricted to anterior or dorsomedial thalamic nuclei present with some of the same memory problems as Korsakoff patients. Aside from major disturbances of long-term memory (see Butters and Stuss (1989) for a review), patients with circumscribed thalamic lesions frequently display impairment on tests of short-term memory that is reminiscent of observations by Cermak and Butters (1972) in their work with Korsakoff patients. Most notably, reports suggest that both types of patient may be impaired on the Brown–Peterson test of short-term memory. There is some controversy regarding this effect (see Baddeley and Warrington 1970), but it appears that conflicting results may be related to variation in testing procedures. In work with BY (Winocur et al. 1984), a severely amnesic patient with bilateral lesions to the dorsomedial nucleus, and a very similar thalamic patient, JG, Winocur et al. noted severe deficits at virtually all delays when stimulus material were presented at a relatively fast (2 second) rate. Both patients improved substantially when stimuli were presented at a 4 second rate. Significantly, the same pattern has been noted in the Korsakoff literature (Cermak and Butters 1972; Baddeley and Warrington 1970; but see Kopelman 1985). This observation led to the suggestion that thalamic damage may produce a basic impairment in encoding new information that could have widespread implications for new learning and memory.

The finding that additional processing time helped to improve short-term memory performance levels in thalamic patients suggested that if some way could be found to overcome the patients' encoding difficulties, long-term memory loss could be reduced. This prediction was, in fact, supported by studies with Korsakoff patients and patients with localized thalamic lesions. In studies involving tests of recognition memory for sentences or pictures, investigators reported that when baseline learning levels were normal, forgetting rates over several days were similar in Korsakoff patients and control subjects (e.g. Huppert and Piercy 1977; Squire 1981). Identical results using similar test material have been observed in NA (Squire 1981), BY (Winocur et al. 1984), and JG (Moscovitch and Winocur, in preparation).

Investigations of implicit memory in thalamic amnesia are less common but the results are generally consistent in showing that Korsakoff patients, as well as patients with restricted thalamic lesions, perform normally on tests of repitition priming and on various tests that involve implicit activation of semantic memory (Warrington and Weiskrantz 1973; Winocur and Weiskrantz 1976; Jacoby and Witherspoon 1982; Graf et al. 1985). There is also evidence that Korsakoff patients normally learn a variety of visuomotor tasks (Cermak et al. 1973; Brooks and Baddeley 1976), but there is some indication that their lack of impairment may not extend to all procedural learning tasks. For example, Butters et al. (1985) found that, contrary to some reports (Cohen 1984), Korsakoff patients were impaired in learning the rule governing the Tower of Hanoi task. This deficit was attributed to a failure in developing appropriate problem-solving strategies that is also evident in other tasks (e.g. Oscar-Berman 1973). There is some evidence that problem-solving abilities, at least to some extent, are compromised in amnesic patients with thalamic lesions. For example, despite showing progressive improvement in acquiring a maze-learning skill when tested over several days, patient NA was impaired relative to normal controls (Teuber et al. 1968). Similarly, the thalamic patient, GG, described by Nichelli et al. (1988) was able to learn a mathematical rule but displayed a lack of skill learning when tested on a visual tracking task. The encoding deficit hypothesis does not make a strong prediction with respect to performance on tests of implicit memory and procedural learning, but deficits on tasks that require processing of relatively complex information would be consistent with this hypothesis.

The encoding deficit hypotheses would not necessarily predict severe retrograde amnesia in thalamic patients, at least for information that was acquired well before the injury. In fact, there is considerable controversy regarding the remote memory capabilities of Korsakoff patients. Although most investigators report severe remote memory loss in such patients, some found temporally graded retrograde amnesia that extended over several decades, but with relative sparing of very old memories (Butters and Albert 1982; Zola-Morgan et al. 1983). Others have reported an even more severe retrograde memory loss with little sparing of events between childhood and adulthood (Sanders and Warrington 1971). However, an important consideration is that remote memory loss in Korsakoff's syndrome is often accompanied by deficits on tests of frontal lobe function (e.g. PI-release, temporal order) and may result from pathology in this region.

Retrograde amnesia has been observed in some thalamic patients (e.g. Graff-Radford et al. 1984; Stuss et al. 1988), but here again frontal involvement may be a factor. In thalamic patients who do not show signs of frontal lobe impairment, the typical finding, at least with respect to public events, is little or no retrograde amnesia, except usually for a brief period preceding the onset of damage (e.g. Squire and Slater 1978; Winocur et al. 1984; Speedie and Heilman 1982; Parkin et al. 1994; Hodges and McCarthy 1993).

There are parallels to the above pattern in the animal literature. Investigators have reported fundamental learning deficits following lesions to anterior and dorsomedial thalamic nuclei on a variety of tasks. For example, several investigators found that rats with lesions restricted to anterior thalamic nuclei were impaired on various delayed non-matching to sample tasks (Aggleton et al. 1991; Mair et al. 1992). Similar results have been observed in studies involving monkeys with localized thalamic damage (Aggleton and Mishkin 1983; Zola-Morgan and Squire 1985). In some studies, thalamic animals were eventually able to reach a normal level of performance when the delay between sample and test trials was minimal. When delay intervals were increased, the performance of thalamic groups declined at a rate that did not differ significantly from normal controls. In a noteworthy study, Hunt and Aggleton (1991) organized rats with thalamic lesions into subgroups that reached an acquisition criterion and those that did not. The thalamic rats that reached the initial learning criterion were no different from controls at longer intervals but, for other subgroups, a lesion x delay interaction approached statistical significance. The latter result relates directly to the finding, reported above, that patients with thalamic lesions, despite having severe amnesia, showed normal forgetting rates on recognition memory tesks in which original learning was found to be normal (Huppert and Piercy 1979; Squire 1981; Winocur, unpublished observations)

Similar results have been reported on tests of spatial (Gross et al. 1965) and non-spatial (Beracochea et al. 1989; Winocur 1985) alternation learning. In the Winocur (1985) study, rats with dorsomedial lesions to the thalamus were administered an operant test of go/no-go alternation with a variable interval between the go and no-go trial. After 12 days of testing, the thalamic group displayed a significant impairment in learning the alternation habit. Of particular interest was the observation that the extent of the thalamic group's deficit, relative to controls, increased with the length of the intertrial interval. This pattern, which indicated a memory loss that was directly related to the learning deficit, contrasted with that seen in a group of rats with hippocampal lesions. The latter group did not differ from controls in alternation learning or performance at short intertrial intervals. In line with the notion that the hippocampus is important for holding information beyond very short intervals, the hippocampal group was impaired only when the intervals reached a critical duration of 20 seconds.

Another study examined the different patterns of memory loss associated with hippocampal or thalamic damage in a test of long-term memory (Winocur 1985). Different groups of rats were administered a test of step-through inhibitory avoidance and tested for recall of the shock experience at intervals varying between one hour and three weeks. Neither lesion group was impaired at brief delays, indicating normal ability to acquire the avoidance response. Hippocampal rats exhibited forgetting of the learned response at longer delays, whereas the thalamic group continued to perform at normal levels. Furthermore, the introduction of interfering experiences during the delay interval exacerbated the rate of forgetting in the hippocampal groups but had no effect on the thalamic groups. The results provide further evidence that memory loss following thalamic lesions is inversely related to original learning, as compared with hippocampal amnesia which appears to be due to some form of consolidation failure.

The dissociable contributions of hippocampus and thalamus to cognitive function must be kept in mind in assessing the apparently similar effects of hippocampal and thalamic lesions on various tests of learning and memory. For example, lesions to either structure reliably impair complex maze learning (Gross *et al.* 1965), response alternation learning (Means *et al.* 1973; Winocur 1985), spatial learning (Kolb 1977; O'Keefe and Nadel 1978), and radial arm maze performance (Olton *et al.* 1979; Stokes and Best 1988). Because the nature and extent of the respective deficits can be similar, the temptation is to attribute poor performance in the two lesion groups to a common underlying deficit. In fact, in most cases the tasks are multidimensional and successful performance depends on the recruitment of several interdependent cognitive operations. Animals can be impaired for quite different reasons but the insensitivity of the outcome measures may well mask the true underlying deficits.

The standard version of the radial arm maze provides an instructive case in point. To perform this task efficiently, the rat must adopt a win-shift strategy, remembering which arms had been previously entered (spatial memory), retain that information while identifying arms not previously entered (working memory), overcome the cumulative effects of proactive interference, and, finally, select and initiate an appropriate response. A breakdown in one or more of these operations could produce large numbers of errors during a single session. The reliable impairment of hippocampal rats on this task can safely be attributed to a failure of spatial memory and, since most of their errors tend to occur late in the session, an exaggerated susceptibility to interference effects (Jarrard 1975; Winocur 1979) is probably also involved. By comparison, when the general pattern of thalamic impairment is considered, it is reasonable to hypothesize that rats with thalamic lesions are impaired on this task because of a basic failure in encoding essential information that enables the development of an efficient strategy (see Stokes and Best 1988). These distinctions can only be made when tasks incorporate measures that are sensitive to the different roles of various brain regions.

A study by Sutherland and Rodriguez (1989) provides another important example of apparently similar memory deficits following thalamic or hippocampal lesions that, in fact, reflect disruption of different mechanisms. These investigators trained rats with lesions to the anterior thalamic nucleus to find and remember the location of a hidden platform in the standard version of the Morris water maze. Since the circular pool is featureless, place navigation in this task is guided by information about the relationships among cues in the distal environment. Rats with damage to the hippocampus are typically impaired at both learning and remembering the location of the platform (Morris *et al.* 1982). By comparison Sutherland and Rodriguez (1989) showed that thalamic-lesioned rats were impaired only on the acquisition measure. When platform location was learned preoperatively, the thalamic group found the platform as well as controls. These results are consistent with the notion that the thalamus plays a crucial role in encoding information during learning, but not necessarily in the expression of learned behaviour.

The dissociable effects of hippocampal and thalamic damage can also be discerned on tests of premorbid memory. As indicated above, patients with thalamic lesions (and no sign of frontal lobe dysfunction) typically show little or no retrograde amnesia. Medial temporal lobe/hippocampal amnesics often show a temporally graded retrograde amnesia and there is evidence of a similar pattern in hippocampal animals. In one study (Winocur 1990), groups of hippocampus- and thalamus-lesioned rats and normal controls were administered tests of memory for an acquired food preference. In a test of anterograde memory, both lesion groups acquired the preference normally but only the hippocampal rats exhibited abnormal forgetting over an 8 day period. This outcome provides further evidence of the differential roles played by the two structures in acquiring and retaining new information. In a second study, the food preference was acquired 0 to 10 days before surgery and the test took place 10 days post-operatively. The results clearly indicated a temporally graded retrograde amnesia in rats with hippocampal lesions and normal memory in thalamic groups at all delays.

The results of the food preference study highlight the important differences between the hippocampus and the thalamus in learning and memory. On the basis of these results, which clearly point to severe anterograde and retrograde memory loss in hippocampus-damaged rats, it is tempting to assert that the thalamus is not directly involved in memory function and, perhaps, that is a reasonable conclusion. On the other hand, other evidence from animal and human studies clearly point to an important role for the thalamus in learning that has direct implications for memory function. While this role has been tentatively related to encoding processes during the early stages of information processing, this is a concept that can be clarified by future research.

PREFRONTAL CORTEX

The challenge of characterizing the various functions of the prefrontal cortex has been taken up in a number of recent reviews to which the reader is referred (Moscovitch and Winocur 1995; Stuss *et al.* 1994; Petrides 1994). In this section, we focus mainly on involvement of the prefrontal cortex in memory-related processes, particularly as they map on to functions associated with other brain regions.

The suggestion that the prefrontal cortex participates in memory was stimulated by the early work of Jacobsen (1936) on monkeys with prefrontal damage. In these studies, monkeys with lesions to prefrontal cortex were reliably impaired on a variety of delayed response and alternation tasks. The common element in these tasks was a delay condition that challenged the ability to recall specific events. While these results pointed to a link between the prefrontal cortex and memory function, a straightforward hypothesis in these terms was undermined by the fact that damage to this area in humans does not produce generalized memory problems.

It is now widely accepted that patients with prefrontal lesions do not suffer the types of memory disturbances seen in patients with damage to medial temporal lobe or diencephalic regions. On the other hand, their memories are far from normal. Prefrontal patients encounter difficulties in recalling information that requires effective search and retrieval operations. Thus, a prefrontal patient may have no trouble engaging automatic processes involved in recalling highly salient experiences but may be impaired when it is necessary to sort through several possible associations in order to isolate and retrieve a less accessible experience. The superiority of prefrontal patients on tasks of recognition that reduce retrieval demands, relative to tests of free recall, further attests to the structure's role in this particular aspect of memory function.

These observations point to the organizational role played by the prefrontal cortex in the retrieval of information during free recall. A similar organizational function is performed when information is encoded as part of new learning. In one study, della Rocchetta (1986) presented patients with damage to prefrontal cortex or medial temporal lobes with a task in which they were required to sort items according to taxonomic categories of their own choosing. Category and item recall were then tested at short and long delays. The impaired organizational skills of prefrontal patients were reflected in their inability to categorize items and in their generally poor recall at short and long delays. Patients with damage to the left temporal lobe were impaired at recalling the names of the pictures, but this deficit was uncorrelated with sorting ability, which was found to be normal.

On the surface, the memory problems of prefrontal patients appear to have little in common with other cognitive deficits reliably associated with such lesions. These include, for example, problems in determining the temporal order of events, estimating frequency, recovering from interference effects (e.g. PI-release), forming hypotheses, and shifting sets. On the other hand, there is an important common element in that these abilities involve conscious strategic processes that require the recollection and use of stored information. To perform these operations successfully, individuals must be capable of working with memory in order to organize information for purposes of generating appropriate goal-directed responses.

Moscovitch and Winocur (1995) have proposed a working-with-memory model that captures a distinctive aspect of frontal lobe function that is basic to its role in selecting responses and organizing behaviour. The concept of working-with-memory stresses the strategic application of remembered events, stored information, or learned skills to a particular task. By incorporating the use of various types of (old or new) information into the organization of behaviour, the working-with-memory concept contrasts with the familiar notion of working memory which typically refers to the retention of small amounts of information while another task is being performed. The latter view is more limited in its application than the more broadly based working-with-memory hypothesis.

The working-with-memory hypothesis is consistent with many of the reliable effects of prefrontal lesions that have been observed in animals and humans. One of the most widely cited symptoms of such damage is a disruption in the temporal organization of information that is reflected in impaired judgment of temporal order. In a series of experiments, Milner *et al.* (1991) presented patients with unilateral frontal or temporal lesions with verbal and non-verbal tests of recency judgment and recognition memory. The results revealed two double dissociations. On the verbal task, left-frontal patients were impaired on judgments of recency but not on recognition memory, while unilateral left temporals exhibited a recognition memory deficit but normal performance on the recency task. The same dissociation pattern was observed in right-hemisphere patients on non-verbal items. Normal temporal ordering has also been reported in the medial temporal lobe amnesic, HM, but a cautionary note is provided by the results of Shimamura *et al.* (1990). These investigators found that frontal lobe patients were impaired in ordering list items and historical events but did not differ from controls in remembering these specific items. By comparison, amnesic patients with damage to medial temporal lobe or diencephalon were found to be impaired in the temporal ordering and content-memory tasks. Shimamura *et al.*'s (1990) results are not necessarily in direct conflict with those of Milner and colleagues but rather may illustrate the point that temporal ordering tasks are multidimensional. The performance of frontal lobe patients on this task is compromised because of the failure to use memory in the strategic process of tagging temporal events. On the other hand, the generalized failure of severely amnesic patients to remember specific events could affect performance on a temporal ordering task if the task challenges episodic memory functions.

The strategic deficit that underlies frontal lobe patients' difficulties on temporal ordering may be related to accompanying problems with remembering other contextual features such as the source of information (Shimamura and Squire 1987; Parkin *et al.* 1988; Janowsky *et al.* 1989). Here again, we find an interesting dissociation in that frontal lobe patients' source memory is independent of their ability to remember content information. By comparison, hippocampal or diencephalic damage typically produces the opposite pattern—impaired memory for targets or facts, but normal memory for target-related contextual information, at least at delays in which the target information can be remembered.

It seems reasonable to conclude that the poor performance on tests of delayed response and delayed alternation following prefrontal damage, as reported initially by Jacobsen and subsequently confirmed in animals (Fuster 1997) and humans (Freedman and Oscar-Berman 1986), is also due to a failure in effectively processing temporally based contextual information. Successful performance on such tasks requires the ability to select a response on the basis of remembering events of the preceding trial. Performance will suffer if individuals lack the strategic ability to distinguish the most recent trial from similar trials of the preceding series. Hippocampal damage can also affect performance on these tasks, but usually only when the duration for recalling critical information exceeds the animal's short-term memory capabilities.

The dissociation of hippocampal and prefrontal function in response-alternation tasks is illustrated in experiments involving the variable interval go/no-go alternation paradigm, described previously. As indicated, hippocampal and thalamic lesions interfere with performance on this task but for different reasons—

hippocampal rats learned the task normally but were impaired at long intertrial intervals, whereas thalamic rats were impaired at all intervals presumably because of a basic deficit in learning the task. The present analysis would expect prefrontal cortex lesions to impair acquisition of the alternation habit because of a working-with-memory deficit that prevents effective segregation and use of trial-specific information in response selection. On the other hand, since the deficit is tied to strategic abilities and not to time-dependent factors, performance should not be seriously affected by increases in the intertrial interval. This prediction was confirmed, demonstrating a triple dissociation between the effects of hippocampal, thalamic, and prefrontal lesions (Winocur 1991). Similar dissociations between the effects of hippocampal and prefrontal lesions on rats' ability to mediate temporally dissociated information have been reported by Kesner on a test of paired-associate learning (Kesner 1993) and by Olton *et al.* (1988) on an operant test of temporal discrimination.

Another task on which the animal and human literature converge in pointing to a critical difference in the effects of prefrontal and hippocampal lesions is conditional associative learning. In this type of learning, subjects must associate different stimuli with different responses so that, on a given trial, the correct response is conditional on the particular stimulus that is presented. Impaired performance on this task is a reliable feature of prefrontal damage that has been observed in rats (Passingham *et al.* 1988), monkeys (Petrides 1982), and humans (Petrides 1985). Under certain conditions, medial temporal lobe/hippocampal damage can produce impairments on this task, but for quite different reasons. For example, Winocur (1991) confirmed that rats with lesions to prefrontal cortex were severely impaired in conditional associative learning. Increasing the delay between presentation of the stimulus and the opportunity to respond did not disproportionately add to the prefrontal group's impairment. By comparison, rats with hippocampal lesions acquired the habit within normal limits but were severely impaired when required to remember the conditional stimulus for more than 5 seconds. Interestingly, at the 5 second delay, accuracy rates were comparable in both groups and, in themselves, might have suggested comparable deficits. However, comparisons at shorter and longer delays clearly revealed that the respective deficits were due to a disruption of different processes. The prefrontal group's deficit was consistent with a working-with-memory hypothesis, while the hippocampal group's behaviour reflected a time-dependent loss of item-specific memory.

The examples provided so far reveal the inability of individuals with prefrontal damage to organize temporally displaced information and select appropriate responses over relatively short intervals. A working-with-memory hypothesis predicts that such deficits will also be manifest when information in long-term storage must be integrated with current information during new learning. Recent research provides two examples of impaired transfer of learning in rats with prefrontal lesions. In one study (Winocur 1992), prefrontal and hippocampal groups initially learned to discriminate between two stimuli (triangles) of different sizes. All groups learned the discrimination equally and performed well when retested two weeks later. However, when administered a new task that demanded the transfer of the size discrimination rule to different stimuli (circles), the prefrontal group was severely impaired in re-establishing criterion.

Another study compared the problem-solving deficits of rats with damage to prefrontal cortex or hippocampus, as measured on a test of complex maze learning. Winocur and Moscovitch (1990) trained the rats on one of the mazes in the Hebb–Williams series and, predictably, observed severe deficits in both groups. Thirty days later, groups were tested on the same maze or a different maze in the same series. The results revealed a clear dissociation. The hippocampal group transferred the maze-learning skill to both mazes but did not display an additional advantage when retested in the original maze. The prefrontal group, on the other hand, showed savings on the familiar maze, indicating maze-specific recall but poor transfer of learning to the new maze. The prefrontal group was able to remember specific information and use it in the same task but was unable to work *with* the memory and apply it to a related task that placed similar demands on the animal.

This brief account does not do justice to the broad range of functions that are affected by damage to the prefrontal cortex. To the examples already provided can be added procedural learning, as reflected in the Tower of Hanoi task (Shallice and Burgess 1991), explicit and implicit versions of cued recall and tests of word-stem completion (Winocur et al. 1996; Nyberg et al. 1997), verbal fluency (Benton 1968), and the process of self-monitoring as reflected on tests of metamemory (Janowsky et al. 1989). It is not surprising then that the prefrontal cortex has been characterized as the executive of the brain that is essential for the expression of complex behaviours. In certain situations, deficits following prefrontal damage may incorporate a type of long-term episodic memory loss that resembles that seen following hippocampal or thalamic damage. It is clear, however, that such similar-looking deficits derive from very different functional impairments. As indicated in this section, with the development of sensitive testing instruments, the respective roles of the prefrontal cortex and other brain regions in complex learning and memory can be experimentally dissociated in a way that advances our conceptual understanding of each structure's unique contribution.

BASAL GANGLIA

The importance of the basal ganglia for motor coordination is well established in the clinical and animal literatures but, until recently, there was little interest in the possible role of this region in cognitive function. Initial investigations indicated that selective lesions to the caudate nucleus in different animal species impaired performance on a variety of learning and memory tasks, especially those with a significant spatial component (Potegal 1982). Neuropsychological studies of patients with focal lesions to the basal ganglia are relatively uncommon and are just beginning to appear. As a result, progress in this area was based largely on clinical observations of cognitive deterioration in patients with Parkinson's disease (PD) or Huntington's disease (HD), two neurodegenerative conditions that attack basal ganglia structures.

Although originating in substantia nigra and anatomically connected basal ganglia structures, PD develops as a result of depletion throughout the dopaminergic neurotransmitter system. Not surprisingly, therefore, a variety of cognitive symptoms have been observed in PD patients, many of whom contract a dementing form of the disease. Demented PD patients exhibit extensive cognitive impairment that includes memory and intellectual loss that is reminiscent of Alzheimer's disease (AD). Non-demented PD patients do not typically suffer problems of conscious recollection but they are reliably impaired in performing cognitive tests that depend on frontal lobe function, an observation that is in line with the close anatomical links between the prefrontal cortex and caudate nucleus. Thus, such patients are reliably impaired on frontal lobe tests that include delayed alternation learning, temporal ordering, conditional associative learning, as well as the Wisconsin card sorting test (WCST), verbal fluency, and other clinical tests of frontal executive function (see Dubois *et al.* (1991) for a review of the cognitive profile associated with PD).

PD patients, like patients with frontal lobe lesions, are not typically impaired on traditional tests of recognition memory that are guided by feelings of familiarity rather than a clear memory for specific information. However, when successful performance requires the use of cognitive processes associated with frontal lobe function, PD patients are impaired. In a recent study, Ergis *et al.* (in preparation) used measures of recognition memory to test patients' ability to detect synonyms of target material, source memory, and the ability to make recency judgments. Parkinson's patients were normal at recognizing target material and in performing basic discriminations but they were impaired on recognition measures that required judgments about similarity, source, and recency. Moreover, there was evidence that such deficits correlated with performance on standard clinical tests of frontal-lobe functions (e.g. verbal fluency, WCST, self-ordered pointing). These results underscore the importance of frontal involvement in at least some of the cognitive disorders of non-demented PD patients.

In line with the pattern of frontal-lobe pathology, PD patients have difficulty on tasks that require strategic planning. This deficit has been reported on a variety of problem-solving tasks, notably the Tower of Hanoi and its various permutations. In the 'tower' task, subjects must transfer a number of blocks from a starting position to a new location according to a prescribed set of rules and in a minimum number of trials. Parkinson's patients are consistently impaired on these tasks and when the use of consciously expressed strategies is taken into account, their deficits can be dissociated from those sometimes seen in patients with diencephalic or medial temporal lobe amnesia (St Cyr and Taylor 1992)

Investigations of patients with HD have also contributed to our knowledge of cognitive disorders associated with basal ganglia damage. Huntington's disease is a neurodegenerative disease that affects the striatal area and the caudate nucleus in particular. It is a progressive disease that is characterized by involuntary choreiform movement and a dementing process that affects a variety of cognitive functions. In the early stages, patients suffer some memory loss that is more apparent on free recall than on recognition tests. In that regard, HD patients differ from medial temporal lobe and diencephalic amnesics whose memory problems are reflected in virtually all measures of declarative memory. Memory loss associated with HD may be the result of disruption of frontal–striatal connections as there is evidence that their impaired memory, like that of PD patients, correlates with performance of tests with frontal executive functions (Pillon et al. 1993). The finding of a flat retrograde amnesia in HD (Beatty et al. 1988), in contrast to the temporally graded retrograde amnesia of general amnesics, is further evidence that frontal lobes are implicated in the memory problems of HD patients.

The defining neuropsychological deficit in HD is a reliable impairment in non-declarative memory as reflected on various tests of perceptuomotor skill learning. In general, the pattern of HD patients on such tasks is similar to that of PD patients and is thought to reflect a response-learning deficit that results from basal ganglia damage.

It is unlikely that the procedural learning deficits associated with HD are simply a function of general dementia. Comparisons of patients with HD or AD on tests of procedural learning and implicit memory reliably yield important differences. For example, Heindel et al. (1989) compared HD and AD patients on a pursuit-rotor, motor-learning task and on a lexical-priming test of implicit memory. The results revealed a clear dissociation in that HD patients were impaired on the pursuit-rotor task and performed normally on the priming task, while the AD group displayed the opposite pattern (see also Pillon et al. 1991).

It is important to note that the procedural learning tasks on which HD and PD patients are typically impaired often have a substantial motor component, and one has to be concerned about the confounding effects of these patients' motor disabilities on neuropsychological test performance. For the most part, however, these deficits were found to be more closely tied to other cognitive problems and independent of motor dysfunction. For example, Heindel et al. (1988) found that HD patients with mild or severe motor abilities did not differ on the pursuit-rotor task nor was their deficit disproportionately affected by increasing the speed of rotation of the disc. Other studies have looked at the broader relationship between motor disability and other aspects of the cognitive deficit in patients with basal ganglia damage. Cooper et al. (1991) and Gabrieli et al. (1996) confirmed that PD patients are impaired on frontal lobe functions (e.g. working memory, temporal ordering, self-ordered pointing, WCST) but, in both cases, the deficits failed to correlate with measures of motor impairments. Finally, Knowlton et al. (1996) tested HD patients on a conditional learning task in which subjects were required to learn a probabilistic rule in order to predict particular outcomes, and a second non-declarative task that involved artificial grammar learning but not the acquisition of new associations. Neither task had a motor component but the HD patients were impaired on the probabilistic rule learning task that involved associative learning.

The pattern that emerges quite clearly from investigations of PD and HD is that such patients are impaired in various aspects of procedural or skill learning, as well as in performing the mnemonic and related functions mediated by frontal–striatal circuits. Similar observations have been made in patients with focal lesions in the basal ganglia area and the caudate nucleus in particular. For example, Hanley et al. (1994) studied a patient (ROB) who suffered an anterior communicating artery aneurysm that produced a left-sided lesion in the caudate nucleus that extended to deep white matter in the left frontal cortex. ROB performed normally on tests of recognition memory but was impaired in verbal free recall, suggesting a retrieval deficit that is typical of frontal–striatal disruption. This patient also displayed a severe source memory deficit but, curiously, recency judgments were intact. A disproportional deficit in free recall, relative to recognition memory, has also been observed in other patients with focal striatal lesions (Irle et al. 1992; Caplan et al. 1990).

The same pattern was also observed by Robbins et al. (1995) in a comprehensive investigation of a patient, FS, who sustained a unilateral lesion to the left caudate-putamen area that spared the ventral striatum and globus palladus. In addition, FS was impaired on a variety of executive function tests, displaying a pattern that was interpreted as a basic failure in working memory. An important feature of FS's test performance is that, while he clearly showed signs of frontal lobe pathology, there were notable departures from the typical frontal lobe pattern. For example, FS was normal on the WCST, the CANTAB tests of attentional set-shifting, and the Cognitive Estimates Test. These results prompted Robbins et al. (1995) to conclude that although restricted lesions to the dorsal striatum produced deficits on frontal tests, there was evidence that the deficit of such patients is qualitatively different from that seen following direct damage to the prefrontal cortex.

In a recent study, Knowlton et al. (1996) used their probabilistic rule learning task to further demonstrate important differences between the cognitive deficits of patients with frontal lobe lesions and PD patients. PD patients were severely impaired on this procedural learning task, relative to amnesic patients who performed normally. The reverse pattern was obtained when the patient groups were administered a declarative memory task, thereby demonstrating a double dissociation with respect to rule learning and memory function. Since PD patients sustained damage to frontal–striatal circuits, it was particularly interesting that patients with circumscribed lesions to the frontal lobes were not impaired on this task. There was no evidence from neuropsychological testing that frontal lobe dysfunction was greater in the PD patients and, in fact, the best predictor of impairment on the task was severity of PD symptoms. These results, in addition to highlighting the dissociation between frontal and striatal function, point to a critical role for the caudate nucleus in incremental habit or rule learning that is independent of frontal lobe involvement. This raises the possibility that striatal damage may have contributed independently to the various procedural learning deficits of HD and PD patients described above.

A similar conclusion may be drawn from the findings of animal investigations of caudate nucleus function. Early research in this area drew attention to the disruptive effects of caudate nucleus lesions on various types of spatial learning and reversal learning tasks. These results were in line with observations that striatal damage interfered with spatial-motor coordination in animals and humans. Spatial deficits were especially pronounced on egocentric spatial tasks in which the subject was the reference point for locating an object in space or for performing a turning response (see Kesner and DiMattia (1987) for a review of caudate nucleus function in egocentric localization).

Subsequent research shows that while animals with caudate damage have particular difficulties on egocentric spatial tasks, the critical factor may not be the spatial component but rather the requirement that critical associations be formed between discrete responses and specific stimuli or reinforcers. In an important study, Packard *et al.* (1989) compared rats with lesions to the caudate nucleus or fornix on two versions of the radial arm maze. In the standard, win-shift, version each of the eight arms was baited once and the most efficient strategy was to obtain all the food without re-entering arms. As expected, the fornix group was impaired on this task but the caudate group performed normally. On a win-stay version, the location of food was signaled by a visual stimulus and rats were required to revisit arms. On the latter task, the opposite pattern was obtained—rats with fornix lesions were actually better than controls but the caudate group was severely impaired. These results indicate that the caudate nucleus is not involved in forming the types of stimulus–stimulus relationships that are necessary in mastering the spatial memory requirements of the standard version of the radial arm maze, but is a critical part of the neural system that mediates stimulus–response learning.

Other work suggests that the types of stimulus–response learning for which the caudate nucleus is important supports the acquisition of procedural or rule-learning tasks. Packard and White (1990) used a different version of the radial arm maze to test the rule-learning ability of rats with caudate nucleus lesions. In this task, only four arms were baited on each trial of testing, but they were always the same four arms. The best strategy was to enter the four arms once each session. Two types of errors were possible—entering arms that were never baited or re-entering baited arms. The caudate group did not re-enter arms, indicating that their spatial memory was intact. However, they consistently entered arms that were never baited, indicating an impairment in learning to respond to a fixed set of stimulus cues. Interestingly, a similar study by Jarrard (1983), involving rats with lesions to the hippocampal system, revealed the opposite pattern of behaviour. That is, hippocampus-lesioned rats learned to restrict their responses to one set of arms, but they performed suboptimally because of a tendency to re-enter arms where food was no longer available.

McDonald and White (1994) showed a similar dissociation in the Morris water maze. Rats with fornix or caudate nucleus damage were initially trained to find a hidden or visible platform. The rats were then required to choose between that spatial location and the visible platform in a new location of the water maze. Fornix lesions did not affect the rats' ability to find the visible platform but they were severely impaired at localizing the platform when it was hidden. Moreover, when the visible platform was moved they swam to the new location. Rats with caudate nucleus lesions located the visible and hidden platforms as well as controls, but, when the visible platform was moved, they swam first to the old location. The results confirmed that rats with damage to the hippocampal system learn little about spatial relationships. On the other hand, rats with lesions to the caudate nucleus are biased towards the use of spatial cues and are impaired on tasks that are best solved on the basis of stimulus–response learning.

The dissociative effects of lesions to caudate nucleus and hippocampus in stimulus–response and spatial learning have been demonstrated by other investigators (e.g. McDonald and White 1993; Packard and McGaugh 1992; Devan *et al.* 1996). In a notable study (McDonald and White 1993), these effects were demonstrated in a triple dissociation that also involved the amygdala (see section on amygdala). In that study, rats with lesions to the fornix, caudate nucleus, or amygdala were administered the standard, win-shift version of the radial arm maze, a win-stay version similar to that used by Packard *et al.* (1989), and a conditional cue preference task that tested rats' abilities to associate cues with primary reinforcements. The results revealed selective deficits associated with each type of lesion. In the context of the present discussion, they confirm that the caudate nucleus is important for forming critical associations between stimuli and responses and that the structure does not contribute to learning stimulus relationships or to learning associations between stimuli and reinforcers.

Evidence from other levels of analysis also supports the view that the caudate nucleus is involved in S–R learning. For example, investigations of evoked potentials in the caudate area have demonstrated a relationship between unit activity of neurons and performance on stimulus–response tasks. In one study, Manetto and Lidsky (1986) tracked single-unit activity in the caudate nucleus of cats during acquisition of a stimulus-guided head turning task. The cats were trained to turn their heads in particular directions following presentation of specific stimulus cues. The investigators found that evoked responses in the caudate nucleus were consistently related to stimulus presentations that elicited appropriate responses.

The animal literature converges with research involving humans in showing that learning and memory functions associated with the caudate nucleus can be differentiated from those associated with the hippocampus and other brain regions. Data from both sources also point to the conclusion that the caudate nucleus contributes to the process of forming stimulus–response associations that enable acquisition of rules or habits. The question arises as to whether the caudate nucleus would also be involved in a type of conditional rule learning that is known to involve frontal lobe function and, if so, whether the respective roles of the two regions can be dissociated. This is an important question because, as has been pointed out already, the two structures are anatomically connected and undoubtedly function in an integrated fashion in the control of various behaviours.

Research into this question is limited, but a recently completed study has provided promising results. Winocur and Eskes (1998) compared the effects of caudate and prefrontal lesions on conditional associative learning in which rats were required to associate one visual stimulus with a particular lever, and a second stimulus with another lever. Following training, rats were switched to a one-lever condition in which, on each trial, the visual stimulus was presented along with the correct or incorrect level. The latter manipulation maintained the same S–R association but reduced the demand on response selection. Both lesion groups were impaired on performing the two-lever task. When switched to the one-lever version, the prefrontal group recovered to near normal levels whereas the caudate group performed at approximately the same level as in the two-lever condition. Other experiments in the series provided evidence that the prefrontal cortex contributed to associative learning and/or response selection, depending on task requirements. By comparison, the behaviour of the caudate groups was much less affected by task manipulation and, in general, appeared to reflect a failure in associative learning.

The results of the Winocur and Eskes (1998) study are consistent with the idea that the caudate nucleus performs a function that is basic to the process of learning new rules or habits. In addition, they show that the caudate's role in this regard can be distinguished from that of other structures that may be involved in the learning process. One issue that remains to be resolved relates to whether it is actually necessary for individuals to perform responses in striatum-mediated S–R learning. Some investigators (e.g. Packard *et al.* 1989; McDonald and White 1993) maintain that response expression is a critical aspect of the representation that is acquired and stored in a dorsal striatal learning and memory system. By comparison, evidence from the human neuropsychological literature (e.g. Knowlton *et al.* 1996*a,b*) suggests that striatal involvement in procedural learning is not restricted to tasks that involve motor activity. At this stage, this apparent discrepancy could reflect differences between human and animal function, the different approaches taken in animal and human research, or a lack of precision in defining relationships between specific striatal structures and behaviour. On the other hand, the issue is an important one and further research is needed to determine if the caudate nucleus and related structures are only critical for forming direct S–R associations or whether they contribute to other types of incremental habit learning.

SUMMARY AND CONCLUSIONS

An important point that emerges from this chapter is that, within the brain's complex organization, differentiated structures can be implicated in specific aspects of learning and memory, and that their respective functions can be dissociated by sensitive behavioural paradigms. A particularly encouraging development is the high degree of convergence between the effects of selective brain damage in animal and human populations. While it has always been assumed that appropriately designed animal models could help describe brain function in humans, this convergence provides strong evidence for functional continuity across species.

While fairly comprehensive in its coverage of specific brain regions, the review in this chapter is not intended to be exhaustive. Rather, its purpose is to show that the highly integrated processes of learning and memory derive from the brain's ability to perform and combine diverse associative and mnemonic functions. Our review points to a hierarchical organization in which the dorsomedial thalamus and the prefrontal cortex are associated with broadly based functions that are essential to most types of learning and memory, whereas structures such as the hippocampus, amygdala, and caudate nucleus are identified with more specialized functions.

The dorsomedial thalamus is seen as contributing in a fundamental way to the registration or encoding of information during the early stages of learning. Such encoding is central to virtually any type of new learning and, in line with this view, damage to this structure is found to affect performance on a wide range of behavioural tasks. Interestingly, in studies where encoding conditions were manipulated to permit thalamic-damaged animals or humans to achieve normal learning levels, long-term memory performance was also normal. There are direct anatomical connections between the dorsomedial thalamus and prefrontal cortex which undoubtedly relate the encoding function of the dorsomedial thalamus to the prefrontal cortex's role in organizing new information and processing it at the appropriate level. However, the prefrontal cortex's complex function extends beyond the acquisition of new information into virtually all cognitive areas that require strategic planning. Invariably, strategic processes directed at appropriate response selection require the integration of stimulus input and stored knowledge, a concept that is embodied in Moscovitch and Winocur's (1995) working-with-memory hypothesis of frontal lobe function.

In contrast to the general functions of the dorsomedial thalamus and prefrontal cortex, the hippocampus is seen as operating within the more limited realm of episodic memory. A large body of evidence points to the hippocampus playing a crucial role in forming associations between unrelated events, defining a particular episode, and committing it to long-term memory. At retrieval, the hippocampus is involved in utilizing available cues and reinstating contextual cues to facilitate conscious recall of the target episode. In rodents, the hippocampus appears to have a special role in processing spatial information, although this may reflect the bias of rodent species to use spatial cues in learning about the environment. A cross-species survey of the animal and human literatures suggest that the hippocampus is needed to learn and remember relationships between spatial and non-spatial information.

The amygdala plays a unique role in encoding emotional correlates of external events. While there is some controversy as to whether the amygdala participates directly in the production of emotional responses, there is convincing evidence that the structure performs an associative function whereby biological significance or emotional salience become conditioned to environmental stimuli. Damage to the amygdala in animals and humans seriously disrupts the ability to process emotion-laden information and interpret social situations.

Historically, the caudate nucleus, like the hippocampus, has been implicated in learning and memory performance that depends on spatial information processing. However, recent evidence clearly shows that the function of the caudate nucleus contrasts dramatically with that of the hippocampus. Whereas the hippocampus is important for learning relationships between stimuli and recalling specific events, the caudate nucleus and related structures are implicated in forming S–R associations and in the type of non-conscious remembering that supports incremental procedural learning. The procedural learning system with which the caudate nucleus can be identified appears to correspond to the 'taxon' system described by O'Keefe and Nadel (1978) in their cognitive map theory. These authors viewed the taxon system as a back-up to the more efficient S–S learning that is controlled by the hippocampus and its 'locale' system. However, it is now apparent that S–R learning that is mediated by the caudate nucleus is crucial for the acquisition of a variety of important habits and skills.

Clearly, memory is not a unitary process but one that consists of multiple components mediated by different brain regions. The evidence in support of the brain–behaviour relationships cited here is, in most cases, quite compelling and speaks to the legitimacy of this view. However, the review and the limited conclusions that can be drawn also underscores challenges that remain. Foremost amongst these challenges is the need to specify the functional significance of other brain regions that are known to be involved in learning and memory. For example, only passing attention was paid to the perirhinal cortex and its relationship to medial temporal lobe function. No mention at all was made of the potential importance of parietal lobe, cingulate gyrus, and cortical association areas. A comprehensive description of neural mechanisms of learning and memory must include the contributions of these and other important structures.

A further limitation of the present approach was the decision to treat each brain region virtually as an undifferentiated unit. In fact, all the structures reviewed in this chapter embody considerable anatomical and functional divesity, most of which is not well understood. Indeed, as we learn more about regional specialization and the finely grained anatomical connections between the subfields of various structures, it may become necessary to revise our notions of functional unity.

Finally, we need as clear a statement as possible as to how the specific brain regions relate to each other. Such a statement needs to be integrative in nature and must show how localized functions combine in an organized fashion. In fact, some investigators are writing in these terms and excellent examples can be found in the attribution and component-process theories advanced respectively by Kesner and DiMattia (1987) and Moscovitch (1994). These theories may be challenged on specific points, but their emphasis on neural networks comprising functionally dissociable brain regions deserves wide support. It is this approach that holds the greatest promise for developing a workable framework for conceptualizing the neural basis of learning and memory.

ACKNOWLEDGEMENTS

Preparation of this chapter was supported by grants to GW from the Medical Research Council of Canada and the Natural Sciences and Engineering Research Council of Canada. Many of the ideas advanced in this chapter derive from a longstanding collaboration between GW and Morris Moscovitch—the latter's contribution is gratefully acknowledged. AME was supported by a post-doctoral fellowship awarded by the Fondation Nationale de Gerontologie de France. RM was supported by a grant from the Natural Sciences and Engineering Research Council of Canada

REFERENCES

Adolphs, R., Tranel, D., Damasio, H., and Damasio, A. (1994). Impaired recognition of emotion in facial expressions following bilateral damage to the human amygdala. *Nature*, **372**, 669–72.

Aggleton, J. P. (1992). The functional effect of amygdala lesions in humans: A comparison of findings from monkeys. In (ed. J. P. Aggleton), *The amygdala: neurobiological aspects of emotion, memory, and mental dysfunction*, pp.485–503. Wiley, New York.

Aggleton, J. P. and Mishkin, M. (1983). Memory impairments following restricted medial thalamic lesions in monkeys. *Experimental Brain Research*, **52**, 199–209.

Aggleton, J. P., Hunt, P. R., and Rawlins, J. N. P. (1986). The effect of hippocampal lesions upon spatial and non-spatial tests of working memory. *Behavioural Brain Research*, **19**, 133–46.

Aggleton, J. P., Keith, A. B., and Sahgal, A. (1991). Both fornix and anterior thalamic, but not mamillary, lesions disrupt delayed non-matching-to-position memory in rats. *Behavioural Brain in Research*, **44**, 151–61.

Amaral, D. G. and Witter, M. P. (1989). The three-dimensional organization of the hippocampal formation: A review of anatomical data. *Neuroscience*, **31**, 571–91.

Baddeley, A. D. and Warrington, E. K. (1970). Amnesia and the distinction between long- and short-term memory. *Journal of Verbal Learning and Verbal Behavior*, **9**, 176–89.

Bagshaw, M. H. and Coppock, H. W. (1968). Galvanic skin response conditioning deficit in amygdalectomized monkeys. *Experimental Neurology*, **20**, 188–96.

Beatty, W. W., Salmon, D. P., Butters, N., Heindel, W. C., and Granholm, E. L. (1988). Retrograde amnesia in patients with Alzheimer's disease or Huntington's disease. *Neurobiology of Aging*, **9**, 181–6.

Bechara, A., Tranel, D., Damasio, H., Adolphs, R., Rockland, C., and Damasio, A. R. (1995). Double dissociation of conditioning and declarative knowledge relative to the amygdala and hippocampus in humans. *Science*, **269**, 1115–18.

Ben-Ari, Y., La Salle, G., and Champagnat, J. C. (1974). Lateral amygdala activity: 1. Relationship between spontaneous and evoked activity. *Electroencephalography and Clinical Neurophysiology*, **37**, 449–61.

Benton, A. L. (1968). Differential behavioral effect in frontal lobe disease. *Neuropsychologia*, **6**, 53–60.

Beracochea, D. J., Jaffard, R., and Jarrard, L. E. (1989). Effect of anterior or dorsal medial thalamic ibotenic lesions on learning and memory in rats. *Behavioral and Neural Biology*, **51**, 364–75.

Bordi, F. and LeDoux, J. (1992). Sensory tuning beyond the sensory system: initial analysis of auditory response properties of neurons in the lateral amygdaloid nucleus and overlying areas of the striatum. *Journal of Neuroscience*, **12**, 2493–503.

Brooks, D. N. and Baddeley, A. D. (1976). What can amnesic patients learn? *Neuropsychologia*, **14**, 111–22.

Butters, N. and Albert, M. S. (1982). Processes underlying failures to recall remote events. In *Human memory and amnesia* (ed. L. S. Cermak), pp.257–74. Erlbaum, Hillsdale, NJ.

Butters, N. and Stuss, D. E. (1989). Diencenphalic amnesia. In *Handbook of neurophyschology*, Vol. 3, (ed. F. Boller and J. Grafman), pp.107–48. Elsevier, Amsterdam.

Butters, N., Wolfe, J., Maytone, M., Granholm, E., and Cermak, L. (1985). Memory disorders associated with Huntington's disease: verbal recall, verbal recognition and procedural memory. *Neuropsychologia*, **23**, 739–43.

Cahill, L. and McGaugh, J. L. (1990). Amygdaloid complex lesions differentially affect retention of tasks using competitive and aversive reinforcement. *Behavioral Neuroscience*, **104**, 532–543.

Cahill, L. F., Babinsky, R., Markowitsch, H. J., and McGaugh, J. L. (1995). The amygdala and emotional memory. *Nature*, **377**, 654–7.

Caplan, L. R., Schmahmann, J. D., Kase, C. S., Feldmann, E. F., Baquis, G., Greenberg, J. P., Gorelick, P. B., Helgason, C., and Hier, D. B. (1990). Caudate infarcts. *Archives of Neurology*, **47**, 133–43.

Cermak, L. S. and Butters, M. (1972). The role of interference and encoding in the short-term memory deficits of Korsakoff patients. *Neuropsychologia*, **10**, 89–96.

Cermak, L. S., Lewis, R., Butters, N., and Goodglass, H. (1973). Role of verbal mediation in performance of motor tasks by Korsakoff patients. *Perceptual Motor Skills*, **37**, 259–62.

Cho, Y. H., Kesner, R. P., and Brodale, S. (1995). Retrograde and anterograde amnesia for spatialdiscrimination in rats: role of hippocampus, entorhinal cortex, and parietal cortex. *Psychobiology*, **23**, 185–94.

Cohen, N. (1984). Preserved learning capacity in amnesia: evidence for multiple memory systems. In *Neuropsychology of memory*, (ed. L. Squire and N. Butters), pp.83–103. Guilford Press, New York.

Cooper, J. A., Sagar, H. J., Jordan, N., Harvey, N., and Sullivan, E. V. (1991). Cognitive impairment in early, untreated Parkinson's disease and its relationship to motor disability. *Brain*, **114**, 2095–122.

Corkin, S. (1965). Tactually-guided maze learning in man: Effects of unilateral cortical excisions and bilateral hippocampal lesions. *Neuropsychologia*, **3**, 339–51.

Corkin, S. (1968). Acquisition of motor skill after bilateral medial temporal lobe excision. *Neuropsychologia*, **6**, 255–65.

Corkin, S. (1984). Lasting consequences of bilateral medial temporal lobotomy: clinical course and experimental findings in HM. *Seminars in Neurology*, **4**, 249–59.

Davis, M. (1992). The role of the amygdala in fear and anxiety. *Annual Review of Neuiroscience*, **15**, 353–75.

della Rocchetta, A. I. (1986). Classification and recall of pictures after unilateral frontal or temporal lobectomy. *Cortex*, **22**, 189–211.

Devan, B. D., Goad, E. H., and Petri, H. L. (1996). Dissociation of hippocampal and striatal contributions to spatial navigation in the water maze. *Neurobiology of Learning and Memory*, **66**, 305–23.

Dubois, B., Boller, F., Pillon, B., and Agid, Y. (1991). Cognitive deficits in Parkinson's disease. In *Handbook of neuropsychology*, Vol. 5, (ed. F. Boller and J. Grafman), pp.195–240. Elsevier, Amsterdam.

Eichenbaum, H., Otto, P., and Cohen, N. J. (1992). The hippocampus—what does it do? *Behavioral and Neural Biology*, **57**, 2–36.

Ennaceur, A., Neave, N., and Aggleton, J. P. (1996). Neurotoxic lesions of the perirhinal cortex do not mimic the effects of fornix transection in the rat. *Behavioural Brain Research*, **80**, 9–25.

Everitt, B. J., Fray, P., Kostarczyk, E., Taylor, S., and Stacey, P. (1987). Studies of instrumental behavior with sexual reinforcement in male rats (*Rattus Norvegicus*): I. Control by brief visual stimuli compared with a receptive female. *Journal of Comparative Psychology*, **101**, 395–406.

Freedman, M. and Oscar-Berman, M. (1986). Bilateral frontal lobe disease and selective delayed response deficits in humans. *Behavioral Neuroscience*, **100**, 337–42.

Fuster, J. M. (1997). *The prefrontal cortex. Anatomy, physiology and neuropsychology of the frontal lobe*, 3rd edn. Raven Press, New York.

Gabrieli, J. D. E., Cohen, N. J., and Corkin, S. (1988). The impaired learning of semantic knowledge following bilateral medial temporal-lobe resection. *Brain and Cognition*, **7**, 157–77.

Gabrieli, J. D. E., Milberg, W., Keane, M. M., and Corkin, S. (1990). Intact priming of patterns despite impaired memory. *Neuropsychologia*, **28**, 417–27.

Gabrieli, J. D. E., Singh, J., Stebbins, G. T., and Goetz, C. G. (1996). Reduced working memory span in Parkinson's disease: evidence for the role of a frontostriatal system in working and strategic memory. *Neuropsychologia*, **10**, 322–32.

Gaffan, D. (1992). Amygdala and the memory of reward. In *The amygdala: neurobiological aspects of emotion, memory, and mental dysfunction*, (ed. J. P. Aggleton), pp.471–83 Wiley, New York.

Gaffan, D. (1994). Dissociated affects of perirhinal cortex ablation, fornix transection and amygdalectomy: evidence for multiple memory systems in the primate's temporal lobe. *Experimental Brain Research*, **99**, 411–22.

Gaffan, D. and Harrison, S. (1987). Amygdalectomy and disconnection in visual learning for auditory secondary reinforcement in monkeys. *Journal of Neuroscience*, **7**, 2285–92.

Goddard, G. V. (1964). Functions of the amygdala. *Psychological Bulletin*, **62**, 89–109.

Graf, P., Shimamura, A. P., and Squire, L. R. (1985). Priming across modalities and priming across category levels: extending the domain of preserved function in amnesia. *Journal of Experimental Psychology: Memory, Learning and Cognition*, **11**, 386–96.

Graff-Radford, N. R., Eslinger, P. J., Damasio, A. R., and Yamada, T. (1984). Non-haemorrhagic infarction of the thalamus: behavioral, anatomic, physiologic correlates. *Neurology*, **34**, 14–23.

Gross, C. G., Chrover, S. L., and Cohen, S. M. (1965). Caudate, cortical, hippocampal, and dorsal thalamic lesions in rats: alternation and Hebb–Williams maze performance. *Neuropsychologia*, **3**, 53–68.

Hanley, J. R., Davies, A. D. M., Downes, J. J., and Mayes, A. R. (1994). Impaired recall of verbal material following rupture and repair of an anterior communicating artery aneurysm. *Cognitive Neuropsychology*, **11**, 543–78.

Heindel, W. C., Butters, N., and Salmon, D. P. (1988). Impaired learning of a motor skill in patients with Huntington's disease. *Behavioral Neuroscience*, **102**, 141–7.

Heindel, W. C., Salmon, D. P., Shults, C. W., Walicke, P. A., and Butters, N. (1989). Neuropsychological evidence for multiple implicit memory systems: a comparison of Alzheimer's, Huntington's and Parkinson's disease patients. *Journal of Neuroscience*, **9**, 582–7.

Hirsh, R. (1974). The hippocampus and contextual retrieval of information from memory: a theory. *Behavioral Biology*, **12**, 421–44.

Hodges, J. R. and McCarthy, R. A. (1993). Autobiographical amnesia resulting from bilateral paramedian thalamic infarction. *Brain*, **116**, 921–40.
Hull, C. L. (1943). *Principles of behavior*. Appleton, New York.
Hunt, P. R. and Aggleton, J. P. (1991). Medial dorsal thalamic lesions and working memory in the rat. *Behavioral and Neural Biology*, **55**, 227–46.
Huppert, F. A. and Piercy, M. (1977). Recognition memory in amnesia patients: a defect of acquisition? *Neuropsychologia*, **15**, 643–52.
Huppert, F. A. and Piercy, M. (1979). Normal and abnormal forgetting in organic amnesia: effect of locus of lesion. *Cortex*, **15**, 385–90.
Irle, E., Wowra, B., Kunert, H. J., Hampl, J., and Kunze, S. (1992). Memory disturbances following anterior communicating artery rupture. *Annals of Neurology*, **31**, 473–80.
Jacobsen, C. F. (1936). Studies of cerebral function in primates. *Comparative Psychological Monographs*, **13**, 1–60.
Jacobson, R. (1986). Disorders of facial recognition, social behavior and affect after combined bilateral amygdalotomy and subcaudate tractotomy—a clinical and experimental study. *Psychological Medicine*, **16**, 439–50.
Jacoby, L. L. and Witherspoon, D. (1982). Remembering without awareness. *Canadian Journal of Psychology*, **36**, 300–24.
Janoswky, J. S., Shimamura, A. P., and Squire, L. R. (1989a). Memory and metamemory: comparisons between patients with frontal lobe lesions and amnesic patients. *Psychobiology*, **17**, 3–11.
Janowsky, J. S., Shimamura, A. P., and Squire, L. R. (1989b). Source memory impairment in patients with frontal lesions. *Neuropsychologia*, **27**, 1043–56.
Jarrard, L. E. (1975). Role of interference in retention by rats with hippocampal lesions. *Journal of Comparative and Physiological Psychology*, **89**, 400–8.
Jarrard, L. E. (1983). Selective hippocampal lesions and behavior: effects of kainic acid lesions on performance of place and cue tasks. *Behavioral Neuroscience*, **97**, 873–89. *Journal of Neurological and Neurosurgical Psychiatry*, **20**, 11–21.
Kesner, R. P. (1993). Paired associate learning in the rat: role of hippocampus, medial prefrontal cortex, and parietal cortex. *Psychobiology*, **21**, 183–92.
Kesner, R. P. and Andrus, R. G. (1982). Amygdala stimulation distorts the magnitude of reinforcement contribution to long-term memory. *Physiological Psychology*, **10**, 55–9.
Kesner, R. P. and DiMattia, B. V. (1987). Neurobiology of an attribute model of memory. *Progress in Psychobiology and Physiological Psychology*, **12**, 207–77.
Kesner, R. P. and Williams, J. M. (1995). Memory for magnitude of reinforcement: Dissociation between the amygdala and hippocampus. *Neurobiology of Learning and Memory*, **64**, 237–44.
Kim, J. J. and Fanselow, M. (1992). Modality-specific retrograde amnesia of fear. *Science*, **256**, 675–77.
Kim, J. J., Rison, R. A., and Fanselow, M. S. (1993). Effects of amygdala, hippocampus, and periaqueductal grey lesions on short- and long-term contextual fear. *Behavioral Neuroscience*, **107**, 1093–8.
Kluver, H. and Bucy, P. C. (1939). Preliminary analysis of the temporal lobes in monkeys. *Archives of Neurology and Psychiatry*, **42**, 979–1000.
Knowlton, B. J., Squire, L. R., Paulsen, J. S., Swerdlow, N. R., Swenson, M. S., and Butters, N. (1996a). Dissociations within nondeclarative memory in Huntington's disease. *Neuropsychologia*, **10**, 538–48.
Knowlton, B. J., Mangels, J. A., and Squire, L. R. (1996b). A neostriatal habit learning system in humans. *Science*, **273**, 1399–402.

Kolb, B. (1977). Studies on the caudate-putamenn and the dorsal medial thalamic nucleus of the rat: implications for mammalian frontal lobe functions. *Physiology and Behavior*, **18**, 237–44.

Kolb, B., Burhman, K., McDonald, R., and Sutherland, R. J. (1994). Dissociation of the medial prefrontal, posterior perirhinal, and posterior temporal cortex for spatial navigation and recognition memory in the rat. *Cerebral Cortex*, **4**, 664–80.

Kopelman, M. D. (1985). Rates of forgetting in Alzheimer's-type dementia and Korsakoff's syndrome. *Neuropsychologia*, **23**, 623–38.

La Bar, K. S., LeDoux, J. E., Spencer, D. D., and Phelps, E. A. (1995). Impaired fear conditioning following unilateral temporal lobectomy in humans. *Journal of Neuroscience*, **50**, 6846–55.

Lashley, K. S. (1929). *Brain mechanisms and intelligence*. University of Chicago Press.

LeDoux, D. E., Iwata, J., Cicchetti, P., and Reis, D. J. (1988). Different projections of the central amygdaloid nucleus mediate autonomic and behavioral correlates of conditioned fear. *Journal of Neuroscience*, **8**, 2517–29.

LeDoux, J. E. (1995). Emotion: clues from the brain. *Annual Review of Psychology*, **46**, 209–35.

Luria, A. R. (1966). *Higher cortical functions in man*. Basic Books, New York.

Mair, R. G., Robinson, J. K., Koger, S. M., Fox, G. D., and Zhang, Y. P. (1992). Delay-non-matching-to-sample performance is impaired by extensive, but not by limited, lesions of the thalamus in the rat. *Behavioral Neuroscience*, **106**, 646–56.

Manetto, C. and Lidsky, T. I. (1986). Caudate neuronal activity in cats during head turning: selectivity for sensory-triggered movements. *Brain Research Bulletin*, **16**, 425–8.

Marslen-Wilson, W. and Teuber, H.-L. (1975). Memory for remote events in anterograde amnesia: recognition of public figures from news photographs. *Neuropsychologia*, **13**, 353–64.

McDonald, R. J. and White, N. M. (1993). A triple dissociation of memory systems: hippocampus, amygdala, and dorsal striatum. *Behavioral Neuroscience*, **107**, 3–22.

McDonald, R. J. and White, N. M. (1994). Parallel information processing in the water maze: evidence for independent memory systems involving dorsal striatum and hippocampus. *Behavioral and Neural Biology*, **61**, 260–70.

Means, L. W., Hunt, M. W., Whiteside, R. R., and Bates, T. W. (1973). Deficient acquisition and retention of single-alternation go/no-go in rats with medial thalamic lesions. *Physiological Psychology*, **1**, 287–91.

Milner, B., Corkin, S., and Teuber, H. L. (1968). Further analysis the hippocampal amnesic syndrome: 14-year follow up study of HM. *Neuropsychologia*, **6**, 215–34.

Milner, B., Corsi, P., and Lanet, G. (1991). Frontal-lobe contribution to recency judgements. *Neuropsychologia*, **29**, 601–18.

Morris, R. M. G., Garrud, P., Rawlins, J. N. P., and O'Keefe, J. (1982). Place navigation is impaired in rats with hippocampal lesions. *Nature*, **297**, 681–3.

Moscovitch, M. (1994). Memory and working with memory: evaluation of a component process model and comparisons with other models. In *Memory systems 1994*, (ed. D. L. Schacter and E. Tulving), pp.269–310. MIT Press Cambridge, MA.

Moscovitch, M. and Winocur, G. (1995). Frontal lobes, memory, and aging. In *Structure and functions of the human prefrontal cortex*, (ed. J. Grafman, K. J. Holyoak, and F. Boller), pp.119–50. New York Academy of Sciences, New York.

Mumby, D. G. and Pinel, J. P. J. (1994). Rhinal cortex lesions impair object recognition in rats. *Behavioral Neuroscience*, **108**, 11–18.

Mumby, D. G., Wood, E. R., and Pinel J. P. J. (1992). Object recognition in rats is only mildly impaired by lesions of the hippocampus and the amygdala. *Psychobiology*, **20**, 18–27.

Muramoto, O., Kuru, Y., Sugishita, M., and Toyokura, Y. (1979). Pure memory loss with hippocampal lesions. A pneumoencephalographic study. *Archives of Neurology*, **36**, 54–56.

Murray, E. A. and Mishkin, M. (1984). Severe tactual as well as visual memory deficits follow combined removal of the amygdala and hippocampus in monkeys. *Journal of Neuroscience*, **4**, 2565–80.

Murray, E. A. and Mishkin, M. (1986). Visual recognition in monkeys following rhinal cortical ablations combined with either amygdalectomy or hippocampectomy. *Journal of Neuroscience*, **6**, 199–203.

Nadel, L. and Moscovitch, M. (1997). Memory consolidation, retrograde amnesia and the hippocampal complex. *Current Opinion in Neurobiology*, **7**, 217–27.

Nichelli, P., Bahmanian-Behbahani, G., Gentilini, M., and Vecchi, A. (1988). Preserved memory abilities in thalamic amnesia. Brain, **111**, 1337–53.

Nyberg, L., Winocur, G., and Moscovitch, M. (1997). Correlation between frontal lobe functions and explicit and implicit stem completion in healthy elderly. *Neuropsychologia*, **11**, 70–6.

O'Keefe, J. and Dostrovsky, J. (1971). The hippocampus as a spatial map. Preliminary evidence from unit activity in the freely-moving rat. *Brain Research*, **34**, 171–5.

O'Keefe, J. and Nadel, L. (1978). *The hippocampus as a cognitive map*. Oxford University Press.

Olton, D. S., Becker, J. T., and Handelmann, G. E. (1979). Hippocampus, space, and memory. *Behavioral and Brain Sciences*, **2**, 313–65.

Olton, D. S., Wenk, G. L., Church, R. M., and Meck, W. H. (1988). Attention and the frontal cortex as examined by simultaneous temporal processing. *Neuropsychologia*, **26**, 307–18.

Oscar-Berman, M. (1973). Hypothesis testing and focusing behavior during concept formation by amnesic Korsakoff patients. *Neuropsychologia*, **11**, 191–8.

Packard, M. G., and McGaugh, J. L. (1992). Double dissociation of fornix and caudate nucleus lesions on acquisition of two water maze tasks: further evidence for multiple memory systems. *Behavioral Neuroscience*, **106**, 439–46.

Packard, M. G. and White, N. M. (1990). Lesions of the caudate nucleus selectively impair acquisition of 'reference memory' in the radial maze. *Behavioral and Neural Biology*, **53**, 39–50.

Packard, M. G., Hirsh, R., and White, N. M. (1989). Differential effects of fornix and caudate nucleus lesions on two radial arm maze tasks: evidence for multiple memory systems. *Journal of Neuroscience*, **9**, 1465–72.

Parkin, A. J., Leng, N. R. C., and Stanhope, N. (1988). Memory impairment following ruptured aneurysm of the anterior communicating artery. *Brain and Cognition*, **7**, 231–43.

Parkin, A. J., Rees, J. E., Hunkin, N. M., and Rose, P. E. (1994). Impairment of memory following discrete thalamic infarction. *Neuropsychologia*, **32**, 39–51.

Pascoe, J. P. and Kapp, B. S. (1985). Electrophysiological characteristics of amygdaloid central nucleus neurons during pavlovian fear conditioning in the rabbit. *Behavioural Brain Research*, **16**, 117–33.

Passingham, R. E., Myers, C., Rawlins, J. N. P., Lightford, V., and Fearn, S. (1988). Premotor cortex in the rat. *Behavioral Neuroscience*, **107**, 101–9.

Penick, S. and Solomon, R. (1991). Hippocampal context, and conditioning. *Behavioral Neuroscience*, **105**, 611–17.

Petrides, M. (1982). Motor conditional associative learning after selective prefrontal lesions in the monkey. *Behavioural Brain Research*, **5**, 407–13.

Petrides, M. (1985). Deficits on conditional associative-learning tasks after frontal- and temporal-lobe lesions in man. *Neuropsychologia*, **23**, 601–14.

Petrides, M. (1994). Frontal lobes and working memory: evidence from investigations of the effects of cortical excisions in non-human primates. In *Handbook of neuropsychology*, Vol. 9, (ed. F. Boller and J. Grafman), pp.59–82. Elsevier, Amsterdam.

Phillips, R. G. and LeDoux, J. E. (1992). Differential contribution of amygdala and hippocampus to cued and contextual fear conditioning. *Behavioral Neuroscience*, **106**, 274–85.

Piggott, S. and Milner, B. (1993). Memory for different aspects of complex visual scenes after unilateral temporal- or frontal-lobe resection. *Neuropsychologia*, **31**, 1–15.

Pillon, B., Dubois, B., Ploska, A., and Agid, Y. (1991). Severity and specificity of cognitive impairment in Alzheimer's, Huntington's, and Parkinson's diseases and progressive supranuclear palsy. *Neurology*, **41**, 634–43.

Pillon, B., Deweer, B., Agid, Y., and Dubois, B. (1993). Explicit memory in Alzheimer's, Huntington's, and Parkinson's diseases. *Archives of Neurology*, **50**, 374–9.

Potegal, M. (1982). Vestibular and neostriatal contribution to spatial orientation. In M. Potegal In *Spatial abilities. Development and physiological foundations*, (ed. M. Potegal), pp.361–87. Academic, New York.

Ranck, J. B. Jr. (1973). Studies on single neurons in dorsal hippocampus formation and septum in unrestrained rats. *Experimental Neurology*, **41**, 461–555.

Reed, J. M. and Squire, L. R. (1997). Impaired recognition memory in patients with lesions limited to the hippocampal formation. *Behavioral Neuroscience*, **111**, 667–75.

Rempel-Clower, N. L., Zola, S. M., Squire, L. R., and Amaral, D. A. (1996). Three cases of enduring memory impairment after bilateral damage limited to the hippocampal formation. *Journal of Neuroscience*, **16**, 5233–55.

Robbins, T. W., Shallice, T., Burgess, P. W., James, M., Rogers, R. D., Warburton, E., and Wise, R. S. J. (1995). Selective impairments in self-ordered working memory in a patient with a unilateral striatal lesion. *Neurocase*, **1**, 217–30.

Rolls, E. P. (1990). A theory of emotion and its application to understanding the neural basis of emotion. *Cognition and Emotion*, **4**, 161–90.

Rosvold, H. E., Mirsky, A., and Pribam, K. H. (1954). Influence of amygdalectomy on social behavior in mokeys. *Journal of Comparative and Physiological Psychology*, **47**, 173–8.

Sanders, H. I. and Warrington, E. K. (1971). Memory for remote events in amnesic patients. *Brain*, **4**, 661–8.

Sarter, M. and Markowitsch, H. J. (1985). The amygdala's role in human mnemonic processing. *Cortex*, **21**, 7–24.

Schacter, D. L. and Tulving, E. (ed.) (1994). *Memory systems 1994*. MIT Press, Cambridge, MA.

Scoville, W. B. and Milner, B. (1957). Loss of recent memory after bilateral hippocampal lesions. *Journal of Neurology, Neurosurgery, and Psychiatry*, **20**, 11–21.

Shallice, T. and Burgess, P. W. (1991). Deficits in strategic application following frontal lobe damage in man. *Brain*, **114**, 727–41.

Shimamura, A. P. and Squire, L. R. (1987). A neuropsychological study of fact memory and source amnesia. *Journal of Experimental Psychology: Learning, Memory, and Cognition*, **13**, 464–73.

Shimamura, A. P., Janowsky, J. S., and Squire, L. R. (1989). Source memory impairment in patients with frontal lobe lesions. *Neuropsychologia*, **27**, 1043–56.

Shimamura, A. P., Janowsky, J. S., and Squire, L. R. (1990). Memory for the temporal order of events in patients with frontal lobe lesions and amnesic patients.. *Neuropsychologia*, **28**, 803–13.

Sidman, M., Stoddard, L., and Mohr, J. (1968). Some additional quantitative observations of immediate memory in a patient with bilateral hippocampal lesions. *Neuropsychologia*, **6**, 245–54.

Smith, M. L. and Milner, B. (1981). The role of the right hippocampus and the recall of spatial location. *Neuropsychologia*, **19**, 781–93.
Solomon, P. R. (1979). Temporal versus spatial information processing theories of hippocampal function. *Psychological Bulletin*, **86**, 1272–9.
Speedie, L. J. and Heilman, K. M. (1982). Amnesic disturbance following infarction of the left dorsal medial nucleus of the thalamus. *Neuropsychologia*, **20**, 597–604.
Squire, L. R. (1981). Two forms of human amnesia and analysis of forgetting. *Journal of Neuroscience*, **1**, 635–40.
Squire, L. R. and Slater, P. C. (1978). Anterograde and retrograde impairment in chronic amnesia. *Neuropsychologia*, **16**, 313–22.
Squire, L. R., Knowlton, B., and Musen, G. (1993). The structure and organization of memory. *Annual Review of Psychology*, **44**, 453–95.
St-Cyr, J. A. and Taylor, A. E. (1992). The mobilization of procedural learning: the 'key signature' of the basal ganglia. In *Neuropsychology of memory*, 2nd edn, (ed. L. R. Squire and N. Butters), pp.188–202. Guilford Press, New York.
Stokes, K. A. and Best, P. J. (1988). Dorsal medial thalamic lesions impair radial arm maze performance in the rat. *Behavioral Neuroscience*, **102**, 294–300.
Stuss, D., Guberman, A., Nelson, R., and Larochelle, S. (1988). The neuropsychology of paramedian thalamic infarction. *Brain and Cognition*, **8**, 348–78.
Stuss, D. T., Eskes, G. A., and Foster, J. K. (1994). Experimental neuropsychological studies of frontal lobe functions. In *Handbook of neuropsychology*, Vol. 9, (ed. F. Boller and J. Grafman), pp.149–85. Elsevier, Amsterdam.
Sutherland, R. J. and Rodriguez, A. J. (1989). The role of the fornix/fimbria and some related subcortical structures in place learning and memory. *Behavioural Brain Research*, **32**, 265–78.
Sutherland, R. J. and Rudy, J. W. (1989). Configural association theory: the role of the hippocampal formation in learning, memory, and amnesia. *Psychobiology*, **17**, 129–44.
Teuber, H. L., Milner, B. and Vaughan, H. G. (1968). Persistent anterograde amnesia after stab wound of the basal brain. *Neuropsychologia*, **6**, 267–82.
Tolman, E. C. (1932). *Purposive behavior in animals and men*. Appleton, New York.
Tolman, E. C. (1948). Cognitive maps in rats and man. *Psychological Review*, **55** 189–208.
Shimamura, A. P., Janowsky, J. S., and Squire, L. R. (1990). Memory for the temporal order of events in patients with frontal lobe lesions and amnesic patients. *Neuropsychologia*, **28**, 803–13.
Ursin, H. (1965). The effect of amygdaloid lesions on flight and defence behavior in cats. *Experimental Neurology*, **11**, 61–71.
Valenstein, E. S. (1973). *Brain control*. Wiley, New York.
Victor, M., Adams, R. D., and Collins, G. H. (1971). *The Wernicke–Korsakoff syndrome*. Davis, Philadelphia.
Warrington, E. K. and Weiskrantz, L. (1973). An analysis of short-term and long-term memory defect in man. In *The physiological basis of memory*, (ed. J. A. Deutsch), pp.365–95. Academic, New York.
Weiskrantz, L. (1956). Behavioral changes associated with ablations of the amygdaloid complex in monkeys. *Journal of Comparative and Physiological Psychology*, **49**, 381–91.
Wickelgren, W. A., (1968). Sparing of short-term memory in an amnesia patient: implications for strength of memory. *Neuropsychologia*, **6**, 235–44.
Winocur, G. (1979). Effect of interference on discrimination learning and recall by rats with hippocampal lesions. *Physiology and Behavior*, **22**, 339–45.
Winocur, G. (1980). The hippocampus and cue utilization. *Physiological Psychology*, **8**, 280–8.

Winocur, G. (1985). The hippocampus and thalamus: their role in short-and long-term memory and the effect of interference. *Behavioural Brain Research*, **16**, 135–52.

Winocur, G. (1990). Anterograde and retrograde amnesia in rats with dorsal hippocampal ordorsomedial thalamic lesions. *Behavioural Brain Research*, **30**, 145–54.

Winocur, G. (1991). Functional dissociation of hippocampus and prefrontal cortex in learning and memory. *Psychobiology*, **91**, 11–20.

Winocur, G. (1992). A comparison of normal old rats and young adult rats with lesions to the hippocampus or prefrontal cortex on a test of matching-to-sample. *Neuropsychologia*, **30**, 769–81.

Winocur, G. (1997). Hippocampal lesions alter conditioning to conditional and contextual sitmuli. *Behavioural Brain Research*, **88**, 219–29.

Winocur, G. and Eskes, G. (1998). Prefrontal cortex and caudate nucleus in conditional associative learning: dissociated effects of selective brain lesions in rats. *Behavioral Neuroscience*, **112**, 1–14.

Winocur, G. and Moscovitch, M. (1990). Hippocampal and prefrontal cortex contributions to learning in memory: analyses of lesion and aging effects on maze-learning in rates. *Behavioral Neuroscience*, **104**, 544–51.

Winocur, G. and Olds, J. (1978). Effects of context manipulation on memory and reversal learning in rats with hippocampal lesions. *Journal of Comparative and Physiological Psychology*, **92**, 312–21.

Winocur, G. and Weiskrantz, L. (1976). An investigation of paired-associate learning in amnesic patients. *Neurospychologia*, **14**, 97–110.

Winocur, G., Oxbury, S., Roberts, R., Agnetti, V., and Davis, C. (1984). Amnesia in a patient with bilateral lesions to the thalamus. *Neuropsychologia*, **22**, 123–43.

Winocur, G., Moscovitch, M., and Stuss, D. T. (1996). Explicit and implicit memory in the elderly: evidence for double dissociation involving medial temporal- and frontal-lobe functions. *Neuropsychologia*, **10**, 57–65.

Young, A. W., Aggleton, J. P., Hellawell, D. J., Johnson, M., Broks, P., and Hanley, J. R. (1995). Face processing impairments after amygdalotomy. *Brain*, **118**, 15–24.

Zola-Morgan, S. and Squire, L. R. (1985). Amnesia in monkeys after lesions of the mediodorsal nucleus of the thalamus. *Annals of Neurology*, **17**, 558–64.

Zola-Morgan, S. and Squire, L. R. (1986). Memory impairment in monkeys following lesions limited to the hippocampus. *Behavioral Neuroscience*, **100**, 155–160.

Zola-Morgan, S. and Squire, L. R. (1990). The primate hippocampal formation: evidence for a time-limited role in memory storage. *Science*, **250**, 288–90.

Zola-Morgan, S., Cohen, N. J., and Squire, L. R. (1983). Recall of remote episodic memory in amnesia. *Neuropsychologia*, **21**, 487–500.

Zola-Morgan, S., Squire, L. R., and Amaral, D. G., (1986). Human amnesia and the medial temporal region: enduring memory impairment following a bilateral lesion limited to field CA1 of the hippocampus. *Journal of Neuroscience*, **6**, 2950–67.

Zola-Morgan, S., Squire, L. R., Amaral, D. G., and Suzuki, W. (1989). Lesions of perirhinal and perihippocampal cortex that spare the amygdala and hippocampal formation produce severe memory impairment. *Journal of Neuroscience*, **9**, 4355–70.

5
Combining disruption and activation techniques to map conceptual and perceptual memory processes in the human brain

TERESA A. BLAXTON

The modern debate between systems and process theories of long-term memory arose primarily from observations that memory performance can sometimes be uncorrelated, or dissociated, across different memory tasks. An early example of a striking dissociation was reported by Warrington and Weiskrantz (1968) who showed that although amnesic patients were impaired on a test of item recognition, they nevertheless showed normal retention of new information as measured on a task of primed picture fragment identification. Similar dissociations began to be reported a few years later in the memory literature testing normal subjects, and widespread interest in this topic area grew rapidly. As further examples of dissociations accumulated, it became apparent that this was a problem of central interest to memory theorists.

As the theme of this book illustrates, the varieties of theories offered to account for these dissociations fall into two primary camps. One group of theorists contends that dissociations reflect the operation of separable underlying memory systems in the brain. Typically one distinguishes between systems supporting memory for events encountered during particular study episodes (for example as tested by recognition) and systems supporting representation of other types of information (such as the type of memory tested by the picture identification task). Depending upon the particular theory, this may be a distinction between declarative and procedural memory (Cohen and Squire 1980), episodic and semantic memory (Tulving 1985), explicit and implicit memory (Graf and Schacter 1985), or episodic and perceptual memory (Tulving and Schacter 1990). Thus, in the case of the Warrington and Weiskrantz (1968) study, the memory system supporting performance on the explicit test of recognition memory is thought to be independent of the system supporting performance on the picture identification task.

The other theoretical camp contends that it is the match in the types of processing engaged at study and retrieval that determine patterns of dissociations across memory tasks, and not the existence of separate memory stores. Specifically, the transfer appropriate processing principle states that memory will be enhanced to the degree that processes performed during encoding are recapitulated at retrieval (Morris et al. 1977). To the degree that there is a mismatch in the type of processing required on those two occasions, memory performance will be poor. Most current instantiations of process theory make a distinction between conceptual processing, which involves the analysis of meaning, and perceptual processing which is geared more to physical features of stimuli apart from their semantic content (e.g. Jacoby 1983). Thus, in the Warrington and Weiskrantz (1968) example, the conceptual test of recognition is dissociated from the perceptual task of picture fragment identification.

As an illustration of the type of dissociation that has been influential with process theorists, consider the now classic example reported by Larry Jacoby in 1983. Testing normal college undergraduates, he showed that although recognition memory was greater for items that were generated rather than read at study, the opposite was true for the task of primed perceptual identification in which participants were better able to identify words that had been read rather than generated during study from antonym cues. This crossover interaction was a dramatic example of a dissociation occurring in normal (non-amnesic) subjects, and was particularly compelling in that it showed a complete reversal of the generation effect which by that time had become a staple of normal memory research.

Jacoby's (1983) interpretation of his findings was that the conceptual processing performed while generating targets from antonym cues during study in the generate condition transferred well to the recognition test in which participants could again process the meaning of target items. On the other hand, the perceptual processing that occurred during a study condition in which participants read target words in the absence of any semantic context transferred well to the perceptual identification task in which they were asked to identify target words presented only briefly (35 ms). From a systems theorist's point of view, however, this dissociation might be said to reflect differences in the operations of two memory stores. The recognition test may be thought of as a measure of explicit or episodic memory, whereas the perceptual identification task might be characterized as an implicit, procedural, or perceptual representation system task, depending upon the particular version of systems theory being considered.

The crossover interaction reported by Jacoby (1983) was later replicated in other paradigms in which performance on some tests such as semantic cued recall and answering general knowledge questions was better following generate study conditions, whereas the read condition produced better performance on other tasks such as word fragment completion and graphemic cued recall (Blaxton 1989). In the context of the debate at that time, the most important aspect of findings such as these was that these dissociations separated tasks according to the types of processing they required, and not according to type of memory system they tapped. Similar findings were subsequently reported using such diverse manipulations as levels of processing (e.g. Hamann 1990), modality effects (e.g. Kirsner et al. 1989; Rajaram and Roediger 1993), effects of imagery during encoding (e.g. Blaxton 1989; Roediger and Blaxton 1987), the picture superiority effect (e.g. Weldon and Roediger

1987), degraded picture naming (Durso and Johnson 1979; Park and Gabrieli 1995), priming in person perception (Smith and Branscombe 1988), and cross-language priming in bilingual subjects (e.g. Dugunoglu and Roediger 1987; Gerard and Scarborough 1989). (For reviews of findings of dissociations among memory measures, see Roediger and McDermott (1993) and Roediger et al. (Chapter 3 this volume).)

The majority of evidence supporting process theory has come from experiments testing normal healthy participants. In contrast, the most compelling evidence against process theory has been observed in studies testing memory-impaired patients with known brain lesions for whom dissociations are often observed between memory systems as opposed to processing dimensions (see Gabrieli, Chapter 8 this volume). Although it is now clear that neither theory is sufficient on its own to explain all of the available data from dissociation experiments, most would agree that any hybrid theory that might be adopted must necessarily encompass a processing component, and that the distinction among classes of processing engaged at study and test is a critical factor in any theory of human memory. When examined in this light, the contributions made by process theory as it has been pursued thus far are laid plain. Aside from the data ensuing from the numerous experimental investigations of the theory, one notable contribution has been the use and promotion of innovative experimental designs in which multiple encoding conditions are crossed with several different memory tasks in a single experiment (see Blaxton 1995). One advantage of this arrangement is that it provides opportunities for the disambiguation of dissociations due to the operation of different types of processing as opposed to different memory systems. Additionally, the introduction of new manipulations of encoding as well as retrieval tasks in process dissociation experiments has led to important discoveries about memory function.

Despite this expertise in experimental methodology and approach, however, process theorists have made very little contribution in other aspects of the science of memory. One important component that has been missing is an account of how conceptual and perceptual processing are subserved by neurological structures in the human brain. Since the process theorist's paradigms of choice can differ substantially from those utilized by systems theorists, there is every reason to presume that the pursuit of this question within the context of process dissociation will yield discoveries not yet uncovered in other investigations reported thus far. With this goal in mind, this chapter will describe converging evidence obtained from several functional mapping techniques in experiments examining dissociations between conceptual and perceptual processing in human memory. As the reader will see, a picture of the neurological structures subserving these types of processing is beginning to emerge. Before presenting this evidence, however, it is important to outline the philosophy with which this formulation is being developed.

IMPORTANCE OF CONVERGING MEASURES

Investigations aimed at the brain mechanisms subserving human memory function are necessarily ones which can visit frustrations upon the researcher. Because of the irrevocable role of language in human memory, animal studies are necessarily limited in the information that they can provide, particularly in terms of questions about verbal memory. It is clear that the most revealing observations derive from studies with human subjects, but there again the limitations are formidable. To address this problem, researchers have developed several approaches to the functional mapping of memory which fall into two categories. There are methods of disruption in which function of known brain regions is blocked, and the ensuing deficits in performance are interpreted as evidence for the critical contribution of the blocked region(s) to the memory function tested. Disruption of function may be permanent as in the case of tests with brain lesioned patients. Alternatively, disruption may be achieved temporarily using either repetitive transcranial magnetic stimulation (rTMS) delivered outside the skull or electrical cortical stimulation delivered directly through electrodes placed on the brain surface. In contrast, there are activation mapping methods which reveal parts of the brain that are active during performance of memory tasks. These include positron emission tomography (PET) and functional magnetic resonance imaging (fMRI).

As shown in Fig. 5.1, each functional mapping measure has its own set of strengths and weaknesses. Although results from each can tell us that a set of structures is involved in a particular processing function, no one method on its own has all of the features that one might wish for in a functional mapping technique. In each case, the reader will note that there are inherent limitations in the types of conclusions that may be drawn from the results produced by the measure of interest.

	Disruption			Activation	
	Behavioural studies with brain lesioned patients	Repetitive transcranial magnetic stimulation (rTMS)	Electrical cortical stimulation	Positron emission tomography (PET)	Functional magnetic resonance imaging (fMRI)
Structure involved in processing function	●	●	●	●	●
Structure critical for processing function	●	●	●		
Precise localization			●	●	●
Time-locked to individual trials		●	●		
Normal control data available	●			●	●

Fig. 5.1. Taxonomy of the types of information that are provided by disruption and activation methods used for functional brain mapping of human memory. Because there are no methods which can provide all of the desired types of information regarding a brain structure's contribution to memory, it is important to acquire converging evidence from as many methods as possible before positing a critical role for a given brain structure.

For this reason, it is of paramount importance that any speculation about the mapping of types of processing onto brain structures be substantiated by as many independent converging measures as possible (Garner *et al.* 1956). The claim that a particular brain region plays a critical role in a processing capability may be made only after similar results have been shown across independent mapping measures. The case is stronger to the degree that results from a variety of measures converge on the same conclusion. In the remainder of this chapter, I will present findings from studies utilizing a series of functional mapping measures that appear to converge on the finding that conceptual and perceptual memory processes are subserved by separable brain regions.† To anticipate, data available thus far suggest that conceptual processing is subserved by left temporal and frontal cortex whereas perceptual processing is subserved by sensory-specific cortical regions involved in the initial perception of stimuli (visual cortex in the case of visual stimuli and auditory cortex in the case of auditory stimuli). As findings from each type of functional mapping measure are presented, the limitations regarding interpretation of data produced by each method will be discussed.

DISRUPTION PARADIGMS

Behavioral studies with brain lesioned patients

On the whole there have not been very many experiments with brain lesioned patients that have included controlled comparisons of conceptual and perceptual transfer. In a paper that I published in 1992, I tested a group of memory-impaired epilepsy patients whose unilateral epileptogenic zones were located in the left mesial and lateral temporal lobe. These patients were impaired on standard memory measures such as recall of prose passages. Their performance was compared with that of a group of patients whose epilepsy was localized in the right mesial and lateral temporal lobe, as well as a group of matched normal controls. There were two study conditions in which patients either read items with no context or generated target words given a synonym and initial letter cue. All subject groups showed normal transfer on perceptual tests of primed word fragment completion and graphemic cued recall with better performance in the read than in the generate condition. The two control groups showed the opposite effect on two conceptual tasks of semantic cued recall and answering general knowledge questions, with better performance in the generate than in the read condition. However, the memory-impaired subjects failed to show a generation effect on either task, revealing deficits in conceptual transfer.

Further evidence for abnormal conceptual transfer in these left temporal patients was observed in a separate experiment in which participants performed a

† For purposes of clarity, the discussion is confined to those experiments in which manipulations of conceptual and perceptual transfer were not confounded with implicit or explicit retrieval mode (i.e. the body of research comparing performance on perceptual implicit tasks with that of conceptual explicit tasks will not be included; see Blaxton (1989) and Neely (1989)).

primed category member production task. In this paradigm patients first studied a list of words containing members of taxonomic categories. Items were either blocked by category on the study list or presented in random order. On a subsequent implicit memory test, patients were given a series of category labels and were asked to name eight members from each category. Both the normal controls and the right temporal patients showed greater priming in a condition in which target items were blocked by semantic category during study as compared with the random order study condition. That is, the additional conceptual organization provided by the blocking manipulation at study transferred well to performance on the conceptual category member generation task. The left temporal patients, however, failed to show differential transfer in these two conditions, again showing evidence of disruption of conceptual processing. The same findings were observed for an explicit version of this task which was identical in construction but which was given with the explicit retrieval instruction to use the category labels as retrieval cues for the previously studied word lists.

In a similar paradigm, memory-impaired patients with Alzheimer's disease have shown deficits in priming on the implicit conceptual category production task, but normal priming on perceptual identification (Keane *et al.* 1991; Monti *et al.* 1995). That is, both the left temporal and Alzheimer's patients show normal perceptual transfer but deficits in conceptual transfer, whether the conceptual memory tasks in question are implicit or explicit. The failure of these memory-impaired patients to show normal conceptual transfer across these paradigms implies involvement of left mesial and/or lateral temporal cortex in conceptual processing.

There is evidence to suggest, however, that not all memory-impaired patients fail to show normal conceptual transfer on implicit memory tasks. Several studies have shown normal conceptual transfer on implicit but not explicit tasks in amnesic patients who have bilateral lesions of the mesial temporal structures and/or diencephalon. For example, a study by Graf *et al.* (1985) showed normal priming for amnesics on a test of primed category member production even though explicit memory on conceptual tests was impaired. Keane *et al.* (1993) reported that amnesic patients with bilateral mesial temporal lesions showed normal priming and normal levels of processing transfer effects on the primed category member production test, again in the context of impaired explicit memory on conceptual retrieval tasks. One possible reason for these discrepant findings is that it is the lateral, rather than mesial, left temporal lobe structures that are critical in conceptual memory transfer. This would account for the findings of global conceptual memory impairment in the epilepsy and Alzheimer's patients who have lateral cortical lesions, as opposed to the other amnesic patient groups whose lesions are confined to the medial structures.

In terms of perceptual processing, there are patient data which suggest involvement of occipital cortex, at least for visual test paradigms. Two patients with occipital lesions have been studied, MS who has a right-hemisphere lesion and patient LH whose lesion is bilateral. Both patients have been tested in a paradigm in which modality of presentation (auditory versus visual) of target words was varied at study, followed by a visual word stem completion test. In this paradigm subjects are shown stems comprised of the initial three letters of words (e.g. 'mot—') and are asked to respond with complete words beginning with those letters (e.g. 'motel'). Many prior demonstrations have shown that priming on this task is affected by manipulation of perceptual variables. In contrast to control subjects, neither MS (Gabrieli *et al.* 1995*a*) nor LH (Keane *et al.* 1995) showed the normal pattern of greater perceptual priming under conditions in which modality matched at study and test (visual–visual) as compared with the non-match condition (auditory–visual). Furthermore, neither patient showed normal repetition priming in a perceptual word identification task in which participants identified words presented for very brief intervals (Fleischman *et al.* 1995; Gabrieli *et al.* 1995*a*; Keane *et al.* 1995). Thus, results from these two case studies imply a critical role for visual cortex in visually based perceptual memory paradigms. Taken together, results from brain lesioned patients suggest a dissociation in the neurological substrates of conceptual and perceptual processing, with left temporal cortex involved in conceptual processing and bilateral occipital cortex mediating visual perceptual transfer.

Limitations of behavioural research with neurologically impaired patients

In the types of studies just described, patients with known memory disorders are tested on an experimental paradigm and their performance compared with that of a control group. To the degree that patient performance is poor on a class of measures, the inference is that the memory function measured is subserved by the brain regions damaged in the patient group. More than any other, this class of investigation has been widely influential in the development of memory theories. It is not without its drawbacks, however. First, patients are often selected for inclusion in memory studies on the basis of poor performance on standardized tests such as the Wechsler Memory Scale and others, rather than on the basis of particular brain lesions. It is therefore not uncommon for patients of mixed aetiologies to be combined into one experimental group, making it impossible to determine precisely which brain regions are implicated in the memory deficits reported. Even in cases such as in the experiments described above in which the make-up of the subject group is more uniform and the lesions well documented, there will still be inevitable individual differences in terms of length of illness, medications, extent of lesion, and so forth that complicate interpretation of results. Additionally, performance measures are typically aggregated across blocks of trials such that information about performance on individual trials is lost. For these reasons, additional evidence for involvement of separable brain regions in different types of processing is required from other disruption methods.

Repetitive transcranial magnetic stimulation (rTMS)

Although relatively new, rTMS holds promise as an aid in the mapping of various cognitive functions in both clinical and research settings. Using this functional mapping technique, rapid-rate repetitive trains of magnetic stimuli (usually lasting from 0.5 to 3 seconds each) are applied using a coil placed on the outside of the skull over the neuroanatomical region of interest. The result of the application of the time-varying magnetic field is the synchronized depolarization of target neurons which can in turn produce a brief suppression of function. Stimulation is usually delivered to several brain regions of the same individual subject within a single experimental session. By timing the delivery of stimulation during encoding or retrieval of to-be-remembered information, memory function can be transiently impaired creating a scenario in which effects of temporary 'lesions' may be studied. Furthermore, because of the discrete nature of the stimulation, mapping effects may be time-locked to individual trials, therefore allowing correlation of stimulation with task performance on a trial by trial basis. Data obtained on trials during which errors were made may be removed from the analysis if desired. Although relatively few studies have been reported in which the effects of rTMS on long-term memory function could be clearly interpreted, some findings are pertinent to the present discussion.

In a study reported by Grafman *et al.* (1994), rTMS was applied as five right-handed normal male subjects studied lists of words. Results from subsequent conceptual tasks of free recall showed that stimulation in left mid-temporal and dorsolateral frontal cortex produced significant impairments for recall of words from the primacy portion of the word lists. That is, stimulation of left frontal and left temporal cortex during encoding disrupted conceptual long-term memory task performance. Recall from the recency portion of the words lists was unaffected by this stimulation, as was word reading.

In an experiment conducted with my colleagues, the effects of rTMS on both implicit and explicit conceptual memory were examined (Blaxton *et al.* 1996*a*). Twelve patients with temporal lobe epilepsy were tested (eight males, four females). All had left brain speech as localized by prior sodium amytal testing. Patients named colour photographs of real objects and read words during an encoding phase. Stimulation was presented with the onset of stimuli for half of these studied items. Across study trials, stimulation was delivered to six neuroanatomical regions, three in each hemisphere. These included a left frontal region in which speech arrest was induced in pre-testing along with its reflection site in the right hemisphere; mid/superior temporal regions stimulated by coil placement 1 cm above the top of the ear; and posterior temporal regions located 2–3 cm posterior the mid/superior temporal sites. Following presentation of study lists, conceptual memory was tested using primed category member generation and semantic cued recall with category labels. The effects of rTMS were much more pronounced in the picture than in the word conditions. The greatest decrements in memory for pictures as measured on the cued recall test followed stimulation in the frontal regions. Picture priming on the category member generation task was disrupted following stimulation in left mid/superior cortex as well as bilateral frontal regions. Thus, the results in common across these rTMS experiments converge with findings from behavioural studies with brain lesioned patients in suggesting involvement of left temporal cortex in conceptual memory processing. In addition, the rTMS results indicate a potential role for left frontal cortex in conceptual memory tasks.

Limitations of rTMS

The primary drawbacks of rTMS have to do with potential risks that the procedure may present to participants. In paradigms such as those described above, subjects may occasionally experience external discomfort on the portion of the head where the coil is placed for stimulation. In all cases in which this has occurred, experimenters immediately ceased stimulation in those regions and no lasting effects were observed. More important is the potential risk that the magnetic stimulation will induce seizures (see Bridgers 1991). Although the overwhelming body of evidence suggests that TMS is safe, there have been a few anecdotal reports of seizures in patients with epilepsy or stroke, and even a few reports of seizures in normal volunteers. For this reason, much rTMS work is now restricted to clinical populations for whom the potential benefits of the procedure far outweigh the remote risk of seizures. The restriction of the use of the procedure to patient groups introduces the limitations one always has under such circumstances, namely the problem of separating the effects of the experimental treatment from the disease itself. In most cases this issue may be addressed by letting each patient serve as his/her own control, and stimulating in a variety of neuroanatomical regions, only some of which will produce an effect on task performance.

A second type of limitation of the rTMS technique is that it is not very precise in terms of localization. Generally speaking, one can describe the area over which stimulation is delivered, but due to warping of the magnetic signal by the skull, and natural diffusion that occurs throughout the various layers of media involved (the coil, bone, dura, blood, neural tissue, etc.), the actual signal is spread over a relatively wide area. Thus localization of rTMS effects is usually described in terms of broad neuroanatomical regions. This particular problem is avoided using the method described next in which low levels of electrical stimulation are delivered directly to points on the cortex.

Electrical cortical stimulation

In the most invasive of the functional mapping techniques described in this chapter, functional mapping is achieved via stimulation of electrodes placed directly on the human cortex. Localization with this procedure can be extremely precise and the results can be time-locked to performance observed on individual trials. In work performed with my colleagues, eight patients (five males, three females) with intractable complex partial seizures were tested (Blaxton *et al.* 1994*a*,*b*). Patients underwent a craniotomy for placement of subdural electrode grids to be used to for seizure recording and language mapping prior to temporal lobectomy, to be given as treatment for epilepsy. Electrodes were placed in the language-dominant hemisphere as determined by previous intracarotid sodium amobarbitol testing. Seven patients had left-brain speech, and one had right-brain speech. Precise neuroanatomical localization of electrodes was determined for every patient by image registration of a CT scan acquired while electrodes were implanted with coplanar pre-surgical MRI (Pelizzari *et al.* 1989). Electrodes were placed over frontal (orbital, inferior, and middle frontal gyri), lateral temporal (middle and superior temporal gyri), inferior temporal (inferior temporal, fusiform, and parahippocampal gyri), and parietal cortex.

Within the context of ongoing language mapping being done for clinical purposes, a memory test of conceptual category production was administered. The language tasks served as the encoding phase for the test of primed category member production. Stimulation (2–15 mA) occurred randomly in half of the study trials in each condition. Across a series of trials, stimulation was initiated at low levels and gradually increased.† To avoid speech arrests during retrieval, no stimulation was delivered during presentation of the memory test. Patients studied items in both visual and auditory presentation conditions. The visual condition was a confrontation naming task in which subjects named colour pictures of real objects. The auditory condition was a responsive naming task in which subjects answered such questions as 'Tell me what is a teacher's red fruit' (answer: apple). Following a filled delay of approximately one to two minutes, the memory probe was given by the experimenter asking the patient to name three items from a semantic category (e.g. 'fruits').

Priming on category member production for items named correctly during encoding was assessed relative to non-studied baseline rates collected prior to and during testing. As may be seen in Fig. 5.2, priming was disrupted by stimulation in inferior temporal, lateral temporal, and frontal cortex. This is in direct contrast to the result observed in parietal cortex in which priming was intact despite stimulation during encoding. There was also an interaction between study modality and site of stimulation in that stimulation of inferior temporal regions disrupted priming more in the visual than in the auditory condition.

A second experiment was conducted in which eight new patients were tested using electrical cortical stimulation. All methods were identical to those just described except that an explicit conceptual task of semantic cued recall was added. Retrieval cues in the form of category labels were identical for the category production and semantic cued recall tasks, but the query presented by the experimenter during semantic cued recall was in the form of 'Do you remember any fruits?' as opposed to 'Name three fruits' on the category member production task. Semantic cued recall queries were presented on half of the memory trials and category member production queries were presented on the other half. As before, no stimulation was presented during retrieval in either condition.

Results from this replication study are presented in Figs. 5.3(a) and 5.3(b). The reader will see in Fig. 5.3(a) that the functional mapping results from the first electrical cortical stimulation study were replicated for the conceptual implicit test

† The gradual increase in amplitude of stimulation was done so as to avoid after-discharges of epileptiform activity. If after-discharges were observed, testing was stopped for several minutes and a new stimulation site was chosen when testing resumed. Since there was great variability in the sensitivity of various electrode sites, this procedure was followed for each stimulation site tested. Data were collapsed across levels of amplitude of stimulation in the reported analyses.

114   *Teresa A. Blaxton*

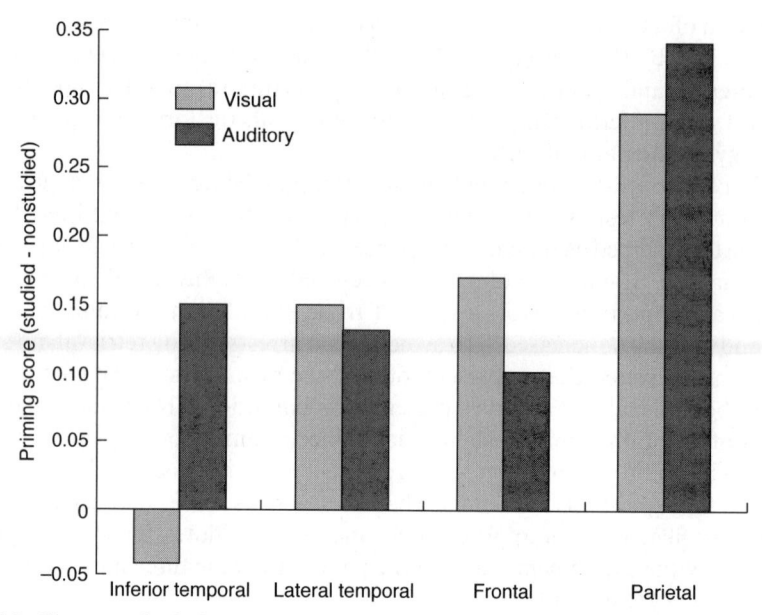

Fig. 5.2. Conceptual priming on implicit category member production as a function of site of cortical stimulation during encoding. Compared with stimulation in parietal cortex, stimulation of inferior temporal, lateral temporal, and frontal cortex in the language-dominant hemisphere disrupted memory for both visually and auditorily presented items.

of primed category member production. As before, stimulation delivered to inferior temporal, lateral temporal, and frontal cortex during encoding disrupted performance on the category member production task. Stimulation in parietal cortex, however, did not interfere with memory on this task. This pattern of results was replicated for the explicit conceptual test of semantic cued recall. As seen in Fig. 5.3(b), overall levels of performance were higher under explicit than implicit retrieval instructions, but the pattern of disruption for conceptual processing was replicated with deficits in performance following stimulation in temporal and frontal regions of the language-dominant hemisphere. These electrical cortical stimulation findings are in agreement with those observed from the other disruption measures in that they implicate left lateral and inferior temporal cortex as well as left frontal cortex in the mediation of conceptual memory processes.

Limitations of cortical stimulation mapping

The most notable limitation of electrical brain stimulation is that, for obvious reasons, there are no normal control data available for comparison purposes. This is a procedure used only in patients being evaluated for neurosurgery in which brain tissue will be removed. These patients have had craniotomies only a few days prior to testing, they have intractable epilepsy (in most cases extending back a decade or more), and they are on anticonvulsant medications. The best that one

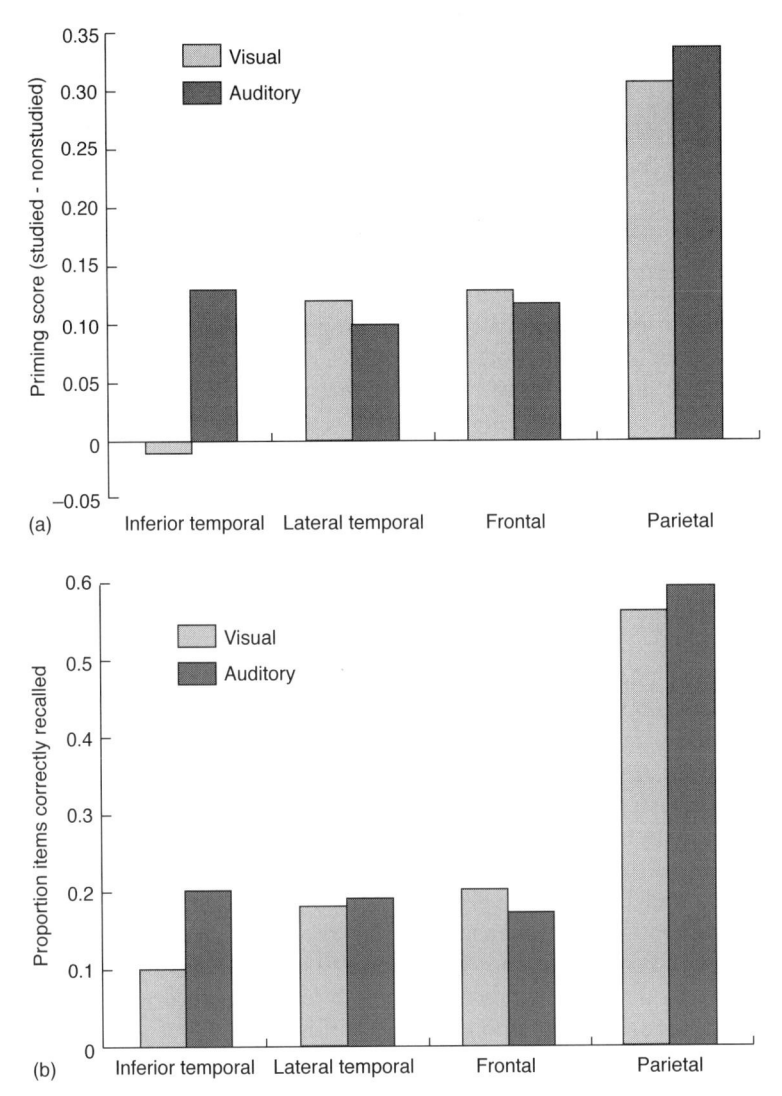

Fig. 5.3. Results from replication experiment showing conceptual priming on implicit category member production (a) and explicit semantic cued recall (b) as a function of site of cortical stimulation during encoding. Compared with stimulation in parietal cortex, stimulation of inferior temporal, lateral temporal, and frontal cortex in the language-dominant hemisphere disrupted memory for both visually and auditorily presented items.

can hope for in terms of a control group is to let each patient serve as his/her own control by demonstrating that stimulation in certain cortical regions leaves performance unaffected. This was achieved in the studies described here in which stimulation in parietal cortex did not produce deficits in conceptual transfer on either the implicit or the explicit tasks.

ACTIVATION STUDIES

PET

PET imaging is based on the principle of mutual annihilation when the positron (a positive electron) emitted from a radionuclide encounters an electron of opposing charge. The annihilation produces two 511 keV gamma rays (photons) that move from the point of encounter at nearly 180° from one another. Simultaneous detection of these opposing photons along their path of radioactive decay by a detector array placed around the head allows for tomographic reconstruction of the location of the point of annihilation. By injecting a radionuclide into the bloodstream and then observing patterns of radioactive decay occurring during performance of a cognitive task, one may infer patterns of regional cerebral blood flow (rCBF) occurring in the brain as subjects perform those tasks. Thus one may use PET to make inferences about the brain structures activated during task performance.

During a PET scan, ^{15}O-labelled water is injected intravenously shortly after subjects begin memory (or control) tasks in the scanner. Conditions are arranged so that only one memory task is performed during each bolus injection. An ^{15}O PET session usually involves from six to twelve bolus injections over a period of 90–120 minutes so that images may be acquired while subjects perform tasks over a series of experimental and control scans. The ^{15}O water technique captures physiological perfusion responses that occur over a 1 minute period. PET scanners have resolutions ranging between 4 and 8 mm. To increase signal to noise ratio, group analyses are usually performed on normalized image data. Although the subject's head is stabilized in the scanner, images are usually corrected for roll, yaw, and head motion occurring between scans. A widely observed convention in the field is the warping of images to the 3D coordinate space derived from the atlas of Talairach and Tournoux (1988) from which localization is derived. A number of PET investigations of human memory have been reported in the past few years which employed paradigms shown elsewhere to involve either conceptual or perceptual processing. Some of these are now briefly described with emphasis on those results reported in common across experiments.

In terms of conceptual encoding, a PET study reported by Kapur *et al.* (1994), compared activation patterns across encoding conditions in which subjects made decisions about presented items. Making semantic decisions about whether words referred to living or non-living things activated left frontal cortex as compared with a condition in which participants decided whether words contained the letter 'a'. Similarly, Shallice *et al.* (1994) reported that left temporal and frontal cortex were activated during an encoding task in which subjects studied semantically related word pairs. These findings are in agreement with those obtained in the disruption paradigms in their implication of left frontal cortical involvement in conceptual memory.

Turning to conceptual retrieval, in a study reported by Rugg *et al.* (1997), subjects studied words in either a deep or shallow encoding condition prior to being scanned while performing either an implicit or explicit conceptual retrieval task. In the deep encoding condition subjects generated sentences containing target words, whereas in the shallow condition subjects made decisions about whether the initial and terminating letters of each word were in alphabetical order. On the implicit memory test subjects made living/non-living decisions about word referents and in the explicit test condition subjects made yes/no decisions about whether the words had been presented earlier. The comparisons of interest for present purposes were made between the deep and shallow conditions. Rugg et al. (1997) observed that, following conceptual processing in the deep encoding condition, regions in left inferior frontal cortex, left superior temporal gyrus, and left hippocampus were activated on both the implicit and explicit conceptual memory tests.

In an experiment described by Raichle et al. (1994), subjects read nouns silently and were asked to perform a conceptual task in which they generated verbs that described what the presented noun might do. On the first occasion in which subjects generated verbs for a given list of nouns, increases in rCBF were observed in left inferior frontal and left mid/superior temporal cortex as compared with a condition in which subjects simply read the nouns aloud. As subjects performed the generation task repeatedly on the same items across several trials, however, a practice effect was observed in the form of rCBF decreases in left frontal and temporal cortex, indicating that as the same items were presented in the conceptual memory task, less and less activation was required to accomplish the same processing.

In terms of perceptual processing, several studies have examined rCBF changes during retrieval using word stem completion tasks. There have been consistent demonstrations of rCBF changes in right visual cortex for both implicit (Buckner et al. 1995; Schacter et al. 1996a; Squire et al. 1992) and explicit (Buckner et al. 1995; Squire et al. 1992) versions of this task as compared with that obtained in non-studied stem completion control conditions. Additionally, memory-related changes have also been observed in left visual cortex during implicit word stem completion (Schacter et al. 1996a).

An experiment reported by Grady et al. (1995) examined rCBF changes during memory for unfamiliar faces. During a study phase, participants were given three presentations of a list of 32 faces. Scanning during a two-alternative forced choice recognition test revealed bilateral activation in ventral occipital cortex as well as in right parietal cortex, as compared with both a face matching and a sensorimotor control task. Interestingly, these activations were observed for young but not for elderly participants, who showed deficits in face recognition performance.

Although the majority of memory paradigms in which perceptual transfer is examined involved memory for visually presented materials, some work has been reported in which memory for auditory stimuli was assessed. An example of perceptual transfer in the auditory domain was reported by Schacter et al. (1996b). In their experiment, normal subjects heard lists of words during a study phase and were subsequently scanned as they performed a recognition test on visually presented items. Activation on the memory task was compared with that observed during a recognition task on all non-studied words. Increases in blood flow were

118   Teresa A. Blaxton

observed in left auditory cortex (in a region bordering areas 42, 22, and 40) during auditory recognition of old items.

Another auditory recognition paradigm was investigated by Tulving et al. (1994). In their experiment normal volunteers first listened to a series of sentences each presented twice via audiotape in a pre-scan session. One day later the subjects were tested in the PET scanner in two conditions. During memory scans subjects listened to tapes of sentences that they had heard previously. In a control condition subjects heard tapes of comparable sentences which had not been previously studied. Relative to the control condition, deactivations were observed in bilateral auditory cortex in superior temporal gyrus in areas 21, 22, 41, and 42. That is, there was less activation in the regions associated with auditory perception of the sentences in the memory condition in which sentences were being processed for the third time as compared with the control condition in which sentences were being perceived for the first time.†

Two PET experiments have directly compared conceptual and perceptual processing in the same subject group. In a study conducted with my colleagues, participants were scanned during retrieval on six tasks as shown in Fig. 5.4 (Blaxton et al. 1996b). Prior to being tested on the conceptual tasks of semantic word association and semantic cued recall, subjects studied weakly related word pairs such as 'sky-eagle'. In the implicit semantic association test, subjects were asked to

	Implicit instructions	Explicit instructions	Baseline
Conceptual tasks	SEMANTIC ASSOCIATION Study: SKY-EAGLE Test Cue: SKY	SEMANTIC CUED RECALL Study: SKY-EAGLE Test Cue: SKY	SEMANTIC NONSTUDIED CONTROL (No Study) Test Cue: SKY
Perceptual tasks	WORD FRAGMENT COMPLETION Study: EAGLE Test Cue: E_G_E	WORD FRAGMENT CUED RECALL Study: EAGLE Test Cue: E_G_E	WORD FRAGMENT NONSTUDIED CONTROL (No Study) Test Cue: E_G_E

Fig. 5.4. Experimental study and test conditions employed in PET experiment reported by Blaxton et al. (1996b). The design allows comparison of blood flow patterns associated with conceptual and perceptual processing in the same group of subjects.

† The discrepancy in these results (activation in the first case and deactivation in the second) may have arisen because the Tulving et al. (1994) paradigm yielded a truer test of auditory priming, in that items were presented in the auditory modality at both study and test. Thus, the auditory cortex deactivations reflect savings in auditory processing for previously studied items as compared with those seen for the first time in the experimental context.

name the first word they thought of that was semantically related to the test cue. The construction of the semantic cued recall test was identical, except that in this case subjects were instructed to think back to the study list and recall the target word that had been paired with the test cue. Blood flow during these tasks was compared with that observed for a semantic non-studied control task in which subjects performed word association on non-studied items. Deactivations compared with the control task were observed in left inferior frontal gyrus, left superior temporal gyrus, and left hippocampal formation.

During the same PET session, participants also performed two perceptual memory tests. The first was an implicit word fragment completion task in which subjects solved fragments formed by the omission of every other letter from test cue words. An explicit version of this task was also presented in which subjects were instructed to refer to the preceding study list in order to solve the fragments. Blood flow during these perceptual memory tasks was compared with that observed during a test of word fragment completion on non-studied items. Deactivations relative to baseline were observed for both perceptual tasks in left visual cortex (area 17).

Although the Blaxton *et al.* (1996*b*) study showed a dissociation in blood flow between conceptual and perceptual memory tasks within a single experiment, an investigation that is in some ways even more compelling showed a dissociation between conceptual and perceptual transfer on the same task in a single experiment (Park *et al.* 1994). In this study, participants were scanned during a task of picture naming primed by prior presentation of either pictures or their word labels. Blood flow on this test was compared with that observed in a control condition in which participants named unprimed pictures. Deactivations relative to baseline were observed in the word-to-picture priming condition in the left superior temporal gyrus and the left inferior frontal gyrus. In contrast, in the picture-to-picture priming condition in which there was an exact perceptual match between studied and tested items, perceptual transfer produced a pattern of deactivation in the bilateral fusiform and inferior occipital gyri (areas 18 and 37).

Taken together, the common results across several PET investigations of memory have now shown consistent modulation of left frontal and temporal cortex during conceptual encoding and retrieval. In contrast, perceptual processing appears to be subserved by the cortical regions supporting initial perception of stimuli—visual cortex in the case of visual tasks and auditory cortex in the case of auditory tasks. These results are largely in agreement with those obtained in the disruption paradigms. The main difference is the added implication from PET studies of the role of auditory cortex in perceptual auditory paradigms, a topic not yet investigated in the disruption literature.

Limitations of PET

The main drawback of PET is that, due to safety restrictions regarding level of exposure to radioactive materials, there is a limitation on the dosimetry of ^{15}O that subjects may receive, and therefore a limit on the number of scans in which any one subject may be tested. With the advent of newer, more sensitive scanners, this problem has been addressed to a certain degree in that less ^{15}O is needed for any one scan in order to achieve a good signal to noise ratio in the reconstructed images. Thus it is now common for activation studies to involve 15 or more scans of a subject in a single session, an arrangement which allows for multiple repetitions of experimental and control scan conditions. (In fact the limitation has now shifted from dosimetry to the length of time that subjects may be reasonably expected to perform cognitive tasks while lying motionless in the scanner.) Despite improvements realized from these technological advances, PET researchers will still encounter roadblocks in situations in which it is desirable to test subjects in multiple sessions over the course of days, weeks, or months since dosimetry restrictions place limitations on the amount of exposure that subjects may have over the course of a year. In order to avoid these restrictions, reduce research costs, and work with a technology that is sometimes more readily available, some investigators have turned to fMRI as an alternative to PET.

fMRI

When the cortex is activated, both blood flow and oxygen saturation increase (Fox and Raichle 1986) and the supply of oxygenated blood exceeds oxygen demand and consumption. The fMRI technique takes advantage of the fact that, under these conditions, activated regions assume a greater proportion of oxygenated to deoxygenated haemoglobin than do non-activated regions. Because oxyhaemoglobin and deoxyhaemoglobin have different paramagnetic properties, haemoglobin can be used as an endogenous contrast agent with the MR scanner measuring increases in signal intensity of oxygenated relative to deoxygenated cortical regions. Most cognitive activation studies utilize this blood oxygen level dependent (BOLD) echoplanar imaging technique.

Findings analogous to the PET result described by Kapur et al. (1994) have been reported in separate studies by Demb et al. (1995) and by Gabrieli et al. (1996). In both experiments subjects encoded to-be-remembered words in either conceptual or perceptual encoding conditions. In the conceptual condition subjects made abstract/concrete item decisions whereas in the perceptual condition subjects monitored the typeface of words for upper or lower case type. Compared with the perceptual condition, imaging of the frontal lobe indicated that conceptual encoding produced activation in left inferior frontal gyrus. A follow-up experiment reported by Wagner et al. (in press) replicated these findings for words and also obtained the same result when nameable pictures were used as the repeated stimulus items.

Blood flow changes during conceptual retrieval have been studied in the frontal lobe using fMRI. In experiments described by Demb et al. (1995) and Gabrieli et al. (1996), subjects were scanned during priming conditions in which they made either conceptual (abstract/concrete) or perceptual (upper/lower case) judgments on words that had been previously encoded under the same conditions. Semantic repetition effects were evidenced by decreases in rCBF in left inferior frontal cortex on the repeated as compared with the initial presentation blocks. These results support those obtained with other functional mapping techniques suggesting that conceptual transfer is subserved by left inferior frontal cortex.

A few fMRI studies have been reported which examined blood flow changes during visually based perceptual memory tasks. In a study reported by Stern *et al.* (1996), subjects were scanned as they studied a series of complex coloured magazine pictures. Subjects were told to study each picture in anticipation of a later memory test. Activation during the encoding task was compared with a baseline condition in which subjects viewed a single colour picture which was presented repeatedly at the same rate as the stimuli in the experimental condition. Results showed bilateral activation of posterior (but not frontal) regions extending from the posterior hippocampal formation back to lingual and fusiform gyri in the inferotemporal and occipital regions.

In a study very similar to the PET paradigm described by Park *et al.* (1994), Martin *et al.* (1995) had subjects silently name line drawings of common objects. Blocks of experimental trials contained a mixture of new and repeated items whereas control blocks contained only previously non-studied items. Just as in Park *et al.*'s (1994) picture-to-picture priming condition, Martin *et al.* (1995) observed deactivations relative to the non-studied control condition in the bilateral occipitotemporal cortex.

Finally, in an experiment described by Poldrack *et al.* (in press), subjects were scanned while performing a very demanding perceptual task in which they made word/non-word decisions to pronounceable letter strings, some of which were presented in mirror-reversed text. Prior to the test session of interest, participants were given several practice trials with a repeated set of items. During the scan session participants performed the mirror reading/lexical decision task on sets of new items as well as on items that were highly practised on nine prior presentations. Item-specific priming for the repeated items was assessed relative to the new baseline condition. Imaging of the posterior regions of the brain during presentation of the practised items revealed bilateral deactivations relative to baseline in occipital and fusiform gyri as well as in parietal cortex. All of these results from perceptual memory paradigms support those described earlier with the other mapping methods. Specifically, perceptual transfer in visually based paradigms is subserved by the region of the brain that is active during initial visual perception, namely bilateral posterior cortex including the occipital and inferior temporal lobes.

Limitations of fMRI

In its present incarnation, the fMRI technique yields a relatively low signal to noise ratio in cognitive mapping studies, often making it difficult to detect significant blood flow changes, at least compared with the PET technique. It is therefore usually necessary to expose subjects to many trials over repeated blocks and average across those blocks in order to obtain a clear result. This means that, on average, subjects are tested in the MR scanner for a longer period (and possibly on more occasions) than might be true with PET. The high number of trials needed to produce a good signal can present a problem in terms of stimulus materials since many more stimuli are needed to fill in the additional trials. Unfortunately some researchers, though none whose work is described here, are sometimes sloppy with regard to this point, often repeating items across trials and thus confounding number of presentations with retention effects so that results are uninterpretable from a memory perspective. (Note that this is really not a limitation of the fMRI technique itself, but rather reflects poor experimental design methodology.)

A second problem with fMRI is that, due to limitations of some head coil designs, experimenters do not usually image the entire brain, but rather restrict their observations to limited regions thought to be of importance *a priori*. Thus we rarely get a picture of whole brain function in an fMRI study, a situation that undoubtedly leads to underestimates of the extent of the neuroanatomical networks subserving memory task performance. This particular problem will be solved with the adoption of new coil designs which will permit imaging of the entire brain.

Perhaps one of the most vexing problems with the fMRI literature at present is that there is no accepted convention among researchers of how statistical analyses are to be performed on functional mapping data. An informal perusal of a dozen papers on this topic yielded nine different statistical approaches, including a few cases of multiple approaches from the same research laboratory. This lack of concensus no doubt reflects the fact that this is a new research area, and one would expect this situation to improve dramatically over the next few years. However, at present, it does present the reader with a problem of interpretation and undermines the influence of this body of work.

Limitations of activation mapping techniques

In the paradigms developed for cognitive mapping thus far using PET and fMRI techniques, activation is integrated over time intervals and statistical comparisons are made between the set of intervals during which one task is performed and the set of intervals in which another control task is performed. During the interval of interest it is always the case that many trials are presented. Thus, the result from these techniques is a picture of activity aggregated across some interval, and there is no information as to what brain regions were activated on a trial by trial basis. Thus, these methods do not allow for separate observation of activation patterns associated with trials in which correct responses were made as opposed to trials on which errors were made.

A second class of limitation has less to do with the techniques themselves than with the conventions that have been adopted for data analysis within the community of neuroimaging researchers. The two most common approaches to the analysis of imaging data are to use either an ANCOVA model such as is embodied in the statistical parametric mapping procedure (Friston *et al.* 1989) or the peak detection approach which searches for outliers in the distribution of signal values (Mintun *et al.* 1989). Both of these methods are performed on grouped data. In gaining the statistical power realized by combining imaging data across all subjects tested in an experiment, however, one loses the capability of examining effects on a subject by subject basis. Thus, most results reported from neuroimaging studies are trends of the group and do not allow the experimenter to explore the question of individual differences. (Note that this criticism applies more frequently to PET than to fMRI studies.)

Beyond these concerns, the greatest limitation in the utility of PET and fMRI findings, as in the case of all activation measures, is that they do not reveal which of the participating brain regions are *critical* for task performance—they merely tell us that activity in a set of brain regions is *modulated* during task performance. Brain regions may be active even though they are not necessary for the function being studied. An instructive example of this principle may be taken from the learning literature on delay eyeblink conditioning. Neurophysiological recordings in animal studies (Berger *et al.* 1983; Disterhoft *et al.* 1986) and PET measurements in humans (Blaxton *et al.* 1996*c*) during delay conditioning have shown that activity of hippocampal neurons changes in a conditioning-specific fashion during and following training. Based on these findings alone one might be tempted to posit a crucial role for the hippocampus in delay conditioning. As it turns out, however, such a conclusion would be inappropriate. Findings from studies using disruption techniques have shown that removal or damage of the hippocampus does not reduce delay conditioning, either in animals (Berger and Orr 1983; Schmaltz and Theios 1972) or humans (Daum *et al.* 1989; Gabrieli *et al.* 1995*b*; Woodruff-Pak 1993). Thus, when evidence from both disruption and activation mapping methods is considered, the results do not converge on the conclusion that the hippocampus is critical for this type of learning. An analogous example occurs in the present context in which PET studies show modulation of the left hippocampal region during conceptual transfer paradigms even though amnesic patients with brain lesions in this area perform normally on implicit conceptual tasks. These examples illustrate why great caution should be exercised in the interpretation of findings obtained in activation studies of learning and memory. It is preferable to base conclusions on converging evidence obtained from both disruption and activation mapping techniques.

NEURAL BASIS OF CONCEPTUAL AND PERCEPTUAL PROCESSING

Based on the data available thus far from disruption and activation mapping methods, a model for the neurological structures subserving conceptual and perceptual memory is presented in Fig. 5.5. The templates in the top row indicate that regions in the left inferior frontal gyrus, left middle temporal gyrus, and left inferior temporal gyrus have been consistently implicated in functional mapping paradigms employing conceptual memory tasks.† This is true whether test items are

† The reader may note that the superior temporal gyrus is not pictured, even though it was identified in several conceptual processing paradigms. At present the role of the superior temporal cortex remains unclear, however, since it has also been identified in auditory perceptual memory paradigms of recognition memory in at least two independent experiments. This question awaits further study.

Conceptual processing regions

Inferior frontal gyrus   Middle temporal gyrus   Inferior temporal gyrus

Perceptual processing regions

Occipital cortex   Superior temporal gyrus

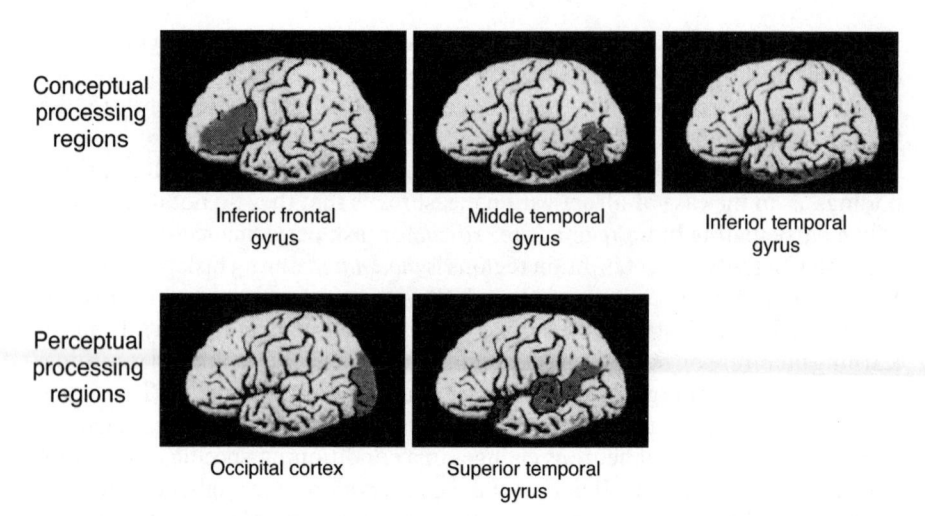

Fig. 5.5. Proposed model for the neurological structures subserving conceptual and perceptual memory. Results available at present from disruption and activation mapping methods converge on left hemisphere structures in the frontal and temporal lobe for conceptual processing. In contrast, mapping studies suggest that perceptual transfer is supported by those brain regions involved in initial perception of stimuli. These would include occipital cortex for visual paradigms and superior temporal cortex for auditory paradigms.

pictures or words and whether modality of presentation is visual or auditory. In contrast, processing for perceptual memory tasks appears to be subserved by those brain regions involved in the initial perception of stimuli. Thus for visual tasks, perceptual transfer is supported by the occipital cortex and related bilateral posterior regions. Transfer observed in auditory paradigms appears to be mediated by primary auditory cortex located in superior temporal gyrus.

CONCLUSION

Having reached the end of this summary of work mapping conceptual and perceptual processing in the human brain, several facts are worth highlighting. First, the general field of functional mapping holds great promise for those who study cognition. We now have available to us an impressive arsenal of mapping tools which, if used properly, can help us to make great strides in mapping function onto structures. We need to be cautious, however, in their use. We should endeavor to establish high standards for interpreting the results we obtain with them, insisting on support from converging measures wherever possible.

That being said, one can nevertheless be encouraged by the progress made on this problem using functional mapping methods thus far. As little as five or certainly ten years ago it would have been virtually impossible to make a convincing case one way or another about the brain structures that might be subserving conceptual and perceptual processing. As the results discussed in this chapter argue, we have now made a good start. Of course there is still much to be done, and there is no doubt that the fledgling model presented in Fig. 5.5 will look very different in a few years from now. That is certainly one of my goals.

As a final point to those readers who count themselves in the systems camp (to the degree that separate camps still exist), it is admittedly ironic that a process theorist would be so concerned with questions of brain structures subserving memory. You might ask whether this is suspiciously close to a systems account, and you may even wonder if I am making the implicit suggestion that there are separable brain systems for conceptual and perceptual memory. My answer is that, to my mind at least, that level of argument is just not relevant to the debate anymore. It has been clear for some time that both the conceptual/perceptual distinction made by process theorists and the implicit/explicit distinction made by systems theorists were valid. In fact, one could easily argue that both are quite necessary in order to explain the totality of results in the literature. The types of data presented in this chapter only make that more evident. It is my belief that we have moved on to bigger questions, and are entering a phase of borrowing from one another's methodologies and ideas to the benefit of all.

REFERENCES

Berger, T. W. and Orr, W. B. (1983). Hippocampectomy selectively disrupts discrimination reversal conditioning of the rabbit nictitating membrane response. *Behavior and Brain Research*, **8**, 49–68.

Berger, T. W., Rinaldi, P. C., Weisz, D. J., and Thompson, R. F. (1983). Single-unit analysis of different hippocampal cell types during classical conditioning of rabbit nictitating membrane response. *Journal of Neurophysiology*, **50**, 1197–219.

Blaxton, T. A. (1989). Investigating dissociations among memory measures: support for a transfer appropriate processing framework. *Journal of Experimental Psychology: Learning, Memory, and Cognition*, **15**, 657–68.

Blaxton, T. A. (1992). Dissociations among memory measures in memory-impaired subjects: Evidence for a processing account of memory. *Memory and Cognition*, **20**, 549–62.

Blaxton, T. A. (1995). A process-based view of memory. *Journal of the International Neuropsychological Society*, **1**, 112–14.

Blaxton, T. A., Malow, B., Bookheimer, S., Figlozzi, F., Sato, S., Kufta, C., Gaillard, W., and Theodore, W. (1994a). Functional mapping of implicit memory via subdural electrode stimulation. *Neurology*, **44**, p. A382-A383.

Blaxton, T. A., Malow, B., Figlozzi, C. M., Sato, S., Kufta, C., Bookheimer, S. Y., and Theodore, W. H. (1994b). Mapping implicit memory with electrical brain stimulation: Dissociations between auditory and visual study modalities. *Society for Neuroscience Abstracts*, **20**, 1289.

Blaxton, T. A., Wassermann, E. M., Hoffman, E. A., Oletsky, H. S., Hallett, M., and Theodore, W. H. (1996a). Functional mapping of implicit and explicit memory using repetitive transcranial magnetic stimulation (rTMS). *Society for Neuroscience Abstracts*, **22**, p.719.

Blaxton, T. A., Bookheimer, S. Y., Zeffiro, T., Figlozzi, C. M., Gaillard, W., and Theodore, W. (1996b). Functional mapping of human memory using PET: Comparisons of conceptual and perceptual tasks. *Canadian Journal of Experimental Psychology*, **50**, 42–56.

Blaxton, T. A., Zeffiro, T. A., Gabrieli, J. D. E., Bookheimer, S. Y., Carrillo, M. C., Theodore, W. H., and Disterhoft, J. F. (1996c). Functional mapping of human learning: a positron emission tomography activation study of eyeblink conditioning. *Journal of Neuroscience*, **16**, 4032–40.

Bridgers, S. L. (1991). The safety of transcranial magnetic stimulation reconsidered: evidence regarding cognitive and other cerebral effects. In *Magnetic motor stimulation: basic principles and clinical experience*, (ed. W. J. Levy, R. Q. Cracco, A. T. Barker, and J. Rothwell), Elsevier, Amsterdam.

Buckner, R. L., Petersen, S. E., Ojemann, J. G., Miezin, F. M., Squire, L. R., and Raichle, M. E. (1995). Functional anatomical studies of explicit and implicit memory retrieval tasks. *Journal of Neuroscience*, **15**, 12–29.

Cohen, N. J. and Squire, L. R. (1980). Preserved learning and retention of pattern-analyzing skill in amnesia: dissociation of 'knowing how' and 'knowing that'. *Science*, **210**, 207–9.

Daum, I., Channon, S., and Canavan, A. G. M. (1989). Classical conditioning in patients with severe memory problems. *Journal of Neurology, Neurosurgery and Psychiatry*, **52**, 47–51.

Demb, J. B., Desmond, J. E., Wagner, A. D., Vaidya, C. J., Glover, G. H., and Gabrieli, J. D. E. (1995). Semantic encoding and retrieval in the left inferior prefrontal cortex: A functional MRI study of task difficulty and process specificity. *Journal of Neuroscience*, **15**, 5870–8.

Disterhoft, J. F., Coulter, D. A., and Alkon, D. L. (1986). Conditioning-specific membrane changes of rabbit hippocampal neurons measured in vitro. *Proceedings of the National Academy of Sciences of the USA*, **83**, 2733–7.

Dugunoglu, A. Y. and Roediger, H. L. (1987). Test differences in accessing bilingual memory. *Journal of Memory and Language*, **26**, 377–91.

Durso, F. T. and Johnson, M. K. (1979). Facilitation in naming and categorizing repeated pictures and words. *Journal of Experimental Psychology: Human Learning and Memory*, **5**, 449–59.

Fleischman, D. A., Gabrieli, J. D. E., Reminger, S., Rinaldi, J., Morrell, F., and Wilson, R. (1995). Conceptual priming in perceptual identification for patients with Alzheimer's disease and a patient with right occipital lobectomy. *Neuropsychology*, **9**, 187–97.

Fox, P. T. and Raichle, M. E. (1986). Focal physiological uncoupling of cerebral blood flow and oxidative metabolism during somatosensory stimulation of human subjects. *Proceedings of the National Academy of Sciences of the USA*, **83**, 1140–4.

Friston, K. J., Passingham, R. E., Nutt, J. G., Heather, J. D., Sawle, G. V., and Frackowiak, R. S. J. (1989). *Journal of Cerebral Blood Flow and Metabolism*, **9**, 690–5.

Gabrieli, J. D. E., Fleischman, D. A., Keane, M. M., Reminger, S. L., and Morrell, F. (1995a). Double dissociation between memory systems underlying explicit and implicit memory. *Psychological Science*, **6**, 76–82.

Gabrieli, J. D. E., McGlinchey-Berroth, R., Carrillo, M. C., Gluck, M., Cermak, L. S., and Disterhoft, J. F. (1995b). Intact delay-eyeblink classical conditioning in amnesia. *Behavioral Neuroscience*, **109**, 819–27.

Gabrieli, J. D. E., Desmond, J. E., Demb, J. B., Wagner, A. D., Stone, M. V., Vaidya, C. J., and Glover, G. H. (1996). Functional magnetic resonance imaging of semantic memory processes in the frontal lobes. *Psychological Science*, **7**, 278–83.

Garner, W. R., Hake, H. W., and Eriksen, C. W. (1956). Operationism and the concept of perception. *Psychological Review*, **63**, 149–59.

Gerard, L. D. and Scarborough, D. L. (1989). Language-specific lexical access of homographs by bilinguals. *Journal of Experimental Psychology: Learning, Memory, and Cognition*, **15**, 305–15.

Grady, C. L., McIntosh, A. R., Horwitz, B., Maisog, J. M., Ungerleider, L. G., Mentis, M. J., Pietrini, P., Schapiro, M. B., and Haxby, J. V. (1995). Age-related reductions in human recognition memory due to impaired encoding. *Science*, **269**, 218–21.

Graf, P. and Schacter, D. L. (1985). Implicit and explicit memory for new associations in normal and amnesic subjects. *Journal of Experimental Psychology: Learning, Memory, and Cognition*, **11**, 501–18.

Graf, P., Shimamura, A. P., and Squire, L. R. (1985). Priming across modalities and priming across category levels: Extending the domain of preserved function in amnesia. *Journal of Experimental Psychology: Learning, Memory, and Cognition*, **11**, 386–96.

Grafman, J., Pascual-Leone, A. Alway, D., Nichelli, P., Gomez-Tortosa, E., and Hallett, M. (1994). Induction of a recall deficit by rapid-rate transcranial magnetic stimulation. *Neuro Report*, **5**, 1157–60.

Hamann, S. B. (1990). Level-of-processing effects in conceptually driven implicit tasks. *Journal of Experimental Psychology: Learning, Memory, and Cognition*, **16**, 970–7.

Jacoby, L. L. (1983). Remembering the data: analyzing interactive processes in reading. *Journal of Verbal Learning and Verbal Behavior*, **22**, 485–508.

Kapur, S., Craik, F. I. M., Tulving, E., Wilson, A. A., Houle, S., and Brown, G. M. (1994). Neuroanatomical correlates of encoding in episodic memory: levels of processing effect. *Proceedings of the National Academy of Science of the USA*, **91**, 2008–11.

Keane, M. M., Gabrieli, J. D. E., Fennema, A. C., Growdon, J. H., and Corkin, S. (1991). Evidence for a dissociation between perceptual and conceptual priming in Alzheimer's disease. *Behavioral Neuroscience*, **105**, 326–42.

Keane, M. M., Gabrieli, J. D. E., Monti, L. A., Cantor, J. M., and Noland, J. S. (1993). Amnesic patients show normal priming and a normal depth-of-processing effect in a conceptually driven implicit memory task. *Society for Neuroscience Abstracts*, **19**, 1079.

Keane, M. M., Gabrieli, J. D. E., Mapstone, H. C., Johnson, K. A., and Corkin, S. (1995). Double dissociation of memory capacities after bilateral occipital-lobe or medial temporal-lobe lesions. *Brain*, **118**, 1129–48.

Kirsner, K., Dunn, J. C., and Standen, P. (1989). Domain-specific resources in word recognition. In *Implicit memory: theoretical issues*, (ed. S. Lewandowsky, J. C. Dunn, and K. Kirsner), pp.99–122. Erlbaum, Hillsdale, NJ.

Martin, A., Lalonde F. M., Wiggs C. L., Weisberg J., Ungerleider L. G., and Haxby J. V. (1995). Repeated presentation of objects reduces activity in ventral occipitotemporal cortex: a fMRI study of repetition priming. *Society for Neuroscience Abstracts*, **21**, 1497.

Mintun, M. A., Fox, P. T., and Raichle, M. E. (1989). A highly accurate method of localizing regions of neuronal activation in the human brain with positron emission tomography. *Journal of Cerebral Blood Flow and Metabolism*, **9**, 96–103.

Monti, L. A., Gabrieli, J. D. E., Reminger, S. L., Rinaldi, J. A., Wilson, R. S., and Fleischman, D. A. (1995). Differential effects of aging and Alzheimer's disease upon conceptual implicit and explicit memory. *Neuropsychology*, **10**, 101–12.

Morris, C. D., Bransford, J. D., and Franks, J. J. (1977). Levels of processing versus transfer appropriate processing. *Journal of Verbal Learning and Verbal Behavior*, **16**, 519–33.

Neely, J. H. (1989). Experimental dissociations and the episodic/semantic memory distinction. In *Varieties of memory and consciousness: essays in honor of Endel Tulving*, (ed. H. L. Roediger and F. I. M. Craik) Erlbaum, Hillsdale, NJ.

Park, S. M. and Gabrieli, J. D. E. (1995). Perceptual and conceptual components of implicit memory for pictures. *Journal of Experimental Psychology: Learning, Memory, and Cognition*, **21**, 1583–94.

Park, S. M., Blaxton, T. A., Gabrieli, J. D. E., Figlozzi, C. M., and Theodore, W. H. (1994). PET activation measures reveal a dissociation between brain regions underlying perceptual and conceptual processes in picture-naming priming. *Society for Neuroscience Abstracts*, **20**, 1230.

Pelizzari, C. A., Chen, G. T. Y., Spelbring, D. R., Weichselbaum, R. R., and Chen, C. T. (1989). Accurate three-dimensional registration of CT, PET, and/or MR images of the brain. *Journal of Computer Assisted Tomography*, **13**, 20–6.

Poldrack, R. A., Desmond, J. E., Glover, G. H., and Gabrieli, J. D. E. The neural basis of visual skill learning: an fMRI study of mirror reading. *Cerebral Cortex*. (In press.)

Raichle, M. E., Fiez, J. A., Videen, T. O., MacLeod, A. K., Pardo, J. V., Fox, P. T., and Petersen, S. E. (1994). Practice-related changes in human brain functional anatomy during nonmotor learning. *Cerebral Cortex*, **4**, 8–26.

Rajaram, S. and Roediger, H. L. (1993). Direct comparison of four implicit memory tests. *Journal of Experimental Psychology: Learning, Memory, and Cognition*, **19**, 765–76.

Roediger, H. L. and Blaxton, T. A. (1987). Effects of varying modality, surface features, and retention interval on priming in word fragment completion. *Memory and Cognition*, **15**, 379–88.

Roediger, H. L. and McDermott, K. B. (1993). Implicit memory in normal human subjects. In *Handbook of neuropsychology*, Vol. 8, (ed. F. Boller and J. Grafman), Elsevier, Amsterdam.

Roediger, H. L., Buckner, R., and McDermott, K. B. (1997). Components of processing. In *Unitary versus multiple systems accounts of memory*, (ed. J. K. Foster and M. Jelicic), Oxford University Press.

Rugg, M. D., Fletcher, P. C., Frith, C. D., Frackowiak, R. S. J., and Dolan, R. J. (1997). Brain regions supporting intentional and incidental memory: a PET study. *Neuro Report*, **8**, 1283–7.

Schacter, D. L., Alpert, N. M., Savage, C. R., Rauch, S. L., and Albert, M. S. (1996a). Conscious recollection and the human hippocampal formation: Evidence from positron emission tomography. *Proceedings of the National Academy of Science of the USA*, **93**, 321–5.

Schacter, D. L., Reiman, E. M., Curran, T., Yun, L. S., Bandy, D., McDermott, K. B., and Roediger, H. L. (1996b) *Neuron*, **17**.

Schmaltz, L. W. and Theios, J. (1972). Acquisition and extinction of a classically conditioned response in hippocampectomized rabbits (*Oryctolagus cuniculus*). *Journal of Comparative Physiology and Psychology*, **79**, 328–33.

Shallice, T., Fletcher, P., Frith, C. D., Grasby, P., Frackowiak, R. S. J., and Dolan, R. J. (1994). Brain regions associated with acquisition and retrieval of verbal episodic memory. *Nature*, **368**, 633–5.

Smith, E. R. and Branscombe, N. R. (1988). Category accessibility as implicit memory. *Journal of Experimental Social Psychology*, **14**, 223–39.

Squire, L. R., Ojemann, J. G., Miezin, F. M., Petersen, S. E., Videen, T. O., and Raichle, M. E. (1992). Activation of the hippocampus in normal humans: a functional anatomical study of memory. *Proceedings of the National Academy of Science of the USA*, **89**, 1837–41.

Stern, C. E., Corkin, S., Gonzalez, R. G., Guimaraes, A. R. Baker, J. R., Jennings, P. J., Carr, C. A., Sugiura, R. M., Vedantham, V., and Rosen, B. R. (1996). The hippocampal formation participates in novel picture encoding: Evidence from functional magnetic resonance imaging. *Proceedings of the National Academy of Science of the USA*, **93**, 8660–5.

Talairach, J. and Tournoux, P. (1988). *Co-planar stereotaxic atlas of the human brain. 3-dimensional proportional system: an approach to cerebral imaging.* Georg Thieme, New York.

Tulving, E. (1985). How many memory systems are there? *American Psychologist*, **40**, 385–98.
Tulving, E. and Schacter, D. L. (1990). Priming and human memory systems. *Science*, **247**, 301–6.
Tulving, E., Kapur, S., Markowitsch, H. J., Craik, F. I. M., Habib, R., and Houle, S. (1994). Neuroanatomical correlates of retrieval in episodic memory: auditory sentence recognition. *Proceedings of the National Academy of Sciences of the USA*,
Wagner, A. D., Desmond, J. E., Demb, J. B., Glover, G. H., and Gabrieli, J. D. E. Semantic repetition priming for verbal and pictorial knowledge: a functional MRI study of left inferior prefrontal cortex. *Journal of Cognitive Neuroscience*. (In press.)
Warrington, E. K. and Weiskrantz, L. (1968). A new method of testing long-term retention with special reference to amnesic patients. *Nature*, **217**, 972–4.
Weldon, M. S. and Roediger, H. L. (1987). Altering retrieval demands reverses the picture superiority effect. *Memory and Cognition*, **15**, 269–80.
Woodruff-Pak, D. S. (1993). Eyeblink classical conditioning in H. M.: delay and trace paradigms. *Behavioral Neuroscience*, **107**, 911–25.

6
How does the brain mediate our ability to remember?

ANDREW R. MAYES

INTRODUCTION

The basic question that needs to be addressed by those wishing to understand the cognitive neuroscience of memory is 'How does the brain mediate our ability to show memory for different kinds of information?' In order to answer this question we have to determine how the psychological processes deemed necessary for memory map on to the brain structures and physiological processes that underlie it. The theme of this book is that over the last few years there has been a dispute between those who believe that there are a number of distinct memory systems and those who believe that all dissociations between different memory tasks can be explained in terms of processing differences within a unitary memory system. The first group is supposed to comprise those whose primary interest is neuropsychological so that they focus on which brain regions mediate memory for different kinds of information, whereas the second group is supposed to comprise those whose primary interest is psychological and who, therefore, focus on the processing differences between different memory tasks. Probably in common with most, if not all, the other contributors to this book, I am uncomfortable with this memory systems versus memory processes contrast, and, in this introduction, I shall say why.

One problem with the supposed contrast between memory systems and memory processes is that the terms are used in different senses by different people. However, Schacter and Tulving (1994a) captured the essence of what most people probably understand by a memory system when they argued that a memory system should be defined in terms of its brain mechanisms, the kind of information which it processes, and the principles of its operation. The notion is that the ability to show memory for specific kinds of information depends on particular parts of the brain which mediate the necessary processes to support the ability. In Schacter and Tulving's definition, it is necessary for different memory systems not only to depend on distinct neural mechanisms that deal with different kinds of information, but also that the mechanisms work in different ways, i.e. by using processes that are qualitatively distinct. They do, however, allow that different memory *subsystems* are only differentiated with respect to the kinds of information with which they deal and the brain regions that do the work. The processes mediating memory in different subsystems do not differ qualitatively.

Logically, memory must comprise three kinds of process, which underlie the encoding, storage, and retrieval of information. Psychologists tend to think of encoding and retrieval as depending on psychological processes whereas storage is regarded as dependent on non-psychological processes such as the biochemical and physiological processes that underlie initial consolidation (Abel et al. 1995). Whether or not this distinction is appropriate, it is clear that if memory systems are distinct, then they must depend on qualitatively different processes. In other words, if there are multiple memory systems, then there must be qualitatively different kinds of processes subserving memory.

If one holds the view that there are distinct memory systems, then one will almost certainly also believe that these systems can be put into a hierarchical scheme. Memory systems at the top of the hierarchy should differ with respect to the qualitative nature of many processes, but systems lower in the hierarchy should differ with respect to the qualitative nature of only one or two processes. Schacter and Tulving (1994a) use the terms system and subsystem for kinds of memory that lie respectively high or low in the hierarchy. For example, procedural (or implicit) memory and declarative (or explicit) memory are regarded by many as memory systems lying high in the hierarchy because they differ with respect to the qualitative nature of many processes, whereas motor and perceptual skills are regarded as lying low in the hierarchy because they probably differ with respect to the qualitative nature of far fewer (if any) processes. The point is that if one wishes to determine how many memory systems there are and how similar the different systems are to each other, then one must analyse the nature of the processes that underlie the ability to perform different memory tasks. Thus, not only does the existence of different memory systems imply the existence of qualitatively distinct memory processes, but the existence across memory tasks of qualitatively distinct processes implies the existence of different memory systems provided the tasks differ systematically with respect to the kinds of information for which memory needs to be shown. Identifying processing differences is also a necessary condition for specifying how similar memory systems are to each other (i.e. where they lie in the hierarchy).

Given the above, there cannot logically be a dispute between those who wish to describe memory in terms of systems and those who wish to describe it in terms of processes. Therefore, the dispute between believers in multiple memory systems and believers in a unitary memory system, although real, cannot be treated as a dispute between those who focus on systems and those who focus on processes. Rather, it is a dispute between those who believe that the ability to show memory for certain kinds of information is mediated by qualitatively different processes from the processes underlying the ability to show memory for certain other kinds of information, and those who believe that this is never the case and that memory for all kinds of information is mediated by basically the same kinds of processes.

This point is clearly illustrated by the dispute that has arisen over whether amnesics have preserved implicit memory and impaired explicit memory or whether they have preserved implicit and explicit memory for perceptual information, and impaired implicit and explicit memory for conceptual information (see Blaxton 1995; Gabrieli 1995). The first position is usually interpreted as the systems theorist's position, whereas the latter position is interpreted as the process theorist's position. This view of the dispute is incorrect and probably arises because many people regard implicit memory as a system distinct from explicit memory. But the dispute is actually about whether this is the correct systems distinction to make or whether one should actually be making a systems distinction between perceptual memory (whether implicit or explicit) and conceptual memory (whether implicit or explicit). Resolution of the dispute will depend on determining whether amnesics and normal people differ with respect to certain encoding, storage, and/or retrieval processes underlying explicit memory or whether they differ with respect to certain encoding, storage, and/or retrieval processes underlying conceptual memory. The substantive dispute is about what memory systems are involved, but its resolution depends on identifying the memory processes affected by amnesia. The way to address the question posed at the beginning of this chapter is to gain a detailed understanding of the *processes* underlying memory for different kinds of information and how the relevant brain structures mediate these processes.

How one specifies processes and the neural structures that mediate them is a theoretical issue that is likely to be guided by working assumptions such as the idea that there is likely to be a one to one relationship between memory for a specified kind of information and activities in specified neural networks. Weldon (Chapter 7, this volume) challenges this particular assumption in her criticism of the memory systems approach, using Marr's (1982) distinction between computational (or functional), algorithmic/representational, and implementational levels of analysis. If memory is the subject of the levels of analysis treatment, then an example of a memory goal that would describe a memory system in functional terms might be 'to enable memories for personally experienced episodes to be achieved'. Weldon's argument is that there may be several ways of achieving this and other kinds of memory goals. In other words, the goals may be achieved by using different kinds of algorithmic operations or processes (or, more generally, different kinds of ways of manipulating information) that may be applied to either the same or slightly different kinds of information. Luria (1973) made the same point very clearly about cognition in general when he suggested that cognitive problems may be solved in a variety of ways each using its own set of processes. The different sets of processes would be mediated by distinct brain structures so there would be a one to many correspondence between the functional and implementational levels respectively.

I want to make two comments on this argument. First, it makes the very important point that it is not enough to specify what is being done at the functional or computational level. One needs to go on to discover in detail what is being done at the algorithmic level and what neural system is doing this. It is unfortunately the case that the term 'process' applies loosely to both levels of analysis (as well as to the implementational level). There will not necessarily be a one to one correspondence between process and neuroanatomy if process is understood to mean the computational goal of a system. But most researchers believe that a particular kind of manipulation, carried out on a specific kind of information, will be mediated by one neural network. So, if process is taken to mean the kind of algorithmic operation carried out on a specific kind of informational representation, then there should be a one to one correspondence between processes and neural structures. For example, the hippocampus is often regarded as part of a group of structures that mediate the ability to show memory for personally experienced episodes. Whether or not episodic memory can also be mediated independently by the activity of other neural structures, it must still be the case that the hippocampus in conjunction with connected structures (some of which are perhaps in Papez circuit) performs certain kinds of algorithmic operations on particular kinds of information. It should be the aim of memory researchers to determine what these processes are. I suggest that memory systems may be characterized by functional/computational level description such as 'enables memory for personally experienced episodes to occur', and that the evidence for the existence of such a system should depend on analysis at *the algorithmic/representational level which might be referred to as the processing level*. If the goal can be achieved in more than one way, then the use of Schacter and Tulving's (1994*a*) definition of a memory system, which requires that separate systems must differ in the information they process, the processes they use, and the neural systems that perform the processes, implies the following: one memory system can make use of more than one set of processes mediated by more than one neural system.

Contrary to this hypothetical implication, the second comment is that there is probably going to be a reasonably good one to one correspondence between the kind of memory being served (i.e. the functional level of description) and neural structures. If functional level descriptions relate to memory for particular kinds of information, then most researchers believe that specified neural systems will process and represent those kinds of information. Furthermore, many researchers believe that memory storage for certain kinds of information will occur within the same neural system that represents those kinds of information as, indeed, Weldon (Chapter 7, this volume) does. The belief receives support from functional brain imaging studies that have found results consistent with it (see e.g. Ungerleider (1995) for a review). If this belief is correct, then it is very improbable that the same information can be stored in distinct systems of neurons in different brain regions. There should, therefore, be a one to one relationship between storage processes for particular kinds of information and specified neural systems.

With memory for facts and personally experienced episodes and possibly for other kinds of information as well, strategic factors may play a role in encoding and retrieval operations so that the precise brain regions mediating encoding and/or retrieval will vary as the strategies and hence the processes used vary. However, the relevant kinds of information have to be encoded and retrieved whatever the strategic variations, if memory for that kind of information is to be shown. Therefore, there must be a core set of brain structures that will always be activated when that kind of memory is shown provided that representation and storage of specific kinds of information occur only in one neural system. Nevertheless, other brain structures may sometimes be involved when the same kind of memory is shown. For example, personally experienced episodes may be remembered after a voluntary strategic and effortful retrieval search or they may be remembered as a result of an involuntary and automatic retrieval. On the basis of much currently available evidence, this would suggest that the frontal association cortex will be involved with episodic memory retrieval, but only when this depends on active search processes (e.g. Mayes 1988). In summary, memory systems, defined at the functional/computational level, are likely to be mediated by one core set of brain structures, which are essential at all times for memory of the relevant kind to be shown. But the memory system will also sometimes depend on other neural systems depending on what strategy is used for retrieval. In other words, on Schacter and Tulving's (1994a) definition, one memory system uses a core set of processes (defined as equivalent to algorithmic operations on certain kinds of informational representation) mediated by a single memory system (which may comprise many brain regions) and may or may not use particular processes that are mediated by other brain regions.

The above analysis suggests that the cognitive neuroscience of memory should be approached by seeking to understand how memory for different kinds of information is achieved in terms of the processes needed and the brain regions that mediate these processes. This approach allows for the possibility that memory for a particular kind of information may be achievable by using different sets of processes and brain regions, or, more modestly, that it sometimes needs the use of particular processes and brain regions and sometimes not. The aim of the approach is quite similar to that of Moscovitch's (1994) components of processing framework. Its focus is that although there may be several memory systems in Schacter and Tulving's (1994a) sense, understanding of memory will be advanced fastest by identifying the processes underlying performance on different memory tasks, showing how the brain mediates these processes, and by determining how the identified processes interact with each other.

Other contributors to this volume (e.g. Roediger *et al.*, Chapter 3, and Gabrieli, Chapter 8) believe that it is likely there will turn out to be many different memory systems. What is the basis of their beliefs? The answer may lie in the four criteria, advanced by Sherry and Schacter (1987), for identifying whether there are two distinct memory systems. These criteria are discussed in some detail by Roediger and his colleagues so I will consider them only briefly here. They are: (1) the occurrence of functional dissociations between performances on tests dependent on the two putative memory systems; (2) the putative systems must depend on brain regions that are at least partially distinct, i.e. there must be neuroimaging and lesion-based dissociations between memory tests dependent on the two systems; (3) performance on such tests must show stochastic independence; (4) performance dependent on the two systems must be based on processes that are functionally incompatible with each other. In my view, criteria (1) and (2) are the important ones because they relate directly to identifying whether two kinds of memory tasks are mediated by different kinds of processes, supported by distinct neural systems. I will return to these two criteria after briefly considering criteria (3) and (4).

As Roediger and his colleagues argue, stochastic independence is much more problematic as a criterion. It is not simply that there are many methodological difficulties with assessing stochastic independence (e.g. Hintzman and Hartry 1990), but also because stochastic independence is sometimes found where two memory tasks are highly similar and no one would want to argue that different kinds of process and memory system exist. This is well illustrated by Hayman and Tulving's (1989) finding of stochastic independence with word fragment completion when different fragments were used as cues for the same words. Whether either the products of one set of memory processes correlate with each other or the products of two qualitatively different sets of memory processes correlate with each other will depend on many, still poorly understood, factors. Just as Hayman and Tulving found that what must have been two nearly identical sets of memory processes can produce products that are stochastically independent of each other, it may be possible for stochastic *dependence* sometimes to exist between the products of two qualitatively different sets of memory processes. For example, if two qualitatively distinct processes, which are components of two memory systems, happen to determine most of the variance in memory performance, and the working efficiency of these two processes is influenced in the same way by external factors, then stochastic dependence may exist between the memory products of the two systems. If this is so, then stochastic independence will be neither a necessary nor a sufficient condition for the existence of two memory systems, or of two qualitatively distinct memory processes.

The fourth criterion, functional incompatibility, is, of course, plausible with the example that Sherry and Schacter (1987) used. It seems probable that, in birds, memory for songs and memory for the location of food are best mediated by processes that work in qualitatively different ways and, hence, are mediated most efficiently by brain systems with different properties each adapted to these processing requirements. Given that song and food location memory are both adaptively valuable to many bird species, then specialized brain regions may have evolved to deal with each form of memory in isolation. Like the other three criteria, the presence of functional incompatibility is supposed to indicate that qualitatively distinct memory processes are mediating performance on tasks that tap memory for distinct kinds of information. Unfortunately, in order to be sure that the criterion is met, one needs already to know that qualitatively distinct memory processes are operating, and, in our current state of knowledge, this is very unlikely to be known. This raises the question of what needs to be known in order to confirm that two processes are qualitatively different from one another when they underlie comparable stages of memory (encoding, storage, or retrieval).

It is generally assumed that the most convincing way of showing that two memory systems exist is to find functional and neuropsychological (which implies neuroanatomical) dissociations between tasks, performance on which depends on memory for different kinds of information. Similar psychopharmacological and developmental dissociations are regarded as strengthening the conclusions that can be drawn from functional and neuropsychological dissociations alone (see Nyberg and Tulving 1996). This assumption is based on the belief that such dissociations show that the processes underlying performance on the two sets of tasks are qualitatively distinct and mediated by partially separate brain regions. Most people would accept that functional and neuropsychological double (but not single) dissociations provide unequivocal support for the existence of qualitatively distinct memory processes, although there are a few researchers who have challenged whether this belief is necessarily or always correct (e.g. Farah 1994). Even if double dissociations do prove that some kind of difference exists, however, they do not by themselves prove the existence of two distinct memory processes.

There are two reasons why this is so. First, dissociations can arise because memory tasks differ with respect to the kinds of information they require to be retrieved, or because they depend on different memory processes, or both of these. Unfortunately, many of the functional dissociations that have been found between information-specific indirect memory and direct memory tasks clearly arise, at least in part, because the two kinds of task involve the retrieval of perceptual and conceptual information respectively. This makes it plausible to suggest that the dissociations arise merely because the tasks require the encoding and retrieval of perceptual and conceptual information respectively. Whenever this kind of suggestion applies to observed functional dissociations between two sets of memory task, no evidence has been found to show that the two kinds of memory task involve different processes. Nevertheless, neuropsychological dissociation between the two sets of tasks would be expected because different kinds of information are almost certainly represented and stored in different brain regions. In brief, neuropsychological dissociations do not in themselves prove that two sets of memory tasks depend on different processes because they may merely mean that the two groups of tasks involve the retrieval of different kinds of information. Functional dissociations may provide evidence that different processes are involved, but to show this they need to be very carefully analysed to determine that the dissociations are caused by variables that are affecting processes rather than the kind of information being encoded and retrieved.

The second reason for scepticism derives directly from the above summary. It has been suggested to me that if performance on two memory tasks requires the retrieval of different kinds of information, then this is very strong prima facie evidence that performance on the tasks is mediated by different kinds of processes. My comments on this are: (1) There is no evidence one way or other for this view and it depends on the existence of clear criteria for determining whether processes are qualitatively different. At present, there are no such criteria although there are heuristic guidelines, and *ex cathedra* assertions are no substitutes for evidence. (2) Given this, it is up to people who believe that different kinds of processes are operating to prove that they are. (3) But, if they are correct, then there may be several hundred thousand memory systems in the Sherry and Schacter (1987) sense. This is one possible answer to the question considered by Roediger and colleagues, and by Gabrieli in this volume. Following the principle that storage of information probably occurs in the same neurons that represent the information, and given that different information is not represented in exactly the same neurons, then, for example, storage of the visual appearance of tulips would involve some neurons that are different from those involved in the storage of the visual appearance of daffodils. In principle, therefore, it should be possible to separate memory for tulips and daffodils by obtaining a functional double dissociation with an appropriate manipulation of information processing at encoding and/or retrieval, and by obtaining a neuropsychological double dissociation with appropriately placed lesions or by recording the activity of large groups of neurons. This argument is supposed to be a *reductio ad absurdum* of the following view: identifying when memory for different information depends on different processes simply requires the identification of functional and neuropsychological double dissociations! One of the aims of research on memory is to find out what kinds of processes are needed in order for memory for different kinds of information to be shown. The nature of the relationship between memory for different kinds of information and different kinds of processes is exactly what needs to be discovered. Nothing about it should be assumed. Therefore, the second reason for scepticism is that there are many instances where one should not assume that memory for different information means that qualitatively different processes are at work. To be sure there are qualitative differences, then there must *always* be evidence beyond simple functional and neuropsychological dissociations.

I should point out that although one can avoid postulating myriad memory systems by requiring stronger evidence for the presence of qualitatively distinct memory processes than functional and neuropsychological dissociations, one cannot avoid a massive multiplication of memory subsystems in Schacter and Tulving's (1994a) sense because separate subsystems are not required to show qualitative processing differences. To prevent the number of subsystems becoming absurdly high, some further restrictive criteria would need to be introduced.

To consider how one might move towards identifying whether memory processes differ qualitatively, one first needs to examine the memory stages of encoding, storage and retrieval in more detail. Whereas it is natural to characterize encoding and retrieval in psychological terms, which correspond to Marr's computational/functional and algorithmic/representational levels, this is not true of storage, which is typically characterized in implementational terms. The neural activities underlying storage can be considered at two levels. The first of these is the microscopic level of the neuron and the synaptic connections between neurons, and the second level is the macroscopic level involving networks of large numbers of neurons. At the first level, it is almost universally believed that long-lasting storage of information in memory depends on structural changes in synapses connecting those neurons, the activity of which represents the stored information. These structural changes in synapses alter the strength of the functional links between the neurons that represent the information. The extent to which the synaptic structural change processes are the same or different with memory for different kinds of information remains only very partially explored. The degree to which differences exist remains polemical. On the one hand, it is known that long-term potentiation (LTP) depends on activity at NMDA receptors in the CA1 and dentate regions of the hippocampal system, but does not do so in the CA3 region of the hippocampus (see Gluck and Granger 1993). As the processes underlying LTP are believed by many to underlie storage of certain kinds of information, this suggests that the microscopic processes underlying storage are likely to be diverse, although it remains unclear whether the above difference in LTP mechanisms has serious implications for other processes involved in memory. On the other hand, Abel *et al.* (1995) have argued that explicit and implicit memory (and presumably their subtypes) 'seem to share a common molecular logic for initial consolidation' so will probably also rely on the same storage operations at the intraneuronal level. There is also evidence that there are marked similarities in the storage processes that exist in very different species such as drosophila, chicks, and mice (see DeZazzo and Tully 1995). Much more, therefore, needs to be learnt about these intraneuronal physiological and biochemical activities, how they differ across brain regions, and what impact, if any, these differences have on the way other memory processes need to operate.

In terms of Marr's (1982) three-level model, the physiological and biochemical operations that underlie storage at the microscopic scale of synapses and neurons correspond to the implementational level. They do not correspond directly to the algorithmic/representational level, which I am equating with processing, although they may well have effects on the kinds of processes that are needed to support memory for a specific kind of information. It needs to be more clearly specified what will indicate whether differences in storage mechanisms are associated with algorithmic processing differences as well. One possibility is that this is indicated when forgetting functions differ from each other, or interference effects on memory work in a very different way (see Wickelgren 1974). Differences in microscopic storage processes may, nevertheless, offer guidelines for the presence of qualitative differences in memory processes.

When one considers storage at the macroscopic level, it seems very likely that some different kinds of information are likely to be represented in qualitatively distinct ways. In general, the representation that was encoded at input will be reactivated at retrieval in a way that depends on how the intraneuronal storage changes are distributed throughout the representing neural network. How this is done may be simulated with varying degrees of precision by connectionist and other kinds of computer-based model (e.g. Gluck *et al.* 1997; Metcalfe 1997). Such models provide strong guidelines about whether different processes are likely to be involved in the representation of distinct kinds of information. Another guideline about whether qualitative differences in processes (in Marr's sense of algorithmic operations on representations) exist that are related to macroscopic level storage operations is the detailed neuronal architecture of the brain regions subserving different memory tasks. If the architecture is radically different, this provides a powerful hint that not only the microscopic storage processes, but also the macroscopic and representational storage processes, may work according to different principles in the two regions.

Encoding and retrieval processes cannot be treated completely independently of storage processes for a reason that is implicit in what is said above. This is that for many, if not all, kinds of memory system, encoding inputs a representation, storage maintains the possibility of reactivating the representation or something closely akin to it, and retrieval carries out this reactivation. Therefore, when memory is successful, there must be a very large overlap in the constraints that apply to interacting encoding, storage, and retrieval processes. Nevertheless, certain kinds of process will be specific to encoding and retrieval operations. An example is the kind of executive processing that is mediating by the prefrontal association cortex and probably other brain regions. Thus, as mentioned above, retrieval can sometimes be carried out automatically whereas there are other occasions when success depends on using an organized search. These effortful search processes are almost certainly qualitatively distinct from the automatic ones that are sometimes sufficient. Provided that effortful search was needed to retrieve some kinds of information, but automatic retrieval was sufficient for other kinds, then there would be strong grounds for postulating separate memory systems.

The human brain not only processes different kinds of information, it also stores this information. Most, if not all, regions of the brain show various kinds of synaptic plasticity (see e.g. Kaas (1997) who focuses on plasticity in primary sensory and motor cortices, regions not often thought of as showing plasticity in adult animals). This suggests that most, if not all, brain regions are capable of storing memories. Indeed, it is likely that storage is an automatic consequence of processing and representing information, although the strength with which this will occur may vary considerably across brain regions. When functional and neuropsychological dissociations are found between tasks that tap memory for different kinds of information, it still needs to be determined whether memory for the different kinds of information is mediated by processes of qualitatively distinct kinds. Only guidelines can currently be used to see whether this is the case. These include: (1) Do the functional dissociations depend on processing manipulations which suggest that distinct processes are operating? (2) Are very different kinds of biochemical and physiological consolidation cascades leading to distinct kinds of synaptic structural change that will underlie storage at the cellular level? (3) Do computer simulations suggest that representation of information in memory is being performed in radically different ways for different kinds of information? (4) Does the architecture and nature of the neurons in the neural system responsible for storing the memory representations differ markedly between brain regions putatively involved with separate memory systems? (5) Are specific encoding and retrieval processes involved with one putative memory system, but not another?

STANDARDLY HYPOTHESIZED MEMORY SYSTEMS— THE CASE OF WORKING MEMORY

Classification schemes for memory systems are hierarchical, as is illustrated by the influential taxonomy used by Squire et al. (1993). At the top level of this scheme, a distinction is made between short-term or working memory and long-term memory. It is well known that Squire and his co-workers subdivide long-term memory into declarative and non-declarative memory, and that these high-level systems are then further subdivided. Thus, declarative memory is subdivided into memory for facts (semantic memory) and memory for events (episodic memory), whereas non-declarative memory is subdivided into skill and habit memory, priming, simple classical conditioning, and non-associative memory. These subdivisions could, of course, be taken further. Thus, in the realm of declarative memory, semantic memory has been subdivided into different categories, such as memory for man-made things and memory for animate things (Warrington and Shallice 1984), and episodic memory could be divided into memory for verbalizable information and memory for hard-to-verbalize information such as faces or complex spatial associations (see Mayes (1988) for a review). The realm of non-declarative memory has perhaps so far been given less attention, but motor, perceptual, and cognitive skills should be distinguishable, priming for perceptual and for conceptual information are generally distinguished from each other, there are different forms of classical conditioning (such as conditioning of motoric responses and conditioning of emotional responses), and there are presumably different kinds of non-associative memory.

Whether even these subdivisions can themselves be further subdivided at a lower level of the hierarchy is unresolved. Indeed, it is unclear whether the distinction which can be made between verbal and non-verbal episodic memory is between what Schacter and Tulving (1994a) would call memory systems, or whether verbal and non-verbal episodic memory are merely separate memory subsystems. To resolve this, one would have to be able to determine whether verbal and non-verbal memory depend on qualitatively distinct processes, which requires more than showing functional and neuropsychological double dissociations between the two possible memory systems.

One implication of this taxonomy for long-term memory is that, for example, different forms of classical conditioning have much more in common with each other than they do with any form of episodic memory. Generally, it is argued that all instances of declarative memory involve an awareness of some kind that a fact or an event is true or has been encountered before, i.e. awareness that in some sense one is remembering. In contrast, all instances of non-declarative memory do not involve an awareness that one is showing memory. The implication is that aware and unaware memory depend on radically distinct processes. I shall return to this issue in the next two sections of this chapter.

Similar subdivisions to those that have been made within the domain of long-term memory can be made between different kinds of short-term or working memory. Thus, there is already good evidence for separate verbal, spatial, and visual object short-term stores, which depend on slightly different cortical regions (see Vallar and Papagno 1995). For example, phonological short-term memory can be disrupted without disrupting visuospatial short-term memory and vice versa (see Vallar and Papagno 1995). Whereas phonological short-term memory is disrupted by lesions to the left parietal lobe, particularly in the left inferior parietal lobe where it conjoins with the left temporal lobe (see McCarthy and Warrington 1990), visuospatial short-term memory is more disrupted by right parietal lesions than by left-sided ones (see Vallar and Papagno 1995). This dissociation is also found with neuroimaging studies, as Paulescu *et al.* (1992) found that activity associated with phonological short-term storage activated the left supramarginal gyrus in normal subjects whereas Jonides *et al.* (1993) reported that using short-term spatial memory activated the right parietal lobe more than the left. In other words, neuropsychological dissociations have been demonstrated between short-term memory for different kinds of information. (See Owen (1997), Courtney *et al.* (1997), and Cohen and Smith (1997) for a discussion of the extent to which neuroimaging studies have identified whether different frontal lobe regions help maintain distinct kinds of information for short periods of time.)

Although in the past, Baddeley (1986) confined the multiplication of short-term storage systems to a phonological store and a visuospatial store, it seems probable that, in the future, neuropsychological dissociations will be found between short-term storage in different sensory systems and between these and short-term storage for motor representations. Indeed, even within single sensory modalities such as vision, it is likely that neuropsychological dissociations will be found. It may also be necessary to postulate a more abstract store capable of holding semantic information for brief periods of time in tasks requiring problem solving or the understanding of stories. Support for this possibility is given by evidence that semantic factors play a role in interference in short-term memory tasks (Dale and Gregory 1966). At this stage, it should be stressed that all these system distinctions are tentative because, in no case, has it yet been proved that different systems of short-term memory exist for different kinds of information. This is so because, although some neuropsychological dissociations have been found, it has not been shown that these arise because of qualitative differences in the kinds of processes underlying the dissociated kinds of short-term memory. Short-term memory for different kinds of information will almost certainly depend on distinct neural networks to hold the information, and, therefore, neuropsychological double dissociations should be found. Nevertheless, these networks may operate according to the same principles.

All the above instances or possible instances of short-term memory involve awareness of and aware memory for whatever is being remembered. If the memory were long-term, it would be referred to by Squire and his associates as declarative memory, and by Schacter and his colleagues (see Schacter and Tulving 1994*b*) as explicit memory. This observation raises the following question: why is there not short-term memory for non-declarative or implicit kinds of memory?

The answer is surely that if short-term memory exists for declarative kinds of information, then very probably it does so as well for non-declarative kinds of information. Subjects would presumably not be aware that they are remembering the non-declarative kinds of information, and, indeed, may not be aware of the information held in their short-term stores at all.

One implication of the above discussion is that short- and long-term memory are likely to be for the same kinds of information. If one follows the Sherry and Schacter (1987) definition, there is a strong reason for saying that short- and long-term memory are not different kinds of memory systems, and certainly not radically distinct kinds of memory system. Indeed, the varieties of short-term memory should all be included within the same memory systems or subsystems as those which control long-term memory for the same information. The reason is simply that short-term memory seems to be for the same kinds of information as does long-term memory, and that, on Sherry and Schacter's definition, differences in the kind of information for which memory is shown is a necessary condition for postulating distinct memory systems.

The empirical claim underlying this reason can be illustrated by the following example. There is evidence that a double dissociation can be demonstrated between impairments of phonological short-term memory and long-term memory for spoken verbal items (see McCarthy and Warrington 1990). However, Baddeley *et al.* (1988) have shown that a patient, PV, who has a severe impairment in phonological short-term memory, was completely unable to learn spoken Russian words, transliterated into her native Italian. She was thus impaired at both short- and long-term memory for these spoken words that were meaningless to her, and which she, therefore, presumably had to represent as phonological sequences. I was very pleased when this result was reported because I had predicted that it would be found several years before (Mayes 1983). The neuropsychological double dissociations that have often been found between phonological short-term memory and auditory verbal long-term memory almost certainly arose because long-term memory was only normal to the extent that incoming information could be rapidly transformed into other codes such as semantic ones. Baddeley *et al.*'s results indicate that, if short-term memory for specific information is impaired, then long-term memory for the *same* information will also be devastated unless the information can be recoded rapidly by the patient so that different information goes into long-term memory. In general, short-term memory may be for phonological combinations, but so surely may long-term memory, and, similarly, if short-term memory can be for visuospatial or another specific kind of information, then so can long-term memory.

A comment on the above is warranted. Even if there are not separate short-term and long-term memory systems, there may still be some important differences in the kinds of processing needed to support short- and long-term memory. Support for this possibility may be derived from the near certainty that there are differences in the biochemical, physiological, and structural storage changes underlying short-term and long-term retention of information at the microscopic level (e.g. Abel *et al.* 1995). Indeed, theorists have argued that storage differences exist not only between short- and long-term memory, but also between these and an intermediate-term memory (and, at least in drosophila, a slightly longer lasting anaesthesia-resistant memory), which have durations ranging from seconds through hours to much longer time periods (see DeZazzo and Tully 1995). Only long-term memory seems to require gene transcription and the manufacture of new kinds of protein presumably to induce enduring structural changes, whereas short-term memory probably depends on the continued activity of the representing neural network. Whereas continued neural activity is present as soon as information is encoded, such activity probably does not continue long after processing is disrupted by other activities. So further memory stores that reach full strength rapidly may well be vital because the changes underlying long-term memory probably take some time to occur. Psychologists have focused on short-term rather than intermediate duration memories because nothing psychological has been found to distinguish intermediate duration memory whereas memories that last a few seconds are very obvious, and clearly are vital for high-level cognitive processes.

The differences between short-term and long-term memory apply at the implementational level so do not have to be accompanied by qualitative processing differences at the algorithmic/representational level. Indeed, Wickelgren (1974) seems to have argued exactly this when he claimed that short- and long-term memory phenomena can be accounted for by a single-trace fragility theory of memory dynamics. Although forgetting from what is regarded as long-term memory follows a power function whereas short-term forgetting follows an exponential function, Wickelgren argued that at a deeper level it can be seen that the forgetting curves follow the same mathematical function. In particular, memory strength declines with time in the same way, and interference disrupts memory in the same way. The different shape of the forgetting curves arises because key parameters in the function have different values for fairly trivial reasons. If Wickelgren was correct, this would presumably mean that basically the same kind of algorithmic *processes* account for short- and long-term forgetting even if there are differences between the two at the microscopic implementational level. At best, therefore, the likely microscopic implementational differences between short- and long-term memory provide guidelines with respect to possible algorithmic/representational processing differences.

The way that memory is organized at the macroscopic level may also differ between long- and short-term memory, and this may influence the kinds of retrieval processes that need to be used. Differences in retrieval processes of a kind that would satisfy a theorist such as Wickelgren have almost certainly not been shown. For example, it may be that only long-term memory involves effortful retrieval processes, but this has not been shown, and introspection suggests to me that it is unlikely to be the case. Also, although maintenance of short-term memory depends more on rehearsal than maintenance of information already in long-term memory, this could be explained trivially by Wickelgren's approach without recourse to postulating qualitatively different kinds of processes.

One striking difference between short- and long-term memory that some might relate to macroscopic aspects of information representation in memory is the following: when retrieval of the same information is involved, as it seems to be with memory for phonological sequences, left inferior parietal lesions disrupt both short- and long-term memory for the sequences, whereas long-term memory alone is disrupted by hippocampal or other lesions that cause amnesia (e.g. Squire et al. 1993). The explanation of this single dissociation constitutes a challenge to the principle enunciated earlier that information is represented and stored (whether long- or short-term) in the same neural system. The principle is not challenged if it is argued that the lesions causing amnesia disrupt a retrieval process that is unique to long-term memory. If correct, this would mean that long-term memory depends on a retrieval process of a qualitatively distinct kind from those used with short-term memory, even though the two kinds of memory involve the same kind of information. This would suggest that memory systems in Sherry and Schacter's (1987) sense (which requires two distinct systems to deal with memory for different kinds of information) may fail to stress important processing differences that apply across memory tasks. If the single dissociation is interpreted to mean that information stored in the parietal cortex short-term is also stored in regions damaged in amnesics in the longer term, then the above principle seems to be challenged. This issue will be considered again briefly in the penultimate section of the chapter, but, once again, here, I merely wish to restress that possible storage differences apply at the implementational level so further evidence is always needed to show whether they are linked to qualitatively distinct processes.

In summary, the full range of kinds of information for which short-term memory can be shown remains to be shown as does whether short-term memory for different kinds of information depends on qualitatively distinct processes. Although there are almost certainly qualitative differences between short- and long-term storage at the implementational level, the question of whether they constitute different memory systems cannot even arise on Sherry and Schacter's definition. This is because short- and long-term memory are likely to be for the same kinds of information. To be consistent with the definition, it would be appropriate to propose that any given memory systems may depend on different implementational mechanisms for short- and long-term storage (and possibly further mechanisms for other durations of storage). Whether these different implementational mechanisms are associated with different processes at the algorithmic level needs further exploration.

It is perhaps appropriate at this stage of the chapter to stress what should be apparent to everyone. This is simply that the most important questions about memory relate to the implementational changes that make storage of information possible. It is of great interest to identify whether memory for different kinds of information depends on distinct kinds of biochemical and physiological changes. Similarly, it is of great interest to know how the biochemical and physiological changes underlying short- and long-term memory (even if these are for the same information) differ from each other. However, as storing information does not involve transforming the information to be stored into other information, then, by definition, storage is not a process in the sense of process at Marr's middle level of analysis. When Nadel (1994) suggested that the duration for which information is stored be used as a criterion for identifying a memory system, he was focusing on storage at the implementational level because different durations of storage are suggestive of different kinds of mediation at this level. This is highly appropriate for understanding memory as storage is its central feature and has to be understood at the implementational level. The sense of memory system, being considered in this chapter, does not focus attention on how storage is mediated at the implementational level. It could only do this by using the term 'process' in two very different senses.

COMPONENT PROCESSES OF LONG-TERM MEMORY: FOUR BASIC KINDS OF PROCESS

In this section I shall advance a framework which proposes that long-term memory comprises four kinds of component processes. These processes are memory representations (see Mayes (1988) for a discussion); enhanced fluency (see Jacoby and Dallas 1981); attributions (see Jacoby *et al.* 1989*a*); and active retrieval search (see Gillund and Shiffrin 1984). These processes will be primarily used to explain explicit or declarative memory, but, by a suitable extension, could be used to explain non-declarative or implicit memory as well.

Memory representations store specific kinds of information and should presumably be specified in terms of what that information is, what the representation processes are, and how the information is stored. Although different kinds of information may be stored in different brain regions, and may depend on distinct physiological and biochemical activities, it remains hard to show whether representation is achieved in algorithmically distinct ways.

Enhanced fluency occurs when studied information has its memory representation activated more rapidly, easily, and strongly after cues that are components of the representation have been encoded (see Jacoby and Dallas 1981). This enhancement is relative to the fluency with which the same cues would have activated the representation on a previous occasion, is typically caused by the strengthening of the information's memory representation, and is, in some sense, automatic (Jacoby and Witherspoon 1992). It is a reasonable assumption that enhanced fluency underlies priming or what I will refer to as information-specific implicit memory (ISIM), and that it can be influenced not only by the strength of a memory, but by the degree of match between the encoding cues and the memory representation as indicated by the encoding specificity principle (e.g. Tulving 1983).

Given the view that memory is stored in the same neural network which represents the remembered information (see Ungerleider 1995), it is of interest that neuroimaging studies of priming have typically found that activation is reduced on the second presentation in the region where the information is likely to be represented.

Thus, Martin et al. (1995), using functional magnetic resonance imaging (fMRI), found that showing pictures for a second time in a silent naming task led to reduced activity in the ventral occipitotemporal region compared with the first time of presentation. Similarly, Demb et al. (1995) found that semantic judgments about words were not only faster on second presentation, but also produced reduced left inferior prefrontal activation as measured by fMRI. This reduced activation may have been specific to semantic representations because it was not seen with non-semantic judgments even though these were also made faster when words were re-presented. If the memory strengthening, which underlies enhanced fluency, involves increasing the degree of connectivity of the representing neural network (via synaptic changes), then the reduced blood oxygenation changes may reflect the more efficient reactivation of the representation (although this needs to be proved).

The notion of attribution, as it is applied to memory, involves a rapid, automatic, and unconscious inference, based on some aspect of enhanced fluency that gives rise to the feeling that the fluently processed representation is a memory. In other words, it gives rise to a feeling of aware or explicit memory. Jacoby and his colleagues have done much to argue for this attributional view of aware memory as providing the mechanism for the non-specific form of episodic memory known as familiarity (see Jacoby and Kelley 1992). In addition, Jacoby et al. (1989a) seemed to propose that the attributional mechanism also accounts for the more specific form of episodic memory, recollection, although this view was not developed nor its implications explored. Before developing this view, which I support, it should be stressed that, according to Jacoby and his colleagues (e.g. Jacoby and Kelley 1992), attributions that are based on enhanced fluency can also be made about perceptual and aesthetic features of more fluently processed information. Whether attributions are made about memory or perceptual/aesthetic features is at least partially determined by whether or not the context directs the subject's attention to memory or non-memory issues.

The fourth kind of mechanism underlying long-term memory is active search, which is typically important in direct tests of memory such as free recall, cued recall, and recognition. In such tasks, subjects receive different amounts of cueing and then search for further cues that are components of the target memory with the aim of increasing the number of components they can encode so as to be able to reactivate the target memory automatically. Subjects use their semantic and episodic memory in a problem-solving fashion to generate cues, which when encoded automatically elicit the target memory. It remains to be discovered how a vague knowledge of the target memory can direct such a non-random search process, but it is clear that there must also be a process which monitors whether reactivated memories are targets or how they relate to targets. This monitoring process is likely to be very important in remembering whether a memory relates to a specific episode because very often one may have reactivated a genuine memory, but one that relates to another episode which is similar to the target one. Search, therefore, involves a process that directs the generation of cues in a non-random manner, a process that monitors how reactivated memories relate to the target memory, and, as will now be argued, a fluency-based and automatic attribution process that leads to aware memories.

It has usually been argued that ISIM and explicit memory are different memory systems, which must mean that they involve memory for different kinds of information, depend on somewhat different brain regions, and are mediated by qualitatively distinct kinds of process (e.g. Schacter and Tulving 1994*a passim*). I wish to suggest an alternative possibility. This is a redundancy model according to which all forms of explicit memory (semantic as well as episodic memory) depend on enhanced fluency and a memory attribution process, but not necessarily on active search processes. Contrary to the multiple systems account of ISIM and explicit memory, this view proposes that these forms of memory are for the same kinds of information. This has, of course, to be shown, but it is just as plausible as the view that ISIM and explicit memory are for different kinds of information. Explicit memory typically includes memory for the kinds of perceptual and conceptual information that are tapped by standard ISIM tasks, and ISIM for the more complex kinds of associative information, typically retrieved in episodic memory, has also been claimed. What needs to be shown is that there is also ISIM for the complex kinds of contextual associative information that are presumably reactivated when we recollect.

The redundancy view proposes: (1) that familiarity is a non-specific feeling of memory that applies to items which are fluently reactivated and, for this reason, have an automatic attribution made about them that leads to the feeling of memory; (2) that this familiarity memory not only underlies item non-specific episodic memory, but may underlie semantic memory in general as one feels one is remembering facts that are fluently reactivated such that one makes an attribution that they are familiar (in this case, enhanced fluency may be for complex associations as well as for single items); (3) the specific form of episodic memory, recollection, where item-experienced context associations are reactivated, occurs when these associations are fluently reactivated so as to lead to a memory attribution and a feeling of memory for the association; (4) both recollection and complex fact memory also often involve the effortful active search processes, which simple item familiarity and ISIM do not seem to require (Jacoby *et al.* 1989*b*). As retrieval may be very non-fluent when effortful search processes have to be used, this produces a complication for point 3. However, it need only be claimed that enhanced fluency occurs in the *final* stage of the search when appropriate cues reactivate the target memory very easily. Assuming that enhanced fluency can be identified at this stage, memory attribution would normally be expected to occur.

The main reason for supporting the above view is that only it provides a plausible mechanism for how the feeling that one is remembering is produced. Just representing information so that one is aware of it is insufficient to tell one whether one is imagining or remembering it because the representing may be accompanied by no feeling of memory or an overwhelming feeling of memory. Of course, one may be able to infer that the information is remembered or imagined on the basis of one's other memories, but this does not solve the problem because such inferences do not lead to automatic feelings of memory, but rather depend on their existence. Neither does Moscovitch's (1995) proposal that aware feelings of memory for episodes are created by an extended hippocampal system acting as a module that receives episodic information of which the subject is aware. This is because the awareness that is relevant is not of the information itself, but of the fact that one encountered that information in the past.

The view, adopted here, is that the content of the information which one is consciously representing cannot of itself lead to an aware feeling of memory. Representations with specific contents may be in mind either because one is remembering or because one is imagining them. Generation of a feeling of memory can only arise from the way in which a representation has been activated leading to an attribution of memory. In other words, it cannot be what is represented *per se* that leads to a feeling of awareness. Given this, all that is left is the way this representation is reactivated. It is insufficient to say that sometimes the representation activates 'an awareness' mechanism because such activation is not random and one needs to specify what features of the reactivated representation trigger the mechanism so that it behaves in a non-random fashion. On the current view, memory attribution is the mechanism triggered by enhanced fluency of the reactivation of the representation.

Several unconfirmed predictions can be derived from this redundancy hypothesis. First, ISIM should occur for complex associations including those between items and experienced context. This has not yet been shown and demonstrations will be difficult because there is growing evidence that performance on indirect memory tasks, which tap memory for previously novel associations, is often driven by effortful search processes related to explicit memory. Recollection of item–context associations often only occurs when it is intentional and involves active search for suitable cues to encode. This implies that, in such cases, enhanced fluency of reactivation of the target memory is only found after an effortful search has been made for the finally encoded cues. Enhanced fluency of activation of item–context associations in tasks that do not depend on active search may, therefore, only be found when such associations have been very strongly learnt so that an active search for appropriate cues is unnecessary. In summary, the key point about this prediction is the following: any person who shows explicit memory for any given information must also have ISIM for exactly the same information. One should be able to show this as long as one tests in an appropriate way, although this may not be easy. This does not, of course, mean that, in any specific instance, ISIM and explicit memory involving the same nominal stimuli, depend on memory for the same information. The example of stem completion (ISIM) and stem cued recall (explicit memory), where the former involves retrieval of primarily perceptual information whereas the latter involves the retrieval of primarily semantic information, shows that this is false, and emphasizes that it is difficult to prove what information is retrieved in a memory task. In other words, it is necessary to show not only ISIM and explicit memory for the same nominal information, but also that they involve retrieval of the same aspects of this information.

Second, Rajaram (1993) has shown that subliminal priming with target items (whether old or new) can selectively enhance the making of know responses in the remember/know procedure, and Jacoby and Witherspoon (1989) have shown a similar effect with the process dissociation procedure. It is plausible that these selective effects on familiarity memory depend on subliminal priming increasing the fluency of reactivation of target items so that memory attributions are enhanced. No effect on recollection and item–context associations should be expected, but an effect would be predicted if subliminal priming was carried out with item–context associations. When such associative subliminal priming is given, the item–context associations should be reactivated with enhanced fluency and make a memory attribution more likely. This critical prediction remains to be tested.

Third, as the view postulates that explicit memory is always accompanied by enhanced fluency, and such fluency seems to lead to less activation in the representing areas of the brain, such reduced activity should also be found with explicit memory. This may be difficult to test properly because confounding factors such as attentional differences will need to be controlled. The significance of this reduced activation still needs to be clarified, preferably by single-unit recording studies. It is, therefore, of interest that many neurons in the anterior inferior temporal cortex respond more the first time that visual stimuli are viewed (see Brown (1996) for a review). However, much more needs to be done before we can interpret what processing changes characterize the reactivation of a representation with enhanced fluency when this occurs as a result of the synaptic changes underlying long-term memory.

Fourth, it seems likely that the mechanisms of enhanced fluency, attribution, and active search each depend on particular brain regions. Neuroimaging and lesion studies should be able to separate attributional and active search processes from enhanced fluency, although the degree to which the neural mediation of the processes will depend on the information being retrieved will almost certainly vary. Thus, fluency should occur in brain regions where the memory is represented, but the location of attribution and active search activations may be relatively independent of where the kinds of information being remembered are being represented in the brain.

IMPLICATIONS OF THE FRAMEWORK

In this section I shall consider some implications of the four-mechanism framework for the kinds of distinction that many wish to make between putative kinds of explicit or aware long-term memory. Particular attention is paid to the possible distinction between semantic and episodic memory because recent work has suggested that neuropsychological dissociations can be found between memory for these two kinds of information. I shall also consider some implications of the framework for the distinction between ISIM and explicit memory.

It is clear that some workers wish to identify not only procedural memory and perceptual representation systems as separate systems from explicit memory, but also to distinguish between episodic and semantic memory. Nyberg and Tulving (1996) support this position by considering a series of converging dissociations involving functional, developmental, psychopharmacological, and neuropsychological dissociations. Although the empirical basis and interpretation of some of this evidence has been disputed by Shanks (1997), most workers would accept that there is an impressive array of dissociations extending across the putative memory systems concerned.

My problem with the suggestion that semantic and episodic memory constitute separate memory systems derives partly from what was said in this chapter's first section and partly from the four-mechanism framework just outlined. It needs to be shown that dissociations arise not because semantic and episodic memory involve retrieval of different kinds of information (which they do), but because they depend on different kinds of processes. One possible kind of evidence, which meets the requirement of being a guideline for there being distinct memory systems, is the interesting and often reported neuroimaging finding that active retrieval of semantic information primarily activates parts of the left prefrontal association cortex whereas active retrieval of episodic information primarily activates parts of the right pre-frontal association cortex (see Nyberg *et al.* (1996) for a review). On the assumption that activation of different frontal cortex regions reflects the operation of different kinds of search operation, this kind of finding would support the separate systems view. Great care needs to be exercised, however, because it is not understood why the effect occurs. It may arise because of non-essential, but typical, differences between semantic and episodic memory. This possibility is illustrated by an elegant study by Wiggs *et al.* (1996), which showed that when difficulty level of episodic memory was matched with that of a very similar semantic task, then fact retrieval produced more right as well as left prefrontal cortex activation than did episodic memory. Although activation differences remained, this study makes the point that many factors must be controlled before one can be sure that any episodic/semantic retrieval activation difference indicates that retrieval of the two kinds of information *must* involve non-overlapping frontal cortex regions, let alone qualitatively distinct active search processes.

Another double dissociation, which suggests that semantic and episodic memory constitute distinct systems, is that hippocampal lesions disrupt episodic memory selectively (Vargha-Khadem *et al.* 1997) whereas anterolateral temporal cortex lesions selectively affect semantic memory (see Patterson and Hodges 1995). Although organic amnesics are known to have problems learning about new facts as well as about new episodes (e.g. Gabrieli *et al.* 1988), Vargha-Khadem *et al.* (1997) have reported that this may not be true of patients with selective hippocampal lesions. They found that three young amnesics, who acquired what may be selective bilateral lesions of the hippocampus many years previously at birth, age four, and age nine, showed impaired free recall of episodic information, but their performance on tests of reading, spelling, reading comprehension, vocabulary, and information revealed performance in the normal range even though normal children perform below ceiling levels on these tests. In contrast, it is generally claimed that what is referred to as semantic dementia leads to a very severe loss of memory for previously well learnt semantic information, but relative preservation of memory for recent personal episodes (see Patterson and Hodges 1995). This form of dementia is caused by progressive atrophy of the anterolateral regions of the temporal lobes usually on the left or bilaterally, leaving the medial temporal lobe region relatively intact (Patterson and Hodges 1995). The double dissociation may, therefore, serve as a guideline that memory for facts and episodes depends on the anterolateral temporal cortex and hippocampus respectively, and that these structures mediate qualitatively distinct processes.

There are three main reasons for doubting this suggestion. First, recent work by Graham and Hodges (1997) suggests that the term 'semantic dementia' is inappropriate. They found that those with semantic dementia are impaired not only at memory for facts acquired in the distant past, but also at memory for personal experiences of a similar age. Unlike Alzheimer's patients, who often show an amnesic-like temporal gradient of impairment for remote memories in which older memories are less impaired, semantic dementia patients show more impairment for older personal memories and very little impairment for such memories that date from the recent past. This suggests that semantic dementia is not specific to fact memory at all, but affects both fact and event memories progressively more severely as time passes. If this is correct, it is also consistent with Squire and Alvarez's (1995) view of the amnesia which is caused by medial temporal lobe lesions. According to this view, maintenance of memories for facts and events initially depends on structures such as the hippocampus in the medial temporal lobes, but through gradual reorganization of storage, older memories are maintained by neocortical structures such as the anterolateral temporal cortex.

Second, with respect to the other half of the dissociation, it is hard to believe that fact memories are acquired normally after selective hippocampal lesions because the cases studied by Vargha-Khadem *et al.* (1997) had very impaired memory for stories even after short delays. As stories are exemplars of factual information, it is very probable that no factual information is acquired normally at least when the test is free recall. The published data are, therefore, puzzling because it is almost certain that the three patients would have been impaired at the initial acquisition of facts, but despite this their eventual memory for the facts appears normal. Whether this impaired initial learning is described as fact learning or episodic learning (as is often claimed although unproved) is not strictly relevant because one still has to be shown how memory for facts such as stories can become normal after initially being very impaired.

Kapur (1994) has attempted to provide an explanation of this puzzle. He found a double dissociation between a patient whose damage was primarily to the mammillary bodies and another patient with necrosis mainly in the perirhinal cortex following radiotherapy. The former patient was immediately impaired on a name–occupation association learning task, but apparently normal at long-term memory of details about famous people, who had been learnt about both pre- and post-morbidly, such as Norman Schwarzkopf. The other patient showed the reverse pattern of deficit. This study requires replication with other similar patients, particularly as the degree of normality of the first patient on remote post-morbid memory may be doubted because this measure was not specifically reported, and would have been based on very few items. However, Kapur argued that there may be two mechanisms for fact learning, a rapid process dependent on the extended hippocampal system (i.e. Papez circuit structures), and a slow, multiple-trial cortical learning process. Long-term fact memories may be more dependent on this hypothetical cortical process because they differ from typical episodic memories in that they have usually received repeated rehearsals over long periods of time. However, this is not a critical difference between fact and episodic memory, and, as we all know, some episodic memories receive all too much rehearsal! These are the remembered personal episodes with which the local bore repeatedly regales us. But most people have some personal episodes which they have mulled over many times over the years. The children studied by Vargha-Khadem and her colleagues, and Kapur's mammillary body patient may all show episodic memory within normal limits on tests of recall for such well rehearsed episodes (like some holidays perhaps) even when ceiling effects do not confound interpretation. It remains to be shown whether similar effects are found at long delays when appropriately matched fact and episodic memories are compared. My suspicion is that they will be because the relevant distinction is not between semantic and episodic memory, but between fast and slow learning mechanisms.

The third reason for doubting the suggestion is a general one, which relates to what functional deficits underlie amnesia. I will argue that the evidence does not suggest that amnesia is a breakdown that separates fact and episode memory. A view that now has strong support is that organic amnesia is a syndrome comprising several different kinds of functional deficit, each with its own anatomy. A distinction that is commonly made is between the effects of damage to the extended hippocampal system (hippocampus, fornix, mammillary bodies, anterior thalamus, and possibly other structures which complete the Papez circuit) and the effects of damage to the perirhinal cortex and its projection site in the thalamus, the dorsomedial nucleus of the thalamus, and possibly its frontal projection site, the orbitofrontal cortex. In humans, a meta-analysis by Aggleton and Shaw (1996) suggested that selective damage to the extended hippocampal system impairs free recall as much as is found in more extensively lesioned patients, but seems to cause little or no deficit in item forced-choice recognition. In contrast, patients with damage to the perirhinal cortex always show very impaired item recognition although the effect of selective perirhinal lesions has not been shown because such lesions occur rarely or never in humans. In animals, however, there is some evidence that there is a double dissociation between the effects of perirhinal and extended hippocampal system damage. For example, in monkeys, Gaffan (1994) has shown that fornix lesions disrupted performance on certain spatial memory tasks whereas perirhinal lesions had no effect. In contrast, he found that perirhinal lesions disrupted visual scene recognition whereas fornix lesions had little effect. In rats, Ennaceur *et al.* (1996) found similar effects with fornix lesions disrupting spatial memory and perirhinal lesions having no apparent effect, whereas only the perirhinal lesions disrupted object recognition. If these findings are reliable, it would seem that although the perirhinal region provides a major input to the hippocampus, the extended perirhinal and hippocampal systems can work, to some degree, independently in mediating complex memory.

What do these two interlinked sets of structures do that is so important for complex memory? Although perirhinal lesions may disrupt item and simple association memory, it is unclear exactly what the perirhinal system does. Nevertheless, it is generally agreed that lesions to this system disrupt the learning and retention of facts as well as episodes. As the focus of this discussion is whether there is a lesion that selectively disrupts episodic memory, I shall concentrate on the nature of the memory disturbance produced by damage to the extended hippocampal system. The dominant view is that lesions to this system disrupt storage of associations between components of information that are represented neocortically (e.g. Teyler and Discenna 1986; Squire and Alvarez 1995; Cohen *et al.* 1997; Mayes 1995). Normally, during retrieval, components of the associative memory are re-encoded and then via the hippocampus reactivate the whole memory which is represented in different parts of the association neocortex. If Squire and Alvarez (1995) are correct, the associations are eventually stored in the neocortex so that the hippocampus is no longer needed. It remains unresolved whether the extended hippocampal system at least temporarily stores all the kinds of association of which fact and episode memory are constituted, or just a subset of these memories. Vargha-Khadem *et al.*'s (1997) results suggest that their patients were only impaired at recognition of object–location and face–voice associations and at free recall (of unspecified kinds of association), but showed normal recognition memory for face–face and non-word–non-word associations as well as for single items.

This preliminary result may not be confirmed by future work on similar patients, but if it is correct, it sits very uneasily with the authors' wish to say that their patients have normal semantic memory. Much semantic memory is for complex associations, which include those between faces and voices, and objects and places. The implication is that semantic memory for these kinds of association must depend on the hippocampus until the memory is reorganized. This will not occur in Vargha-Khadem *et al.*'s patients, so very long-term memory for such associations should be very impaired. The long-term deficit should apply to both episodic and semantic memory when these depend on the affected kinds of association.

There is, in my view, therefore, no good evidence that semantic and episodic memory involve different processes. Rather, they seem to use similar brain mechanisms and processes to retrieve memory for overlapping but not completely identical kinds of information. Their mediation must involve some non-overlapping brain regions (as only episodic memory involves the representation of personally experienced episodes), but this is insufficient to prove the existence of distinct processes, and, therefore, systems. For those who wish to postulate separate systems for verbal and non-verbal memory, the same point applies. Neuropsychological dissociations occur between these two kinds of memory (see Mayes 1988), but probably merely show that representing different kinds of information involves distinct brain regions. What seems most likely is that left and right sides of the structures disrupted in amnesics normally perform the same processes on different kinds of information. Unless representation of these kinds of information is performed in radically distinct ways, there is no reason to postulate separate systems.

In their chapter, Roediger and his colleagues suggest that there may be no lesser a reason for postulating that recognition and recall are different memory systems than there is for popular distinctions such as that between explicit and implicit memory. In fact, there is. One needs to specify what kinds of information recall and recognition are for, and this may be hard because even when the nominal targets are the same, the information being retrieved may be very different. For example, there is good evidence that organized word list recall is typically of associations between words whereas recognition words from a list is typically much less dependent on retrieving associations between the words and more dependent on retrieving single items (e.g. Bruce and Fagan 1970). However, as was done by Vargha-Khadem *et al.* (1997), recognition tests can be devised for associations.

In brief, in Sherry and Schacter's (1987) terms, systems are defined in terms of the kind of information being remembered. If recall and recognition of facts and episodes constitute different systems, then it first has to be shown that they necessarily involve retrieval of different kinds of fact and event information (which given what has just been said is unlikely), and then it has to be shown that dissociations must be explained in terms of qualitative differences in the processes used. My suspicion is that if double dissociations between item recognition and 'associative' recall could be shown, they would also be found when associative recognition tests are substituted for recall. In other words, the dissociation is not related specifically to recall, but to the kind of information being remembered. It remains to be shown whether recall and recognition of the *same* kinds of information involve different kinds of processes.

I shall now return briefly to the problem, raised in the section on short-term memory, of whether the evidence that many amnesics have normal short-term or working memory (Cave and Squire 1992) contradicts the principle that information is stored where it is represented. There are two resolutions of this problem, both of which allow one to maintain the essence of this very useful and plausible principle. First, it may be that long-term memory for things like phonological sequences, although nominally for the same information as short-term memory, actually involves the retrieval of complex associations between the sequences and the context in which they were experienced whereas short-term memory merely involves retrieval of the phonological sequences. The retrieval of item–context associations would be represented in additional brain regions to those used for representing the phonological sequences. As indicated before, identifying the information retrieved in a memory task is not easy, and as yet no-one has specified clear principles for achieving this. The second resolution is that the anatomical long-term memory system stores markers (see Teyler and Discenna 1986) which enable the same information that is retrieved from short-term memory to be activated in the identical neocortical representing sites. Short-term memory does not require this because the representing site retains some level of activity from initial encoding. If Squire and Alvarez (1995) are correct in their view that eventually the storage of facts and episodes is mediated neocortically, then this resolution of the problem carries the implication that memory of very practised phonological sequences will be disrupted by exactly the same lesions that impair phonological short-term memory.

The final implication that I wish to draw from the framework outlined in the previous section is that one should be very careful before identifying perceptual, conceptual, or any other kind of ISIM as a distinct system from explicit memory of either facts or events. This is because the framework suggests that enhanced fluency in reactivating specific kinds of information (ISIM) is a necessary process together with memory attribution, and, often, active search for producing aware (explicit) memory for the same information. As enhanced fluency is likely to depend on readier reactivation of the representing neural network, it should be mediated by the representing neurons themselves. It seems less likely that memory attribution will be mediated by the representing neurons. This suggests another view of the function of the extended hippocampal system to the one that is popularly given. The popular view is that the hippocampus at least temporarily stores explicit (aware) memory for events and possibly facts (e.g. Squire *et al.* 1993). Instead, if the above account is correct, then the hippocampal system may simply store associations of certain kinds. Whether these lead to unaware or aware memory will depend on whether the conditions for triggering memory attribution in a brain region that has not yet been identified are met.

This view can be tested by appropriate use of neuroimaging procedures. As single-trial averaging procedures are now being developed for fMRI (e.g. Josephs *et al.* 1997), it may soon be possible to compare conditions where memories of object–location associations are reactivated with enhanced fluency, but without aware memory, and conditions where aware memory is present as well. With the former condition, one might expect to see reduced activation of the hippocampus compared with when old spatial associations are reactivated without enhanced fluency. With the latter condition, other brain regions responsible for attributions of aware memory may be activated. The view also predicts that hippocampal lesions will disrupt ISIM as well as explicit memory for spatial and perhaps some other kinds of associations. Interestingly, impaired amnesic performance on indirect memory tasks that tap memory for novel associative information is often found (e.g. Curran 1997) although it is currently very hard to show that this reflects an amnesic deficit in ISIM for associations rather than the more effective use by control subjects of intentional retrieval strategies (e.g. McKone and Slee 1997).

One of the implications of the above suggestion that extended hippocampal system lesions, and perhaps amnesia in general, involve disruptions of both unaware and aware memory is that the distinction between explicit and implicit memory may not be as radical as many have supposed (see Schacter and Tulving 1994a passim). It has been said that explicit memory often, but not always, involves active search whereas there is no good evidence that ISIM ever does. In everyday life, active search is not always needed for explicit memory because retrieval sometimes results as an automatic consequence from cues that have been incidentally encoded during ongoing processing. There is also evidence that familiarity is always dependent on an automatic retrieval process, and as familiarity should be regarded as a form of explicit memory, ISIM may well share this feature with at least one kind of explicit memory.

Even if the memory system supported by the extended hippocampal system is distinct from the one that supports other forms of non-declarative or implicit memory, such as motoric classical conditioning, the way these systems interact may have been misdescribed. It is well known that cerebellar lesions in humans as well as animals disrupt this form of conditioning, but leave semantic and episodic memory intact (e.g. Daum et al. 1993). In contrast, hippocampal or medial temporal lobe lesions have no effect either on simple delay tone–airpuff conditioning or on two-tone discriminative conditioning (see Daum and Schugens 1995). However, the hippocampus does monitor what is going on during conditioning, and hippocampal lesions in animals abolish the normal decrement in conditioned responses that occurs when the conditioned stimuli are presented in a new background context (e.g. Honey and Good 1993). Similarly, Daum and Schugens (in press) have shown that amnesics, who probably had damage to the extended hippocampal system, unlike control subjects, failed to show reversal of discriminative classical conditioning although they acquired the initial discrimination normally. The usual interpretation of these effects is that the normal hippocampal modulation involves the mediation of conditioning by aware memory of the context or other aspects of the conditioning situation. It is supposed that such aware memory mediation is important for more complex conditioning phenomena to occur normally. It is far from clear, however, that awareness of relevant contingencies is either necessary or sufficient for conditioning to occur (see Daum and Schugens 1995). This possibility needs to be properly assessed, but if true, it would mean that some complex types of classical conditioning depend on the use of memory for *kinds of information supported by the hippocampus* (for example spatial context) for which there may be no aware memory. The critical information modulates performance via a two-way interaction between the hippocampus and cerebellum. On this view, the extended hippocampal system supports memory for certain kinds of association, which can be used either to produce aware memories (declarative or explicit memory) or unaware memories (non-declarative, procedural, or implicit memory).

The distinction between declarative/explicit memory and non-declarative/procedural/implicit memory is a messy one. There is no dispute that the two kinds of memory depend on somewhat different brain regions and often involve memory for different kinds of information. What is less clear is whether they are mediated by different kinds of process. Cohen et al. (1997) have recently argued that the two kinds of memory do differ with respect to both compositionality (that the components of a complex thing are represented as well as the thing itself) and flexibility (the memories are not tied to a specific context) so that only declarative memory shows the properties. This would be strong support for different kinds of process mediating the two kinds of memory. Willingham (in press) has recently challenged both these claims and argues that procedural memory is often both compositional and flexible. If he is correct, then it remains unproved that there are any interesting kinds of processing difference between these two kinds of memory.

CONCLUSION

The basic message I want to convey is simple. The brain is a plastic system in the sense that as it processes information it also stores it by modifying the connectivity of at least some of the same neurons that are representing the processed information. As different kinds of information are represented in different neural regions, memory for those kinds of information will also be found in the corresponding brain regions. Functional and neuropsychological and other kinds of double dissociation should, therefore, be found between tests of memory for different kinds of information.

In our present state of ignorance, it is of some interest to know which are the brain regions that keep the stored representations for different kinds of information. However, there are at least three further and deeper questions to which it is vital to learn the answers. The approach that is concerned with identifying how many different memory systems there are focuses attention only on the first of these questions. This question is whether memory for the different kinds of information is mediated by qualitatively distinct kinds of process. This is not established by functional and neuropsychological double dissociations. At present, only guidelines are available which suggest that qualitative processing differences may be present. What is most heuristically valuable is identifying the kinds of process that mediate memory for different kinds of information. In order to do this with confidence, we need to clarify the concept of process, perhaps by developing Marr's (1982) notion of particular kinds of algorithmic or other operation carried out on particular kinds of representation, and use this to specify criteria, not guidelines, for identifying specific kinds of process. Although there are currently no good criteria for distinguishing between processes, it is, in my view, highly probable that memory for some kinds of information is mediated by distinct processes from memory for other kinds of information. For example, active search processes may not be used for most, if not all, kinds of implicit (including ISIM) or non-declarative memory whereas they are often used in order to produce fact or event memories.

The second question that is strangely sidestepped by the memory systems approach is whether any processes are optionally used to retrieve the same kinds of information. Reference to this has already been made in pointing out that active search processes need not always be used to retrieve complex episodic or semantic memories. It remains to be seen whether similar phenomena occur with non-aware forms of memory.

The third question, which in my view is central to the understanding of memory, concerns the storage processes used by neurons to hold information for different periods of time, and whether these are different for any different kinds of information. To maintain focus on this and the second question, one would have to modify the notion of memory system so that different memory systems could be identified either by their use of different algorithmic transformation processes for their representations or by their use of different kinds of neuronal (implementational) processes to store these representations. Unless one argues that any given memory system of this kind may use different physiological and biochemical processes to store their representations for different periods of time, one would also have to modify the notion of a memory system further to allow that two distinct systems could support the retrieval of the same kind of information for different durations. I am proposing that the concept of memory system should be used so that there are two systems even when they retrieve the same kind of information provided they use qualitatively distinct implementational and algorithmic/representational processes. The stress should be on the different processes (in the broad sense) that underlie memory, which brain structures mediate them, and, in the long run, how they do so.

The framework of four kinds of process or mechanism underlying long-term memory, considered earlier, offers a processing approach to questions about putatively different kinds of memory system. Use of such an approach suggests modifications to common beliefs, such as that ISIM and explicit memory are different memory systems. It also suggests that identifying whether processes like memory attribution, enhanced fluency, and active search are or are not required in order to show memory for different kinds of information is a good way of determining whether distinct memory systems are present. Future work will be assisted by even fancier technology than we have now. This will not be enough to solve the difficult problem of determining how memory for different kinds of information is mediated. For that, we will need to use and develop a theoretical framework of memory processes of which the four-mechanism framework is an initial crude example.

REFERENCES

Abel, T., Alberini, C., Ghirardi, M., Huang, Y.-Y., Nguyen, P., and Kandel, E. R. (1995). Steps toward a molecular definition of memory consolidation. In *Memory distortion* (ed. D. L. Schacter), pp.298–328. Harvard University Press, Cambridge, MA.

Aggleton, J. P. and Shaw, C. (1996). Amnesia and recognition memory: a reanalysis of psychometric data. *Neuropsychologia*, **34**, 51–62.

Baddeley, A. D. (1986). *Working memory*. Clarendon, Oxford.

Baddeley, A. D., Papagno, C., and Vallar, G. (1988). When long-term learning depends on short-term storage. *Journal of Memory and Language*, **27**, 586–95.

Blaxton, T. A. (1995). A process-based view of memory. *Journal of the International Neuropsychological Society*, **1**, 112–14.

Brown, M. W. (1996). Neuronal responses and recognition memory. *Seminars in the Neurosciences*, **8**, 23–32.

Bruce, D. and Fagan, R. L. (1970). More on the recognition and free recall of organized lists. *Journal of Experimental Psychology*, **85**, 153–4.

Cave, C. B. and Squire, L. R. (1992). Intact verbal and nonverbal short-term memory following damage to the human hippocampus. *Hippocampus*, **2**, 151–64.

Cohen, D. and Smith, E. E. (1997). Response. *Trends in Cognitive Sciences*, **1**, 126–7.

Cohen, N. J., Poldrack, R. A., and Eichenbaum, H. (1997). Memory for items and memory for relations in the procedural/declarative memory framework. *Memory*, **5**, 131–78.

Courtney, S. M., Ungerleider, L. G., and Haxby, J. V. (1997). Response. *Trends in Cognitive Sciences*, **1**, 125–6.

Curran, T. (1997). Higher-order associative learning in amnesia: evidence from the serial reaction time task. *Journal of Cognitive Neuroscience*, **9**, 522–33.

Dale, H. C. A. and Gregory, M. (1966). Evidence of semantic encoding in short-term memory. *Psychonomic Science*, **5**, 153–4.

Daum, I. and Schugens, M. M. (1995). Classical conditioning after brain lesions in humans: the contribution to neuropsychology. *Journal of Psychophysiology*, **9**, 109–18.

Daum, I. and Schugens, M. M. Impairment of eyeblink discrimination reversal learning in amnesia. *Society for Neuroscience Abstracts*. (In Press.)

Daum, I., Schugens, M. M., Ackermann, H., Lutzenberger, W., Dichgans, J., and Birbaumer, N. (1993). Classical conditioning after cerebellar lesions in humans. *Behavioral Neuroscience*, **107**, 748–56.

Demb, J. B., Desmond, J. E., Wagner, A. D., Vaidya, C. J., Glover, G. H., and Gabrieli, J. D. E. (1995). Semantic encoding and retrieval in the left inferior prefrontal cortex: a functional MRI study of task difficulty and process specificity. *Journal of Neuroscience*, **15**, 5870–8.

DeZazzo, J. and Tully, T. (1995). Dissection of memory formation: from behavioral pharmacology to molecular genetics. *Trends in Neurosciences*, **18**, 212–18.

Ennaceur, A., Neave, N., and Aggleton, J. P. (1996). Neurotoxic lesions of the perirhinal cortex do not mimic the behavioural effects of fornix transection in the rat. *Behavioral Brain Research*, **80**, 9–25.

Farah, M. (1994). Neuropsychological inference with an interactive brain: a critique of the 'locality' assumption. *Behavioural and Brain Sciences*, **17** (1), 43–61.

Gabrieli, J. D. E. (1995). A systematic view of human memory processes. *Journal of the International Neuropsychological Society*, **1**, 115–18.

Gabrieli, J. D. E., Cohen, N. J., and Corkin, S. (1988). The impaired learning of semantic knowledge following bilateral medial temporal-lobe resection. *Brain and Cognition*, **7**, 525–39.

Gaffan, D. (1994). Dissociated effects of perirhinal cortex ablation, fornix transection and amygdalectomy: evidence for multiple memory systems in the primate temporal lobe. *Experimental Brain Research*, **99**, 411–22.

Gillund, G. and Shiffrin, R. M. (1984). A retrieval model for both recognition and recall. *Psychological Review*, **91**, 1–67.

Gluck, M. A. and Granger, R. (1993). Computational models of the neural bases of learning and memory. *Annual Review of Neuroscience*, **16**, 667–706.

Gluck, M. A., Ermita, B. R., Oliver, L. M., and Myers, C. E. (1997). Extending models of hippocampal function in animal conditioning to human amnesia. *Memory*, **5**, 179–212.

Graham, K. S. and Hodges, J. R. (1997). Differentiating the roles of the hippocampal complex and the neocortex in long-term memory storage: evidence from the study of semantic dementia. *Neuropsychology*, **11**, 77–89.

Honey, R. and Good, M. (1993). Selective hippocampal lesions abolish the contextual specificity of latent inhibition and conditioning. *Behavioral Neuroscience*, **107**, 23–33.

Hayman, C. A. G. and Tulving, E. (1989). Is priming a fragment completion based on a 'traceless' memory system? *Journal of Experimental Psychology: Learning, Memory, and Cognition*, **14**, 941–56.

Hintzman, D. L. and Hartry, A. L. (1990). Item effects in recognition and fragment completion: contingency relations vary for different subsets of words. *Journal of Experimental Psychology: Learning, Memory, and Cognition*, **16**, 955–69.

Jacoby, L. L. and Dallas, M. (1981). On the relationship between autobiographical memory and perceptual learning. *Journal of Experimental Psychology: General*, **110**, 306–40.

Jacoby, L. L. and Kelley, C. M. (1992). Unconscious influences of memory: Dissociations and automaticity. In *The neuropsychology of consciousness*, (ed. A. D. Milner and M. D. Rugg), pp.201–34. Academic, New York.

Jacoby, L. L. and Whitehouse, K. (1989). An illusion of memory: false recognition influenced by unconscious perception. *Journal of Experimental Psychology: General*, **118**, 126–35.

Jacoby, L. L. and Witherspoon, D. (1989). An illusion of memory: false recognition influenced by unconscious perception. *Journal of Experimental Psychology: General*, **118**, 126–35.

Jacoby, L. L. and Witherspoon, D. (1992). Remembering without awareness. *Canadian Journal of Psychology*, **36**, 300–24.

Jacoby, L. L., Kelley, C. M., and Dywan, J. (1989a). Memory attributions. In *Varieties of memory and consciousness: essays in honour of Endel Tulving*, (ed. H. L. Roediger III and F. I. M. Craik), pp.391–422. Erlbaum, Hillsdale, NJ.

Jacoby, L. L., Woloshyn, V., and Kelley, C. M. (1989b). Becoming famous without being recognized: unconscious influences of memory produced by dividing attention. *Journal of Experimental Psychology: General*, **118**, 115–25.

Jonides, J., Smith, E. E., Koeppe, R. A., Awh, E., Minoshima, S., and Mintun, M. A. (1993). Spatial working memory in humans as revealed by PET. *Nature*, **363**, 623–5.

Josephs, O., Turner, R., and Friston, K. (1997). Event-related fMRI. *Human Brain Mapping*, **5**, 1–6.

Kaas, J. H. (1997). Functional plasticity in adult cortex. *Seminars in Neurscience*, **9**, 1.

Kapur, N. (1994). Remembering Norman Schwarzkopf: evidence for two distinct long-term fact learning mechanisms. *Cognitive Neuropsychology*, **11**, 661–70.

Luria, A. R. (1973). *The working brain: an introduction to neuropsychology*. Penguin, Harmondsworth.

Marr, D. (1982). *Vision*. Freeman, San Francisco.

Martin, A., Lalonde, F. M., Wiggs, C. L., Weisberg, J., Ungerleider, L. G., and Haxby, J. V. (1995). Repeated presentation of objects reduces activity in verntral occipitotemporal cortex: an MRI study of repetition priming. *Society for Neuroscience Abstracts*, **21**, 1497.

Mayes, A. R. (1983). Human and animal memory: some basic questions. In *Memory in humans and animals*, (ed. A. R. Mayes), pp.1–19. Van Nostrand Reinhold, Wokingham.

Mayes, A. R. (1988). *Human organic memory disorders*. Cambridge University Press.

Mayes, A. R. (1995). Memory and amnesia. *Behavioral Brain Research*, **66**, 29–36.

McCarthy, R. A. and Warrington, E. K. (1990). *Cognitive neuropsychology*. Academic, San Diego.

McKone, E. and Slee, J. A. (1997). Explicit contamination in 'implicit' memory for new associations. *Memory and Cognition*, **25**, 352–66.

Metcalfe, J. (1997). Predicting syndromes of amnesia from a composite holographic associative recall/recognition model (CHARM). *Memory*, **5**, 233–53.

Moscovitch, M. (1994). Memory and working with memory: evaluation of a component process model and comparisons with other models. In *Memory systems 1994*, (ed. D. L. Schacter and E. Tulving), pp.269–310. MIT Press, Cambridge, MA.

Moscovitch, M. (1995). Recovered consciousness: a hypothesis concerning modularity and episodic memory. *Journal of Clinical and Experimental Neuropsychology*, **17**, 276–90.

Nadel, L. (1994). Multiple memory systems: what and why, an update. In *Memory systems 1994*, (ed. D. L. Schacter and E. Tulving), pp.39–63. MIT Press, Cambridge, MA.

Nyberg, L. and Tulving, E. (1996). Classifying human long-term memory: evidence from converging dissociations. *European Journal of Cognitive Psychology*, **8**, 163–83.

Nyberg, L., Cabeza, R., and Tulving, E. (1996). PET studies of encoding and retrieval: the HERA model. *Psychonomic Bulletin and Review*, **3**, 135–48.

Owen, A. M. (1997). Tuning in to the temporal dynamics of brain activation using functional magnetic resonance imaging (fMRI). *Trends in Cognitive Sciences*, **1**, 123–5.

Patterson, K. and Hodges, J. (1995). Disorders of semantic memory. In *Handbook of memory disorders*, (ed. A. D. Baddeley, B. Wilson and F. N. Watts), pp.167–86. Wiley, Chichester.

Paulescu, E., Frith, C. D., and Frackowiak, R. S. J. (1993). The neural correlates of the verbal component of working memory. *Nature*, **362**, 342–5.

Rajaram, S. (1993). Remembering and knowing: two means of access to the personal past. *Memory and Cognition*, **21**, 89–112.

Schacter, D. L. and Tulving, E. (1994*a*). What are the memory systems of 1994? In *Memory systems 1994* (ed. D. L. Schacter and E. Tulving), pp.1–38. MIT Press, Cambridge, MA.

Schacter, D. L. and Tulving, E. (ed.) (1994*b*). *Memory systems 1994*. MIT Press, Cambridge, MA.

Shanks, D. R. (1997). Dissociating long-term memory systems: comment on Nyberg and Tulving (1996). *European Journal of Cognitive Psychology*, **9**, 111–20.

Sherry, D. F. and Schacter, D. L. (1987). The evolution of multiple memory systems. *Psychological Review*, **99**, 195–231.

Squire, L. R. and Alvarez, P. (1995). Retrograde amnesia and memory consolidation: a neurobiological perspective. *Current Opinion in Neurobiology*, **5**, 169–77.

Squire, L. R., Knowlton, B., and Musen, G. (1993). The structure and organization of memory. *Annual Review of Psychology*, **44**, 453–95.

Teyler, T. J. and Discenna, P. (1986). The hippocampal memory indexing theory. *Behavioral Neuroscience*, **100**, 147–54.

Tulving, E. (1983). *Elements of episodic memory*. Oxford University Press.

Ungerleider, L. G. (1995). Functional brain imaging studies of cortical mechanisms for memory. *Science*, **270**, 769–75.

Vargha-Khadem, F., Gadian, D. G., Watkins, K. E., Connelly, A., Van Paesschen, W. and Mishkin, M. (1997). Differential effects of early hippocampal pathology on episodic and semantic memory. *Science*, **277**, 376–80.

Vallar, G. and Papagno, C. (1995). Neuropsychological impairments of short-term memory. In *Handbook of memory disorders*, (ed. A. D. Baddeley and B. A. Wilson), pp. 135–65. Wiley, Chichester.

Warrington, E. K. and Shallice, T. (1984). Category specific semantic impairments. *Brain*, **107**, 829–55.

Wickelgren, W. A. (1974). Single-trace fragility theory of memory dynamics. *Memory and Cognition*, **2**, 775–80.

Wiggs, C. L., Weisberg, J., Garber, S., and Martin, A. (1996). Brain regions associated with semantic and episodic memory. *Neuroimage*, **3**, 568.

Willingham, D. B. What differentiates declarative and procedural memories: reply to Cohen, Poldrack and Eichenbaum (1997). *Memory*. (In Press.)

7

The memory chop shop: issues in the search for memory systems

MARY SUSAN WELDON

The standard psychology building provides an interesting mirror of psychologists' view of the human being. The human is carved up and distributed throughout the building: the first floor might contain phobias and addictions, the second floor might house childhoods, the third floor a variety of cognitive processes, and the fourth floor a social world. Emotions or motivations might be given a lab somewhere, or they might not, depending on the decade. We tell ourselves that it is only of necessity that we divide the human in this manner—the system is simply too complicated to study in an integrated fashion. But what view of the human does this dissection create? What does it mean when scientists treat the components of the human system as if they are independent of one another, when components are dropped in or out of the human as is fashionable or convenient?

Memory has been treated in a similar fashion. Assorted kinds of memory are strewn throughout various laboratories, with procedural memory in one, semantic memory in another, memory for faces somewhere else, and conscious and unconscious memory divided up elsewhere. Although the idea that memory may comprise more than one system is not new, recent developments in behavioural research and neuroimaging appear to have given unprecedented impetus to the idea that there are qualitatively different kinds of memory, that each is associated with unique brain structures, and that the number of possible memory systems to be discovered is limited only by one's time on the fMRI machine.

The goal of this book is to address the question of whether memory is unitary or comprised of multiple systems, and I have been assigned the task of arguing against the systems view and in favour of the unitary view. But given the widespread, almost unquestioning acceptance of the idea that memory is composed of multiple systems, arguing for a unitary view of memory at this time seems akin to arguing for a geocentric theory of planetary motion. Further, it is not at all clear what it would mean to say that memory is unitary, any more than to say memory is comprised of multiple systems, since neither concept is well defined. So instead of arguing for a unitary view of memory, I will address some problems with many current approaches to delineating memory systems, and challenge the prevalent assumption that the concept of multiple systems is the necessary or best alternative to the unitary view.

THE LOGIC OF THE COGNITIVE NEUROSCIENCE APPROACH

Whenever investigators have discovered dissociations between memory tests, the question usually arises as to whether different memory systems subserve performance on the tests. For example, dissociations between the recency and asymptotic portions of the serial position curve were interpreted as support for a distinction between the short-term and long-term memory stores (Atkinson and Shiffrin 1968), dissociations between semantic and episodic memory tests as evidence of a distinction between semantic and episodic memory systems (Tulving 1972), and dissociations between implicit and explicit tests as evidence for two systems which have been characterized in a variety of ways (see Schacter and Tulving 1994a). (An interesting exception is that dissociations between recognition and recall tests did not lead to the postulation of the recognition and recall memory systems.) More recently, investigators have become quite skilled at producing dissociations, and nearly everyone now agrees that if task dissociations were the only criteria for postulating separate systems, memory systems would multiply beyond sense (Roediger 1990).

Schacter (1992) has therefore suggested that multiple sources of converging data must point to the existence of multiple systems. He recommends adopting a *cognitive neuroscience* approach in which evidence from functional dissociations, brain lesion studies, neuroimaging studies, and non-human primates converge to suggest the existence of a distinct memory system. This certainly seems to suggest reasonable criteria for postulating multiple memory systems, but on close examination even these criteria do not provide sufficient constraints on determining what evidence is necessary to postulate the existence of a memory system. First, the criteria do not provide clear operational definitions indicating what empirically observable conditions must be met to designate a memory system. Second, a variety of problems exist with the logic and assumptions underlying efforts to link behavioural data with brain functions and structures. Finally, evidence derived from brain lesion and neuroimaging studies presents special inferential difficulties. This chapter examines these problems as they relate to attempts to discover memory systems (see summary in Table 7.1), suggests that this approach to characterizing non-unitary memory needs to be reconceptualized, and briefly suggests approaches that may be fruitful in understanding the relation between memory processes and brain functions.

CHARACTERIZING A MEMORY SYSTEM

One of the most difficult issues for the multiple-system view of memory is how to define a system. To determine whether memory is composed of multiple systems, one must have a clear idea of just what criteria must be met to designate a memory system (Roediger *et al.* 1990).

Table 7.1 Summary of issues and problems in the demarcation and localization of memory systems

1. Reconciling the architecture of functional cognitive models with the actual properties of the brain
2. Mapping relations among the levels of description: functional, algorithmic, implementational
   a. Clearly specifying the level of description
   b. Determining the appropriate grain and units of analysis at each level of description
   c. Determining whether the elements, organization, and vocabulary used at one level are appropriate for a different level
3. Determining the operational criteria for defining a system (operational definition)
4. Accounting for many-to-one and one-to-many mappings between neural units and functions
5. Determining the actual function of the brain locus in the memory process of interest
   a. Necessity versus sufficiency of the locus
6. Process purity: all tasks involve multiple cognitive functions, making separation of functions difficult.
7. Determining the units of analysis that should be employed to distinguish one system from another
   a. At the functional level: task? kinds of information? learning mechanism? behaviour?
   b. At the implementational level: anatomical features? Fibre paths? physiological changes? biochemical mechanisms?
8. Interpreting brain lesion data
   a. Determining the functional relation between a brain locus and a mental process
   b. Subtractive logic: removing one brain component may not leave the rest of the system intact.
   c. Generalizing from the functioning of the damaged brain to that of the intact brain
   d. Lesion studies may exaggerate the independence of intact cognitive functions.
   e. Interpreting recovery of function after brain damage: neurological repair versus learning new task strategies
   f. Hot-spot approach may exaggerate apparent importance, size, and specificity of localized function.
9. Interpreting brain-imaging data
   a. Paired-image subtraction and subtractive logic: assuming that task components can be inserted and subtracted independently (assumptions of additivity, pure insertion, and serial processing)
   b. Selecting an appropriate control task
   c. Disentangling changes in levels of activation that are due to the addition or subtraction of processes of interest, from those due to concomitant changes in strategy, attention, difficulty, modality, etc.
   d. Small differences in tasks can produce large differences in neuroimaging results.
   e. Valid statistical criteria for determining whether differences in levels of activation are functionally significant
   f. Applying the same statistical criteria to all brain regions, regardless of possible differences in neural and vascular density, thresholds for synaptic transmission,

efficiency of connectivity, haemodynamic response functions, or the degree to which the mental functions are highly distributed versus relatively localized
   g. Interpreting differences in levels of activation, which is not evidence for unique or specific involvement of a brain locus in two different tasks or systems
   h. Interpreting the *lack* of differences in activation in brain loci in two tasks: is the area critical in both tasks, or unimportant?
   i. Standardizing brain images to correct for individual differences in brain anatomy and activation levels may introduce artifacts in pinpointing brain loci and measuring differences in activation.
   j. The time course of metabolic changes lags behind behavioural and neurological activity
   k. Specifying the functional role of neurons; interpreting increases versus decreases in activation; interpreting activation versus inhibition
   l. Highly distributed functions can diffuse signal strength and be difficult to detect
   m. Assumption that brain location is the critical defining feature of a memory system
   n. Interpreting discrepancies between lesion and neuroimaging data
10. Evolutionary arguments currently are *post hoc* and lack testable hypotheses
11. Bias in task selection emphasizes the study of dissociable tasks, which may exaggerate the independence of memory processes
12. Need to account for the integration of memory with other cognitive processes

One might think it satisfactory to use the term 'system' in a loose fashion. People refer to many things as systems—such as the educational system, the highway system, or the cardiovascular system—without worrying too much about their precise features, such as whether they are modular, independent, uniquely dedicated, or clearly bounded. For example, the cardiovascular system is intimately intertwined with all aspects of human physiological structures and function, to the extent that if the cardiovascular system fails all other physiological systems die, yet there does not seem to be a lot of angst about referring to cardiovascular structures and functions as a system (at least, not to my knowledge). So why does it seem so difficult to settle on a taxonomy of memory systems?

The problem can be traced at least to Descartes' dualism in which he drew a sharp distinction between mind and body. Historically psychologists have been able to theorize about mind without paying much attention to the neurological substrate, and neurologists have been able to study the nervous system without needing to account for how its anatomical and physiological features gave rise to the complex aspects of mental life. This is not to say that there was no interest in the connections between the mental and physical, but merely that the two ventures could proceed quite successfully despite enormous gaps in understanding their interrelations. But recently numerous factors, mainly technological advances in neuroimaging, have enabled investigators to say much more about the mind–body relation, and so the interdisciplinary venture of cognitive neuroscience is working to meld the two data bases. The problem is that the theories contributed by cognitive psychologists and neurologists tend to be specified at different levels of description. Cognitive psychologists have tended to work at the functional behavioural level, and neurologists at the physical level. However, there is no reason to assume that the functionally described cognitive systems will map onto the physically described brain system in a direct fashion. This is why the definition of a system is so critical in this domain, and so much more difficult than defining those physiological systems that do not entail mental expression.

How then is one to conceptualize a memory system? The effort to delineate memory systems depends heavily on how one relates cognition and brain, and in the remainder of this section some of the difficulties that arise in this effort are examined. Because current endeavours to differentiate memory systems depend so heavily on neuroanatomical evidence, the following arguments are based on the assumption that the goal of systems theorizing is to account for mnemonic activity in terms of brain functions and structures.

Models of cognition versus properties of brain

Consider the box-and-arrow model traditionally favoured in cognitive psychology. A familiar example is presented in Fig. 7.1. Such models have tended to assume

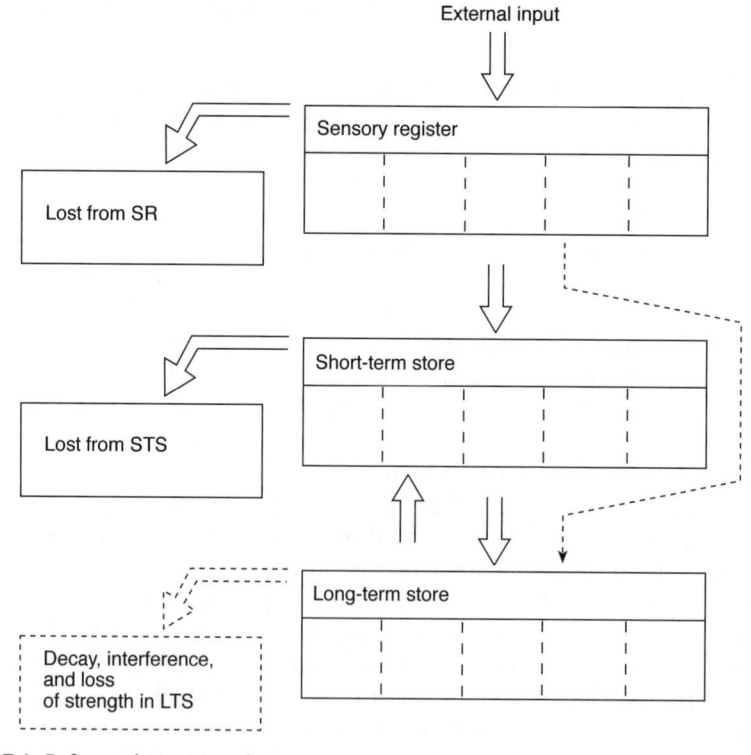

Fig. 7.1. Information-processing model depicting Atkinson and Shiffrin's hypothesized functional architecture of the stages of memory. (From Ellis and Hunt (1993, p.78) adapted from Atkinson and Shiffrin (1968), with permission.)

a few things. First, they are *sequential*. They start with an input from the environment, which is then processed through several successive stages, and which ultimately produces an output (mental product or behavioural response). There may be an occasional feedback loop, but overall input-to-output is unidirectional, or at least stepwise. Second, they are *hierarchical*. Processing proceeds from low-level analyses (e.g. sensation, perception), to mid- and high-level analyses (retrieval, decision). Third, they are *computational*. That is, an input is typically transformed into abstract codes or symbols which are transported through successive stages, each stage performing its computations and conveying the output to the next stage, like an assembly line.

This type of model lends itself rather easily to the concept of memory systems. First, the model in itself could be construed as representing a system, since it seems to stand alone and perform its duty in a relatively self-contained fashion. Second, the individual boxes that comprise the model, or subsets of paths and boxes, could also be construed as systems which perform specialized functions and then pass their results to another system. Conceptually this characterization of systems seems straightforward. That is, systems can be specified at a functional level, based on (1) theories about what kinds of mental computations need to be performed to accomplish certain behavioural outcomes, as well as (2) evidence for functional dissociations between the postulated systems (but see Dunn and Kirsner 1988; Farah 1994). Of course, until recently, it was not commonly believed that if one opened up the brain one would actually find the boxes and arrows delineated in such models, but the boxes and arrows captured the critical functions at an abstract level.

Now, consider approaching the question of brain function from a neurological standpoint. Early neuroanatomists carved up the brain in several different ways, such as by gross anatomical features (e.g. lobes and fissures), evolutionary age (old reptilian, limbic system, cortex (MacLean, 1949)), cytoarchitecture (cellular arrangements (e.g. Brodmann 1909)), and standard topological and functional zones (e.g. hippocampal formation, perirhinal area). Attempts were then made to link these topographical features with specific functions. Until recently, the standard model of brain function has embodied three concepts, roughly analogous to those that characterize cognitive models: (1) *sequential* flow of neural impulses; (2) *hierarchical* organization, with the cortex dominating the old brain and limbic system; and (3) *localizability* of mental and physical functions in discrete parts of the brain, with inputs and outputs (computations) passed from locus to another (Cytowic 1996). In neurocognitive theory, then, this model would lend itself quite easily to integration with the box-and-arrow models of cognitive psychology, since the assumptions and architectures of the models bear an obvious similarity to one another, and even encourage the idea that there could be a one-to-one mapping between functional cognitive models and neuroanatomical architecture, producing a coherent functional neurocognitive model.

More recently, however, the standard sequential hierarchical model of brain function has been replaced by one in which neural propagation is characterized as parallel, recursive, and multiplex (Cytowic 1996). Multiplexity refers to the fact that information is transmitted through the nervous system in multiple ways which include the familiar structures and mechanisms (neurons, neurotransmitters, synapses), but also include volume transmission (the action of hormones, peptides, and other chemicals through extracellular fluid), as well as the functioning of neurons with multiple possible outputs, such as neurons containing multiple neuromodulators (Nieuwenhuys 1985), or capable of different firing patterns (Huguenard *et al.* 1995), and even chaotic patterns of neural activity (Freeman 1991). This view of the brain challenges the standard model.

In this modern view, sequentiality is rejected because of the extensive recursivity between cortical and subcortical areas, and the presence of simultaneous activity across multiple brain sites. The standard hierarchical notion is rejected because the cortex is no longer recognized as the highest or most advanced level of processing. Instead, interconnections between cortical and subcortical areas are reciprocal, rendering them interdependent and interactive. Finally, psychological functions are not assumed to be localized in one-to-one mappings between function and brain locus, but instead are characterized as distributed networks, involving many-to-one mappings and one-to-many mappings. That is, a chunk of neural tissue may be involved in several different functions, and a function may be distributed over multiple areas. Evidence for chaotic activity during the perception of familiar stimuli (Freeman 1991) also suggests that traditional information-processing models cannot describe some fundamental brain processes.

With this more recent model of neurological activity, the marriage between cognitive models and neuroanatomy becomes much more difficult, and hence so does the effort to characterize a memory system. One cannot simply take a model (or operational definition) of a system at the functional level and assume that it characterizes the implementation at the neuronal level, because the properties of the two levels of description may not be the same.

Levels of description

In defining a memory system, then, one must first be careful to specify the level at which the model is operating. For example, Marr (1982) has distinguished between the *computational, representational/algorithmic*, and *implementational* levels of analysis. The computational level specifies the goals of the activity, that is, *what* functions need to be performed (computed) to accomplish the task; the algorithmic level specifies *how* these functions will be performed, that is, what are the representations for the input and output, and what is the algorithm for the computation; and the implementational level specifies the physical substrate of the representation and algorithm. (I will refer to Marr's computational level as the 'functional' level, to avoid theoretical commitments that may be associated with the term computational.) A description specified at one level may not map into another level in a straightforward fashion. As Marr expresses it, although the levels are coupled, each level only loosely constrains the others, and a wide choice of options is available at each level.

The importance of clearly specifying the level at which one is describing a cognitive system is illustrated in a recent debate in the literature. Farah (1994) demonstrated that a parallel distributed processing (PDP) framework can account for double dissociations between semantic memory for living and non-living things (e.g. Warrington and Shallice 1984; Warrington and McCarthy 1983). Therefore, she argued, the dissociation data did not demand an explanation in terms of specialized functional systems localized in the brain. However, Oaksford (1994) argued that locality was not refuted if localization was specified at the computational level, that is, in terms of the functional architecture of a box-and-arrow model. For example, in Fig. 7.2, someone who has difficulty naming and defining living things (e.g. animals, plants) may have impairment to a category-specific component of the semantic memory system (i.e. for living things), and so the deficit is 'localized' in this box. Thus, even if the functions engaged to identify living things are distributed at the algorithmic or implementational level, they *are* localized at the functional (computational) level. Thus, Oaksford claims, Farah's PDP model does *not* refute locality. Unfortunately, Oaksford's interpretation is not what theorists typically mean by localization of function, since locality is generally assumed to refer to where the function is implemented in the brain, not in the box-and-arrow representation. Nevertheless, the more general point raised by this debate is apt. The way that a system and its subsystems are specified at one level may not characterize their organization at another level; for example, a localized functional unit in a cognitive model may be widely distributed in its neurological implementation. In other words, the organization of cognitive tasks at the functional level may bear little resemblance to their organization and implementation within the neural substrate. Failure to address this issue contributes to confusion about how to define and identify memory systems.

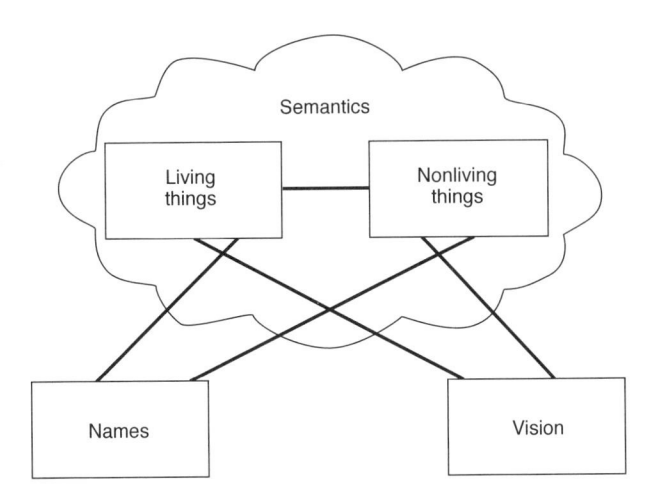

Fig. 7.2. Category-specific functional architecture for semantic memory. (From Farah (1994) with permission.)

Some current definitions of memory systems

Many attempts have been made to specify the requisite criteria for delineating a system (see examples in Table 7.2). One way in which they can loosely be distinguished is in terms of the stringency of the proposed criteria. At one extreme is the strong modularity view of Fodor (1983), who argued that a cognitive system must possess several properties to be considered modular, including: (1) *domain specificity*, that is, having specialized processors such that only a restricted class of stimulus features is processed; (2) *mandatory operation*, such that the operations are applied whenever the appropriate input is present; (3) *cognitive impenetrability*, such that central systems have restricted access to the modules' internal representations; (4) *information encapsulation*, such that processing is bottom-up and unaffected by feedback, beliefs, or expectations; and thus (5) *neural hard-wiring*, accepting only limited, privileged neural inputs.

Table 7.2 Definitions of systems

Authors	System
Fodor (1983)	Modularity includes domain specificity, mandatory operation, cognitive impenetrability, information encapsulation, neural hard-wiring, autonomous and not assembled
Tulving (1983)	Systems can operate independently of one another (although efficiency may be lost). The operation of systems can be enhanced or impaired independently. Systems are governed at least partially by different principles
Tulving (1985)	Systems are organized structures of more elementary operating components, consisting of a neural substrate and its behavioural or cognitive correlates. Different learning and memory situations involve different concatenations of components from one or more systems
Sherry and Schacter (1987)	Memory system: interaction among the component processes of acquisition, retention, and retrieval, characterized by certain rules of operation
	Multiple memory systems: systems characterized by fundamentally different rules of operation
	Functional incompatibility: the specialized functional problems each system handles cannot be handled by another system.
	Strong view: system is functionally autonomous, and component processes interact exclusively with one another. Different systems operate by different rules and share no component processes
	Weak view: component processes can interact with other processes outside the system. Different systems may share components, but the specific interactions among the processes define the system

Schacter and Tulving (1994b)	Three criteria: (1) class inclusion operations—a memory system can process any particular input or information of a specific kind; (2) properties and relations—properties include rules of operation, kind of information, and neural substrates; one or more statements about what the system is for; functional incompatibility; and (3) convergent dissociations (dissociations of different kinds, observed with different tasks in different populations using different techniques)
Squire (1994)	Forms (systems) of memory are different in terms of what kind of learning occurs in each case, what is stored as knowledge, and what brain systems are involved
Moscovitch (1994)	Memory modules are computational devices that have propositional content and satisfy all of the following criteria: domain specificity, informational encapsulation or cognitive impenetrability, and shallow output; essentially a stupid closed computational device that delivers its shallow output to interpretive central systems. Central systems give meaning and assign relevance to module output. None of the criteria of modularity apply to central systems. Central systems integrate information from superficially dissimilar domains and are open to top-down influences. Output is deep or meaningful and the interlevel representations that give rise to the final output may be available to consciousness
Nadel (1994)	Two criteria for a memory system: (1) computational differences in different neural architectures; and (2) length of time information is stored in them
Johnson and Chalfonte (1994)	Differences between subsystems: (1) initiation of processes (perceptual stimuli or more centrally generated); (2) learning with or without production of phenomenal experience of objects and events; (3) reflective processes that work with simple self-generated goals or between multiple goals or agendas

Fodor's (1985) concept of modularity seems impractical for defining memory systems for two reasons. First, although these properties may characterize some types of memory systems that have been proposed to exist (e.g. perhaps perceptual memory or classical conditioning systems), they certainly would not apply to all types of memory systems or functions that have been identified, particularly those involving the hippocampal circuit or the frontal lobe, or those labeled explicit or intentional retrieval. Second, Fodor drew a sharp distinction between modular systems and cognitive processes which are sensitive to beliefs and desires, and so Fodor himself would be unlikely to suggest that modularity could serve as a way to distinguish one type of memory from another, given that remembering is not usually informationally encapsulated. On the other hand, Moscovitch (1994) has adopted Fodor's distinction between modular and central systems, and has proposed that some kinds of retrieval are mediated primarily by modules (e.g. perceptual priming arises in perceptual input modules; recognition is mediated by the hippocampal module), whereas other types of remembering are mediated primarily by central systems that are sensitive to top-down influences and are not domain-specific, informationally encapsulated, or cognitively impenetrable (e.g. free recall is strategic and mediated by the frontal lobes).

Table 7.2 summarizes some of the other criteria that have been proposed to distinguish between memory subsystems. While these are not as stringent as Fodor's (1983) modularity, they do vary in the degree to which they require subsystems to be isolatable and independent. These definitions present a variety of interesting proposals for delineating subsystems, but several problems are apparent. Most notably, it is often not clear how one would determine whether the system met a particular criterion (i.e. what empirical observations must be made), and this is largely because the distinctions between levels of descriptions are not taken into account. For example, consider Schacter and Tulving's (1994b) requirement that systems must be described in terms (1) what they are for (function); (2) their rules of operation (algorithms); (3) their neural substrates (implementation); (4) the kind of information they process; (5) their relations to other systems; and (6) their functional incompatibility with other systems (Sherry and Schacter 1987). In terms of Marr's framework, items 1–3 map onto Marr's functional, algorithmic, and implementational level of description, respectively. And implicit in this set of criteria is the assumption that the organization and properties of a system described at one level will be coherently maintained as they are mapped through each of the other levels; that is, neurological systems are isomorphic with the functional categories of mental operations that are used by cognitive psychologists. But, as discussed above, current neurological theories of brain function do not correspond well with traditional cognitive box-and-arrow models. Thus, the assumption that a memory system can be simultaneously defined in terms of both its psychological function and neurological implementation has great paradigmatic significance. Yet, the viability and implications of this most fundamental assumption have not been seriously discussed or debated within the memory literature. Many other system definitions in Table 7.2 also seem to assume that a mapping between the functional and implementational levels is necessary to differentiate the systems, without questioning whether it is feasible or even realistic.

Mapping across levels of description

The problem of operationally defining memory systems raises several interesting questions. First, as implied above, one must ask if it is *possible* to map functional level systems isomorphically into implementational level systems. The answer is not clear. While recent technological advances in neuroimaging have certainly kindled optimism, and they have undeniably yielded many interesting hypotheses about the relation between brain and behaviour, one has to worry that the interpretation of neuroimaging results is exceeding the data. For example, while some functions do appear to be subserved by local specializations (e.g. sensory cortex, motor cortex, aspects of language production), it is not clear that similar principles hold for all or even many cognitive functions. In fact, the field of neurology has been very conservative about making any such claims. Morton (1984) has argued that the assumption of functional and anatomical modularity is unlikely to be justified for higher mental functions.

While most investigators concede that more than one brain structure may be necessary for the performance of a particular cognitive function, the problems with localization go beyond simply identifying the multiple locations. There is good evidence for the existence of brain loci that subserve multiple functions, as well functions that are distributed across multiple loci. To take an example from the literature on attention, a quite specific deficit such as hemispatial neglect can arise from cortical lesions in the posterior parietal cortex, premotor–prefrontal cortex, or cingulate gyrus, as well as subcortical lesions in the superior colliculus, striatum, or thalamic pulvinar nucleus. These findings have led Mesulam (1994) to suggest that spatial attention is subserved by a large-scale distributed network with different components providing slightly different spatial coordinate systems.

Figure 7.3 illustrates Mesulam's (1994) model of this network. In Fig. 7.3(a), behaviour α corresponds to directed spatial attention, with three major neural computations A_1, A_2, and A_3 distributed across three anatomical sites, site I (frontal eye fields (FEF)), site II (area PG), and site III (cingulate gyrus). Each anatomical site belongs to several intersecting neural networks supporting particular behaviours comprising directed spatial attention, specifically exploratory behaviour, perceptual representation, and motivational mapping. As such, spatial attention involves multiple brain sites, and these sites also participate in multiple functions. Thus, one might include a box for spatial attention in a box-and-arrow model of attention at the functional level, but one is not going to find that the neural level components are organized in this way—there is more than one brain location for each functional box, and each brain location subserves more than one box. The point is that the behavioural, neurocomputational, and neuroanatomical levels do not preserve the same organization at each level. Thus, Mesulam's model suggests that 'the anatomical mapping of behavior is both localized and distributed, but neither equipotential (holistic) nor modular (insular or phrenological)' (p. 75). Finally, because of tight interconnectivity between many brain regions (e.g. area PG, the frontal eye fields, and areas 23–24 of the cingulate gyrus) damage in one area can induce dysfunction or diaschisis in another (Fiorelli et al. 1991), a result incompatible with a strong locality assumption.

It turns out that in the case of motor responses as well, lesions at different locations can yield the same clinical deficits (e.g. motor neglect (Laplane and Degos 1983)), so the true nature of locality is poorly understood even in the case of motor cortex, considered to be one of the canonical examples of localized function. Even individual cells can be multimodal, for example visual neurons may respond to sounds or touch, and different types of modality-specific cells can be intermixed in the same area, making it difficult to localize function in even the

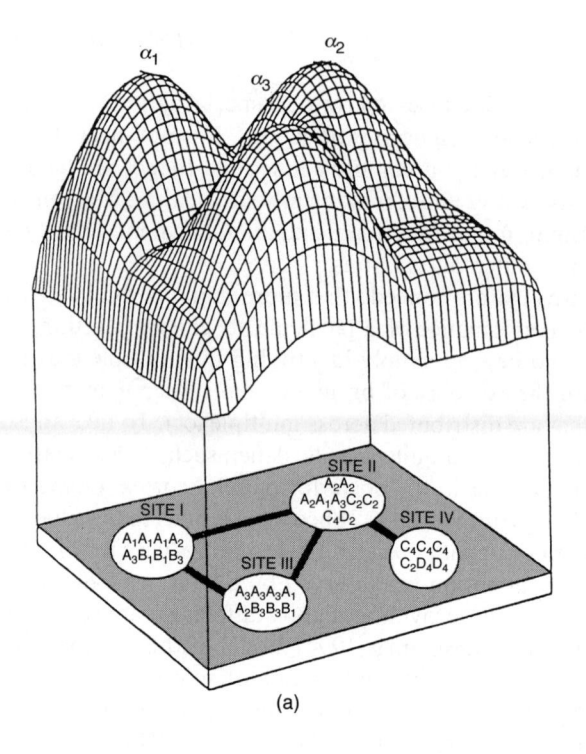

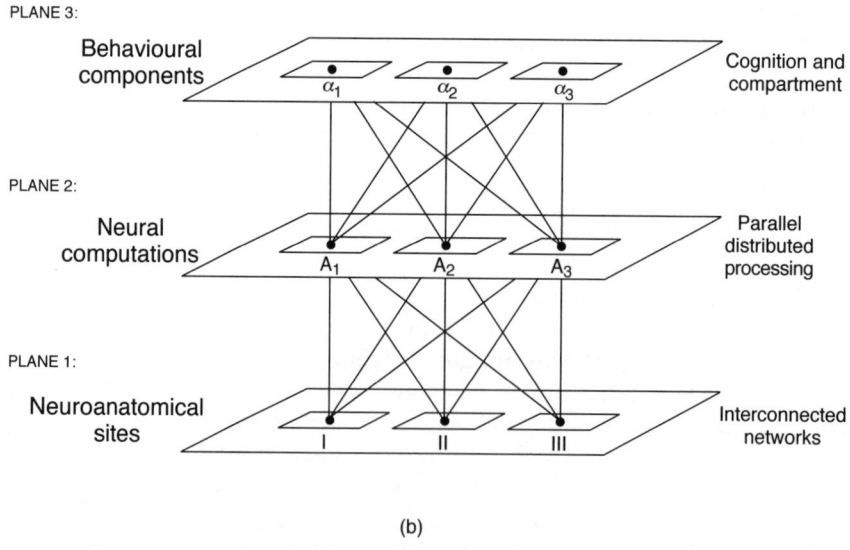

Fig. 7.3. (a) A schematic illustration of the interrelations between behavioural (functional) and anatomical components of an hypothesized attentional network. Alphas (α) refer to behavioural components of directed spatial attention (exploratory behaviour, perceptual representation, motivational mapping), sites refer to anatomical structures, and A, B, and C refer to the distributed neural components underlying the behaviours. (b) The vertical organization of the relations between anatomical, computational (algorithmic), and cognitive planes. (From Mesulam (1990) with permission.)

smallest structural units of the brain (Cytowic 1996). Of course, these examples do not demonstrate that similar multiple mappings between brain structures and functions exist in memory, although the complex functions of the frontal lobe and hippocampus do suggest the possibility. (For example, two studies have identified a site in the hippocampus engaged during activities such as reading words aloud (Bookheimer et al. 1995) and also detecting a salty taste (Kinomura, 1994).) But these examples do demonstrate the existence of such complex mappings, and suggest that they should also be considered for understanding the neural organization of memory.

Process purity of cognitive tasks

The issue of the process purity of cognitive tasks is of paramount concern in the effort to demarcate memory systems. In its most extreme form, process purity is the assumption that a task engages a single process or memory system. But no task, no matter how trivial, involves only a single cognitive process. Thus, the assumption of task purity represents a particularly big problem in efforts to map memory systems. A person is never just remembering. Dozens of mental operations are taking place at any particular moment, including those directly relevant to the task (e.g. access to memory for an event), those supporting the task (e.g. language processing, sensory processing, strategy development, executive control), those relevant to the social situation (e.g. trying to figure out what is expected, performance anxiety, etc.), and those that are irrelevant to the task (e.g. how to itch one's nose when strapped into the fMRI machine). The problem of separating the memory component from these other operations is non-trivial. It may even be impossible because hundreds of operations occurring in real-time normal functioning may not be neurologically separable. For example, a neural network may simultaneously participate in many different dimensions of processing, or the manner in which the task is performed may vary as a function of the particular constellation of operations that are being performed simultaneously.

In its weaker form, the idea that tasks are process-pure assumes that tasks can be designed in which a particular process or system dominates performance, and so one can determine what the fundamental process categories or system structures are, even if all the individual components cannot be precisely discriminated. But even this assumption can be problematic. For example, in the case of classical conditioning, which is considered one of the most simple and primitive of learning mechanisms, cerebellar lesions that impair the acquisition of a conditioned eye-blink response have no effect on electrodermal conditioning, indicating that damage to the cerebellar circuitry does not lead to a generalized associative learning deficit (Daum and Schugens 1996). Conditioning studies comparing delay versus trace conditioning paradigms also reveal dissociations, such that hippocampally lesioned animals are impaired in acquiring conditioned responses in a trace conditioning task, but not in delay conditioning (Moyer et al. 1990). Thus, even the most basic functional categories of learning tasks exhibit dissociations and specializations in the neural machinery. The assumption of process purity thus presents a particularly thorny problem for traversing the different levels of description in a neurocognitive model, because the categories of cognitive process that are designated at the functional level (e.g. classical conditioning) may not be preserved at the implementational level, and vice versa.

Necessity versus sufficiency

Even if one can successfully identify the multiple brain regions engaged during a task, one is still confronted with the issue of the necessity versus sufficiency of the site for the memory process of interest. Theoretically, a particular neurological site may be sufficient for a task, it may be necessary but not sufficient in itself, or it may be involved but neither necessary nor sufficient. How one determines the actual status of an area is unclear. Again, operational criteria are lacking. Even lesion data can be misleading in determining the necessity of a brain site, since a lesion may produce impaired performance on a critical task by damaging a component that stores or transmits information in an earlier or later stage of the information-processing stream. Does such a function qualify the area for membership in the system, or not?

But assuming for the moment that it is possible to perform isomorphic mappings between levels of description, one needs to ask a second question, which is whether it is *necessary* to do so. The answer to this might depend to some degree on how one feels about the so-called mind–body problem. While this issue creates great consternation for some, others are more perplexed that such a problem is believed to exist in the first place. For example Searle (1994) argues that 'mental states are simply higher-level features of the brain' (p. 31) in the same way that liquidity of water is a higher-level feature of molecules of H_2O. One does not find liquidity in molecules, and one will not find consciousness in a neuron. From this standpoint, one might argue that it is not really necessary to seek the features of the functional level in the implementational level, since they are simply different levels at which to describe features of the brain. Of course, clinical considerations and scientific curiosity will continue to motivate scientists to understand these links, regardless of individual philosophical positions. Nevertheless, one is confronted with the problem that the components of a system described at the implementational level may not provide the appropriate elements, organization, or vocabulary to describe what the system is doing or how it is organized at the functional level. Therefore, if it is necessary to map complex functional models of memory systems into localized brain structures, it is also necessary to develop a vocabulary and organizational architecture that enables one to traverse these levels while maintaining coherence in the framework.

Units of analysis

Suppose that one decides that it is both possible and necessary to map cognitive models to brain models, then a further question arises: how does one go about it?

Should one start with a functional model and then look for the neural underpinnings, or start by mapping the neural circuits and then figuring out what they do? In practice investigators use both sources of information in an iterative fashion, but this does not circumvent the problem of which constraints should receive the most weight.

A further problem is hiding here—what units of analysis should one adopt at the functional and implementational levels? The lack of realistic criteria for determining the appropriate units and grain of analysis for delineating memory functions or neural systems becomes clear when one considers some of the systems models that have been hypothesized. Three prominent examples are summarized in Table 7.3, although many other models exist and encounter similar problems.

Schacter and Tulving's (1994*b*) and Squire's (1994) architectures, although differing in the number and organization of systems, adopt similar approaches in that they propose a set of systems, the corresponding neural substrates, and some important properties. Moscovitch's (1994) approach is somewhat different, in that he starts by classifying tasks according to the degree to which performance is mediated primarily by modules or central systems, and although he postulates neural substrates, he does not suggest system names. In looking across these three different schemes, one sees a clear lack of agreement about how to characterize the critical features of the proposed systems. For example Schacter and Tulving specify some of their systems and subsystems in terms of the *kind of information* they process (e.g. visual word form; relational), but others in terms of the *learning mechanism* (e.g. simple conditioning), or the *kind of behaviour* (e.g. motor skills). Squire specifies the declarative system in terms of the kind of information it handles (i.e. facts and events), but the non-declarative system in terms of learning mechanisms (e.g. simple classical conditioning), kind of behaviour (i.e. skills and habits), or *empirical outcome* (i.e. priming). Moscovitch organizes his systems in terms of the *type of test* (e.g. implicit item-specific perceptual; explicit associative). Therefore, there are no clear criteria specifying the appropriate units of analysis for the functional level of description. When one specifies the goal of a system, should it be specified in terms of the kind(s) of information it processes, the learning mechanism it employs, the kind of processing it does, or the behaviours it supports?

The same problem arises when working at the implementational level. Should memory systems be described in terms of anatomical features, neural pathways, or biochemical mechanisms, for example? Because topographic features of the brain do not typically correspond to functional boundaries, and because a variety of functions may be supported by the same brain structure, gross anatomical features of the brain will not suffice to delineate memory systems. At the hodological level (the structure of fibre paths in the brain) one is confronted by such massive interconnectivity and reciprocal connectivity that delineating the boundaries of many systems is difficult, if not impossible or meaningless. Furthermore, because more than one neuroactive principle is present in many individual neurons, and many individual neurons are capable of producing different outcomes, in many instances it may be impossible to localize systems even at the neuronal level. That

Table 7.3 Models of memory systems
(i) Schacter and Tulving (1994b)

System	Subsystems	Neural substrate	Retrieval	Properties
Procedural	Motor skills Cognitive skills Simple conditioning Simple associative learning	Basal ganglia, premotor, and motor cortices	Implicit	Non-cognitive; automatic; independent of hippocampal structures; gradual incremental learning
Perceptual representation (PRS)	Visual word form Auditory word form Structural description		Implicit	Cognitive
Semantic	Spatial Relational	Medial temporal lobe	Implicit	Cognitive
Primary	Visual Auditory		Explicit	Cognitive; short-term retention
Episodic		Prefrontal-cortical area Medial temporal lobe	Explicit	Cognitive

(ii) Squire (1994)

System	Components	Neural substrate	Retrieval	Properties
Declarative	Facts Events	Medial temporal lobe (hippocampal system) and diencephalon	Explicit	Conscious recollection of facts and events; recall and recognition; fast; flexible
Nondeclarative	Skills and habits (motor, perceptual, and cognitive) Priming Simple classical conditioning Non-associative learning	Visual neocortex and neostriatum; right extrastriate cortex Cerebellum	Implicit	Non-conscious; knowledge expressed through performance; learning not consciously accessible; gradual, cumulative learning of new associations; less flexible

(iii) Moscovitch (1994)

Test type	Neural Substrate	Properties
Implicit		
Item-specific, perceptual	Perceptual input modules in posterior neocortex (representational systems)	Identification or classification of stimuli based on sensory cues
Item-specific, conceptual	Interpretative multimodal central systems in the lateral, temporal, parietal, and possibly frontal lobes	Production or classification of items in response to conceptual cues
Procedural, sensorimotor	Basal ganglia, cerebellum	Acquisition and improvement of motor or sensory skills
Procedural, ordered/rule-based	Dorsolateral and midlateral frontal lobes	Learning to solve problems with rules or organized response contingencies
Explicit		
Associative	Hippocampus and related limbic structures in the medial temporal lobes and diencephalon	Conscious recollection of episodes in which the cue is sufficient for retrieval
Strategic	Dorsolateral and ventromedial frontal lobes, cingulate cortex	Conscious recollection of episodes in which extracue strategic factors and critical

is, the same neuron may participate in very different types of activities. And of course, since the effect of a neurotransmitter depends on a variety of factors (e.g. the nature of the receptor with which it combines, the activity of neuromodulators), biochemistry alone cannot define brain systems, either.

The problem of selecting the appropriate unit of analysis within any level of description further demonstrates that the organization of systems may not map isomorphically through the functional, algorithmic, and implementational levels. For example, suppose one specifies a functional system whose goal is to store and retrieve personal experiences (an episodic system). It is possible that at the representational/algorithmic level it will employ a variety of learning mechanisms (e.g. associative learning, long-term potentiation), some of which will be shared by other functional systems. Furthermore, these different brain locations may employ different subsets of these mechanisms, and the mechanisms may even have different behavioural consequences depending on where in the brain they are implemented (e.g. long-term potentiation (see Lynch and Granger 1994)). A possible implication is that theorists will have to be content with a variety of different systems models, dynamically organized for different purposes and according to different criteria, but none of which represents a direct or complete description in and of itself.

In summary, before delineating a set of memory systems, one needs to be clear about the operational definitions to be employed, the appropriate types of empirical observations that must be made, the level of description at which one is working, and the unit of analysis that is deemed appropriate. Without these clear operational criteria, systems cannot be identified and the models cannot be tested. Although ideally systems should be described at multiple levels, such as the functional, representational/algorithmic, and implementational levels, at this time it is not clear that memory systems can be mapped through these different levels isomorphically and simultaneously.

STUDYING THE DAMAGED BRAIN

An important source of evidence for the claim of multiple memory systems is data from populations with organic brain damage, specifically amnesics of various aetiologies. When a particular part of the brain is damaged, and a particular functional deficit is observed, it is assumed that that brain region plays a critical role in that function, which can be a rather tenuous inference in itself. However, the further suggestion that the brain region is the locus of that function is an unwarranted leap of logic. Several problems exist with this logic, including those of validating the assumptions that (1) such data reveal the relevance and function of the area, (2) there is a one-to-one mapping between function and brain locus, (3) the function of the damaged brain can be generalized to describe the function of the intact brain, and (4) there is only one way to accomplish a task.

Localization of function, converging operations, and complex interactions

Consider the scientist studying the leaping ability of frogs. He (or she) places his frog on the floor, says 'Jump frog, jump!' and the frog leaps 15 feet. In his notebook he jots, 'Frog leaps 15 feet'. He then cuts off one front leg, says, 'Jump frog, jump!' and the frog leaps 12 feet. He jots down, 'Three legs—frog leaps 12 feet'. He cuts off the other front leg and says, 'Jump frog, jump!'. The frog jumps, and he jots down, 'Two legs—frog leaps 8 feet'. He cuts off one back leg, says 'Jump frog, jump!'. The frog jumps, and he writes, 'One leg—frog leaps 2 feet'. Finally, he cuts off the last leg and says, 'Jump frog, jump!'. The frog does nothing. Again he says, 'Jump frog, jump'. Again no response. He writes in his notebook, 'No legs—frog loses hearing'.

The moral of course is that even if damage to a physical component results in an observable impairment, it is not necessarily the case that the component is the locus of the function. In the worst case scenario, it might have nothing to do with the function, as in the case of the frog's legs and its hearing. In the case of human brain function, problems can arise in determining the specific functions and relative importance of a brain region in the behaviours of interest. A site can be the main locus of a function, it can be one of several critical components, it may serve as a relay to a critical area, or it may support a related critical function such as maintaining attention during a recall task. Thus, studying a system with a damaged component may reveal little about the function or importance of the component. If one takes the transistor out of radio, it will not produce any sound, but that does not mean that the transistor produces sound. Of course, converging evidence from other sources, such as neuroimaging, primate, and drug studies, can be helpful in interpreting lesion data, but it is also the case that these other sources can produce contradictory evidence that complicates rather than simplifies interpretation.

According to the logic of interpreting lesion data, if a structure is lesioned and a behavioural impairment results, then the structure plays a critical role in the behaviour. But an implicit assumption is also that if the lesion has no effect on behaviour, then the structure is not involved. The problem with this logic is illustrated by recent work examining the role of the hippocampus in classical conditioning (Solomon and Yang 1994). Early work indicated that lesions to the hippocampus did not affect acquisition of a conditioned eye-blink response in rabbits, suggesting that the hippocampus was not necessary for conditioning. (This type of finding underlies the assignment of classical conditioning to the non-declarative or procedural memory system in Table 7.3.) However, later work showed that drugs that disrupt the neuronal activity of the hippocampus (e.g. scopolamine) do interfere with conditioning, and the disruption may occur through interactions with the cerebellum. Also, electrophysiological activity associated with conditioning and occurring in the hippocampus is affected by cerebellar activity, suggesting that learning mechanisms in the hippocampus may be influenced by learning processes in other brain areas. Thus, the effects of isolated lesions may be misleading because they have limited ability to capture complex interactions among components. Similar problems arise in work with humans. Lesions in one area may affect cortical metabolism in other areas (Fiorelli et al. 1991; Fazio et al. 1992), or a lesion in one area may affect the blood supply or a neural or chemical pathway providing input to another area, and thus miscue an investigator about the function of the lesioned area. Therefore, lesion data may be misinterpreted to suggest that a function is more localized than it really is.

Subtractive logic and task performance

Using data from patients with brain lesions to map out memory systems incorporates *subtractive logic*, that is, the assumption that when one component of the system is removed the remainder of the system continues to function normally and in the same manner. This assumption, which was also an important underpinning of Donders' (1868) work, has been viewed with scepticism for a long time. A corollary of this assumption is that there is only one way to do the task. This corollary has three problematic aspects, (1) the assumption that all normal individuals perform the task in the same way, (2) the assumption that individuals with brain damage cannot perform the task at normal levels, and (3) people with brain damage have not developed alternative strategies that enable them to perform the task at normal levels. It is unlikely that these assumptions hold true for all tasks that involve memory. Given what is known about the high degree of interactivity in the brain, in many cases it will be difficult to justify the assumption that the addition or subtraction of one brain component has no impact on how the rest of the brain executes tasks.

Recovery of function and generalizing from impaired function

Over a period of time following brain injury patients can make significant recovery of functions. However, the correct interpretation of this recovery is usually unclear. Did the neurological system repair itself or did the patient develop a new strategy to perform the task? Even if the patient does not perform the task at a normal level, yet performs it better than immediately after the injury, it is still not clear whether this is due to the less-than-complete recovery of the neurological system or to the adoption of a less-than-adequate new strategy.

A system component may be involved in many different tasks in the normal human, but after injury, alternative strategies may work well for only a subset of these tasks, in which case dissociations may reflect the operation of a reorganized system, not the original intact system (Shallice 1988). Relatively little is known about the bases of recovery processes in human patients, making it difficult to determine the degree to which one is justified in generalizing from the damaged to the intact system (cf. McCarthy 1994). This may become a problem when hypothesizing about memory systems because the intact brain may perform memory functions in a relatively integrated fashion, whereas a damaged brain may not have this option, and so dissociations between groups (e.g. amnesics and normals) may create the appearance that mental functions are splintered into independent systems, or exaggerate the degree to which the postulated systems actually function independently in the intact brain.

Level of description and analysis

The lesion method assumes that systems are both functionally and anatomically modular, but as noted earlier, at this time there is insufficient evidence to suggest that organizational schemes employed at the functional level have the same structure at the anatomical level. Because a brain area may subserve more than one mental function, because multiple brain areas subserve a particular mental function, and because lesions do not respect functional boundaries in the brain, lesions may produce the appearance that certain activities are subserved by the same neurocognitive system. Whether this is true depends on how one operationalizes a system, such as whether one defines it in terms of functional categories (e.g. implicit memory tasks or classical conditioning), specific mechanisms (e.g. long-term potentiation), or neuronal components (e.g. tasks that involve the posterior cingulate gyrus). Furthermore, stable functional deficits usually involve fairly large lesions, and so localizing specific cognitive processes, which may be implemented at a fine-grained level, will be difficult.

The 'hot spot' approach

A further problem in using lesion data to localize memory systems can arise from the hot spot approach (Shallice 1988, Ch. 9). In this technique, a critical functional area is located by superimposing the lesions of patients who have a particular deficit, and looking for the area of collective overlap. However, areas that are more likely to be damaged due to differential probabilities of certain diseases or injuries may be overrepresented in the sample, and thus are more likely to be included because of their frequency rather than their demonstrated functional importance.

Furthermore, such techniques can lead to serious imprecision in localizing function. To take an example from the language literature, Fig. 7.4 shows a map of essential language areas in the left hemisphere in 117 patients dominant for language in the left hemisphere, based on electrical stimulation mapping during a naming task conducted during surgery (Ojemann *et al*. 1989). The map is striking because it illustrates that whereas each individual patient showed localization over a relatively small mosaic of sites, across patients there was substantial variability. Ojemann *et al*. suggest that one implication of this finding is that the traditional maps for Broca–Wernicke areas are too large because they have been based on aggregate data, so language cannot be reliably localized using anatomical criteria alone. This is consistent with the fact that anatomical boundaries based on early descriptions of brain topography do not necessarily conform to

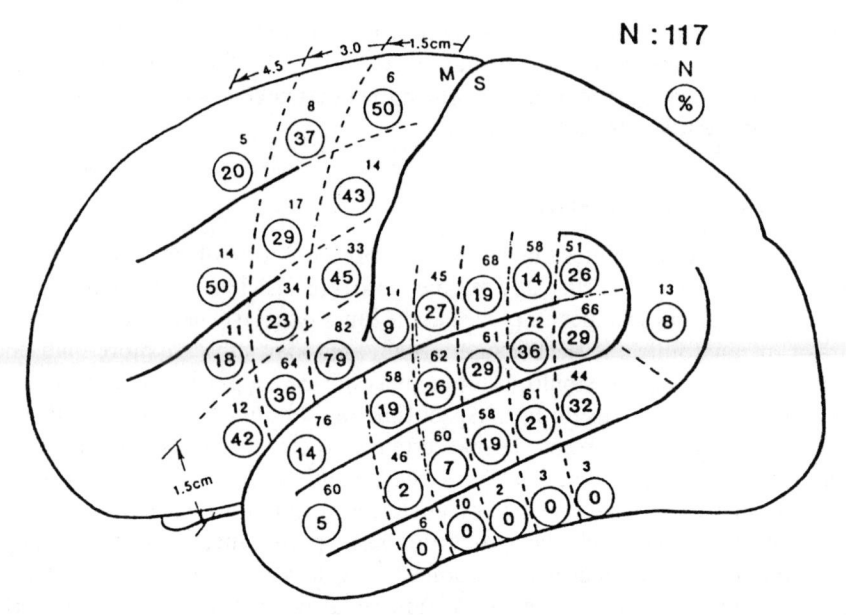

Fig. 7.4. Electrical stimulation mapping during picture naming in 117 left-dominant language patients reveals variability in location of essential language areas in the left hemisphere. In each zone, the upper number indicates the number of patients tested in that zone, and the circled number indicates the percentage of those tested who showed essential language function in that zone. (From Ojemann et al. (1989) with permission.)

functional boundaries, and so trying to localize functions in terms of anatomical features is of limited value.

Across individuals, the degree to which higher mental functions are localized within specific anatomical structures is unclear at this time. Although many functions seem localized with some consistency across individuals, particularly sensory and motor functions, other functions may not be correlated with specific anatomical structures to the same degree. Ojemann and colleagues' work reveals that across individuals, language functions are spread across very large areas of the brain and a wide variety of anatomical sites. The degree to which this might be true for memory functions is unknown, but Ojemann et al.'s data demonstrate that it is possible in principle. Thus, it is not clear that seeking a precise correspondence between anatomical structures and higher mental functions will lead to an accurate characterization of all memory functions in terms of their neural substrates. This is particularly true for very mentalistic concepts like consciousness and free will (Sarter et al. 1996).

Shallice (1988, Ch. 9) has argued that for the most part the localization of lesions, particularly in group studies, is not essential for cognitive neuropsychology (see also Caramazza 1986). However, he also states that this is not a matter of principle, but rather due to limitations in the methodology currently available, which may change in the future.

STUDYING THE RADIANT BRAIN

Another important source of data for identifying memory systems is neuroimaging, including electroencephalography (EEG), positron emission tomography (PET), and functional magnetic resonance imaging (fMRI). The latter two techniques have been particularly important in the search for memory systems, and these techniques essentially provide images of metabolic activity in the brain by recording regional cerebral blood flow (rCBF) or the blood oxygenation level-dependent (BOLD) signal respectively. The assumption is that the level of metabolic activity in a brain region is an index of the level of involvement of that area in a task, although the actual mechanisms of neurovascular coupling are poorly understood at this time.

Paired image subtraction

In the typical brain-imaging paradigm, investigators employ a paired image subtraction method to identify brain regions critical to various cognitive tasks. In this method, a baseline task is developed which allegedly involves all the cognitive activities engaged during the memory task, *except* for the memory component of interest. For example, in a study of category cued recall to locate the episodic memory system (Shallice *et al.* 1994), subjects heard a list of category–exemplar pairs (e.g. *poet–Browning*), and then later were presented the category labels (*poet*), and asked to recall the exemplar (*Browning*). In the control condition, a different group of subjects was given the same category labels (e.g. *poet*) and asked to generate their own exemplars from semantic memory. PET scans were performed during these tasks. The logic was that differences in patterns of activation in these conditions would identify regions specifically associated with retrieval from episodic memory.

Several problems arise in this approach to identifying memory systems. First, as with lesion studies, the method rests on subtractive logic which makes a series of questionable assumptions, including: (1) the brain works in a serial, hierarchical, and feed-forward fashion (contradicting what is known about the extensive recursivity of neural networks); (2) adding or subtracting task components directly includes or excludes the involvement of the brain area hypothesized to correspond to that task component; (3) *additivity*, the idea that system components are independent and their functions can be considered in isolation from each other; and (4) *pure insertion*, the idea that adding or subtracting designated task components does not affect the involvement, organization, or operations of other task components or brain areas (also see Sergent 1994).

The problems of the subtractive method are tied to a second problem, that of creating an appropriate control task. Patterns of differential brain activation are not absolute, but are defined only relative to the control task. Different patterns of activation can emerge when different control tasks are used, and inconsistencies across studies may arise from differences in the control tasks employed (Sergent

1994). Furthermore, the assumption that the control task lacks only the component of interest is often difficult to validate. For example, in the Shallice *et al.* (1994) study, the episodic and semantic conditions differed not only in whether they engaged an episodic memory component, but also in the exact words that the subjects produced during the task. In the episodic retrieval task the targets were low-dominant exemplars of the categories (e.g. *poet–Browning*), but it is unlikely that subjects produced such items in the semantic generation task, because people normally generate familiar high-dominance exemplars in open-ended response tasks (e.g. *poet–Longfellow*). Thus, not only did the two tasks differ in terms of their memory demands, but also in terms of the knowledge accessed and the relative difficulty of each task. It is possible that the rCBF was discriminating the high- and low-dominant exemplar systems, rather than the episodic and semantic systems.

Similarly, to test recognition memory, Andreasen *et al.* (1995) compared brain activity during an oral yes/no recognition task with a control task in which subjects simply read the words aloud. Note that the oral outputs are different in the two tasks ('yes/no' versus a word read aloud), which may confound the comparison of the patterns of activation that arise due to the different memory demands. (It is important to note that not all neuroimaging experiments involve such striking examples of these problems, but the examples discussed here were chosen because they are able to clearly illustrate the fundamental issues.)

The control and experimental tasks may differ in many dimensions not accounted for in the memory model under consideration, such as task difficulty, general interest, attentional requirements, working memory load, and strategic factors. Thus, the two tasks will differ in many processes other than the ones of interest. As an example, Johnson *et al.* (1996) reported patterns of event related potentials (ERPs) associated with two different recognition test paradigms. The first paradigm was the traditional recognition test in which old and new items are randomly mixed in the test list. The second paradigm was that typically used in PET studies in which the old items are presented in one block, and the new items presented in a separate block. This is done because it takes 30–40 s to complete a scan, and so if old and new items are mixed together, the scan would mix the patterns of activation for recognition of old items with those comprising processing of new items. The ERP patterns for the old and new items in each test paradigm were then examined. The old and new test items produced the same patterns of ERP activity when the test items were randomly mixed, but different patterns of activity when the items were blocked. That is, ERP patterns dissociated as a function of word order on the recognition test. The two recognition tests were nominally identical and should have behaved similarly if the ERP was simply tapping into recognition processes. However, the patterns of activation appeared to be influenced by expectations and strategies in the two different testing conditions. Johnson *et al.* expressed concern that brain imaging does not provide direct evidence about memory processes and representations *per se*, but rather reflects a whole constellation of cognitive processes, including those related to strategy, task difficulty, and attention.

Similarly, small differences in task requirements can lead to significant differences in the subset of brain areas identified as the critical components of the neural substrate of the task. For example, Sergent *et al.* (1994) found that in a face identification task, merely reducing stimulus presentation time from 3 s to 2 s eliminated differential activation of the right anterior temporal cortex. As another example, Table 7.4 shows the *XYZ* coordinates of the critical brain areas identified in three different experiments comparing verbal free recall on subspan and supraspan memory tasks. Presumably, in all three experiments, this comparison should

Table 7.4 Brain areas underlying auditory-verbal long-term memory in three different experiments (*XYZ* coordinates)

Grasby *et al.* (1993*a*)	Backer *et al.* (1994)	Grasby *et al.* (1993*b*)
(i) Regions of increased rCBF		
−2.6 5.2 0.4	−2.2, 5.4 −0.4	−2.4 −3 −0.4
left prefrontal cortex	left superior frontal gyrus	left hippocampal formation
2 5.6 −0.4	2.2 5.4 −0.4	Loci mentioned, without
right prefrontal cortex	right superior frontal gyrus	coordinates: right hippocampal formation, posterior, hypothalamus, precuneus, angular gyrus, posterior cingulate
	−3.4 4.6 −0.4	
0.2 −3.8 1.2	−2.8 1.6 3.2	
cingulate gyrus (retrosplenial area)	left middle frontal gyrus	
	3.2 4.6 −0.4	
1.6 −6.2 3.2	0.4 2 3.2	
cingulate gyrus (precuneus area)	right middle frontal gyrus	
	−3.6 0.2 0.8	
	left inferior frontal gyrus	
	4 4.2 0.8	
	right inferior frontal gyrus	
	−0.6 3.2 2	
	−1 3.4 2.4	
	left cingulate cortex	
	0.4 3 1.2	
	1 4.6 1.6	
	right cingulate cortex	
	−2.6 −7 2.4	
	left occipital cortex	
(ii) Regions of decreased rCBF		
−4.6 −1.8 0.8		
left superior temporal gyrus/insular		
4.4 −1.4 0.8		
right superior temporal gyrus/insular		

yield the memory system underlying long-term episodic memory, but as one can see, across the three experiments quite different areas emerge as the critical brain areas, as defined by statistically significant changes in rCBF on the supraspan task. Almost no consistency emerges across the three studies. Furthermore, only one study identifies the hippocampus as a critical component, a surprising outcome given that lesion studies indicate that the hippocampus is essential for long-term episodic learning. The fact that relatively small or insignificant changes in the tasks can produce large variability in patterns of activation suggests the need for more conservative interpretations of these data, and the need to carefully compile data across multiple experiments (e.g. Blaxton *et al.* 1996).

The effort to identify unique memory systems through paired-image subtraction may produce misleading maps of the neurological system that underlies an activity. For example, if area *XYZ* is not differentially activated during two tasks, it will be eliminated from consideration as a system component. However, such a finding in no way implies that the area is *not* a critical component of the neurological substrate (or system) for both tasks (e.g. consider the hippocampus, mentioned above). Nevertheless, as an artifact of this methodology, the area cannot be included as a system component, even if it is equally critical on both tasks. The importance of operational definitions once again comes into play. To what degree are two systems required to be functionally and neurologically independent? If the criterion is that systems must be functionally and neurologically incompatible (e.g. Sherry and Schacter 1987), then the operational definition precludes the inclusion of any neurological components shared by two different memory operations, even if that component is essential to successful performance of both. Therefore, a system can include *only* neurological components that are not shared by other systems. In many cases, however, defining the system only in terms of mutually exclusive neurological components will give a false representation of how the task is actually accomplished. Brain loci other than those in the mutually exclusive subsets of neural elements may be necessary to accomplish the task. The mere fact that a few regions are more activated in the memory condition than in the control condition does not mean that those few regions comprise all the essential components of the system that subserves successful performance on the memory task. The converse is also true. That is, the fact that one brain area is more activated in an experimental than a control task is not direct evidence for its causal role in the function of interest, much less its inclusion in the hypothesized memory system that underlies the task. This is because increased activation may arise from other cognitive processes that co-vary with a change in the target task, such as difficulty, attentional demands, input and output modalities, etc. For example, consider an area that exhibits increased activation in an episodic memory task (experimental task) relative to a word naming task (the control task). The activation might reflect the development of a strategy to search recent memory rather than reflecting a central component of the episodic memory system *per se*. In summary, the presence or absence of differences in activation levels do not reveal the functional significance of an area with respect to the memory system of interest, that is, they do not reveal what specific process or processes the area is engaged in nor whether these processes constitute an integral part of the system.

This problem is related to an even more curious upshot of neuroimaging. The subtractive method identifies areas of significant *differences* in activation, but the data are often presented and interpreted in a manner suggesting that this hot spot is *uniquely* activated. In fact, an area may be highly active during both the baseline and memory tasks, but just *more* activated during the memory task. This clearly does not serve as evidence of 'specific' involvement. Simply because an area is more activated in the experimental task than in the control task does not mean that its function is irrelevant to performing the control task. This misrepresentation permeates many reports of such data, in which authors refer to 'activated' areas instead of 'differentially activated' areas. Such a presentation begs the question of how much activity is needed to decide whether or not a brain area is critically involved in a task, or whether it constitutes a component of the system that underlies the task. Is the best criterion for the inclusion or exclusion of neural components in a hypothesized memory system the finding that differential activation is statistically significant with a *z-score* at $p < 0.05$? In fact, there is no evidence that this is the appropriate criterion to apply in determining if a brain area is playing an important role in a cognitive task, or if it comprises a necessary or critical component of a memory system.

It is probably because of the paired-image subtractive method that some odd results arise, such as failures to identify the hippocampus as a unique critical component of the episodic memory system (e.g. Shallice *et al*. 1994; Squire 1992; Grasby *et al*. 1993*a*; but see Grasby *et al*. 1993*b*), despite the fact that lesion data have led many investigators to believe this structure is a critical component of the system that underlies episodic or explicit memory. However, if the hippocampus is involved in forming associations (e.g. Moscovitch 1994), then there might be hardly a time when a person is not forming associations, even when retrieving a past experience. This may be an example of a case in which a critical system component is equally active in both the control and experimental tasks, so is dropped out of the system model.

Finally, Sarter *et al*. (1996) discuss how the need to standardize brain images for individual differences in activation levels can lead to artifactual effects in paired image subtraction. For example, activation in each pixel may be represented as a proportion of total brain activation. However, if total brain activation is significantly higher in a stimulating experimental task than in its passive control task, an area that is relatively inactive on both tasks may spuriously appear to diminish in activity because it becomes a smaller portion of overall activity in the stimulating task.

Spatial and temporal resolution

Another area of concern in using neuroimaging data to identify memory systems is the spatial and temporal resolution of the measures. Although the temporal resolution of EEG is very good, its spatial resolution is poor. The spatial resolutions of PET and fMRI are considerably better, but their temporal resolutions are poor, with PET scans requiring about 40–70 s and fMRI scans requiring less time but still much slower than the neural events of interest (Posner and Raichle 1994). Coupled with the fact that the dynamics of neurovascular activity are poorly understood, it is clear that the metabolic activity measured in brain scans is occurring on a quite different time scale from the real-time behaviours and neural activities of interest, complicating the mapping between the two. Furthermore, over the long scan time, periods of increase and decrease in rCBF may cancel each other out, and the involvement of the area will be lost. Thus, the durations and sequences of specific neural activities relative to the cognitive activities of interest cannot be determined. Finally, different brain regions vary dramatically in the time course of their haemodynamic responses, complicating the interpretation of patterns of activation that co-occur across multiple brain loci.

Problems in spatial localization can be compounded when data from several individuals are averaged together, as is the usual practice in experimental work. Because there is large individual variation in the size and topology of brains, different brain images are usually adjusted to fit the Talairach and Tournoux (1988) standard atlas, which provides a standardized proportional grid system. However, the electrical stimulation work by Ojemann *et al.* (1989) illustrated in Fig. 7.4 demonstrates that even the Talairach proportional grid system will not necessarily remove individual differences in the localization of functions. When mosaics of distributed neural activity are aggregated, it may give the appearance that functions are localized in large coherent anatomical sites, when in fact they are distributed in idiosyncratic patterns.

Functional role of the neurons

The problems of spatial and temporal resolution also compound the problems that arise when there are many-to-one mappings of functions to brain sites in the loci of interest. Not only do the images fail to reveal exactly which neurons are involved or the time course of their activity, but they also fail to reveal what the neurons are doing. Because neurons in the same area may perform both excitatory and inhibitory functions, increasing local activity in two different tasks may have the same radiological outcome (i.e. evidence of heightened metabolic activity), while having completely different functional implications (Sarter *et al.* 1996). Furthermore, because some neurons are capable of producing different outputs (e.g. releasing different neurotransmitters), depending on a host of other physiological and biochemical factors, then even when the same collection of neurons is active during two different tasks, it is not actually known if the neurons are performing the same function or different functions in both tasks. Neural assemblies showing equivalent levels of activation across two tasks are thus dropped out of consideration as system components without knowing whether they are in fact critical to the tasks or whether they are performing the same functions in the tasks.

Sergent (1994) lists several problematic assumptions that underlie the interpretation of rCBF in brain imaging. Among these is the assumption that higher increases in rCBF indicate a higher contribution of the cerebral area to the task. This assumption is unwarranted because in the cases of habituation or practice *less* activation may characterize the critical role of a cortical area, as has been observed with the right posterior cortex in word stem completion priming (Squire *et al.* 1992; see also Table 7.4). Second, the method assumes that the degree to which neuronal activity increases serves as an index of the relative involvement or importance of the structure. This assumption is instantiated in practice by using the same statistical criterion for all brain regions when determining whether a region exhibits significant differences in neural activity in two different tasks. However, relatively small increases in rCBF may be correlated with important increases in neuronal activity in areas with highly efficient connectivity, relatively low thresholds for synaptic transmission, or dense vascularization. The problems that may arise in trying to map memory systems are clear, because rCBF does not provide the level of detail needed to determine the *functional* significance of various brain areas in different memory tests. Currently, similar problems exist with the interpretation of other measures of haemodynamic response.

Weak distributed activity

The case in which the neural substrate of a cognitive function is widely distributed presents a special problem for neuroimaging. The signal strength for such diffuse circuitry may be weak in any particular area, and therefore difficult to discriminate from noise or activity in the control task (Sarter *et al.* 1996). Therefore, the contribution of this circuit will be lost, and the architecture of the critical neural substrate will be misrepresented. This introduces a systematic bias into system models because only strongly localized components will have the opportunity to be detected, and thus the models may exaggerate the extent to which the functions of interest are localized and segregated from other functions.

Critical system properties

Another problem with paired-image subtraction is the implicit assumption that the defining feature of a system is its location, which may be a red herring. Other properties may be equally or more important, such as chemical systems, physiological mechanisms, and higher-order organizational properties of the brain. Current neuroimaging methods are unable to analyse these dimensions.

A note on developing methodologies

Efforts are ongoing to develop methodologies that address some of the weaknesses of the methods and technology discussed here. For example, McIntosh and colleagues have questioned the validity of subtractive logic and have demonstrated how covariance analysis techniques such as structural equation modelling

(McIntosh and Gonzalez-Lima 1994) and partial least squares analyses (Jennings et al. 1997) can be used to map functional neural networks by assessing intercorrelations in activity among neural regions, instead of employing the traditional univariate analyses of activation in individual areas. These techniques enable one to take a systemic view of neural function which is more consistent with the known reciprocity of neural connectivity, avoiding the assumption of feed-forward serial processing. Using partial least squares analyses, Jennings et al. (1997) also demonstrated that the additivity assumption of paired-image subtraction is untenable, because patterns of activity attributable to semantic processing varied as a function of the response requirements (e.g. mouse-click versus spoken response).

Brain imaging technology is also developing rapidly. Functional MRI has improved the temporal resolution of brain images, enabling haemodynamic changes to be measured within a few seconds of the stimulus event. In addition, a technique known as event-related fMRI, or single-trial methodology (e.g. Buckner et al. 1996; Dale and Buckner 1997), enables haemodynamic responses to be extracted for individual response trials. Although the time course of the measured haemodynamic response is still considerably longer than that of the neural events of interest, the method nevertheless represents an improvement in the temporal resolution of maps of neural activation and a step toward closer coupling between brain and behavioural events. For example, Courtney et al. (1997) have used dynamic measures of neural activity to identify brain areas predominantly related to either perception or the maintenance of information in a working memory task. Furthermore, event-related fMRI improves experimental flexibility by permitting the use of designs more similar to those used in behavioural studies, such as randomly mixed presentations of different types of stimuli. In the future, one can anticipate that theoretical, statistical, technological, and methodological developments will continue to improve the utility of brain imaging in formulating and testing theories of cognition. However, it remains to be seen whether such innovations can resolve many of the fundamental problems that confront efforts to map discrete memory systems (e.g. see Table 7.1).

CONSIDERING THE EVOLVED BRAIN

One popular argument in systems theories is that evolutionary pressures offer a rationale for the development of multiple memory systems (Sherry and Schacter 1987; Tulving 1985). Tulving has argued that because evolution is characterized by sudden jumps and shifts, one might expect that separate memory systems evolved abruptly as well, providing new specialized capabilities not available in the more primitive brain mechanisms. Sherry and Schacter argue that various learning and memory abilities are adaptive specializations which evolve in response to functionally incompatible demands in the environment. That is, when a system that evolved to handle one set of problems is unsuited for a different set of problems, then a new memory system is required to handle the new problems.

Evolutionary arguments run a particular risk of being weak hypotheses when they are invoked *post hoc*. Any feature of any organism can be 'explained' in terms of evolution, but evolution in itself does not provide a theoretically useful idea in this domain if it is not presented as a well-developed testable and falsifiable set of hypotheses. The claim that an attribute is adaptive does not meet this criterion, and hence is non-explanatory, since nearly anything can be argued to be adaptive or maladaptive, depending on the perspective one wishes to take (e.g. Gould and Lewontin 1979). Sherry and Schacter (1987) acknowledge this point.

Functional incompatibility seems like a reasonable condition for the evolution of a new memory system, but in practice it is unclear what constitutes functional incompatibility such that a new memory system would be required. For example, in the case of memory functions, it is unclear why the demands of retrieving a personal experience (episodic memory) would be incompatible with the processes that make a recent event accessible without requiring conscious access (implicit memory), even though these two functions are assigned to separate systems (see Table 7.3). In fact, if anything, it seems that retrieval would be well served by having these postulated systems work in concert. This seems to be even more true for episodic and semantic memory in which the links between personal experience and general knowledge can be very tight. Indeed, it seems just as reasonable to suggest that as new cognitive and memory capabilities evolved they developed as integrated functions, exploiting and expanding existing memory capacities, as it is to suggest that they evolved in a disconnected fashion in which they worked independently from one another. For example, the intact brain may learn that if one picks up a hot pan one gets burned, but it could be argued that classical conditioning, episodic memory, and general knowledge ideally will all work together to help one avoid getting burned on future occasions.

The fact that some task requirements may be incompatible with other task requirements (e.g. some kinds of learning should be rigid whereas other should be flexible, such as song learning versus food finding in birds (Sherry and Schacter 1987)) does not mean that *in toto* the mechanisms underlying learning and memory for the two tasks must comprise independent systems. The systems may share some mechanisms, but this does not justify the conclusion that these shared mechanisms are not critical components of each of the systems.

The suggestion that new memory systems probably emerged in dramatic leaps that gave rise to new and dedicated neural systems also runs into difficulties. For example, many systems theories identify the hippocampus as the structure associated with the most highly evolved aspect of memory, episodic memory. However, rats and humans both have hippocampi, although the rat hippocampus is relatively more primitive. Therefore, it is plausible that memory skills evolved with the expansion of existing primitive structures, rather than requiring entirely new structures.

Evolutionary arguments run into problems with other aspects of current proposals about multiple memory systems. To take just one example, consider the visual word form subsystem proposed by Schacter and Tulving (1994*b*). An evolutionary argument would suggest that this system developed to enable people to read words. However, widespread literacy is a relatively new development in human history, occurring only within the last hundred years, too short a period for a word form system to evolve. Furthermore, a significant number of people who use written languages do not use alphabetic words, but instead use ideographic representational systems such as kanji. Would these groups lack a visual word form system, and if not, then how would they have evolved one? It seems unlikely that a special system has evolved to process written words; rather, processing written language probably engages more general perceptual, memory, and language processes. Evolutionary arguments run the risk of leading to teleological oddities and overly specialized views of memory mechanisms.

In general, evolutionary adaptation is a weak point of departure for arguments for memory systems, particularly when ideas about what is adaptive are based on *ad hoc* analyses of particular tasks.

BIAS IN TASK SELECTION

The effort to define memory systems leads to bias in the types of tasks and processes that are studied to develop the system models. Evidence for a system depends heavily on the presence of dissociations (e.g. task dissociations in normal individuals and patients with lesions), and so tasks that dissociate provide the major source of data for studies of memory. Such an approach may exaggerate the extent to which memory processes are fractionated and systems are specialized or independent. Tasks that do not easily fit into the hypothesized systems or do not appear to be primarily memory tests are not studied, and the wide range of tasks in which memory supports cognitive activity but is not the focus of activity (e.g. reading, reasoning), does not contribute to the data base about the neurological organization of memory. Thus, while it seems reasonable to assume that in a majority of instances many different types of memory processes are contributing to performance in an integrated fashion, the emphasis on task dissociations makes it difficult to explore this possibility in efforts to characterize the organization of memory.

THE DISSECTED MIND

Historically, investigators of memory have often suggested that there is more than one type of remembering. Aristotle distinguished between recollection and memory, James (1890) between primary and secondary memory, and Ebbinghaus (1885/1964) between voluntary, involuntary, and unconscious memory. More recently, dissociations between various memory tasks led to Atkinson and Shiffrin's (1968) distinction between the short-term and long-term stores, Tulving's (1985) distinctions between episodic, semantic, and procedural memories, and Schacter's

(1990) hypothesis about the perceptual representation system (PRS). However, most recently, as investigators have produced or discovered increasing numbers of dissociations, even more types of memory have been labelled, such as semantic, episodic, procedural, lexical, declarative, non-declarative, generic, singular, working, primary, perceptual, visual word form, simple associative learning, non-associative learning, simple classical conditioning, priming, etc. Along with extraordinary developments in neuroimaging technology, the identification of all these kinds of memory processes and systems has compelled many investigators to seek their various loci.

In this venture, memory seems to have been severed from the rest of cognition. Memory is treated as if it exists for its own sake, when in fact most of the time memory is operating in the background in the service of other tasks, such as driving to work, having a conversation, reading a newspaper, and using oven gloves to pick up a hot pan. Most of the time, one need not attend to the memory processes that support daily activity. Rarely are we conscious of the indispensable role that memory is playing in each moment of thought and action. Instead, memory functions are almost always integrated into some other task, and recruited to support performance on these tasks. Thus, how does one arrive at the assumption that different kinds of memory exist as systems separate from other cognitive processes, and that these memory systems reside within their own circumscribed locations in the brain? Because memory processes are often integrated with the process of performing particular tasks, such as perceiving and speaking, it seems unlikely that the neural activity underlying the mnemonic component of the task will necessarily reside in a location separate from the neural activity supporting the task itself. Yet, current developments in the quest for memory systems have made this idea nearly a pre-theoretical assumption.

There is no reason to assume that because one divides the mind into functionally distinct operations (e.g. memory, attention, perception, or even procedural versus episodic memory), that one is going to find brain areas that uniquely correspond to these functions. Furthermore, to search for different memory systems seems to assume that memory is the only function of the brain area in which it is localized, when in fact neural activity in the region may give rise to more than just a memory process. This is not to say that there are not brain circuits devoted primarily to storing and retrieving information. There do seem to be mechanisms and neural circuitry that enable humans to form representations and engage in conscious recollections that are not embodied in the re-enactment or re-experience of the original event, and that may be represented to at least some degree in neural circuitry different from that engaged during the original experience. However, this kind of intentional remembering represents only a fraction of the kinds of memory that support human activity during attention, perception, language, reasoning, problem-solving, reading, intention, motivation, emotion, consciousness, etc. It seems unlikely that each of these expressions of memory has a dedicated neural circuit that performs only the memory part of the task, especially when one considers how many different types of memory may be working together at any particular time. For example, while reading one may be drawing on general knowledge, personal experience, lexical knowledge, syntactic knowledge, orthographic knowledge, and other reading skills (e.g. Levy 1993) to perform the task, and these may not necessarily comprise independent memory representations or processes.

The idea that memory comprises independent and separable subsystems seems to have emerged from our inclination to study tasks in which it is relatively easy to focus on the memory component, such as recalling a list of words or performing a word stem completion test. While such tasks may be useful in helping us isolate processes of interest, they can also be misleading in that they emphasize the separation of remembering from other cognitive processes, while ignoring the integration of memory with all mental processes. This then can mislead one into looking for a dedicated area somewhere in the brain for each different kind of memory that has been postulated to exist, based on the study of a few carefully selected tasks. The way that memory tasks have been constructed and classified for clinical and laboratory use does not ensure their anatomical identifiability.

REFRAMING THE QUESTION

The goal of this chapter was to discuss several issues attending the effort to conceptualize memory in terms of distinct, anatomically identifiable systems. Problems were discussed concerning the operational definition of systems, the appropriate units of analysis, mapping across levels of description, inferential problems in interpreting lesion and neuroimaging data, and how memory is conceptualized in relation to other cognitive activities. Where do these difficulties leave us in terms of trying to characterize the relations between memory processes and brain structures? Memory clearly is not unitary in the sense that a single mechanism or set of principles describes all learning and memory phenomena. However, the problems discussed above do present strong challenges to the assumption that the appropriate alternative to the unitary view is that memory is best characterized in terms of multiple independent systems. The fact that there are diverse memory processes and mechanisms does not necessitate that they all be conceptualized as functionally and anatomically separate systems.

The work that has been conducted in an effort to map memory systems has been of great importance. The knowledge and ideas that have resulted from the last decade of work on memory dissociations, brain lesions, and neuroimaging has had significant theoretical, empirical, and heuristic value. The preceding discussion of the inferential difficulties in developing operational definitions and in using lesion and neuroimaging data to map memory systems is not intended to suggest that these methods have no value in the development of memory theory. Such work has been and will continue to provide important data that must be accounted for in theories of memory. But it is also necessary to assess the coherence of the direction in which the current approach is leading, and to examine some of the underlying assumptions that guide this venture. As more is learned about the nature of neural physiology, chemistry, and organization, as well as the limitations of neuroimaging and lesion data, it becomes clear that the mapping of memory systems with any certainty seems premature.

On the one hand, the hippocampal circuitry does seem like a possible candidate for a relatively distinct memory system, even though it is unclear exactly what role the hippocampus plays in remembering. To some extent the hippocampal formation, along with its inputs and outputs, comes closest to qualifying as an anatomically identifiable memory system. However, there is little evidence that the other types of memory functions and mechanisms that have been identified (e.g. Table 7.3) exist as anatomical entities separate from the broader activities that they support (e.g. perception, language). Thus, many memory functions may be best characterized *not* as separate anatomical systems, but rather as *properties* of neural networks that accomplish other tasks.

Consider 'implicit memory' for example. Although many investigators are looking for the system or systems in which implicit memory is 'located', this does not seem likely to be a fruitful search because implicit memory processes themselves are not unitary (e.g. Blaxton 1989; Marsolek *et al.* 1992; Weldon and Coyote 1996), and in at least in some cases they appear to be *properties* of neural systems that support multiple functions, rather than separate neural systems in themselves. As an example, perceptual and mnemonic activity appear to be integrated in perceptual priming effects. Evidence from PET suggests that repetition priming on the word stem completion task is accompanied by reduced blood flow in the posterior cortex, the site of early visual perceptual processing (Squire *et al.* 1992). The reduced blood flow may be associated with increased efficiency of visual processing, suggesting that the memorial and perceptual components are integrated within the same neural circuitry. To call this a memory system would be to misrepresent the actual activity of the area. Perceptual memory processes may not function separately from perceptual processes, but rather be mechanisms integrated with perceptual processes.

Other data provide relatively more direct evidence that the same neurons that register perception can also record perceptual memory through mechanisms that alter the neurons themselves, and although the specifics of these processes are not well understood, structural, electrical, and chemical mechanisms all seem to be involved. For example, Freeman (1991) has demonstrated that patterns of neural activity produced by various odours in the olfactory bulbs of rabbits depend on their histories of associative learning with the set of stimuli. Freeman suggests that cell assemblies are both 'a crucial repository of past associations and an essential participant in formation of the collective bulbar burst' (p.81), that is, memory and perception are integrated within the same neural assembly, and the process of perception configures these neural assemblies through stimulus-specific patterns of activity. Thus, memory and perception are inseparable, since perceptual acts occur within a neural network that has been shaped by past experience (i.e. memory). Of course, this is not proof that all rabbit sensory systems or any human sensory systems work in this same way, but it does suggest that some types of memory may not be separate neural systems in the way that the hippocampal circuit might be. Thus, it would be misleading to characterize such neural networks as memory systems *per se*, since memory is a property of a neural system subserving a complex mental function.

There also are likely to be memory functions that cannot readily be classified as either separate systems or as integrated properties of neural networks. Consider the evidence in humans that some of the same cortical visual areas that are engaged during visual perception are also engaged when people imagine objects and scenes (Farah 1988). Measures of electrophysiological activity and rCBF have revealed heightened activity in occipital regions during both visual perception and mental imagery tasks. In addition, individuals with right parietal lobe damage accompanied by left hemifield visual neglect have difficulty accessing the left sides of imagined objects and scenes (Bisiach and Luzzatti 1978). These data would seem to suggest an integrated system subserving visual perception and image memory. But limitations in interpreting lesion and neuroimaging data suggest caution in interpreting these data as such, because they do not enable one to determine whether the same neural assemblies are engaged while looking at an object as while imagining that object. In fact, evidence that visual memory can be separate from the visual perceptual apparatus is provided by the fact that when Bisiach and Luzzatti's patients were asked to imagine a familiar location from one direction they neglected details on the left, but when asked to imagine the scene from the opposite direction, such that these neglected details would now be on the right side, the patients were able to describe them. This suggests that at least some knowledge about the scene is represented independently of the apparatus actually employed to visually imagine the scene. Do Bisiach and Luzzatti's patients have damage to their visual perceptual system, or to their visual memory system? Such findings suggest that for many kinds of remembering, efforts to treat remembering either as an activity separate from other cognitive activities or as wholly integrated with these activities will likely oversimplify the picture of how remembering is organized functionally and anatomically.

One fruitful approach might be to identify the kinds of mechanisms employed in the brain to represent experience through structural, chemical, electrical, and physiological modifications. This effort should be free of any commitment to a classificatory scheme based on task types, such as implicit, explicit, semantic, procedural, or conditioning. That is, no *a priori* assumptions should be made that any category of memory tasks is characterized by a unique locus or neural mechanism. For example, long-term potentiation (LTP) may be a mechanism that operates in many different brain regions, and there may even be different varieties of LTP (Lynch and Granger 1994). Thus, LTP likely subserves a variety of memory functions, but it should not be assumed that its particular instantiations respect the functional task boundaries developed in laboratory tasks. Thus, rather than seeking the gross anatomical structures that allegedly comprise the memory system underlying a particular class of memory task, it would be useful to understand the varieties of neurophysiological activities that subserve various component processes, and the neural-level mechanisms that capture and reflect experience in the performance of the task. That is, if one is interested in understanding how experience is processed, stored, and retrieved in the brain, then it will be valuable to identify the memory mechanisms used by the brain, rather than focusing on brain loci *per se*. In the future, it may turn out that these mechanisms are organized into discrete systems identifiable by their anatomical, physiological, or chemical properties. But it may also be the case that different memory tasks engage many different combinations of mechanisms or components, depending on the task demands at any particular time, and that many functional systems are organized flexibly to some degree.

It might also be useful to devote more serious attention to task analyses (e.g. Moscovitch 1984), that is, a more process-oriented analyses of tasks, rather than trying to map out neurological mechanisms on the basis of gross task categories. Currently, most memory systems have been carved up by considering the general category of task that is being performed. That is, there is a tendency to identify tasks with systems (e.g. recognition with the declarative system), but this has not led to a coherent or internally consistent organization of memory systems. One problem is that independent criteria for classifying tasks have not been established. A second problem is that this level of analysis may be too gross for understanding the underlying brain mechanisms, because even the simplest tasks involve a large number of processes. It might be worthwhile to try to decompose tasks into the specific activities or processes that need to be performed in each. In other words, it may be that a taxonomy of memory should not be based on memory tests *per se*, but on the kinds of processes that need to be performed. Consider the difference between recognition and recall, two memory tasks that can be dissociated. Most investigators have not proposed the existence of separate recognition and recall systems, but rather have tried to identify the specific processes that distinguish recognition from recall. In particular, Moscovitch (1994) has hypothesized that different neural circuits underlie recognition and recall, but this idea is based on an analysis of the different task requirements and the different process they engage, not on a search for recognition and recall systems *per se*.

Perhaps it is the focus on memory tasks rather than component processes that has led to the search for a memory system that underlies each category of memory test, while overlooking more complex, integrative uses of memory, such as those involved in reading a book or engaging in a conversation. However, not all memory processes are likely to be associated with distinct anatomical memory systems, so other possible relations between memory and cognitive activities should be imagined and examined.

SUMMARY AND CONCLUSIONS

The goal of this chapter is to challenge the idea that the best alternative to a unitary view of memory is the hypothesis that memory comprises multiple anatomically and functionally distinct systems. The search for multiple memory systems seems to be proceeding without appropriate attention to several fundamental issues concerning how a system is to be defined, whether functional categories of description will map isomorphically to anatomical structures, and whether neuroanatomy provides the most appropriate physical characteristic by which to specify memory mechanisms. Furthermore, many significant inferential problems accompany the interpretation of brain lesions and neuroimaging data as evidence for the existence of multiple systems, and their use as tools to map these postulated systems. This discussion is not intended to discount the potential value of these techniques, nor to suggest that they be abandoned. Rather, it is intended to suggest that in these ventures we need to be forthcoming about their limitations, so that the credibility of the work and its interpretation will not be at issue.

Finally, the notion that all classes of memory functions are necessarily implemented in independent memory systems should be critically examined, and alternative models explored. For example, some memory mechanisms may be integrated within neural networks subserving other mental or physical functions, and these networks should not be characterized as memory systems *per se*. Other kinds of memory functions may require both integrated and separate representations. Rather than trying to map multiprocess memory tasks into isolable memory systems, more fine-grained analyses of the component processes that comprise memory functions should be performed, since this may yield a more accurate picture of the multiple mechanisms underlying the complex and constant play of memory.

ACKNOWLEDGMENTS

Preparation of this chapter was supported by National Institute of Mental Health Grant #1R03MH53857-01, and a Faculty Research Grant from the University of California, Santa Cruz. I thank Julie B. Holloway and Humberto Guitierrez-Rivas for their assistance with portions of this chapter, Randy McIntosh and Kathleen McDermott for helpful discussions about current work, and Michael Wenger and Nameera Akhtar for helpful comments on an earlier draft.

REFERENCES

Andreasen, N. C., O'Leary, D. S., Arndt, S., Cizadlo, T., Hurtig, R. R., K., Watkins, G. L., Boles Ponto, L. L., and Hichwa, R. D. (1995). Short-term and long-term verbal memory: A positron emission tomography study. *Proceedings of the National Academy of Sciences of the USA*, **92**, 5111–15.

Atkinson, R. C. and Shiffrin, R. M. (1968). Human memory: a proposed system and its control processes. In *The psychology of learning and motivation: advances in theory and research*, Vol. 2, (ed. K. W. Spence and J. T. Spence), pp.89–195. Academic, New York.

Becker, J. T., Mintun, M., Diehl, D. J., Dobkin, J., Martidis, A., Madoff, D., and DeKosky, S. T. (1994). Functional neuroanatomy of verbal free recall: a replication study. *Human Brain Mapping*, **1**, 284–92.

Bisiach, E. and Luzzatti, C. (1978). Unilateral neglect of representational space. *Cortex*, **14**, 129–33.
Blaxton, T. (1989). Investigating dissociations among memory measures: support for a transfer-appropriate processing framework. *Journal of Experimental Psychology: Learning, Memory, and Cognition*, **15**, 657–68.
Blaxton, T. A., Bookheimer, S. Y., Zeffiro, T. A., Figlozzi, C. M., Gaillard, W. D., and Theodore, W. H. (1996). Functional mapping of human memory using PET: comparisons of conceptual and perceptual tasks. *Canadian Journal of Experimental Psychology*, **50**, 42–56.
Brodmann, K. (1909). *Vergleichende Lokalisationslehere der Grosshirnrinde in ihren Prinzipien dargestellt auf Grund des Zellenbaues*. Barth, Leipzig.
Bookheimer, S. Y., Zeffiro I. A., Blaxton, T., and Gaillard, W. (1995). Regional cerebral blood flow during object naming and word reading. *Human Brain Mapping*, **3**, 93–106.
Buckner, R. L., Bandettini, P. A., O'Craven, K. M., Savoy, R. L., Petersen, S. E., Raichle, M. E., and Rosen, B. R. (1996). Detection of cortical activation during averaged single trials of a cognitive task using functional magnetic resonance imaging. *Proceedings of the National Academy of Sciences of the USA*, **93**, 14878–83.
Caramazza, A. (1986). On drawing inferences about the structure of normal cognitive systems from the analysis of patterns of impaired performance: the case for single-patient studies. *Brain and Cognition*, **5**, 41–66.
Courtney, S. M., Ungerleider, L. G., Keil, K., and Haxby, J. V. (1997). Transient and sustained activity in a distributed neural system for human working memory. *Nature*, **386**, 608–11.
Cytowic, R. E. (1996). *The neurological side of neuropsychology*. MIT Press, Cambridge, MA.
Dale, A. M. and Buckner, R. L. (1997). Selective averaging of rapidly presented individual trials using fMRI. *Human Brain Mapping*, **5**, 329–40.
Daum, I. and Schugens, M. M. (1996). On the cerebellum and classical conditioning. *Current Directions in Psychological Science*, **5**, 58–61.
de Haan, E. H., Bauer, R. M., and Greve, K. W. (1992). Behavioural and physiological evidence for covert face recognition in a prosopagnosic patient. *Cortex*, **28**, 77–95.
Donders, F. C. (1868). Over de snelheid van psychische processen. *Onderzoekingen gedaan in het psyiologish laboratorium der Utrechtsche Hoogeschool: tweede reeks*, **II**, 92–120.
Dunn, J. C. and Kirsner, K. (1988). Discovering functionally independent mental processes: the principle of reversed association. *Psychological Review*, **95**, 91–101.
Ebbinghaus, H. (1964). *Memory*, (transl. H. A. Ruger and C. E. Bussenius) Dover, New York.
Ellis, H. C. and Hunt, R. R. (1993). *Fundamentals of cognitive psychology*. Brown and Benchmark, Madison, WI.
Farah, M. J. (1988). Is visual imagery really visual? Overlooked evidence from neuropsychology. *Psychological Review*, **95**, 307–17.
Farah, M. J. (1994). Neuropsychological inference with an interactive brain: a critique of the 'locality assumption'. *Behavioral and Brain Sciences*, **17**, 43–104.
Fazio, F., Gilardi, M. C., Colombo, F., Cappa, S. F., Vallar, Bettinardi, V., Paulesu, E., Alberoni, M., and Bressi, S. E. (1992). Metabolic impairment in human amnesia: a PET study of memory networks. *Journal of Cerebral Blood Flow and Metabolism*, **12**, 353–8.
Fiorelli, M., Blin, J., Bakchine, S., Laplane, D., and Baron, J. C. (1991). PET studies of cortical diaschisis in patients with motor hemi-neglect. *Journal of the Neurological Sciences*, **104**, 135–42.
Fodor, J. A. (1983). *The modularity of mind*. MIT Press, Cambridge, MA.

Fodor, J. A. (1985). *Precis of 'The modularity of mind'*, (pp.73–7). Cambridge University Press.
Freeman, W. J. (1991). The physiology of perception. *Scientific American*, 78–85.
Gould, S. J. and Lewontin, R. C. (1979). The spandrels of San Marco and the Panglossian paradigm: a critique of the adaptationist programme. *Proceedings of the Royal Society of London*, B, **205**, 581–98.
Grasby, P. M., Frith, C. D., Friston, K. J., Bench, C., Frackowiak, R. S., and Dolan, R. J. (1993*a*). Functional mapping of brain areas implicated in auditory-verbal memory function. *Brain*, **116**, 1–20.
Grasby, P. M., Frith, C. D., Friston, K., Frackowiak, R. S., and Dolan, R. J. (1993*b*). Activation of the human hippocampal formation during auditory-verbal long-term memory function. *Neuroscience Letters*, **163**, 185–8.
Huguenard, J. R., McCormick, D. A., and Coulter. D. (1995). Thalamocortical interactions. In *The cortical neuron*, (ed. M. J. Gutnick and I. Mody), pp.156–73. Oxford University Press, New York.
James, W. (1890). *The principles of psychology*, Vol. 1. Holt, New York.
Jennings, J. M., McIntosh, A. R., Kapur, S., Tulving, E., and Houle, S. (1997). Cognitive subtractions may not add up: the interaction between semantic processing and response mode. *Neuroimage*, **5**, 229–39.
Johnson, M. K., and Chalfonte, B. L. (1994). Binding complex memories: the role of reactivation and the hippocampus. In *Memory systems 1994*, (ed. D. L. Schacter and E. Tulving), pp. 311–50. MIT Press, Cambridge, MA.
Johnson, M. K., Nolde, S. F., and Kouniou, J. (1996). Event-related potentials associated with source monitoring. *Annual Meeting of the Psychonomics Society*.
Kinomura, S., Kawashima, R., Yamada, K., Ono, S., Itoh, M., Yoshioka, S., Yamaguchi, T., Matsui, H., Miyazawa, H., and Itoh H. (1994). Functional anatomy of taste perception in the human brain studied with positron emission tomography. *Brain Research*, **659**, 263–6.
Laplane, D. and Degos, J. D. (1983). Motor neglect. *Journal of Neurology, Neurosurgery, and Psychiatry*, **46**, 152–8.
Levy, B. A. (1993). Fluent reading: an implicit indicator of reading skill development. In *Implicit memory: new directions in cognition, development, and neuropsychology*, (ed. P. Graf and M. E. Masson), pp.49–73. Erlbaum, Hillsdale, NJ.
Lynch, G. and Granger, R. (1994). Variations in synaptic plasticity and types of memory in corticohippocampal networks. In *Memory systems 1994*, (ed. D. L. Schacter and E. Tulving), pp.65–86. MIT Press, Cambridge, MA.
MacLean, P. D. (1949). Psychosomatic disease and the 'visceral brain': recent developments bearing on the Papez theory of emotion. *Psychosomatic Medicine*, **11**, 338–53.
Marr, D. (1982). *Vision*. Freeman, San Francisco.
Marsolek, C. J., Kosslyn, S. M., and Squire, L. R. (1992). Form-specific visual priming in the right cerebral hemisphere. *Journal of Experimental Psychology: Learning, Memory, and Cognition*, **18**, 492–508.
McCarthy, R. A. (1994). Neuropsychology: going loco? *Behavioral and Brain Sciences*, **17**, 73–4.
McIntosh, A. R. and Gonzalez-Lima, F. (1994). Structural equation modeling and its application to network analysis in functional brain imaging. *Human Brain Mapping*, **2**, 2–22.
Mesulam, M. M. (1994). Distributed locality and large-scale neurocognitive networks. *Behavioral and Brain Sciences*, **17**, 74–6.
Mesulam, M. M. (1990). Large-scale neurocognitive networks and distributed processing for attention, language and memory. *Annals of Neurology*, **28**, 597–610.

Morton, J. (1984). Brain-based and non-brain based models of language. In *Biological perspectives in language*, (ed. D. Caplan, A. R. Lecours and A. Smith). MIT Press, Cambridge, MA.
Moscovitch, M. (1984). The sufficient conditions for demonstrating preserved memory in amnesia: a task analysis. In *The neuropsychology of memory*, (ed. N. Butters and L. R. Squire), pp.104–14. Guildford Press, New York.
Moscovitch, M. (1994). Memory and working with memory: evaluation of a component process model and comparisons with other models. In *Memory systems 1994*, (ed. D. L. Schacter and E. Tulving), pp.269–310. MIT Press, Cambridge, MA.
Moyer, J. R., Deyo, R. A., and Disterhoft, J. F. (1990). Hippocampectomy disrupts trace eye-blink conditioning in rabbits. *Behavioral Neuroscience*, **104**, 243–52.
Nadel, L. (1994). Multiple memory systems: what and why, an update. In *Memory systems 1994* (ed. D. L. Schacter and E. Tulving), pp. 39–63. MIT Press, Cambridge, MA.
Nieuwenhuys, R. (1985). *Chemoarchitecture of the brain*. Springer, Berlin.
Oaksford, M. (1994). Computational levels again. *Behavioral and Brain Sciences*, **7**, 76–7.
Ojemann, G. A., Ojemann, J., Lettich, E., and Berger, M. (1989). Cortical language localization in left-dominant hemisphere. *Journal of Neurosurgery*, **71**, 316–26.
Posner, M. I. and Raichle, M. E. (1994). *Images of the mind*. Freeman, New York.
Posner, M. I., Petersen, S. E., and Fox, P. T., M. W. (1988). Localization of cognitive operations in the human brain. *Science*, **240**, 1627–31.
Roediger, H. L. III (1990). Implicit memory: retention without remembering. *American Psychologist*, **45**, 1043–56.
Roediger, H. L. III Rajaram, S., and Srinivas, K. (1990). Specifying criteria for postulating memory systems. *Annals of the New York Academy of Sciences*, **608**, 572–95.
Sarter, M., Berntson, G. G., and Cacioppo, J. T. (1996). Brain imaging and cognitive neuroscience: toward strong inference in attributing function to structure. *American Psychologist*, **51**, 13–21.
Sartori, G. and Job, R. (1988). The oyster with four legs: a neuropsychological study on the interaction of visual and semantic information. *Cognitive Neuropsychology*, **5**, 105–32.
Schacter, D. L. (1990). Perceptual representation systems and implicit memory: toward a resolution of the multiple memory systems debate. In *The development and neural bases of higher cognitive functions*, (ed. A. Diamond), pp.543–71. New York Academy of Sciences, New York.
Schacter, D. L. (1992). Understanding implicit memory: a cognitive neuroscience approach. *American Psychologist*, **47**, 559–69.
Schacter, D. L. and Tulving, E. (ed.) (1994*a*). *Memory systems 1994*. MIT Press, Cambridge, MA.
Schacter, D. L. and Tulving E. (1994*b*). What are the memory systems of 1994? In *Memory systems 1994*, (ed. D. L. Schacter and E. Tulving), pp.1–38. MIT Press, Cambridge, MA.
Searle, J. R. (1994). Some relations between mind and brain. In *Neuroscience, memory, and language*, (ed. R. D. Broadwell), pp.25–34. Library of Congress, Washington, DC.
Sergent, J. (1994). Brain-imaging studies of cognitive functions. *Trends in Neuroscience*, **17**, 221–7.
Sergent, J., MacDonald, B., and Zuck, E. (1994). Structural and functional organization of knowledge about faces and proper names: a positron emission tomography study. In *Attention and performance XV*, (ed. C. Umilta and M. Moscovitch), pp.204–28. MIT Press, Cambridge, MA.
Shallice, T. (1988). *From neuropsychology to mental structure*. Cambridge University Press
Shallice, T., Fletcher, P., Frith, C. D., Grasby, P., Frackowiak, R. S., and Dolan, R. J.

(1994). Brain regions associated with acquisition and retrieval of verbal episodic memory. *Nature*, **368**, 633–5.

Sherry, D. F. and Schacter, D. L. (1987). The evolution of multiple memory systems. *Psychological Review*, **94**, 439–54.

Solomon, P. R. and Yang, B. Y. (1994). What are the best strategies for understanding hippocampal function? *Behavioral and Brain Sciences*, **17**, 494–5.

Squire, L. R. (1994). Declarative and nondeclarative memory: multiple brain systems supporting learning and memory. In *Memory systems 1994*, (ed. D. L. Schacter and E. Tulving), pp.203–32. MIT Press, Cambridge, MA.

Squire, L. R., Ojemann, J. G., Miezin, F. M., Petersen, S. E., Videen, T. O., and Raichle, M. E. (1992). Activation of the hippocampus is normal humans: a functional anatomical study of memory. *Proceedings of the National Academy of Sciences of the USA*, **89**, 1837–41.

Talairach, J. and Tournoux, P. (1988). *Co-planar stereotaxic atlas of the human brain*. Thieme, New York.

Tulving, E. (1972). Episodic and semantic memory. In *Organization of memory*, (ed. E. Tulving and W. Donaldson), pp. 381–403. Academic, New York.

Tulving, E. (1983). *Elements of episodic memory*. Oxford University Press.

Tulving, E. (1985). How many memory systems are there? *American Psychologist*, **40**, 385–8.

Warrington, E. K. and McCarthy, R. (1983). Category specific access dysphasia. *Brain*, **106**, 859–78.

Warrington, E. K. and Shallice, T. (1984). Category specific semantic impairments. *Brain*, **107**, 829–53.

Weldon, M. S. and Coyote, K. C. (1996). Failure to find the picture superiority effect in implicit conceptual memory tests. *Journal of Experimental Psychology: Learning, Memory, and Cognition*, **22**, 670–86.

8
The architecture of human memory

JOHN D. E. GABRIELI

What is the functional architecture of human memory? This book constitutes a dialogue between two perspectives, one psychological and another neuropsychological, about how to answer this question. The psychological perspective grows from a distinguished line of experimentation with normal subjects that began with Ebbinghaus (1885). Over the next century, this line of research revealed a great deal about the characteristics of human memory performance through verbal learning research and information-processing models (e.g. Atkinson and Shiffrin 1968; Bower 1967; Craik and Lockhart 1972; Tulving 1964; Underwood 1983). Few, if any, of these researchers posited a truly monolithic account of memory, with many models containing multiple representations or processes. Memory, however, was often seen as a unitary capacity comprising highly interactive component processes governed by broad principles that determine what is remembered and what is forgotten.

A separate tradition of neuropsychological research has emphasized the non-unitary nature of memory. This line of research has interpreted dissociations between various forms of intact and impaired memory that occur in patients with brain lesions as indicating that human memory is composed of multiple systems. Each memory system has a unique brain location and unique mnemonic capacity. Although there were some interactions between psychological and neuropsychological perspectives, such as the distinction between short-term and long-term memory, the intellectual influences were unidirectional. Neuropsychologists working in hospitals and medical schools took advantage of ideas and findings from the study of normal human memory in order to analyse and interpret mnemonic deficits following brain injuries. Memory research in academic psychology departments was, however, minimally influenced by neuropsychological findings. For example, a widely used and influential textbook on memory published in 1980 contains only two brief mentions of neuropsychological findings (Klatzky 1980).

These two traditions have interacted with increasing frequency and vigour over the past 45 years, beginning with the discovery of HM's amnesia in 1953 and exploding with the development of functional neuroimaging techniques such as positron emission tomography (PET) and functional magnetic resonance imaging (fMRI). It is common nowadays to find memory researchers engaged in an integrated programme of investigation including behavioural studies of normal subjects, neuropsychological analysis of patients, and functional neuroimaging.

Nevertheless, a residual tension between psychological and neuropsychological approaches to studying memory has remained and has been labelled as a debate between unitary and multiple systems or between processing and systems accounts of memory. In this chapter I first review briefly the intellectual history of the systems approach to memory which can be viewed as three generations of inquiry. Then, I consider some particular points of debate between processing and systems views of memory. Finally, I offer some suggestions about future directions in memory research which integrate psychological and neuropsychological perspectives.

A BRIEF HISTORY OF MEMORY SYSTEMS RESEARCH

First generation: is memory unitary?

In the early 1950s, on the basis of lesion studies with rats, Karl Lashley proposed that mammals had a unitary memory system: 'It is not possible to demonstrate the isolated localization of a memory trace anywhere in the nervous system... the engram is represented throughout the region' (Lashley 1950, p.478). In one sense, Lashley's view remains correct: memory for an event or fact is still thought to be recorded, retained, and retrieved by a large network of brain regions. In another sense, however, Lashley's proposal has been shown to be incorrect because it is clear now that different brain regions participate in different kinds of memory.

The modern era of memory systems research began with the noted case of the amnesic patient HM who, in 1953, underwent bilateral resection of medial-temporal lobe regions for the treatment of otherwise intractable epilepsy (Scoville and Milner 1957). The result was a profound and pervasive anterograde amnesia such that, for all practical purposes, HM has not been able to remember any events or learn any facts since 1953, including wars, assassinations, humans landing on the moon, or the deaths of his own parents. His short-term memory remained intact, as did most perceptual, cognitive, motivational, and motor abilities. HM retained most of his preoperative memories, although it appears that he has a subtle retrograde amnesia extending back eleven years prior to his surgery (Sagar *et al.* 1985). Thus, HM's case showed that the resected medial-temporal regions were essential for remembering events and facts, but were not required either for short-term memory or for many aspects of perception, thought, and action.

HM also provided the first well documented evidence that some kinds of long-term memory do not depend upon the brain structures and psychological processes that are essential for remembering events and facts. He acquired and retained normally a skill for mirror-tracing across days despite an absence of conscious memory for the experiences in which he gained that skill (Milner 1962). Indeed, when tested years later, HM showed complete retention of mirror tracing skill after delays of not only a day, but also a week, two weeks, and a year (Gabrieli *et al.* 1993). HM also showed a substantial, but slightly less than normal, benefit of repeatedly identifying incomplete pictures (Milner *et al.* 1968) (Warrington and Weiskrantz

(1968) had a contemporaneous report of the same phenomenon). This change in the processing of a stimulus due to prior processing of the same or a related stimulus is now defined as repetition priming. HM's slightly reduced priming was due to testing conditions that encouraged normal subjects to explicitly consult their memory for prior experience with identical incomplete pictures. When those conditions are avoided, amnesic patients show entirely normal priming in the identification of incomplete pictures (Verfaellie *et al*. 1996).

These studies revealed that memory is not composed of a unitary engram distributed throughout the nervous system. Specifically, the engrams underlying HM's intact short-term memory, skill learning, and repetition priming cannot be represented in the medial-temporal structures that were vital for most aspects of memory. Thus, different kinds of memory traces or engrams are represented discretely in the nervous system.

Second generation: what kinds of memory are impaired and intact in amnesia?

Dichotomies of memory

The second generation of memory systems research attempted to provide a theoretical framework characterizing the different kinds of representations and processes mediated by neurally distinct memory systems. Tulving and Kinsbourne and their colleagues proposed that amnesia reflected a dissociation between neural systems subserving episodic memory processes (memory for temporally and spatially specific autobiographical events) and semantic memory processes (memory for generic knowledge such as words, concepts, and history) (Kinsbourne and Wood 1975; Schacter and Tulving 1982; Tulving 1972). This interpretation was challenged by other researchers who showed that amnesic patients failed to acquire both episodic and semantic memories (Gabrieli *et al*. 1988; Zola-Morgan *et al*. 1983). For example, HM did not know the meaning of words or phrases that came into the language after the onset of his amnesia. He defined 'jet lag' as 'when jets slow down', a 'half-way house' as 'a house that's half way there', 'nuke' as 'neutral', and 'soul food' as 'forgiveness' (Gabrieli 1986). Similarly, he knew practically nothing of people who came into public prominence after 1953 (Gabrieli *et al*. 1988; Marslen-Wilson and Teuber 1975). Thus, the semantic/episodic framework provoked debate amongst systems researchers.

Two other frameworks received more widespread acceptance. First, Cohen and Squire (1980) proposed that amnesia reflects a dissociation between declarative and procedural forms of memory. Declarative memory was defined initially as 'knowing that' or data-based knowledge 'concerned with the accumulation of facts and data derived from learning experiences' (Cohen and Eichenbaum 1993). Procedural memory was defined as 'knowing how' or rule-based information (Cohen and Squire 1980) that 'involves the tuning and modifying of the particular processors engaged during training' (Cohen and Eichenbaum 1993). Cohen and Squire diverged in their later conceptions of 'procedural' memory. Cohen classified all forms of memory that share a set of features and characteristics as procedural, including forms of repetition priming and conditioning that are intact in amnesia (Cohen and Eichenbaum 1993). Squire classified forms of preserved learning in amnesia as 'non-declarative', and reserved the term procedural for only skill learning (Squire 1992).

Second, Graf and Schacter (1985) proposed a distinction between implicit memory, 'revealed when performance on a task is facilitated in the absence of conscious recollection', and explicit memory 'revealed when performance on a task requires conscious recollection of previous experience'. Implicit and explicit forms of memory were posited to be 'tapped by priming tests on the one hand, and by recall and recognition tests on the other hand'. The implicit/explicit distinction is widely used, but two different senses of that distinction are often confused. One sense is that of retrieval instructions for a memory test. A memory test is explicit when subjects are asked to intentionally retrieve memories from a specified episode, and it is implicit when subjects are asked to perform a task and no reference is made to any prior episode. A second sense refers to retrieval processes. In this sense, explicit retrieval entails conscious recollection and implicit retrieval occurs without conscious recollection. There is not, however, an equivalence between test instructions and the memory processes used to perform a test. As will be reviewed below, people often intentionally or incidentally invoke conscious recollection on implicit tests, and sometimes resort to implicit retrieval on an explicit test.

These two distinctions motivated many studies of learning and memory to determine the scope and limits of intact memory in amnesia. Thus, it was found that preserved skill learning in amnesia extended from sensorimotor tasks, such as mirror tracing and rotary pursuit (Corkin 1968), to perceptual tasks, such as reading mirror-reversed text (Cohen and Squire 1980), and to cognitive tasks, such as the Tower of Hanoi and probabilistic classification (Cohen et al. 1985; Knowlton et al. 1994; Saint-Cyr et al. 1988; Schmidtke et al. 1996). Amnesic patients have shown intact learning for classical delay eyeblink conditioning (Gabrieli et al. 1995b) and fear conditioning (Bechara et al. 1995).

Repetition priming was intensively studied in amnesia. Amnesic patients showed intact priming for meaningful words or pictures on tests of visual (Cermak et al. 1985) and auditory (Schacter et al. 1995) threshold identification, word stem completion (Graf et al. 1984; Warrington and Weiskrantz 1970), word fragment completion (Vaidya et al. 1995), picture naming (Cave and Squire 1992; Verfaellie et al. 1996), word association generation (Shimamura and Squire 1984; Vaidya et al. 1995), and category–exemplar generation (Graf and Schacter 1985; Keane et al. 1997). They exhibited intact priming for novel verbal information on tests of threshold identification of pronounceable pseudowords (Haist et al. 1991) and unpronounceable letter strings (Keane et al. 1995a) and for novel non-verbal information on tests with dot patterns (Gabrieli et al. 1990; Knowlton and Squire 1993; Musen and Squire 1992) and shapes (Schacter et al. 1991). They demonstrated normal priming for novel associations created by arbitrary study-phase pairing of stimuli on tasks of word identification (Gabrieli et al. 1997b), reading time (Moscovitch et al. 1986), and colour-word naming (Musen and Squire 1993).

Thus, many islands of preserved learning were found in the vast ocean of global amnesia.

There are, however, many instances in which amnesic patients show impaired performance on implicit tests of memory. For example, when HM defines 'jet lag' as 'when jets slow down', no explicit reference is made to any prior episode. Yet, unlike healthy control subjects, he cannot define that term. Amnesic patients also have deficits in later stages of some cognitive skill learning tasks (Knowlton et al. 1994), and in more complex forms of eyeblink conditioning, including trace conditioning (McGlinchey-Berroth et al. 1997) and discrimination reversal (Daum et al. 1989). Amnesic patients have impaired priming for word stems with unique completions (Squire et al. 1987), impaired associative priming for word stem completion (Cermak et al. 1988; Schacter and Graf 1986; Shimamura and Squire 1989), impaired voice-specific priming on auditory word identification (Schacter et al. 1995), impaired priming on visual identification of incomplete words or pictures (Cermak et al. 1993; Gabrieli et al. 1994; Milner et al. 1968; Verfaellie et al. 1996; Warrington and Weiskrantz 1968), and impaired priming for general knowledge (Vaidya et al. 1996). Because theoretical interest has focused on spared learning in amnesia, few investigators have pursued areas of impaired implicit test performance in amnesia. Therefore, the range of impaired amnesic performance on implicit tests of memory is likely to be far greater than this brief list indicates.

Limitations of dichotomies: the problem of relating tasks to processes

Amnesic deficits on implicit tests that do not ask for declarative knowledge are theoretically important and problematic. Neither the explicit/implicit nor the declarative/procedural distinction can explain, *a priori*, why amnesic patients show intact priming for word stems with multiple completions but not with single completions, or intact priming of new associations between words on an identification but not a word stem completion test, or intact cognitive skill learning for early but not later phases of probabilistic classification, or intact priming for identifying incomplete drawings after studying complete but not incomplete drawings (Verfaellie et al. 1996), or intact font-specific priming in visual word stem completion (Vaidya et al. 1998) but impaired voice-specific priming in auditory word identification (Schacter et al. 1995).

These deficits may be explained in a number of ways. One is that subjects with intact declarative memory recognize the opportunity to use that memory and simply perform, on their own, explicit retrieval of relevant declarative knowledge. This may occur when it is evidently advantageous to support test-phase performance accuracy with intentional retrieval of study-phase experience (e.g. Knowlton et al. 1994; Vaidya et al. 1996). It does not explain amnesic deficits when test-phase accuracy is not enhanced by study-phase memories, such as associative word stem completion where any completion is satisfactory (e.g. Cermak et al. 1988; Schacter and Graf 1986; Shimamura and Squire 1989). In those cases, implicit tests may incidentally invoke some declarative memory processes. In both cases, intact declarative memory processes augment implicit test performance in normal subjects, but are unavailable to augment the implicit test performance of amnesic patients. These *single-deficit* explanations treat impaired implicit test performance as another measure of the same impairments that underlie impaired explicit test performance. Alternatively, amnesic impairments on implicit tests could reveal additional processing deficits beyond those that underlie impaired explicit test performance.

A limitation of the single-deficit interpretation is that it is circular in logic—every implicit test failed by amnesic patients is treated as a covert explicit test. An advantage of the single-deficit interpretation is that it is parsimonious—it does not posit a new processing deficit for every amnesic failure. This parsimony has been assumed for amnesic declarative failure on explicit tests. It is assumed that impaired memory for abstract words, concrete words, short words, long words, common words, and uncommon words does not reflect multiple, distinct processing failures. Instead, the near constant correlation of these deficits in amnesia makes it more parsimonious to consider them as multiple expressions of a common processing deficit. By the same logic, in the absence of other qualifying findings, it seems prudent to ascribe correlated amnesic deficits on implicit and explicit tests to a common cause.

The foregoing discussion highlights the difficulty in discerning what memory processes are engaged by a memory task. The experimenter controls whether the test instruction is explicit or implicit, but it is the laws of memory that determine which processes and underlying neural substrates are engaged by a person in performing the test. Thus, the mapping between retrieval instructions and memory processing must be discovered through experimental analysis. This analysis is particularly salient in the comparison of explicit and implicit cued-retrieval tasks. Such comparisons are theoretically powerful because the retrieval cues are held constant, and only retrieval instructions are varied. For example, if subjects see SOUTH in a study phase, they later see SOU at test and are asked either to recall what study word began with those letters (explicit test) or to generate the first word that comes to mind beginning with those letters (implicit test). Indeed, amnesic patients show intact priming and impaired cued recall with only such a change in retrieval instructions on tests such as word stem completion (Graf *et al.* 1984), word fragment completion (Vaidya *et al.* 1995), word associate generation (Shimamura and Squire 1984; Vaidya *et al.* 1995), and category–exemplar generation (Keane *et al.* 1997). Further, normal subjects provide significantly more study words when performing explicit than implicit cued retrieval, but amnesic patients often show little change in performance across the two retrieval instructions (e.g. Graf *et al.* 1984; Vaidya *et al.* 1995). These findings suggest that amnesic patients may often be providing primed responses rather than intentionally retrieved episodic memories on cued recall tests. In other words, amnesic patients are providing cue-driven guesses, scored as correct explicit retrievals, which reflect no more than the first response that comes to mind.

Providing primed responses to retrieval cues in an explicit test is not limited to amnesic patients. For example, one study compared the performance of HM with that of normal control subjects on three tests of memory for meaningless patterns that had been drawn to connect dot configurations in a study phase (Gabrieli *et al.* 1990). In an implicit test, subjects were given with the same dot configurations seen earlier, and were asked to connect them with the first pattern that came to mind. HM showed intact priming by having a normal bias to draw patterns copied earlier. He was impaired on an explicit multiple-choice recognition test of memory for the patterns. Finally, there was a cued recall test in which subjects were provided with the same dot configurations seen earlier, and asked explicitly to connect them with same pattern they had copied earlier. Surprisingly, HM and control subjects performed equally on this test and were no more likely to produce the study patterns than they had been on the implicit test. This was interpreted as indicating that explicit memory for the incidentally encoded, meaningless, non-verbal patterns was so poor that neither HM nor control subjects could do more than produce the first pattern that came to mind on both the explicit and implicit cued-retrieval tests.

Others have objected that this interpretation is circular, because it characterizes memory retrieval as conscious or non-conscious on the basis of impaired or intact amnesic performance respectively, rather than the explicit or implicit nature of test instructions (Ostergaard and Jernigan 1993; Ratcliff and McKoon 1996). This concern about the circularity of the logic is well taken, but consider the merit of the non-circular alternative that these researchers would have to embrace. The alternative interpretation is that HM has intact declarative memory for dot-cued patterns despite his amnesia for letters, digits, words, pictures, non-verbal designs, sentences, paragraphs, the war in Vietnam, Watergate, the name of the current President, the current decade, his current age, the invention and widespread use of the computer, and the deaths of his parents. Further, this preserved explicit memory for meaningless patterns is available for cued recall but not multiple-choice tests, and is coincidentally equivalent in the implicit and explicit test performance of both HM and control subjects. This alternative interpretation has the merit of not being circular because it assumes an equivalence between explicit test instructions and conscious memory processes, but has the demerit of being unlikely to be correct.

Third generation: multiple memory systems

The seeds of a third generation of research were planted as researchers discovered multiple components of declarative memory. Immediate or short-term memory capacities intact in amnesia are impaired in patients with neocortical lesions. These domain-specific immediate memory stores appear to be separable both by a verbal/non-verbal dimension in left and right hemispheres, and by an auditory/visual dimension in temporal and parieto-occipital regions. Most strikingly, some of these material-and-modality specific immediate memory stores participate minimally in long-term memory processes, with exceptions such as learning a foreign language (reviewed in Smith and Jonides 1994).

Multiple components of long-term declarative memory were also discovered. Declarative memory depends not only on the medial-temporal region, but also diencephalic and basal forebrain regions (e.g. Press *et al.* 1989). Left and right medial-temporal regions play specific roles in verbal and non-verbal long-term memory respectively (Milner 1971). Within the medial-temporal region, there is now evidence for dissociable declarative memory processes occurring in the amygdala (Cahill *et al.* 1995, 1996), subiculum, and parahippocampal cortex (Gabrieli *et al.* 1997*a*). There also appears to be a frontostriatal system with multiple components involved in working memory modulation of the encoding and retrieval of declarative memories (e.g. Demb *et al.* 1995; Gabrieli *et al.* 1996*a*, *b*; Janowsky *et al.* 1989; Kapur *et al.* 1994; Milner 1971; Petrides and Milner 1982; Schacter *et al.* 1996; Shallice *et al.* 1994; Singh *et al.* 1992; Squire *et al.* 1992; Stebbins *et al.* 1995; Tulving *et al.* 1994). Thus, there are multiple systems involved in different components of both short-term and long-term declarative memory.

Many systems of non-declarative memory have also been discovered in studies of patients with lesions in brain regions that are intact in amnesia. Thus, the cerebellum plays a critical role in classical eyeblink conditioning (Daum *et al.* 1993) and the amygdala in fear conditioning (Bechara *et al.* 1995; LaBar *et al.* 1995). A contribution of the basal ganglia to skill learning has been suggested by the deficits of Huntington's disease patients on motor, perceptual, and cognitive skill learning tasks (Gabrieli *et al.* 1997*c*; Heindel *et al.* 1988, 1989; Knowlton *et al.* 1996; Martone *et al.* 1984; Willingham and Koroshetz 1993). A neocortical basis of repetition priming is indicated by priming deficits in patients with Alzheimer's disease or focal cortical lesions (Gabrieli *et al.* 1994, 1995*a*; Keane *et al.* 1991, 1995*b*; Shimamura *et al.* 1987).

Thus, there are many dissociable forms of declarative and non-declarative memory with separable processing and neural bases. With so many brain regions implicated in various forms of memory, there is a sense in which Lashley was correct that the 'engram is represented throughout the region'. Systems research, however, has shown that there are different engrams in different memory systems. With the advent of brain imaging techniques, memory systems research can progress in a systematic fashion instead of depending upon the happenstance pathologies of nature that lead to focal or neurodegenerative brain injuries. Imaging and lesion evidence can provide powerful mutual constraints upon the neural identification and psychological characterization of memory systems (reviewed in Gabrieli 1998).

THE PROCESSING/SYSTEMS DEBATE

The processing/systems debate was spurred by an important set of ideas and experimental findings from Roediger and his colleagues (Blaxton 1989; Roediger and Blaxton 1987; Roediger *et al.* 1989, 1990; Srinivas and Roediger 1990). The debate was waged at two levels. One level was a broad claim about the limited value of memory systems theories altogether. Roediger (1990) cited a statement from Tulving and Bower (1974) that 'it has not yet been made clear by anyone how the task of explaining memory phenomena is materially aided by the hypothesized existence of different memory stores and systems' (p.273). Roediger (Roediger *et al.* 1990) concurs by stating that 'We have still not seen a satisfactory answer to this query' (p.585).

Understanding the brain organization of human memory, however, does explain the dissociations one sees in brain-injured patients. It is unclear how else such memory phenomena can be explained. Further, the modern study of implicit memory is built upon the discovery of spared memory in amnesic patients (Warrington and Weiskrantz 1970). Although there is a long history of ideas about implicit memory (Schacter 1987), no memory theory predicted or pursued such phenomena until studies of amnesia (Cohen and Squire 1980; Milner *et al.* 1968; Warrington and Weiskrantz 1968, 1970) motivated such research (e.g. Graf *et al.* 1982, 1984; Jacoby and Dallas 1981; Tulving *et al.* 1982). Thus, the actual existence in the brain of different stores and systems, revealed via amnesia, allowed for the discovery of forms of memory that were unknown and unanticipated by the traditional psychological study of memory.

Knowledge of the existence of multiple memory systems also provides important constraints on the interpretation of behavioural studies. Memory systems are not only physically distinct in the brain, but also have different processing characteristics. Therefore, when a study manipulates encoding or retrieval demands and comes to some conclusion about memory processes and representations, that conclusion is appropriate only for the form of memory that has been studied. Indeed, this appreciation about the manifold natures of multiple memory systems has spurred not only a great deal of research in repetition priming, but has also reinvigorated studies of skill learning and conditioning in humans. Thus, the mnemonic uniqueness of memory systems has both sharpened the scope of memory research, system by system, and broadened the range of human learning abilities that are under active investigation.

At a more specific level, Roediger and his collaborators took aim at the procedural/declarative and explicit/implicit distinctions that guided amnesia research. Roediger and his students emphasized another distinction, that between conceptual and perceptual tests of memory, which are based upon stimulus meaning or form respectively. Performance on conceptual tests of memory are enhanced by semantic analysis at study. Thus, conceptual memory is superior after semantic than non-semantic encoding and after generating a word to a semantic cue than merely reading the word. Conceptual memory is unaffected by study-phase shifts in stimulus form, such as between auditory and visual stimuli, or between verbal and pictorial visual stimuli. Perceptual memory, in contrast, is superior when stimulus form is the same at study and test, and is unaffected by variation in semantic analysis at study. The perceptual/conceptual distinction built upon findings from other researchers who emphasized related processing distinctions, most notably Jacoby's distinction between recollection and a more perceptually based familiarity component of recognition memory (Jacoby and Dallas 1981; Jacoby and Witherspoon 1982; Jacoby 1983).

Many early studies reported dissociations in amnesic patients between impaired performance on explicit memory tests and intact performance on implicit memory tests involving repetition priming. These findings were commonly interpreted as a dissociation between explicit and implicit retrieval demands. The perceptual/conceptual processing distinction, however, raised another interpretation. The explicit tests involved memory measures of recall or recognition, and both of these measures are classified as being largely conceptual because they are superior after semantic versus non-semantic encoding and after generating than reading a word. Many of the implicit memory tests yielding intact priming in amnesia were perceptual in nature, including word identification (Cermak et al. 1985), word stem completion (Graf et al. 1984; Warrington and Weiskrantz 1970), and word fragment completion (Vaidya et al. 1995). Therefore, these dissociations, by themselves, did not indicate whether preserved priming in amnesia reflected spared performance on implicit tests or on perceptual tests.

Blaxton (1989) investigated systematically the relation between explicit and implicit retrieval, on the one hand, and perceptual and conceptual processing, on the other hand. She found that in normal subjects manipulations of conceptual encoding had parallel effects upon performance on an implicit test (general knowledge) and explicit tests of free and semantic cued recall. She also found that manipulations of perceptual encoding had parallel effects upon performance on an implicit test (word fragment completion) and an explicit test (graphemic cued recall). Thus, it was the perceptual or conceptual nature of study-and-test phase processing that determined performance, and not the implicit or explicit test instructions.

These findings led Blaxton (1992) to question the idea that intact and impaired memory in amnesia reflected implicit and explicit test demands. Instead, she hypothesized that 'memory impaired patients are characterized as having deficits in conceptual, but not data-driven, processing capabilities'. The claims about conceptual and perceptual processing capabilities in amnesia are considered in turn.

Are conceptual processing capabilities impaired in amnesia?

Even at the outset, there were empirical and theoretical reasons to doubt the claim that the core problem in amnesia was one of 'conceptual processing capabilities'. The empirical reasons were that two studies had already been published in which amnesic patients had shown normal magnitudes of priming on tasks generally considered as conceptual—word association generation (Shimamura and Squire 1984) and category–exemplar generation (Graf et al. 1985). The sole caveat was that neither study had used a study-phase processing manipulation to verify the conceptual basis of the observed priming. Priming on these tasks, however, cannot logically be anything but conceptual. First, subjects are asked to generate associates or exemplars on the basis of conceptual relations between words. Second, there is no perceptual mechanism that can support priming when the study-phase items (e.g. QUEEN or MUSHROOM) bear no perceptual relation to test-phase cues (what word is related to KING? or what are eight examples of VEGETABLES?).

The theoretical concern was the claim that amnesia is characterized by a pervasive deficit in 'conceptual processing capabilities'. Global amnesia is defined as a syndrome with a circumscribed deficit in declarative memory performance, with other motivational, motor, perceptual, and conceptual abilities being intact. Amnesic patients are commonly selected for research studies on the basis of scoring well on IQ tests of non-mnemonic mental abilities, such as the Wechsler Adult Intelligence Scale—Revised (WAIS-R) (Wechsler 1981), but scoring poorly on the long-term memory portions of tests of mnemonic abilities, such as the Wechsler Memory Scale—Revised (WMS-R) (Wechsler 1987). In the case of HM, for example, his IQ score increased from 104 pre-operatively when he was not amnesic in 1953 to 112 post-operatively in 1955 when he was amnesic (Corkin 1984). Patients with widespread 'conceptual processing' deficits would perform poorly on tests involving many aspects of language and thinking, such as the WAIS-R. Therefore, one would have to posit a complete dissociation between mnemonic and non-mnemonic conceptual processes. Such a dissociation is contrary to the view that priming reflects experience-induced plasticity in the same system that mediates initial processing of a percept or concept. This view seems to be central to processing theory, and is now well supported by functional neuroimaging studies of perceptual (Buckner *et al*. 1995; Schacter *et al*. 1996; Squire *et al*. 1992) and conceptual (Demb *et al*. 1995; Gabrieli *et al*. 1996*a*; Wagner *et al*. 1997*a*) priming.

Despite the above objections, no study had shown directly that amnesic patients would perform normally on a conceptual implicit test that was empirically demonstrated to be conceptual. Several such studies, therefore, were conducted with amnesic patients and all yielded findings contradicting the processing claim of a global conceptual deficit in amnesia. Amnesic patients showed normal priming on word association generation where priming was demonstrated to be conceptual by being unaffected by a shift in study-test modality (Vaidya *et al*. 1995). Amnesic patients also showed normal priming on category–exemplar generation where priming was demonstrated to be conceptual by being affected by the degree of conceptual encoding at study (Keane *et al*. 1997). In both studies, amnesic patients were impaired on explicit tests that used the same cues, i.e. had the same conceptual processing demands, as the implicit tests. Related studies have found similar dissociations between implicit and explicit conceptual memory performance with amnesic patients (Carlesimo 1994; Cermak *et al*. 1995), schizophrenic patients (Schwartz *et al*. 1993), and healthy older relative to younger people (Light and Albertson 1989; Monti *et al*. 1996).

These results resolve two arguments of the processing systems debate. First, they show that amnesic patients cannot be 'characterized as having deficits in conceptual processing capabilities'. Amnesic patients showed normal priming on several conceptual tests, including normal sensitivity to conceptual encoding and insensitivity to perceptual encoding. Second, they demonstrate that conceptual processes are not unitary. Merely shifting instructions from implicit to explicit retrieval yielded dissociations between conceptual test performances in amnesia, schizophrenia, and aging. Further, following these amnesia studies, there has been growing evidence for multiple conceptual memory mechanisms (e.g. McDermott and Roediger 1996; Vaidya et al. 1997; Weldon and Coyote 1997).

Amnesic patients have, however, shown a deficit on another conceptual implicit test, general knowledge (Vaidya et al. 1996). In this test, subjects in the study phase are exposed to words (such as BUTTERFLY). In the test phase, they attempt to answer questions such as 'What insect is the Monarch and Queen Alexandria?' Priming is measured as how much more often subjects answer questions for which the answer was seen in the study phase than baseline questions. This implicit test is validated as being conceptual because priming is greater after semantic than non-semantic study-phase processing (Blaxton 1989; Carlesimo 1994; Cermak et al. 1995; Challis and Sidhu 1993; Hamann 1990; Srinivas and Roediger 1990; Vaidya et al. 1996) and unaffected by study-test changes in stimulus modality (Blaxton 1989; Srinivas and Roediger 1990).

Blaxton (1992) interpreted impaired amnesic priming on this task as evidence for a global conceptual memory deficit in amnesia. An alternative interpretation is based on the fact that normal subjects showed identical test-phase performance when given implicit or explicit test-phase instructions (Vaidya et al. 1996). This contrasts with other tasks, reviewed earlier, in which normal subjects provided more study-phase responses under explicit than implicit test instructions. Thus, it appears that on the general knowledge task normal subjects spontaneously engaged in explicit retrieval of declarative memories for study-phase items in answering test-phase questions regardless of test-phase instructions. One can gain an intuition about what is likely to be occurring on the general knowledge test with this exercise. Imagine that I ask you to study the name 'Mortenson'. Then, a few moments later, I ask you 'What was Marilyn Monroe's real last name?' You note a possible relation between the test-phase question and a study-phase answer and say 'Mortenson'. Does it seem that this answer emerged without deliberate consultation of the study phase?

The general knowledge test demonstrates the danger of equating a feature of a test with an underlying process. Because the test was conceptual and involved implicit retrieval instructions, it was assumed to be invoking the same processes as word association and category–exemplar generation tasks. The processes underlying general-knowledge priming are, however, dissociable from those underlying priming on word association and category–exemplar generation. In normal subjects, a switch from implicit to explicit instructions increases the number of study-phase responses provided on word association and category–exemplar generation, but the same switch in retrieval instructions has no effect on general-knowledge priming (Keane et al. 1997; Vaidya et al. 1995, 1996).

The dissociation is even more apparent in amnesia. Direct comparison of amnesic priming on category–exemplar generation and general-knowledge tasks can be made by examining the performance of nine patients who participated in two different studies that used the two tasks (Keane *et al.* 1997; Vaidya *et al.* 1996). Both studies used the same semantic (natural/manufactured) and non-semantic (upper case/lower case) questions to manipulate conceptual encoding at study. Relative to control subjects, the nine amnesics had impaired priming on the general knowledge test but intact priming on the category–exemplar generation test (Fig. 8.1).

Amnesic and normal performance, therefore, indicate that general-knowledge priming shares more processes in common with those invoked by most explicit memory tests than those invoked by category–exemplar generation. It seems more important to classify memory tests by the memory processes they invoke than by features such as test instructions or sensitivity to experimental manipulations.

Are perceptual processing capabilities spared in amnesia?

The second major processing claim about amnesia was that perceptual memory processes are spared. Indeed, amnesic patients have shown normal priming on many perceptual tasks, including normal sensitivity to the influences of modality, font, and form in their visual priming (Cave and Squire 1992; Graf and Schacter 1985; Vaidya *et al.* 1998). They have, however, often shown impaired priming on other perceptual tasks (Cermak *et al.* 1993; Gabrieli *et al.* 1994; Milner *et al.* 1968; Verfaellie *et al.* 1996; Warrington and Weiskrantz 1968). The critical question is whether amnesic patients fail a perceptual explicit test that has the same test cue as a matched implicit test. Indeed, amnesic patients have consistently shown im-

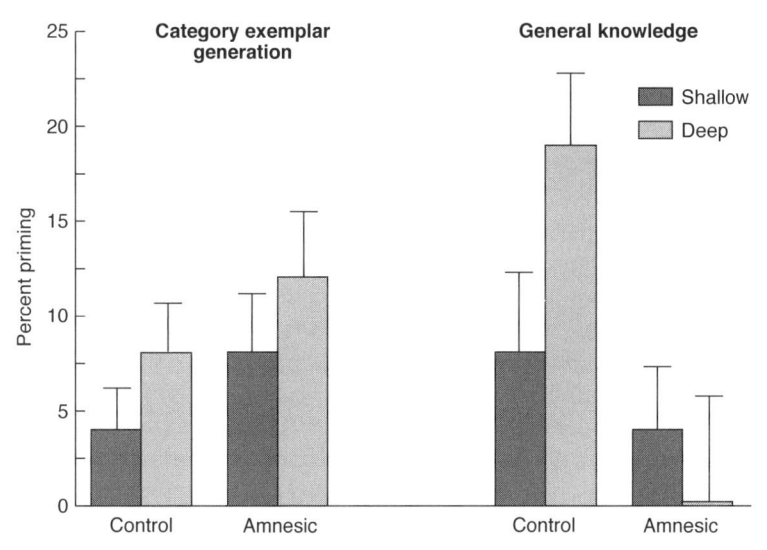

Fig. 8.1. Amount of priming following shallow (solid bars) and deep (hatched bars) conceptual processing on the category–exemplar generation and general knowledge tests in control subjects and amnesic patients. Bars are standard errors of the means.

paired explicit memory performance on perceptual cued-recall tests such as stem-cued recall (Graf et al. 1984) and word fragment cued recall (Vaidya et al. 1995). Thus, amnesic patients show intact and impaired memory performance, respectively, on implicit and explicit tests where the perceptual relation of study and test items are identical. These results refute the processing claim of a global preservation of perceptual memory processes in amnesia.

Blaxton and others have used tasks such as a graphemic cued recall to provide an explicit measure of the same perceptual memory process they believe to underlie priming on perceptual tasks such as word identification or word stem completion. There is, however, an alternative possibility. Patients with unilateral right medial temporal lobe lesions show explicit memory impairments for non-semantic visual information such as meaningless non-verbal patterns (e.g. Kimura 1963; Milner 1971; Taylor 1969). Presumably these right-hemisphere declarative memory mechanisms represent perceptual details of stimuli that serve to differentiate one stimulus from another in visual memory. These memory mechanisms may be insensitive to conceptual (linguistic) manipulations that influence left-hemisphere encoding of verbal and meaningful pictorial stimuli. Impaired amnesic performance on explicit perceptual tests may be the consequence of injury to right-hemisphere memory mechanisms that represent perceptual rather than conceptual declarative memories. Thus, dissociations in amnesia between intact and impaired perceptual memory may reflect separable systems mediating declarative and procedural memories for visual experience.

There is also another, longer-standing, view about the potential role of perceptual processes in explicit memory performance. Dual-process models posit that recognition performance reflects two distinct processes—conscious, controlled recollection, and unconscious, automatic familiarity (Jacoby and Dallas 1981; Mandler 1980). Study-phase perceptual processing of a stimulus makes the later reprocessing of that stimulus more fluent. This fluency could underlie priming on implicit perceptual tests of word identification or word stem completion. The same fluency could render studied stimuli as feeling more familiar in an explicit recognition memory test. Thus, a common process could mediate perceptual priming and the familiarity component of recognition memory. This speculation became testable with the development of methods aimed at dissociating the roles of recollection and familiarity in explicit recognition performance. The process dissociation procedure (PDP) uses inclusion and exclusion tasks that have recollection and familiarity working in concert or in opposition so that separate values for recollection and familiarity can be calculated (Jacoby 1991).

There is now considerable evidence, however, that different processes mediate perceptual priming and the familiarity component of recognition memory. In most PDP studies, recognition familiarity is influenced by conceptual rather than perceptual factors. Thus, semantic relative to non-semantic encoding, generating versus reading words, and naming pictures versus naming words all increase familiarity (and recollection) when recognition is tested with visually presented words (Jacoby 1991; Toth 1996; Wagner et al. 1997b; Wagner and Gabrieli 1998). In contrast, semantic versus nonsemantic encoding has no effect upon perceptual priming and generating versus reading words or naming pictures versus naming words decreases perceptual priming with visually presented words (e.g. Jacoby and Dallas 1981; Jacoby 1983; Wagner *et al.* 1997*b*). Taken together, these findings constitute double dissociations between conceptually driven recognition familiarity and perceptual priming.

The separation between perceptual priming and recognition familiarity is further supported by neuropsychological evidence. MS, a patient with severely impaired visual perceptual priming (Fleischman *et al.* 1995; Gabrieli *et al.* 1995*a*), shows normal familiarity in recognition performance as assessed with the PDP method (Wagner *et al.* in press). Conversely, EP, an amnesic patient who does not score above chance on recognition tests, shows intact visual perceptual priming (Hamann and Squire 1997). The fact that intact perceptual priming fails to support EP's recognition and that impaired perceptual priming fails to compromise MS's recognition familiarity argues against the participation of visual priming in visual recognition.

Thus, neither healthy nor brain-injured people appear to consult occipitally based early visual processes when recalling or recognizing prior experience. Although some experimental manipulations could force such a consultation, it is not one that occurs naturally (even when it would be useful for amnesic patients). The idea that relatively early modality-specific perceptual processes play little if any role in declarative memory is consistent with a great deal of evidence that people remember the conceptual gist rather than the perceptual details of experience. The minimal role of perceptual experience is dramatically shown in the powerful false memory effects for words that were neither seen nor heard but are conceptually related to study-phase words (Roediger and McDermott 1995).

Perceptual/conceptual distinctions in the brain: a proposal for a conceptual representation system (CRS)

Although the perceptual/conceptual distinction does not illuminate disorders of explicit retrieval performance, it does provide an important distinction between two major classes of priming. This distinction corresponds well with a memory-systems account positing that perceptual priming is mediated by modality-specific cortical regions and conceptual priming by association frontal and temporal regions (Gabrieli 1989; Keane *et al.* 1991). Alzheimer's patients exhibit severely reduced conceptual priming (Monti *et al.* 1996), but intact perceptual priming on visual tasks (Gabrieli *et al.* 1994; Fleischman *et al.* 1995; Keane *et al.* 1991, 1994). This pattern of impaired conceptual and intact perceptual priming may be interpreted in terms of the characteristic neocortical neuropathology in Alzheimer's. *In vivo* metabolic imaging studies (e.g. Frackowiak *et al.* 1981) and post-mortem studies of late-stage Alzheimer's patients (e.g. Brun and England 1981) find substantial damage to association neocortices in the frontal, parietal, and temporal lobes but relatively little compromise of primary perceptual cortices. The sparing of modality-specific cortices and the compromise of association cortices may account, respectively, for intact perceptual and impaired conceptual priming.

There is more direct evidence about the separate identities of memory systems underlying perceptual and conceptual priming. Patients with right occipital lesions have shown an absence of priming on visual word identification tasks, and of modality and font specificity on word stem completion priming (Fleischman *et al.* 1995; Gabrieli *et al.* 1995*a*; Keane *et al.* 1995*b*; Vaidya *et al.* 1998). Priming on visual word stem completion tasks is associated with reduced activity, relative to baseline word stem completion, in bilateral occipito-temporal regions (Schacter *et al.* 1996; Squire *et al.* 1992). Priming on conceptual tasks is associated with reduced activity in left frontal neocortex on tasks involving abstract/concrete decisions about words (Demb *et al.* 1995; Gabrieli *et al.* 1996*a*), living/non-living decisions about words and pictures (Wagner *et al.* 1997*a*), generation of verbs to nouns (Raichle *et al.* 1994), and generation of semantically related words (Blaxton *et al.* 1996). Thus, the behavioural dissociation between perceptual and conceptual processes corresponds well with separate neural systems underlying visual-perceptual and conceptual forms of priming.

Tulving and Schacter (Tulving and Schacter 1990; Schacter 1990) posited the existence of perceptual representation systems (PRS) distinct from declarative memory on the basis of four sources of convergent evidence: preservation of perceptual priming in densely amnesic patients, developmental dissociations (e.g. aging), functional independence in normal subjects, and drug-induced dissociations. The distinction between declarative and conceptual priming processes has been more difficult to substantiate because these two memory processes share many features in common, such as sensitivity to semantic encoding. There is now, however, convergent evidence for such a distinction. Conceptual priming is preserved in densely amnesic patients (Graf and Schacter 1985; Keane *et al.* 1997; Seger *et al.* 1997; Shimamura and Squire 1984; Vaidya *et al.* 1995) who, like normal subjects, show reduced activity in left inferior prefrontal cortex in association with conceptual priming (Gabrieli *et al.* 1996*c*). Conceptual priming is dissociable from declarative memory in aging (Light and Albertson 1989; Monti *et al.* 1996), in normal subjects (McDermott and Roediger 1996; Vaidya *et al.* 1997; Weldon and Coyote 1997), and by pharmacological manipulations (Curran 1994).

There is now, therefore, sufficient evidence to warrant proposal of conceptual representation systems (CRS). These systems may represent knowledge about words and ideas. It may be hypothesized that conceptual priming reflects a constant experiential modulation of the organization of conceptual knowledge. It is common, for example, to have subjects list category exemplars as a means of characterizing the organization of category knowledge in terms of prototypes and semantic distances. Category–exemplar priming, therefore, may reflect plasticity that normally modulates the structure and content of conceptual knowledge. Such experiential modulation could provide a learning mechanism that allows conceptual knowledge to be changed so as to reflect ongoing experience.

FUTURE MEMORY SYSTEMS RESEARCH

Two issues may be considered in the future development of memory systems research. First, as indicated earlier, it is likely that there are many memory systems when one considers the many forms of memory that have already been dissociated from one another. A concern has been raised that so many dissociations will result in the positing of too many memory systems, 25 or more (Roediger 1990).

It would indeed be convenient to have all human learning accounted for by four systems, or at most seven so that all could be kept in short-term memory at once, but there is no reason to believe that the long evolutionary history of the human brain and mind minimized how many memory systems we possess rather than maximized what we can learn. Nature is often comfortable with large numbers. Early theories about matter aimed for an efficient theory of four elements (water, air, wind, and earth), but the modern periodic table contains over 100 elements. More relevant to memory systems are brain numbers such as 52 or 58. There are 52 cortical Brodmann areas each distinguished by their cytoarchitecture and these do not include large, multicomponent parts of the brain such as the cerebellum, basal ganglia, basal forebrain, or hippocampus that are already known to be critical for various forms of memory. There are 58 well characterized neurotransmitter receptors for just the biogenic amines, aceylcholine, GABA, histamine, opiates, and amino acid transmitters.

Not every cortical region or neurotransmitter may constitute a system, but it is too early to know what sorts of numbers about the brain are relevant for thinking about how many memory systems exist. There may be a fairly limited number of memory systems in the human brain. Indeed, we should seek to explain all known dissociations with the fewest number of memory systems possible. There is, however, no *a priori* reason to expect a small number of systems. The number of systems that make human memory has been determined already by nature and it is our goal to discover that number.

Second, I have emphasized in my critique of certain processing claims the dangers of equating features of tasks with underlying memory processes. Many different memory processes have features in common. For example, performances on almost all tests of memory share the feature of being superior after a short relative to a long study-test delay or after many versus few study trials. This does not mean that all those forms of memory depend upon a common process. Finding performance on two memory tests to be similarly affected by a manipulation indicates that the processes underlying performance on the two tests have a similar feature, not that they are the same process.

As discussed earlier, some processing theorists have emphasized a distinction between perceptual (or data-driven) and conceptual processes (e.g. Blaxton 1989; Roediger and Blaxton 1987; Roediger *et al.* 1989). 'Perception' is not, however, a process *per se*. Visual, auditory, tactual, olfactory, and gustatory perception are mediated by separate processes and neural networks. Further, each modality probably contains multiple processes. Perceptual memories related to each of the five senses share an abstract common *feature* of being tied to sense-specific stimulus dimensions. That shared abstract feature, however, is not a process. There are also likely to be multiple conceptual processes that are also mediated by separable neural networks. Of course, processing theorists never claimed that there is a unitary perceptual process; they used modality manipulations in order to illuminate the modality-specific nature of visual versus auditory or pictorial versus verbal processing. Nevertheless, interpretations of results were almost always described in terms of perceptual/conceptual distinctions. It is a bit ironic that some early 'processing' accounts were aimed less at specific processes than at two abstracted features of many different, dissociable processes.

The equation of features and processes occurs also in biologically inspired and cogent analyses about how memory systems ought to be defined (e.g. Cohen and Eichenbaum 1993; Roediger *et al.* 1990; Schacter and Tulving 1994; Sherry and Schacter 1987; Squire *et al.* 1992; Tulving 1985; Weiskrantz 1987). Thus, Cohen and Eichenbaum (1993) emphasize 'features and characteristics' of 'the declarative system' and procedural memory systems (pp.73–4). Schacter and Tulving (1994) posit five memory systems, each bound together by 'property lists and relations': Procedural, perceptual, semantic, primary or working, and episodic. Within these systems are 'subsystems' that 'share the principal rules of operation' within a system but that operate on different 'kinds of information'. For example, within the procedural subsystem are motor and cognitive skills and 'simple conditioning'. No subsystems are proposed for the 'episodic system'.

There are, however, many dissociations that are problematic for such accounts. For example, there is a well established dissociation between left and right medial-temporal lobe involvement in verbal and non-verbal declarative or episodic memory performance (e.g. Milner 1971). All of the above processing and systems investigators are aware of this dissociation, but they choose to equate the left and right medial-temporal regions because they can be described by common features. There are also many dissociations within non-declarative memory. There are dissociable procedural systems mediating motor skill learning and simple conditioning (Woodruff-Pak and Papka 1996), motor skill learning for mirror-tracing and rotary pursuit (Gabrieli *et al.* 1997c), for two variants of rotary pursuit (Willingham *et al.* 1996), and for two variants of serial reaction time (Willingham and Koroshetz 1993). There are neuropyschological dissociations between two kinds of visual perceptual priming and between two kinds of conceptual priming (Gabrieli et al. 1994, submitted; Keane *et al.* 1991). Yet, these and other dissociable forms of memory are grouped together as episodic, procedural, perceptual, or semantic because they share features such as how they are measured.

I propose that if two expressions of memory are psychologically and neurally dissociable, they ought to be interpreted as reflecting the operations of two different memory systems of the brain (similar to what Schacter and Tulving describe as subsystems). This applies equally to dissociations between classes of memory (e.g. declarative and procedural) as to dissociations within classes of memory (e.g.

two kinds of motor skill learning or two kinds of conceptual priming). Memory systems are specific neural networks that mediate specific mnemonic processes. In contrast, classes of memory (e.g. procedural, perceptual, semantic, working, and episodic) represent our current thoughts about useful groupings of mnemonic tasks, features, and measures. There is no reason to believe that the natural organization of memory processes in the brain is ordered by such useful but artificial classifications.

CONCLUSION

There are now many points of theoretical agreement and empirical convergence among a variety of processing and systems researchers. There may, however, be a remaining intellectual tension that fuels a variety of continuing debates that reflect different views on how human memory ought to be understood. The traditional psychological view is that the basics of human memory are to be understood through behavioural experimentation with healthy subjects. Neuropsychological sources of evidence, such as patient or functional neuroimaging studies, constitute a parallel, separate line of research that offers some constraints or clues for behavioural experimentation (e.g. the existence of implicit or procedural memory).

Another perspective, and one that I favour, is that we have entered a new era where equal weight ought to be given to mnemonic processes and neural networks in comprehending the functional architecture of human memory. Memory systems may constitute the finite processing elements of human memory that are combined in many ways to perform a wide range of tasks. Such systems will be defined with increasing psychological and neural precision and yield close mappings between brain form and memory function. The natural mapping between form and function may explain why there has been a remarkable concordance between kinds of memory that are spared in amnesia and kinds of memory that are functionally dissociable from declarative memory in healthy people.

In vision, the separate views accorded to the two eyes enhance the perception of depth. Analogously, a theory of the functional architecture of human memory that is equally constrained by biological and psychological views ought to have more depth than any theory limited to one view only.

ACKNOWLEDGEMENTS

I thank Debra Fleischman, Maggie Keane, Russ Poldrack, and Dan Willingham for helpful comments on this chapter and Marion Zabinski for assistance with the manuscript.

REFERENCES

Atkinson, R. C. and Shiffrin, R. M. (1968). Human memory: a proposed system and its control processes. In *The psychology of learning and motivation: advances in research and theory*, (ed. K. W. Spence), pp.89–195. Academic, New York.

Bechara, A., Tranel, D., Damasio, H., Adolphs, R., Rockland, C., and Damasio, A. R. (1995). Double dissociation of conditioning and declarative knowledge relative to the amygdala and hippocampus in humans. *Science*, 269, 1115–18.

Blaxton, T. A. (1989). Investigating dissociations among memory measures: support for a transfer-appropriate processing framework. *Journal of Experimental Psychology Learning, Memory, and Cognition*, 15, 657–68.

Blaxton, T. A. (1992). Dissociations among memory measures in memory-impaired subjects: evidence for a processing account of memory. *Memory and Cognition*, 20, 549–62.

Blaxton, T. A., Bookheimer, S. Y., Zeffiro, T. A., Figlozzi, C. M., William, D. G., and Theodore, W. H. (1996). Functional mapping of human memory using PET: comparisons of conceptual and perceptual tasks. *Canadian Journal of Experimental Psychology*, 50, 42–56.

Bower, G. H. (1967). A multicomponent theory of the memory trace. In *The psychology of learning and motivation*, (ed. K. W. Spence and J. T. Spence), pp.229–35. Academic, New York.

Brun, A. and Englund, E. (1981). Regional pattern of degeneration in Alzheimer's disease: neuronal loss and histopathological grading. *Histopathology*, 5, 549–64.

Buckner, R. L., Petersen, S. E., Ojemann, J. G., Miezin, F. M., Squire, L. R., and Raichle, M. E. (1995). Functional anatomical studies of explicit and implicit memory retrieval tasks. *Journal of Neuroscience*, 12, 12–29.

Cahill, L., Babinsky, R., Markowitsch, H. J., and McGaugh, J. L. (1995). The amygdala and emotional memory. *Nature*, 377, 295–6.

Cahill, L., Haier, R. J., Fallon, J., Alkire, M. T., Tang, C., Keator, D., *et al.* (1996). Amygdala activity at encoding correlated with long-term, free recall of emotional information. *Proceedings of the National Academy of Sciences of the USA*, 93, 8016–21.

Carlesimo, G. A. (1994). Perceptual and conceptual priming in amnesic and alcoholic patients. *Neuropsychologia*, 32, 903–21.

Cave, C. B. and Squire, L. R. (1992). Intact and long-lasting repetition priming in amnesia. *Journal of Experimental Psychology: Learning, Memory, and Cognition*, 18, 509–20.

Cermak, L. S., Talbot, N., Chandler, K., and Wolbarst, L. R. (1985). The perceptual priming phenomenon in amnesia. *Neuropsychologia*, 23, 615–22.

Cermak, L. S., Bleich, R. P., and Blackford, S. P. (1988). Deficits in the implicit retention of new associations by alcoholic Korsakoff patients. *Brain and Language*, 7, 312–23.

Cermak, L. S., Verfaellie, M., and Letourneau, L. (1993). Episodic effects of picture identification for alcoholic Korsakoff patients. *Brain and Cognition*, 22, 85–97.

Cermak, L. S., Verfaellie, M., and Chase, K. A. (1995). Implicit and explicit memory in amnesia: an analysis of data-driven and conceptually driven processes. *Neuropsychology*, 22, 85–97.

Challis, B. H. and Sidhu, R. (1993). Dissociative effect of massed repetition on implicit and explicit measures of memory. *Journal of Experimental Psychology: Learning, Memory, and Cognition*, 19, 115–27.

Cohen, N. J. and Eichenbaum, H. (1993). *Memory, amnesia and the hippocampal system*. MIT Press, Cambridge, MA.

Cohen, N. J. and Squire, L. R. (1980). Preserved learning and retention of pattern-analyzing skill in amnesia: dissociation of knowing how and knowing that. *Science*, 210, 207–10.

Cohen, N. J., Eichenbaum, H., Deacedo, B. S., and Corkin, S. (1985). Different memory systems underlying acquisition of procedural and declarative knowledge. *Annals of the New York Academy of Sciences*, **444**, 54–71.

Corkin, S. (1968). Acquisition of motor skills after bilateral medial temporal-lobe excision. *Neuropsychologia*, **6**, 255–65.

Corkin, S. (1984). Lasting consequences of bilateral medial temporal lobectomy: clinical course and experimental findings in H.M. *Seminars in Neurology*, **4**, 252–62.

Craik, F. I. M. and Lockhart, R. S. (1972). Levels of processing: a framework for memory research. *Journal of Verbal Learning and Verbal Behavior*, **11**, 671–84.

Curran, H. V. (1994). What aspects of memory and information processing are affected by benzodiazepines and alcohol? *Behavioural Pharmacology*, **5**, 14.

Daum, I., Channon, S., and Canavan, A. G. M. (1989). Classical conditioning in patients with severe memory problems. *Journal of Neurology, Neurosurgery and Psychiatry*, **52**, 47–51.

Daum, I., Ackermann, H., Schugens, M. M., Reimold, C., Dichgans, J., and Birbaumer, N. (1993). The cerebellum and cognitive functions in humans. *Behavioral Neuroscience*, **117**, 411–19.

Demb, J. B., Desmond, J. E., Wagner, A. D., Vaidya, C. J., Glover, G. H., and Gabrieli, J. D. E. (1995). Semantic encoding and retrieval in the left inferior prefrontal cortex: a functional MRI study of task difficulty and process specificity. *Journal of Neuroscience*, **15**, 5870–8.

Ebbinghaus, H. (1885). *Uber das Gedachtnis*. Duncker & Humblot, Leipzig.

Fleischman, D. A., Gabrieli, J. D. E., Reminger, S., Rinaldi, J., Morrell, F., and Wilson, R. (1995). Conceptual priming in perceptual identification for patients with Alzheimer's disease and a patient with a right occipital lobectomy. *Neuropsychology*, **9**, 187–97.

Frackowiak, R. S. J., Pozzilli, C., Legg, N. J., Du Boulay, G. H., Marshall, J., Lenzi, G. L., et al. (1981). Regional cerebral oxygen supply and utilization in dementia: a clinical and physiological study with oxygen-15 and positron tomography. *Brain*, **104**, 753–78.

Gabrieli, J. D. E. (1986). Memory systems of the human brain: dissociations among learning capacities in amnesia. Unpublished D.Phil. thesis. Massachusetts Institute of Technology.

Gabrieli, J. D. E. (1989). Dissociation of memory capacities in neurodegenerative disease. In *Alzheimer's disease: advances in basic research and therapies*, (ed. R. J. Wurtman, S. Corkin, J. H. Growdon, and E. Ritter-Walker), pp.317–27. Center for Brain Sciences and Metabolism Charitable Trust, Cambridge.

Gabrieli, J. D. E. (1998). Cognitive neuroscience of human memory. In *Annual Review of Psychology*, **49**, 87–115.

Gabrieli, J. D. E., Cohen, N. J., and Corkin, S. (1988). The impaired learning of semantic knowledge following bilateral medial temporal-lobe resection. *Brain and Cognition*, **7**, 525–39.

Gabrieli, J. D. E., Milberg, W., Keane, M. M., and Corkin, S. (1990). Intact priming of patterns despite impaired memory. *Neuropsychologia*, **28**, 417–27.

Gabrieli, J. D. E., Corkin, S., Mickel, S. F., and Growdon, J. H. (1993). Intact acquisition and long-term retention of mirror-tracing skill in Alzheimer's disease and in global amnesia. *Behavioral Neuroscience*, **107**, 899–910.

Gabrieli, J. D. E., Keane, M. M., Stanger, B. Z., Kjelgaard, M. M., Corkin, S., and Growdon, J. H. (1994). Dissociations among structural-perceptual, lexical-semantic, and even-fact memory systems in amnesic, Alzheimer's, and normal subjects. *Cortex*, **30**, 75–103.

Gabrieli, J. D. E., Fleischman, D. A., Keane, M. M., Reminger, S. L., and Morrell, F. (1995a). Double dissociation between memory systems underlying explicit and implicit memory in the human brain. *Psychological Science*, **6**, 76–82.

Gabrieli, J. D. E., McGlinchey-Berroth, R., Carillo, M. C., Gluck, M. A., Cermak, L. S., and Disterhoft, J. F. (1995b). Intact delay-eyeblink classical conditioning in amnesia. *Behavioral Neuroscience*, **109**, 819–27.

Gabrieli, J. D. E., Desmond, J. E., Demb, J. B., Wagner, A. D., Stone, M. V., Vaidya, C. J., *et al.* (1996a). Functional magnetic resonance imaging of semantic memory processes in the frontal lobes. *Psychological Science*, **7**, 278–83.

Gabrieli, J. D. E., Singh, J., Stebbins, G. T., and Goetz, C. G. (1996b). Reduced working-memory span in Parkinson's disease: evidence for the role of a fronto-striatal system in working and strategic memory. *Neuropsychology*, **10**, 322–32.

Gabrieli, J. D. E., Sullivan, E. V., Desmond, J. E., Stebbins, G. T., Vaidya, C. J., Keane, M. M., Wagner, A. D., Zarella, M. M., Glover, G. H., and Pfeferbaum, A. (1996c). Behavioral and functional neuroimaging evidence for preserved conceptual implicit memory in global amnesia. *Society for Neuroscience Abstracts*, **22**, 1449.

Gabrieli, J. D. E., Brewer, J. B., Desmond, J. E., and Glover, G. H. (1997a). Separate neural bases of two fundamental memory processes in the human medial temporal lobe. *Science*, **276**, 264–6.

Gabrieli, J. D. E., Keane, M. M., Zarella, M. M., and Poldrack, R. A. (1997b). Preservation of implicit memory for new associations in global amnesia. *Psychological Science*, **4**, 326–9.

Gabrieli, J. D. E., Stebbins, G. T., Singh, J., Willingham, D. B., and Goetz, C. G. (1997c). Intact mirror-tracing and impaired rotary-pursuit skill learning in patients with Huntington's disease: evidence for dissociable memory systems in skill learning. *Neuropsychology*, **11**, 272–81.

Gabrieli, J. D. E., Vaidya, C. J., Stone, M., Francis, W. S., Thompson-Schill, S. L., Fleischman, D. A., Tinklenberg, J. R., Yesavage, J. A., and Wilson, R. S. The role of attention in repetition priming: convergent behavioral and neuropsychological evidence. (Submitted.)

Graf, P. and Schacter, D. L. (1985). Implicit and explicit memory for new associations in normal and amnesic subjects. *Journal of Experimental Psychology: Learning, Memory, and Cognition*, **11**, 501–18.

Graf, P., Mandler, G., and Haden, P. E. (1982). Simulating amnesica symptoms in normal subjects. *Science*, **218**, 1243–4.

Graf, P., Squire, L. R., and Mandler, G. (1984). The information that amnesic patients do not forget. *Journal of Experimental Psychology: Learning, Memory, and Cognition*, **10**, 164–78.

Haist, F., Musen, G., and Squire, L. R. (1991). Intact priming of words and nonwords in amnesia. *Psychobiology*, **19**, 275–85.

Hamann, S. B. (1990). Level-of-processing effects in conceptually driven implicit tasks. *Journal of Experimental Psychology: Learning, Memory, and Cognition*, **16**, 970–7.

Hamann, S. B. and Squire, L. R. (1997). Intact perceptual memory in the absence of conscious memory. *Behavioral Neuroscience*, **111**, 850–4.

Heindel, W. C., Butters, N., and Salmon, D. P. (1988). Impaired learning of a motor skill in patients with Huntington's disease. *Behavioral Neuroscience*, **102**, 141–7.

Heindel, W. C., Salmon, D. P., Shults, C. W., Wallicke, P. A., and Butters, N. (1989). Neuropsychological evidence for multiple implicit memory systems: a comparison of Alzheimer's, Huntington's and Parkinson's disease patients. *Journal of Neuroscience*, **9**, 582–7.

Jacoby, L. L. (1983). Remembering the data: analyzing interactive processes in reading. *Journal of Verbal Learning and Verbal Behavior*, **22**, 485–508.
Jacoby, L. L. (1991). A process dissociation framework: separating automatic from intentional uses of memory. *Journal of Memory and Language*, **30**, 513–41.
Jacoby, L. L. and Dallas, M. (1981). On the relationship between autobiographical memory and perceptual learning. *Journal of Experimental Psychology: General*, **110**, 306–40.
Jacoby, L. L. and Witherspoon, D. (1982). Remembering without awareness. *Canadian Journal of Psychology*, **36**, 300–24.
Janowsky, J. S., Shimamura, A. P., and Squire, L. R. (1989). Source memory impairment in patients with frontal lobe lesions. *Neuropsychologia*, **8**, 1043–56.
Kapur, S., Craik, F. I. M., Tulving, E., Wilson, A. A., Houle, S. H., and Brown, G. M. (1994). Neuroanatomical correlates of encoding in episodic memory: levels of processing effect. *Proceedings of the National Academy of Sciences of the USA*, **91**, 2008–11.
Keane, M. M., Gabrieli, J. D. E., Fennema, A. C., Growdon, J. H., and Corkin, S. (1991). Evidence for a dissociation between perceptual and conceptual priming in Alzheimer's disease. *Behavioral Neuroscience*, **105**, 326–42.
Keane, M. M., Gabrieli, J. D., Growdon, J. H., and Corkin, S. (1994). Priming in perceptual identification of pseudowords is normal in Alzheimer's disease. *Neuropsychologia*, **32**, 343–56.
Keane, M. M., Gabrieli, J. D. E., Noland, J. S., and McNealy, S. I. (1995*a*). Normal perceptual priming of orthographically illegal nonwords in amnesia. *Journal of the International Neuropsychological Society*, **1**, 425–33.
Keane, M. M., Gabrieli, J. D. E., Mapstone, H., Johnson, K. A., and Corkin, S. (1995*b*). Double dissociation of memory capacities after bilateral occipital-lobe or medial temporal-lobe lesions. *Brain*, **118**, 1129–48.
Keane, M. M., Gabrieli, J. D. E., Monti, L. A., Fleischman, D. A., Cantor, J. M., and Noland, J. S. (1997). Intact and impaired conceptual memory processing in amnesia. *Neuropsychology*, **11**, 59–69.
Kimura, D. (1963). Right temporal-lobe damage: perception of unfamiliar stimuli after damage. *Archives of Neurology*, **8**, 264–71.
Kinsbourne, M. and Wood, F. (1975). Short term memory processes and the amnesic syndrome. In *Short-term memory*, (ed. J. A. Deutsch), pp.258–91. Academic, New York.
Klatzky, R. L. (1980). *Human memory: structures and processes*. W. H. Freeman, New York.
Knowlton, B. J. and Squire, L. R. (1993). The learning of categories: parallel brain systems for item memory and category knowledge. *Science*, **262**, 1747–9.
Knowlton, B. J., Squire, L. R., and Gluck, M. (1994). Probabilistic classification learning in amnesia. *Learning and Memory*, **1**, 106–20.
Knowlton, B. J., Squire, L. R., Paulsen, J. S., Swerdlow, N. R., Swenson, M., and Butters, N. (1996). Dissociations within nondeclarative memory in Huntington's disease. *Neuropsychology*, **10**, 538–48.
LaBar, K. S., Ledoux, J. E., Spencer, D. D., and Phelps, E. A. (1995). Impaired fear conditioning following unilateral temporal lobectomy in humans. *Journal of Neuroscience*, **15**, 6846–55.
Lashley, K. S. (1950). In search of the engram. In *Symposia of the Society for Experimental Biology, no. 4*., pp. 454–82. Cambridge University Press, London.
Light, L. L. and Albertson, S. A. (1989). Direct and indirect tests of memory for category exemplars in young and older adults. *Psychology and Aging*, **4**, 487–92.
Mandler, G. (1980). Recognizing: the judgment of previous occurrence. *Psychological Review*, **87**, 252–71.

Marlsen-Wilson, W. D. and Teuber, H. L. (1975). Memory for remote events in anterograde amnesia: recognition of public figures from news photographs. *Neuropsychologia*, 13, 353–64.
Martone, M., Butters, N., Payne, M., Becker, J. T., and Sax, D. (1984). Dissociations between skill learning and verbal recognition in amnesia and dementia. *Archives of Neurology*, 41, 965–70.
McDermott, K. B. and Roediger, H. L. (1996). Exact and conceptual repetition dissociate conceptual memory tests: problems for transfer appropriate processing theory. *Canadian Journal of Experimental Psychology*, 50, 57–71.
McGlinchey-Berroth, R., Carrillo, M., Gabrieli, J. D. E., Brawn, C. M., and Disterhoft, J. F. (1997). Impaired trace eyeblink conditioning in bilateral medial temporal lobe amnesia. *Behavioral Neuroscience*, 111, 873–82.
Milner, B. (1962). Les troubles de la memoire accompagnant des lesions hippocampiques bilaterales. In *Physiologie de l'hippocampe*, (ed. P. Passouant). Centre de la Recherche Scientifique, Paris.
Milner, B. (1971). Interhemispheric differences in the localization of psychological processes in man. *British Medical Journal*, 27, 272–7.
Milner, B., Corkin, S., and Teuber, H. L. (1968). Further analysis of the hippocampal amnesia syndrome: 14 year follow-up study of H. M. *Neuropsychologia*, 6, 215–34.
Monti, L. A., Gabrieli, J. D. E., Reminger, S. L., Rinaldi, J. A., Wilson, R. S., and Fleischman, D. A. (1996). Differential effects of aging and Alzheimer's disease upon conceptual implicit and explicit memory. *Neuropsychology*, 10, 101–12.
Moscovitch, M., Winocur, G., and McLachlan, D. (1986). Memory as assessed by recognition and reading time in normal and memory-impaired people with Alzheimer's disease and other neurological disorders. *Journal of Experimental Psychology: General*, 115, 331–47.
Musen, G. and Squire, L. R. (1992). Nonverbal priming in amnesia. *Memory and Cognition*, 20, 441–8.
Musen, G. and Squire, L. R. (1993). Implicit learning of color-word associations using a stroop paradigm. *Journal of Experimental Psychology: Learning, Memory, and Cognition*, 19, 789–98.
Ostergaard, A. L. and Jernigan, T. L. (1993). Are word priming and explicit memory mediated by different brain structures? In *Implicit memory: new directions in cognition, development, and neuropsychology*, (ed. P. Graf and M. E. J. Masson), pp.327–49. Erlbaum, Hillsdale, NJ.
Petrides, M. and Milner, B. (1982). Deficits on subject-ordered tasks after frontal and temporal lobe lesions in man. *Neuropsychologia*, 20, 601–14.
Press, G. A., Amaral, D. G., and Squire, L. R. (1989). Hippocampal abnormalities in amnesic patients revealed by high-resolution magnetic resonance imaging. *Nature*, 341, 54–7.
Raichle, M. E., Fiez, J. A., Videen, T. O., MacLeod, A. K., Pardo, J. V., Fox, P. E., et al. (1994). Practice-related changes in human brain functional anatomy during nonmotor learning. *Cerebral Cortex*, 4, 8–26.
Ratcliff, R. and McKoon, G. (1996). Bias effects in implicit memory tasks. *Journal of Experimental Psychology: General*, 4, 403–21.
Roediger, H. L. (1990). Implicit memory: a commentary. *Bulletin of the Psychonomic Society*, 28, 373–80.
Roediger, H. L. and Blaxton, T. A. (1987). Effects of varying modality, surface features, and retention interval on priming in word-fragment completion. *Memory and Cognition*, 15, 379–88.

Roediger, H. L. and McDermott, K. B. (1995). Creating false memories: remembering words not presented in lists. *Journal of Experimental Psychology: Learning, Memory, and Cognition*, **21**, 803–14.

Roediger, H. L., Weldon, M. S., and Challis, B. H. (1989). Explaining dissociations between implicit and explicit measures of retention: a processing account. In *Varieties of memory and consciousness: essays in honour of Endel Tulving*, (ed. H. L. Roediger and F. I. M. Craik), pp.3–14. Erlbaum, Hillsdale, NJ.

Roediger, H. L., Rajaram, S., and Srinivas, K. (1990). Specifying criteria for postulating memory systems. *Annals of the New York Academy of Sciences*, **608**, 572–89.

Sagar, H. H., Cohen, N. J., Corkin, S., and Growden, J. M. (1985). Dissociations among processes in remote memory. *Annals of the New York Academy of Sciences*, **444**, 533–5.

Saint-Cyr, J. A., Taylor, A. E., and Lang, A. E. (1988). Procedural learning and neostriatal function in man. *Brain*, **111**, 941–59.

Schacter, D. L. (1987). Implicit memory: history and current status. *Journal of Experimental Psychology: Learning, Memory, and Cognition*, **13**, 501–18.

Schacter, D. L. (1990). Perceptual representation systems and implicit memory: toward a resolution of the multiple memory systems debate. *Annals of the New York Academy of Sciences*, **608**, 543–71.

Schacter, D. L. and Graf, P. (1986). Preserved learning in amnesic patients: perspectives from research on direct priming. *Journal of Clinical and Experimental Neuropsychology*, **8**, 727–43.

Schacter, D. L. and Tulving, E. (1982). Memory, amnesia, and the episodic/semantic distinction. In *Expression of knowledge*, (ed. R. L. Isaacson and N. E. Spear), pp.33–61. Plenum, New York.

Schacter, D. L. and Tulving, E. (1994). What are the memory systems of 1994? In *Memory systems 1994*, (ed. D. L. Schacter and E. Tulving), pp.1–38. MIT Press, Cambridge, MA.

Schacter, D. L., Cooper, L. A., Tharan, M., and Rubens, A. B. (1991). Preserved priming of novel objects in patients with memory disorders. *Journal of Cognitive Neuroscience*, **3**, 117–30.

Schacter, D. L., Church, B. A., and Bolton, E. (1995). Implicit memory in amnesic patients: impairment of voice-specific priming. *Psychological Science*, **6**, 20–5.

Schacter, D. L., Alpert, N. M., Savage, C. R., Rauch, S. L., and Albert, M. S. (1996). Conscious recollection and the human hippocampal formation: Evidence from positron emission topography. *Proceedings of the National Academy of Sciences of the USA*, **93**, 321–5.

Schmidtke, K., Handschu, R., and Vollmer, H. (1996). Cognitive procedural learning in amnesia. *Brain and Cognition*, **32**, 441–67.

Schwartz, B. L., Rosse, R. B., and Deutsch, S. I. (1993). Limits of the processing view in accounting for dissociations among memory measures in a clinical population. *Memory and Cognition*, **21**, 63–72.

Scoville, W. B. and Milner, B. (1957). Loss of recent memory after bilateral hippocampal lesions. *Journal of Neurology, Neurosurgery, and Psychiatry*, **20**, 11–21.

Seger, C. A., Rabin, L. A., Zarella, M., and Gabrieli, J. D. E. (1997). Preserved verb generation priming in global amnesia. *Neuropsycholgia*, **35**, 1069–74.

Shallice, T., Fletcher, P., Frith, C. D., Grasby, P., Frackowiak, R. S. J., and Dolan, R. J. (1994). Brain regions associated with acquisition and retrieval of verbal episodic memory. *Nature*, **368**, 633–5.

Sherry, D. F. and Schacter, D. L. (1987). The evolution of multiple memory systems. *Psychological Review*, **94**, 439–54.

Shimamura, A. P. and Squire, L. R. (1984). Paired-associate learning and priming effects in amnesia: a neuropsychological study. *Journal of Experimental Psychology: General*, **113**, 556–70.
Shimamura, A. P. and Squire, L. R. (1989). Impaired priming of new associations in amnesia. *Journal of Experimental Psychology: Learning, Memory, and Cognition*, **15**, 721–8.
Shimamura, A. P., Salmon, D. P., Squire, L. R., and Butters, N. (1987). Memory dysfunction and word priming in dementia and amnesia. *Behavioral Neuroscience*, **101**, 347–51.
Singh, J., Gabrieli, J. D. E., Stebbins, G. T., and Goetz, C. G. (1992). Impairment of working memory in patients with Huntington's disease. *Neurology*, **42**, 280.
Smith, E. E. and Jonides, J. (1994). Working memory in humans: neuropsychological evidence. In *The cognitive neurosciences*, (ed. M. Gazzaniga), pp.1009–20. MIT Press, Cambridge, MA.
Squire, L. R. (1992). Memory and the hippocampus: A synthesis from findings with rats, workings, and humans. *Psychology Review*, **99**, 195–231.
Squire, L. R., Shimamura, A. P., and Graf, P. (1987). Strength and duration of priming effects in normal subjects and amnesic patients. *Neuropsychologia*, **25**, 195–210.
Squire, L. R., Ojemann, J. G., Miezin, F. M., Petersen, S. E., Videen, T. O., and Raichle, M. E. (1992). Activation of the hippocampus in normal humans: a functional anatomical study of memory. *Proceedings of the National Academy of Sciences of the USA*, **89**, 1837–41.
Srinivas, K. and Roediger, H. L. (1990). Classifying implicit memory tests: category association and anagram solution. *Journal of Memory and Language*, **29**, 389–412.
Stebbins, G. T., Singh, J., Weiner, J., Goetz, C. G., and Gabrieli, J. D. E. (1995). Selective impairments of memory functioning in unmedicated adults with Gilles de la Tourette's syndrome. *Neuropsychology*, **9**, 329–37.
Taylor, L. B. (1969). Localisation of cerebral lesions by psychological testing. *Clinical Neurology*, **16**, 269–87.
Toth, J. P. (1996). Conceptual automaticity in recognition memory: levels-of-processing effects on familiarity. *Canadian Journal of Experimental Psychology*, **50**, 123–38.
Tulving, E. (1964). Intratrial and intertrial retention: notes towards a theory of free recall verbal learning. *Psychological Review*, **71**, 219–37.
Tulving, E. (1972). Episodic and semantic memory. In *Organization of memory*, (ed. E. Tulving and W. Donaldson), pp.381–403. Academic, New York.
Tulving, E. (1985). How many memory systems are there? *American Psychologist*, **40**, 385–98.
Tulving, E. and Bower, G. H. (1974). The logic of memory representations. In *The psychology of learning and motivation*, (ed. G. H. Bower), pp.265–301. Academic, New York.
Tulving, E. and Schacter, D. L. (1990). Priming and human memory systems. *Science*, **247**, 301–6.
Tulving, E., Schacter, D. L., and Starke, H. (1982). Priming effects in word-fragment completion are independent of recognition memory. *Journal of Experimental Psychology: Learning, Memory, and Cognition*, **8**, 336–42.
Tulving, E., Kapur, S., Markowitsch, H. J., Craik, F. I. M., Habib, R., and Houle, S. (1994). Neuroanatomical correlates of retrieval in episodic memory: auditory sentence recognition. *Proceedings of the National Academy of Sciences of the USA*, **91**, 2012–15.
Underwood, B. J. (1983). *Attributes of memory*. Scott, Foresman, Glenview, IL.
Vaidya, C. J., Gabrieli, J. D. E., Keane, M. M., and Monti, L. A. (1995). Perceptual and conceptual memory processes in global amnesia. *Neuropsychology*, **9**, 580–91.
Vaidya, C. J., Gabrieli, J. D. E., Demb, J. B., Keane, M. M., and Wetzel, L. C. (1996).

Impaired priming on the general knowledge task in amnesia. *Neuropsychology*, **10**, 529–37.
Vaidya, C. J., Gabrieli, J. D. E., Keane, M. M., Monti, L. A., Gutierrez-Rivas, H., and Zarella, M. M. (1997). Evidence for multiple mechanisms of conceptual priming on implicit memory tests. *Journal of Experimental Psychology: Learning, Memory, and Cognition*, **23**, 1324–43.
Vaidya, C. J., Gabrieli, J. D. E., Verfaellie, M., Fleischman, D., and Askari, N. (1998) Font-specific priming following global amnesia and occipital lobe damage. *Neuropsychology*, **12**, 183–92.
Verfaellie, M., Gabrieli, J. D. E., Vaidya, C. J., and Croce, P. (1996). Implicit memory for pictures in amnesia: Role of etiology and priming task. *Neuropsychology*, **10**, 517–37.
Wagner, A. D. and Gabrieli, J. D. E (1998). On the relationship between familiarity in implicit and explicit memory: evidence for multiple, distinct familiarity processes. *Acta Psychologica*, **98**, 211–30.
Wagner, A. D., Desmond, J. E., Demb, J. B., Glover, G. H., and Gabrieli, J. D. E. (1997a). Semantic memory processes and left inferior prefrontal cortex: a functional MRI study of form specificity. *Journal of Cognitive Neuroscience*, **9**, 714–26.
Wagner, A. D., Gabrieli, J. D. E., and Verfaellie, M. (1997b). Dissociations between familiarity processes in explicit-recognition and implicit-perceptual memory. *Journal of Experimental Psychology: Learning, Memory, and Cognition*, **23**, 305–23.
Wagner, A. D., Stebbins, G. T., Masciari, F., Fleischman, D. A., and Gabrieli, J. D. E. (in press) Neuropsychological dissociation between recognition familiarity and perceptual priming in visual long-term memory. *Cortex*.
Warrington, E. K. and Weiskrantz, L. (1968). A new method of testing long-term retention with special reference to amnesic patients. *Nature*, **217**, 972–4.
Warrington, E. K. and Weiskrantz, L. (1970). The amnesic syndrome: consolidation or retrieval? *Nature*, **228**, 628–30.
Wechsler, D. (1981). *Manual for the Wechsler Adult Intelligence Scale—revised*. The Psychological Corporation, New York.
Wechsler, D. (1987). *Wechsler Memory Scale—revised manual*. The Psychological Corporation, San Antonio.
Weiskrantz, L. (1987). Neuroanatomy of memory and amnesia: a case of multiple memory systems. *Human Neurobiology*, **6**, 93–105.
Weldon, M. S. and Coyote, K. C. (1997). There is no picture superiority effect on implicit conceptual tests. *Journal of Experimental Psychology: Learning, Memory, and Cognition*, **22**, 670–86.
Willingham, D. B. and Koroshetz, W. J. (1993). Evidence for dissociable motor skills in Huntington's disease patients. *Psychobiology*, **21**, 173–82.
Willingham, D. B., Koroshetz, W. J., and Peterson, E. W. (1996). Motor skills have diverse neural bases: spared and impaired skill acquisition in Huntington's disease. *Neuropsychology*, **10**, 315–21.
Woodruff-Pak, D. S. and Papka, M. (1996). Huntington's disease and eyeblink classical conditioning: normal learning but abnormal timing. *Journal of the International Neuropsychological Society*, **2**, 323–34.
Zola-Morgan, S., Cohen, N., and Squire, L. (1983). Recall of remote episodic memory in amnesia. *Neuropsychologia*, **21**, 487–500.

9
Not one versus many, but zero versus any: structure and function in the context of the multiple memory systems debate

JEFFREY P. TOTH AND R. REED HUNT

PRELUDE

Imagine the following five scenarios. Each begins with a person, let's call him John, who has purchased a new house and, before going to bed on his first night there, hangs his car keys on a nail in the kitchen closet. That following morning his wife asks 'where are the car keys, John?'. In the first scenario, John replies 'they're in the kitchen closet', while in the second he says, 'they're hanging on that nail in the kitchen'. In the third scenario, John says, 'I don't remember, but check that nail in the kitchen closet'. In the fourth scenario, John says, 'I don't remember where they are', but then immediately walks over to the kitchen closet, retracing his steps of the previous evening, and finds the keys. Finally, in a fifth scenario, John doesn't say anything but simply points to the kitchen closet.

All of these scenarios reflect pretty run-of-the-mill stuff, the kinds of things that happen to us every day. What makes them interesting is that all of John's various responses, as well as numerous others not considered, could easily have arisen from the exact same encoded event. The question is: what kind of memory system mediates John's various responses?

The act of hanging the keys on that first night was a novel event for John, something that had happened only once in his life. This might lead one to believe that, upon hearing his wife's question, John experienced an episodic memory of hanging the keys the previous evening. This possibility is consistent with John's reply in the first two scenarios, but notice that his answer is not exactly the same. In the first case he refers to the closet, while in the second he refers to the nail. Do we need to postulate different episodic memories in the two cases?

In contrast to the first two, the third scenario ('I don't remember, but check that nail') does not seem consistent with an episodic memory interpretation. Here, John does not exhibit an episodic recollection of key placement, but only a vague knowledge (or *knowing*) of where the keys might be. In this case, therefore, John's response seems most consistent with the operation of semantic memory. But note that both the first and second scenarios are also consistent with a semantic memory interpretation, as there is nothing in what he says to indicates a vivid episodic recollection. This interpretive difficulty is a bit troublesome but, ignoring minor details, perhaps we could at least be sure that in all three cases John had some form of *declarative* (propositional) memory of the keys' location. Or could we?

In scenario four, John does indeed utter a declaration ('I don't know'), but it suggests no memory for the keys' location. Yet, despite the lack of evidence for declarative memory, by 'retracing his steps' he walks directly to where the keys were hung the previous evening. In this case, therefore, based on a series of motor movements nearly identical with those executed the previous evening, we might say that a procedural memory mediated John's finding of the keys.

Scenario five, where John simply points to the closet, also lends itself to a procedural interpretation. But imagine that, upon seeing him point, his wife says, 'how do you know they're in the closet?', to which John replies, 'because I distinctly remembering putting them there last night... I remember the smell of mildew when I opened the closet'. Here, then, we would have verbal evidence that John did in fact have an episodic memory of the keys' location. Would we now want to say that, upon hearing the original inquiry as to the keys' location, John retrieved an episodic memory that then *directed* the motor system to raise his arm and point?

Finally, imagine a slight twist to our scenario. Instead of keys, John hangs a heavy vacuum cleaner on the nail in the kitchen closet. The next morning his wife asks, 'John, do you think that the nail in the kitchen closet is strong enough to hold an ironing board?', to which John answers 'yes', confidently and without hesitation. What memory system is mediating John's response? Is it that John first experiences an episodic memory of hanging the vacuum cleaner, and then uses this memory as a basis for reasoning about the strength of the nail? Or perhaps in originally hanging the vacuum cleaner on the nail, John acquired the semantic fact of the nail's strength. What if John correctly answers the strength-of-the-nail question, but moments later exhibits no memory for hanging the vacuum cleaner; or claims no declarative memory for its location but walks over to the closet, thus exhibiting procedural memory? Can procedural memories form the basis of propositional (declarative) reasoning?

The above examples were designed to raise a few questions about the notion of memory systems. Most importantly, how does a systems theorist unambiguously identify a particular memory as being in one system or another (episodic or semantic, declarative or procedural)? What are the rules by which an event gets encoded *into* any particular system? Is it based on the content of the to-be-remembered information; whether it is verbal or motoric; the state of the rememberer? And when is a measure of performance (e.g. talking, pointing, walking) taken as indicative of, say, episodic memory as opposed to procedural memory? More generally, what is the relation between proposed memory systems and other aspects of cognition such as reasoning and acting? Before answering these questions, we suggest that memory researchers step back and ask an even broader question: does the theoretical machinery underlying the multiple systems approach clarify or obscure our understanding of memory?

INTRODUCTION

One of the most important developments in modern cognitive psychology has been the realization that past experience can affect subsequent performance in a multitude of different ways. In addition to traditional expressions of memory such as recall and recognition, people also show effects of prior experience that are unaccompanied by conscious recollection of the past, and these effects may manifest themselves as changes in perception, categorization, reasoning, or motor behaviour. A major issue concerns the most appropriate way of characterizing and explaining such variety, with two general perspectives defining the theoretical landscape. The most popular view is that the various expressions of memory reflect the operation of multiple, relatively independent memory systems. The alternative 'processing' view does not postulate multiple systems, but rather views mnemonic variety as reflecting the different ways in which task demands and processing goals can alter how prior experience gets expressed in subsequent performance.

Proper understanding of the current debate between the 'multiple system' and 'processing' approaches to memory requires an appreciation of their underlying assumptions. Insight into these assumptions is revealed by examining the historical legacies of the two frameworks, legacies which can be traced to the beginnings of psychology as a science. During those formative years, two opposing metatheoretical approaches dominated conceptions of the mind. One approach, structuralism, advocated studying the contents of the mind; complex mental abilities such as perception and memory were viewed as separate phenomena, to be understood by decomposing and analysing their constituent elements. An opposing view, functionalism, rejected this 'mental chemistry', arguing that the various faculties of mind (perception, memory, reasoning) operate in an integrated fashion to bring about adaptive, goal-directed thought and behaviour; thus, rather than analysing the structure and content of mental acts (what they *are*), functionalists emphasized the role that such acts play in an organism's response to changing environmental demands (what they *do*).

In the context of modern theories of human memory, structuralism is represented by the multiple memory systems approach. In this approach, one postulates a multitude of distinct memory representations, and the systems in which these representations are stored. Memory, then, is the process of activating the representations stored in a particular system. Once activated, the representations are able to influence a person's performance with the nature of that influence being dependent on the kind of information 'contained in' the representation. Thus, for the systems approach, memory is explained by reference to structural concepts—specifically, memory systems (the 'architecture' of memory) and memory representations (the fundamental components from which these large-scale systems are built).

In contrast, modern processing approaches exemplify a more functional orientation to the study of memory. For these approaches, little is gained in talking about underlying memory representations or the systems in which they are stored, because memory is not something to be found *in* those representations and systems. Rather, memory emerges in the interaction between a person with a prior history of experiences, and the environmental situations (e.g. the memory tasks) in which those prior experiences can be identified as influencing performance. Here, then, the dominant metaphor is one of process rather than structure.

Of course, these are caricatures of current approaches to memory. Process theorists regularly talk in terms of representations, mental attributes, and the like, while systems theorists are obviously concerned with functional uses of memory. However, we believe there are important insights to be gained from psychology's initial attempt to wrestle with mental structure and function, insights that have wide-ranging implications for the current debate over multiple memory systems. We shall say more later about the historical antecedents of current processing approaches, but for the moment we wish to focus on the lineage of structuralism in the multiple systems approach to memory.

The legacy of structuralism in multiple systems theory

Perhaps the clearest rendition of the structuralist's program was provided by Titchener (1898). In particular, Titchener drew an analogy between structuralism in psychology and morphology in biology, and saw the structural approach as providing a kind of morphology of mind: 'The primary aim of the experimental psychologist has been to analyze the structure of the mind. . . . His task is a vivisection, but a vivisection which shall yield structural results.' (p.450). Moreover, this morphological approach was viewed as necessarily primary to the analysis of psychological processes advocated by the functionalists. Just as the biological study of a physiological process is predicated on an understanding of its underlying morphology, so too psychological processes and functions had to reflect the operation of some underlying parts, and it was a structural analysis that was required to discover and describe these parts: 'In a word, the historical conditions of psychology rendered it inevitable that, when the time came for the transformation from philosophy to science, problems should be formulated, explicitly or implicitly, as static rather than dynamic, structural rather than functional' (Titchener 1898, p.453).

A strikingly similar metatheory underlies current systems approaches to the study of memory. Thus, advocates of this approach are adamant that 'some sort of systematic classification of memory is fundamental to our theoretical understanding of mnemonic processes' (Schacter and Tulving 1994*b*, p.2) and is required to 'guide functional research on learning and memory' (Tulving 1985*b*, p.72). The claim, then, is that understanding the structure or 'morphology of memory' is a prerequisite to understanding mnemonic processes and functions, just as understanding the morphology of a bird's wing is necessary for understanding its ability to fly.

The main argument of this chapter is that this strategy, although logical and sound in biology, is seriously flawed in the psychological study of memory.

Interestingly, the major flaw can be traced to a fundamental *difference* between the structuralism advocated by Titchener and that advocated by modern systems theorists, a difference we spell out more clearly below. First, however, we provide a brief description of the more popular memory systems proposed in the literature, and a general critique of those proposals.

THE MEMORY SYSTEMS OF 199X

There are a number of different proposals regarding human long-term memory systems. Most of them, however, derive from two early dichotomies; first, between declarative and procedural memory (Cohen 1984; Cohen and Squire 1980) and second, between episodic and semantic memory (Tulving 1972, 1983). In general, declarative memory ('knowing that') is defined as memory for *facts and events* that can be consciously accessed and verbalized. Procedural memory ('knowing how') is memory for *cognitive or motor skills* that cannot be consciously accessed or verbalized. Episodic and semantic memory, although sometimes treated as distinct systems (e.g. Tulving 1983), can also be viewed as subclasses of declarative memory (see Schacter and Tulving 1994b; Squire 1994); both are viewed as propositional in the sense of having a truth value and being expressible in words or statements. Episodic memory is memory for specific autobiographical events. Semantic memory is closely tied to language and involves memory (or 'knowledge') of facts, ideas, and concepts.

Two other dimensions that appear critical in the classification of memory are those of consciousness (or awareness) and intent, dimensions captured in the distinction between explicit and implicit memory (see Schacter 1987; Roediger and McDermott 1993). Explicit memories are both conscious, in the sense that the person is aware of remembering prior events, and intentional, in the sense that the person in some sense wants, or voluntarily intends, to retrieve them. In contrast, implicit memories are unconscious, in the sense that the person is unaware of retrieving or otherwise being influenced by prior events, and their retrieval is thought to occur involuntarily or without intent (see Jacoby 1984; Jacoby and Witherspoon 1982). Some researchers (e.g. Squire 1994) view the distinction between explicit and implicit memory as co-extensive with that between declarative and procedural memory, thus implying that explicit, but not implicit, memories can be expressed verbally. Moreover, explicit memories are considered to be *cognitive*, concerned with 'information' or 'symbolic knowledge', whereas implicit memories are *noncognitive*, concerned with 'stimulus–response bonds' or 'response probabilities' (see Petri and Mishkin 1994).† It is not clear whether implicit and explicit memory

---

† The connection between the explicit/implicit distinction and that between declarative and non-declarative memory is potentially problematic both with regards to their verbalizability and in terms of what is thought to be stored in the memory trace or system. First, in terms of verbalizability, it is often unclear whether researchers are referring to the processes underlying particular forms of memory, or the mnemonic 'products' of those processes. If it is the underlying processes that are viewed as central,

are supposed to be treated as memory systems *per se*, or simply as descriptive terms that are indicative of separate systems (see Ratcliff and McKoon 1996).

Procedural memory, also referred to as 'non-declarative memory', has recently been subdivided into a number of other systems (see Schacter and Tulving 1994*b*; Squire 1987, 1994). These include (1) skills and habits, (2) simple associative learning or conditioning, (3) non-associative forms of learning such as habituation and sensitization, and (4) the perceptual representation systems, a collection of pre-semantic subsystems used in the perception of objects and words. The latter system is simply called 'priming' by Squire (1994).

Finally, in addition to the more general systems described above, a number of more content-specific memory systems have also been proposed, or at least hinted at. For example, Schacter (1989) (see also Moscovitch 1989, 1992), proposed a number of distinct 'knowledge modules' that seem likely candidates for being memory systems, including the lexical, conceptual, facial, spatial, and self modules. Given that each of these domains reflect 'overlearned or unitized information', additional systems of this kind could also be postulated, such as the music and mathematics systems. Moreover, given that memory modules may be assembled through experience (Moscovitch 1989), systems specific to particular areas of expertise may also be possible; experts in fields such as radiology, entomology, and cosmology, for example, may be expected to have x-ray, insect, and stellar memory systems, respectively.

CRITICAL ANALYSIS OF THE MULTIPLE SYSTEMS PROJECT

The systems described above reflect a concerted attempt to provide a comprehensive morphology of memory, a theoretical classification of the different ways in which prior experience may affect subsequent thought and behaviour. In this section, we discuss some of the difficulties for these classification schemes. Central to our analysis is consideration of the criteria that have been proposed for identifying memory systems. Although proposed criteria undergo almost constant modification‡, three general criteria seem to recur in the literature, so we assume that

then nether implicit or explicit memory seem declarative as people can provide little or no verbal description of the processes underlying either type of memory. If, alternatively, it is the mnemonic product (i.e. what 'comes to mind') that is most important, then both forms of memory seem declarative (verbally describable), at least in situations in which words, signs, pictures, objects, or other language-related stimuli are retrieved (as if often the case in studies of implicit memory).

A second problem concerns the issue of what is stored 'in' an implicit or explicit memory. Although it is intuitively appealing to say that explicit ('cognitive') memory is concerned with *information*, whereas implicit ('non-cognitive') memory reflects stimulus–response (SR) connections (strengths, biases, or response tendencies), it is unclear what this information/SR-connection difference is supposed to correspond to in the memory trace. Stated as a question, what difference in the brain should one expect to see between an explicit/cognitive memory and an implicit/non-cognitive memory such that 'information' could be discerned in the former case but not the latter?

‡ In presenting the case 'for the possible heuristic usefulness of a taxonomic distinction between semantic and episodic memory', Tulving (1972) enumerated four major differences between these two

these form the fundamental core of the multiple systems proposal. These criteria are (1) that memory systems can be functionally dissociated, (2) that each system stores a different kind of information, and (3) that each system has a distinct neural implementation. Evidence for any one of these criteria is usually sufficient to suggest the possibility of a memory system; in general, however, confident postulation of a system requires that all three criteria be met.

In exploring these criteria, our analysis appeals to two issues that have recently become central in the study of memory: the relation between tests and processes, and the relation of memory to other aspects of cognition such as perception, reasoning, and action. Consideration of these issues sets the stage for further analysis of the relation between current system-based approaches to memory and earlier (Titchenerian) approaches to mind.

Functional dissociations and the process-pure problem

Functional dissociations are one of most important criteria for the postulation of memory systems. A functional dissociation occurs when an experimental manipulation produces different effects on two or more tests of memory. For example, variations in encoding—attending to the meaningful versus perceptual aspects of a word—have been shown to have a large influence on explicit tests such as recall and recognition, but little or no effect on implicit tests such as perceptual identification or stem completion (e.g. Jacoby and Dallas 1981; Graf *et al.* 1982). Similarly, amnesic patients show deficits on explicit/declarative tests of recall and recognition, but not on implicit/procedural tests such as mirror-reading (e.g. Cohen and Squire 1980). These results have been taken as strong evidence for the existence of separate memory systems.

A major problem with the functional dissociation criterion is that dissociations are known to occur between tasks that supposedly tap the same memory system (Blaxton 1989; Dunn and Kirsner 1989; Hayman and Tulving 1989; Hintzman

kinds of memory: (1) the nature of the stored information (basically, 'facts' versus 'events'); (2) autobiographic versus cognitive reference; (3) conditions of retrieval; and (4) vulnerability to interference. In Tulving (1983), episodic and semantic memory were no longer useful heuristic categories but were regarded as distinct 'functional systems' with 28 diagnostic features. Also, these two systems were to be distinguished from a third, procedural, system of memory. In 1984, Tulving identified five major criteria for distinguishing between memory systems: (1) their functions and the kinds of information they process; (2) their laws of operation; (3) their basis in the brain; (4) their phylogenetic and ontogenetic development; and (5) their format for representing information. A possible sixth criterion proposed in this period (Tulving 1985*a*) concerned the different kinds of consciousness associated with each memory system. More recently, three 'broad criteria' have been proposed for identifying different memory systems: class inclusion operations, properties in relation to other systems, and convergent dissociations (see Schacter and Tulving (1994*b*) for an explanation). In one way or another, these recent additions include the three 'general criteria' discussed in this chapter.

Squire (e.g. 1987) has been less explicit about criteria; however, in 1994 he notes that 'forms of memory are different in terms of what kind of learning occurs in each, what is stored as knowledge, and what brain systems are involved' (Squire 1994, p.215), thus enumerating the three criteria we examine here. Other criteria, proposed in the animal literature for example (Nadel 1992), have included length of storage time and computational differences. The latter notion is similar to Sherry and Schacter's (1987) notion of 'incompatibility' and is discussed in more detail below.

1990; McKoon *et al.* 1986; Ratcliff and McKoon 1996; Witherspoon and Moscovitch 1989). For example, using normal subjects, Blaxton (1989) showed a dissociation between two tasks thought to tap episodic memory (semantic cued recall and graphemic cued recall) and between two tasks thought to tap semantic memory (word fragment completion and answering general-knowledge questions). Dissociations between various procedural memory tests as a function of neurological dysfunction have also been identified (see Moscovitch *et al.* 1993).

How are such findings handled by multiple systems theory? One strategy is to simply postulate new systems for the dissociated tasks; for example, rather than reflecting the operation of semantic memory (Tulving 1983) performance on word fragment completion is now thought to reflect the operation of a perceptual representation (Tulving and Schacter 1990) or priming (Squire 1994) system.

A second way to explain apparent within-system dissociations is to note that tasks are not pure with regard to the mnemonic processes or systems they access. That is, rather than selectively measuring a single kind of memory, it is now widely agreed that most, if not all, memory tasks engage multiple forms of memory. This is known as the 'process-pure' problem (see Jacoby 1991) but it could as easily be called the 'system-pure' problem. Thus, the episodic system may contribute to both semantic and graphemic cued recall, but these tasks may also reflect contributions from other systems; semantic cued recall, for example, may reflect contributions from semantic memory, while graphemic cued recall may draw on the word-form subsystem of the perceptual representation system.

There is a serious problem, however, in appealing to the process- (or system-) impurity of memory tests if one's goal is to use functional dissociations to discover and verify the existence of proposed memory systems. What is crucial is not that two *tasks* differ in their information-processing requirements; this is known by definition (they are, after all, *different* tasks). Rather, the researcher is interested in evidence that the hypothetical *systems* proposed to mediate performance on those tasks are fundamentally different with respect to their *mnemonic*-processing requirements. The problem, then, is the following: if test performance reflects the operation of multiple mnemonic systems, how can one be sure that distinctions made at the task level (i.e. on the basis of dissociations) accurately reflect the underlying structure of memory? In general, researchers postulating multiple memory system are cognizant of this problem and thus advocate 'converging dissociations . . . of different kinds, observed with different tasks, in different populations, and using different techniques' (Schacter and Tulving 1994*b*, p.18). Unfortunately, converging dissociations, rather than solving the process-pure problem, may simply exacerbate it if the nature of the impurity is consistent across a particular method of testing, or is inherent to the kinds of mnemonic content being contrasted.

To illustrate, consider a recent study by Glisky *et al.* (1995). These researchers were interested in the difference between item memory and source memory, and the possibility that these two forms of memory reflect the operation of different brain systems. To investigate these issues, Glisky *et al.* used neuropsychological test performance to separate elderly subjects into 'high frontal' or 'low frontal' groups, and (in a separate analysis) into 'high temporal' and 'low temporal' groups. All subjects were then exposed to a list of sentences, half spoken in a male voice, the other half in a female voice. Subsequent testing revealed an impressive double dissociation between item memory (recognition of previously presented sentences) and source memory (recognition of the voice in which the sentences had been spoken). In particular, the 'high frontal' group exhibited better source memory than the 'low frontal' group, but the two groups showed equivalent item memory; conversely, the 'high temporal' group showed better item memory than the 'low temporal' group, but the two groups did not differ in their ability to discriminate source.

Such data would seem to constitute promising evidence for separate memory systems, an item-based system mediated by the temporal lobes, and a source-based system mediated by the frontal lobes. Indeed, by concluding that 'memory for the content and for the context [source] of an event may be functionally dissociable and may rely on different parts of the brain' (Glisky *et al.*, p.229) they invoke two of the main criteria used to postulate memory systems, functional dissociation and different underlying neurology. Moreover, this claim was noted to gain additional credibility by the existence of other, *converging* studies showing that individuals with frontal dysfunction often are impaired on tests of source memory (e.g. Craik *et al.* 1990; Janowsky *et al.* 1989; Schacter *et al.* 1984).

The problem with this interpretation concerns the fundamentally different processing demands made by the item and source tests. In particular, the item test used by Glisky *et al.* involved presentation of two sentences, one that had been previously presented in the experiment, another that had not been presented in the experiment or, possibly, at any other time in the subject's prior history. In contrast, the source test involved two presentations of the same previously presented sentence in each of two voices, *both of which had been heard at study*. Thus, despite the fact that '[t]he form of the source memory test was identical to the item memory tests' (i.e. both were two-alternative forced choice), the stimuli used and discriminations required were actually quite different.

Rather than tapping distinct systems, then, an alternative explanation is that the item and source tests simply differed in the *specificity* of the mnemonic judgment they required. Stated in 'processing' terms, performance on the item memory test may have been largely mediated by familiarity (an automatic form of memory), while performance on the source test required conscious recollection of the sentence–voice configuration. If one makes the further assumption that more fine-grained ('configural') distinctions recruit controlled processes dependent on frontal-lobe structures (e.g. Rudy and Sutherland 1992; Shallice 1988), then the apparent 'double dissociation' between item and source, rather than reflecting the operation of distinct systems, is more appropriately seen as a consequence of the way in which the two tests required a different balance of mnemonic automaticity and control.

Regardless of the accuracy of this account of Glisky *et al.*'s item/source dissociation, the general point is that the relation between test performance and hypothetical underlying memory systems (or processes) can be quite complex.† Few researchers would argue with the claim that modern research on memory is just beginning to unravel the complex arrangement of processes that underlie memory performance; and that even relatively simple tasks, such as recognition of isolated words or sentences, involves a complex combination of processes and processing relationships. An obvious implication of this fact is that currently proposed memory systems are based on test performance that reflects different combinations of mnemonic processes or systems; that is, they are based on data from process *impure* tests. The impurity of available memory tests, relative to the presumed discrete nature of proposed memory systems, undermines the use of task dissociations to cleanly identify memory systems.

Wider implications of process-impurity

The process-pure problem extends beyond the interpretation of specific tasks and may well be the Achilles' heel of the multiple systems approach. By definition, any particular act of memory draws on more than one (ostensibly defined) system. The most obvious example of this is the reliance of episodic memory on semantic memory. When we remember a specific autobiographical event, we understand its meaning. Episodic events are always interpreted in relation to other facts we know about the world. Memory is never purely episodic.

The problem extends beyond episodic and semantic memory. Motor and cognitive skills are classified as procedural (Schacter and Tulving 1994b) or non-declarative (Squire 1994), but the concept of skill is equally applicable to declarative knowledge. Witness our descriptions of mathematicians, philosophers, and politicians (to name a few) who have acquired 'skill with language' or 'skill in the manipulation of concepts'. And as shown in our 'key' example that started this chapter, single episodes (episodic memories?) regularly mediate motoric acts such as pointing or walking. On a memory systems account, examples such as these require the postulation of complex, but rarely specified, communication routes between systems (e.g. the episodic system directing the procedural system) in addition to the systems themselves.

Moreover, the mixture of declarative and procedural memory is not restricted to just the skill and habit system. 'Simple associative learning' is held to be non-declarative, a position that seems reasonable when the discussion is restricted to sensory-affective forms of classical conditioning. However, a large literature shows that classical conditioning operates in the declarative domain. For instance, conditioned responding to *words* has been shown using both salivation and GSR as the conditioned response (Razran 1939; Riess 1940) (see also Phillips 1958; Raskin 1969). Importantly, stimulus generalization in these paradigms has been shown to

---

† Additional evidence for such complexity is provided by Jacoby *et al.* (1993) who showed that apparent null effects of an experimental manipulation on implicit test performance (i.e. reading versus solving anagrams), can be produced by differential contributions of controlled and automatic uses of memory that offset one another in overall performance (see also Toth *et al.* 1994).

be greater for synonyms (i.e. 'urn' to 'vase') than homonyms ('urn' to 'earn'). Such results place 'simple' conditioning squarely in the declarative/semantic domain.

Conversely, if non-declarative memory systems are implicit (unconscious and unintentional), and thus independent of explicit/declarative systems, then it seems difficult to explain the modulation of simple (non-declarative?) conditioning as a function of verbal instructions and intentions to learn (e.g. Hilgard and Humphreys 1938; Hill 1967; Nicholls and Kimble 1964). These findings constitute direct evidence that lower-level ('implicit') forms of memory are penetrable by higher-level ('explicit') processes.

Of course, it is always possible for the multiple systems theorist to appeal to the impurity of their paradigms. That is, observed responses in conditioning experiments may reflect influences from higher-level systems that are nevertheless independent of the lower-level systems the conditioning paradigms were designed to index. However, such arguments beg the question of which results can be taken as contaminated and which as pure, as all paradigms seem equally suspect.

Perhaps because of problems like these, Tulving (1984, 1985a) proposed a 'monohierarchical arrangement' of memory systems such that episodic memory is dependent on semantic memory which, in turn, is dependent on procedural memory. Ironically, the monohierarchical conceptualization simply formalizes the problem of using task dissociations to identify discrete systems and, however implicitly, acknowledges that multiple systems theories are not open to empirical confirmation or falsification (see McKoon et al. 1986; Ratcliff and McKoon 1996). In addition, the monohierarchical concept entails the implication that similar basic mechanisms, both psychological and neurological, are at work in all forms of memory, a position with which we agree and explore more fully below.

The problems that provoked Tulving's monohierarchical arrangement go far beyond the inextricable coaction of different forms of memory, as it is never purely 'memory' that is being assessed in memory tasks but a host of other, supportive abilities such as perception, comprehension, and reasoning. Abilities such as these set the context for mnemonic processing in such an way as to form an integral part of the very definition of memory (Bransford et al. 1977). Thus arises another difficult issue for the multiple systems approach: The degree to which memory systems can be considered separate from other aspects of cognition.

Systems defined by contents: the artificial separation of memory, perception, reason, and action

In describing his original reasons for making a distinction between semantic and episodic memory, Tulving (1984) nicely captures an important, but under-appreciated problem posed by the postulation of multiple memory systems. Specifically, he noted that researchers such as Rumelhart et al. (1972), Kintsch (1972), and Collins and Quillian (1972) 'were concerned with what I thought were the processes involved in the understanding of language, whereas they suggested that they were studying memory in a broader sense than had been used in the past. . . . I thought that the extension of the concept of memory to the comprehension of language, question answering, making of inferences, and other such cognitive skills was inappropriate' (Tulving 1984, p.223).

Of course, history shows that Tulving was actually of two minds about this issue. What he apparently found inappropriate was the extension of traditional definitions of memory—in terms of conscious, explicit recollection—to the domains of language, question answering, etc. Yet his solution to this problem was, in fact, to extend the concept of memory, *in the form of a semantic memory system*, into these very domains. From our perspective, however, memory permeates every form of cognitive processing from perception to language to reasoning to action. Thus, just as it seems inappropriate to extend traditional notions of memory into the domain of language, so it seems inappropriate to extend the concept of memory, *in the form of memory systems*, to every aspect of cognitive processing that shows sensitivity to prior experience. Stated simply, postulation of 'separate' or 'independent' memory systems erects artificial boundaries between memory and other aspects of cognition that should eventually be incorporated into a more comprehensive theory of thought and behaviour.

The problem appears in sharp relief when considering the second criterion for the postulation of memory systems, the notion that different systems store different kinds of contents or forms of information.† As noted above, one distinction between kinds of information is that between declarative knowledge (facts and events) and procedural/non-declarative knowledge (cognitive and motor skills). Also noted was the possibility that more specific kinds of mnemonic contents, such as faces or music, may also qualify for memory system status. Consistent with the modularity-of-mind hypothesis (Fodor 1983), Sherry and Schacter (1987) argued that specialization for one kind of content may make a system unable to process another kind of content, an idea referred to as 'functional incompatibility'. For example, it might be argued that a system specifically devoted to the processing and storage of faces would be unable to process and store music.

A potentially serious problem with the different-contents/incompatibility criterion is that it confounds incompatibility of memory function with incompatibility of other psychological functions such as perception. That is, it might be the case that the neural machinery devoted to the perception of faces is incompatible with that required for the perception of music, yet the principles of memory could be the same. Sherry and Schacter were aware of this problem and thus argued that postulation of a distinct memory system or 'memory module' necessitates that it have 'its own acquisition, retention, and retrieval processes and that the rules of

---

† The different-contents criterion has always been a staple of distinguishing between systems (see footnote to p.237). Its role in more recent formulations, however, is somewhat unclear. In particular, under the 'properties and relations' criterion, Schacter and Tulving (1994*b*) state that 'The properties of any system include rules of operation, *kind of information*, and neural substrates' (p.16; emphasis added). However, under the 'class-inclusion' criterion we are told that 'An intact memory system enables one to perform a very large number of tasks of a particular class or category, *regardless of the informational contents of the tasks*' (p.15; emphasis added). We can only assume that 'kind of information' and 'informational contents' mean something different to Schacter and Tulving.

operation of these processes differ across modules' (Sherry and Schacter 1987, p.440). This is one of the stricter criteria for postulation of a memory system, but it is still problematic because it assumes a separation between the neural and psychological mechanisms underlying memory, and those underlying other aspects of processing. If, alternatively, memory and other forms of processing (e.g. perception, action) share underlying mechanisms, it may be difficult, if not impossible, to ever show mnemonic incompatibility between different mental contents.

An analogy with the distinction between implicit and explicit memory may help make this idea clear. A major advance in determining whether performance on a task reflects implicit (unintentional) or explicit (intentional) memory involved keeping retrieval cues constant and varying only the test instructions, a strategy known as the retrieval intentionality criterion (Schacter et al. 1989). The intentionality criterion was important because dissociations produced with different retrieval cues (e.g. faces versus music) can logically reflect not differences in consciousness, intentionality, or underlying principles of memory, but less interesting differences associated with the information-processing requirements of the retrieval cues themselves (Dunn and Kirsner, 1989); for example, that we *see* faces but *hear* music. On the basis of this criterion, then, a direct comparison of memory mechanisms for different content domains, *keeping all other information-processing demands constant*, is impossible.

Note that this is a logical problem rather than an empirical one, and stems directly from treating memory as an independent mental act separate from other cognitive functions such as perceiving, reasoning, and acting. This compartmentalization of function is a throwback to the faculty psychology of Gall and, more generally, to the structuralist enterprise of analysing the mind into separable components. And although it is often claimed that modern research on the brain has revitalized these ideas in the form of Fodorian modularity, it is worth noting that modern brain science can also been seen as providing the opposite lesson—that there are no hard and fast distinctions between perception, memory, reasoning, and action (see, e.g., Deacon 1989; Milner and Goodale 1995; Mesulam 1990).

Commenting on the proliferation of memory systems, Nadel (1992) makes this point concisely: 'The view that processing and memory storage occur in the same circuits. . . emerged from the neurobiological literature, largely because it is hard to imagine how in the nervous system these activities could be kept entirely separate from one another. One might almost argue that we have gone too far in this regard—everything the nervous system does could be construed as "memory-like" in some sense, as just about every form of activity in the nervous system leaves some relatively nontransient trace behind' (Nadel 1992, p.180). Indeed, we would count ourselves among those who feel that multiple system theorists have 'gone too far', treating almost every aspect of cognition (e.g. learning, language, object perception) as a distinct kind of memory system. As noted by Dennett (1991), 'the very idea that there are important theoretical divisions between such presumed subsystems as "long-term memory" and "reasoning" (or "planning") is more an artifact of the divide-and-conquer strategy then anything found in nature' (Dennett 1991, p.39).

The point, of course, is not to abandon the divide-and-conquer strategy, but rather to be vigilant against reifying *in* nature (i.e. in the mind or brain) heuristic divisions made in the interest of clarity or scientific understanding. As discussed in the next section, one must also guard against viewing the divided-and-conquered parts as recently discovered, alternative versions of the whole.

Lower-forms of learning as separate systems?

What is the difference between learning and memory? Most textbooks describe learning as the process of *acquiring* information about the world whereas memory is the storage and subsequent expression of that leaning. If we accept this definition, then characterization of different forms of learning as separate memory systems seems inappropriate; learning is a component of memory, not a qualitatively different form of memory. Moreover, even if we take learning to incorporate both acquisition and subsequent expression, it is not at all clear that lower (non-declarative) forms of learning operate independently of higher (declarative) forms (see pp.241–2).

'Simple associative learning' is now commonly described as one of the many memory systems, as are the non-associative processes of habituation and sensitization (e.g. Squire 1987, 1994). This expansion of the definition of memory to include 'lower' forms of learning plays an interesting *rhetorical* role in the multiple systems debate because their 'discovery' by memory theorists produces a relatively large increase in the number of putative long-term memory systems. Yet most neurobiologists would agree that these phenomena are ubiquitous in the nervous system, cutting across numerous content domains as well as both perceptual and motor systems. They are also likely to play a role in perceptual priming, as well as other rapid motor and sensorimotor adaptations, thus making it difficult to see how they can be considered as 'separate' memory systems.

On the basis of evidence that the cellular mechanisms underlying classical conditioning are an extension of those underlying sensitization, Hawkins and Kandel (1984) (see also Lynch and Granger 1992) have suggested that higher forms of learning may reflect combinations of the neurobiological mechanisms underlying basic habituation and sensitization. In particular, they suggest that 'whereas single neurons may possess only a few fundamental types of plasticity which are used in all forms of learning, combining the neurons in large numbers with specific synaptic connections (as occurs for example in the mammalian cortex) may produce the much more subtle and varied processes required for more advanced types of learning' (Hawkins and Kandel 1984, p.380).

Such observations are fascinating and could have widespread implications for our understanding of both the neural and cognitive bases of memory. In particular, they suggest the possibility that lower (procedural/non-declarative) forms of learning may be on a continuum with, and thus partially underlie, higher 'cognitive' forms of memory including explicit/episodic recollection. Of course, this is not to deny the differences that certainly emerge from the combined operation of basic neural mechanisms, or from the operation of large-scale neural collectives. But a continuum of learning and memory is consistent with the idea that memory tasks, although dissociable, also have numerous shared components (e.g. Humphreys *et al.* 1989; Moscovitch 1992; Ratcliff and McKoon 1996). Conceptualization of different forms of learning and memory as independent from one another, residing in isolated systems, draws attention away from such commonalties, and thus undermines the possibility of finding unifying principles of memory. As discussed more fully in the next section, we believe that multiple system theorists may be confusing dissociable memory *tasks* with ontologically 'real' memory systems.

Memory systems: a psychological theory or a taxonomy of tasks?

It is often unclear whether the postulation of multiple memory systems is to be taken as a formal theory, a taxonomic classification of memory, or simply an intuitive description. Thus, writing in 1986 about the episodic/semantic distinction, Tulving stated that 'what had been a "potentially useful" heuristic in 1972 has now become a full-fledged hypothesis, or theory, of the basic nature of memory' (Tulving 1986, p.307). Yet, in the same paper he writes that '[t]he idea of differentiable episodic and semantic systems, in its most rudimentary form, is simply a hunch . . .' (Tulving 1986, p.308). Most recent work seems to emphasize the classificatory nature of the multiple systems approach (e.g. Schacter and Tulving 1994*b*, p.26). But what exactly is being classified?

Tulving (1985*b*) provided an insightful discussion of the classification problem in the study of learning and memory, focusing on the conceptual problems involved in defining the fundamental unit of analysis for the field. In particular, he noted that 'Systematic biology . . . differs from systematic learning and memory in many ways. One of the more conspicuous differences is the fact that there is little difficulty in determining the to-be-classified things in biology: They are concrete things that occupy space, that have boundaries, and that have perceptually identifiable and objectively measurable characteristics. In learning and memory, it is not necessarily clear what the objects of classification are or what they should be' (Tulving 1985*b*, p.77).

Identifying the fundamental unit of analysis for the study of learning and memory is indeed central if one's goal is to offer a taxonomy of memory tasks and, ultimately, of underlying memory structures. Tulving (1985*b*) explored the possibility that *tasks* may be the appropriate unit of analysis for memory, but this approach was quickly dismissed given the multiple ways in which tasks can be performed, and the way a particular response may reflect very different processes (recall our discussion of the process-pure problem, and our examples of 'John' at the beginning of the chapter). Tulving's solution to this problem was to draw an analogy with the biological concept of species and suggests that, instead of specific tasks, classes of tasks may be a more appropriate unit of analysis in learning and memory. And, indeed, this seems to be the strategy adopted by multiple system theorists, as examination of their classification schemes reveal them to essentially be lists of the various tasks and paradigms that have been used to study the effects of prior experience.†

But if a single task is inappropriate as the unit of analysis in a study of memory, is a class of tasks any better? In both cases we are still left with the fundamental difficulty that, unlike biological organisms, neither the covert processes that determine test performance, nor the memory structures to be inferred from that performance, have any 'perceptually identifiable characteristics'. Indeed, as described in the next section, the only observable 'units' in memory are functional relations, but functional relations provide a poor basis for structural classification.

The central problem facing the multiple systems project: can you build psychological structures using only functional relations?

Multiple system theorists are faced with a fundamental problem: their goal is to provide a theory of observed memory performance based on underlying systems/structures, but they have no means for identifying or isolating the 'units of analysis' that would unambiguously identify those systems. To understand the problem, let us return to our analogy between current multiple systems approaches to memory and earlier structural approaches to mind. Recall that, as is true for the multiple systems theorist, structural psychologists such as Titchener believed that a 'morphological' analysis of mind was a prerequisite to understanding its processes and functions. Importantly, however, there is a critical methodological difference between Titchener's structuralism and the renovated structuralism advocated by current system theorists. In particular, structuralists such as Titchener believed they were in possession of a scientific methodology that would allow them to *directly* observe the structure that necessarily underlies mental experience. That method was introspection. Irrespective of its shortcomings, introspection held out the possibility of directly 'looking' at the structure of mind in the much the same way that one might visually inspect the structure (morphology) of a bird's wing.

However, because the method of introspection has become unacceptable in experimental psychology, largely because of its subjectivity, the analogy between morphological analysis in biology and structural analysis in psychology has lost its meaning. That is, elimination of introspection as a viable method in psychology also removes any means of directly observing the structure of the mind, and thus of hypothetical memory systems. Of course, what has taken the place of introspection is the analysis of something more objective and directly observable, but which is necessarily *functional*, namely task performance.

† An important exception to this is the more functionally oriented multiple-entry, modular memory (MEM) system advanced by Johnson (1983). Critically, MEM is concerned with processing requirements *among* tasks, rather than distinctions *between* tasks as a function of their content (see Johnson and Hirst 1993; Johnson and Chalfonte 1994). Thus, unlike many other multiple systems theories (e.g. Schacter and Tulving 1994b; Squire 1994) the subsystems in MEM are not assumed to be coextensive with particular memory tasks.

The point is this: multiple systems approaches to memory are attempting to describe the underlying structure of memory. However, that structure cannot be directly observed but can only be inferred on the basis of task performance. Task performance, however, is not structural, but rather reflects the functional relationship between prior experience and subsequent task demands. But this leads to a fundamental circularity because if mental structures (i.e. memory systems) are being inferred though a functional task analysis, how can these structures then be used to explain performance on those very same tasks?

As a concrete example of this circularity, consider semantic-cued recall and graphemic-cued recall, discussed earlier in the context of the process-pure problem. Both tests were/are ostensibly episodic as they both probe memory for a specific prior event. Yet, as shown by Blaxton (1989) these two tasks respond very differently to experimental manipulations. Specifically, semantic-cued recall shows a positive generation effect (i.e. self-generated items are better remembered than read items) while graphemic-cued recall shows the opposite relation (read greater than generate). Results such as these have led multiple system theorists to view graphemic-cued recall as tapping a perceptual memory system, and semantic-cued recall as tapping semantic memory (Tulving and Schacter 1990). Thus, classification of these memory tests is entirely based on functional relations; that is, in terms of the pattern of results they exhibit. They are not defined *a priori* as episodic, but rather functionally, in terms of their relation to experimental variables. No structure (system) has been 'discovered' by these observations, and to explain the results by appeal to such hypothetical structures confuses more than clarifies our understanding of the observed functional relations.

In the light of these arguments, it is worth considering Sherry and Schacter's (1987) claim that multiple systems theorists need to consider more thoroughly the functions of the systems they propose. Sherry and Schacter recognized the need for 'a well-specified set of criteria' for determining functional incompatibility between memory tests, but went on to acknowledge that such criteria cannot currently be specified because 'the necessary information concerning the operation of memory is unavailable' (Sherry and Schacter 1987, p.449). What information is required? Sherry and Schacter state: 'To provide a convincing analysis of functional incompatibility, it would be necessary to possess (a) an understanding of the demands of a particular memory problem, (b) a description of the *architecture* of the hypothesized system that allegedly handles the problem, and (c) a description of the properties of some other hypothetical system that allegedly cannot handle the problem' (Sherry and Schacter 1987, p.449, emphasis added). Our analysis suggests that such a program could never be realized because it is impossible to obtain 'a description of the architecture of a hypothesized system' independently of 'the demands of a particular memory problem'.†

---

† Sherry and Schacter do provide two examples of functionally incompatibility, one concerning dual visual systems in flying insects, the other concerning dual blood supply systems in the wings of bats. What is most notable about these biological examples is that both are predicated on a morphological analysis of observable anatomical characteristics.

Perhaps it is the tacit recognition of this conundrum that has spurred the feverish activity and rhetoric of the system theorist about the importance of neuroscience to the study of memory. Thus, one increasingly hears that 'brain systems' provide the best explanation of memory, or sees the terms 'brain systems' and 'memory systems' used synonymously. One might go so far as to say that this trend reflects the realization on the part of multiple system theorists that they lack the psychological grounding for the memory structures (the 'architectures') they have built. That is, knowing at some level that their postulated memory structures can never be truly observed or verified, they appeal to the more substantive and objectively observable structures found in the brain.

Memory and brain

The third major criterion for the postulation of memory systems is that they are based on the operation of different brain systems. For instance, Squire (1994) describes different 'forms' of memory, and then notes how these 'multiple memories' are most consistent with a 'brain-systems' view. Similarly, Schacter and Tulving (1994b, p.13) state that different memory systems reflect 'different neural substrates (neural structures and mechanisms)'.

The brain systems manoeuvre is often taken as the most scientifically compelling criterion for the postulation of multiple memory systems, but for all of its technological appeal, it may well be the most obfuscating of the three criteria. Examination of the literature reveals very few clear statements about exactly what is meant by the terms 'brain system' or 'neural mechanism'. For example, is the hippocampus a 'brain system' and is it the same thing as the episodic or declarative memory system? Exactly what are the necessary and sufficient structures that define the 'medial-temporal lobe memory system'? And is it just the neural structures or do we also include in this brain system neural *processes* and other 'non-neural' components (e.g. glial cells, blood flow, hormonal influences, etc.)? And what of 'neural mechanism'? If we were to discover that all long-term memory in the brain is mediated by a similar form of long-term potentiation (Lynch and Granger 1992), or that all learning reflects variations on the basic neural processes of habituation and sensitization (Hawkins and Kandel 1984), would this mean that there is a single memory system? In short, serious evaluation of the brain systems criterion requires a precision in theoretical definition that is currently lacking in both psychology and neurology.

Even if the lack of precision were ignored, however, and the relationship between 'memory systems' and 'brain systems' was assumed to be isomorphic, available functional neuroimaging evidence does not bear out the tidy compartmentalization of memory systems implied by current system classifications. That is, rather than seeing a circumscribed Episodic Memory System being activated for all episodic memory tasks, or a Semantic Memory System underlying performance on all semantic tasks, instead what one observes are highly distributed and often overlapping patterns of activations that suggest numerous components, both shared and distinct, among tasks. That is, the picture one gets is much more compatible with a processing, or a components-of-processing view (Witherspoon and Moscovitch 1989), in which various neural processes are recruited or assembled for the task at hand (see Mesulam 1990). Two recent studies bare out this point.

Cabeza *et al.* (1997) used PET to directly compared the neural activity underlying recall and recognition. Versions of each task were specifically designed to be matched in terms of visual input, verbal output, and cognitive effort, thus raising the possibility that a core episodic system might be identified. However, although there were overlapping areas of activation (right prefrontal and anterior cingulate), the two tasks also produced very distinct patterns of activations. In particular, whereas recognition produced higher levels of activation than did recall in the inferior parietal cortex, recall resulted in significantly greater activation in the anterior cingulate, globus pallidus, thalamus, and cerebellum. This would seem to provide direct evidence that, although both tasks are thought to tap the same episodic/declarative memory system, they are nevertheless mediated by different neural networks (i.e. distinct 'brain systems' or 'neural mechanisms').† Thus, the Cabeza study provides little evidence for a core system underlying episodic memory.

Even more dramatic evidence of the variable relation between memory performance and brain activation is shown in a PET study by Jennings *et al.* (1997). These researchers attempted to determine if the neural activation underlying a *single* semantic task would be the same across different modes of responding (vocal versus mouse-clicks versus silent thought). In separate scans, subjects used each response mode to make yes/no decisions to visually presented words in either a semantic task (living/non-living) or a non-semantic task (does the word contain the letter 'a'). Within a particular response mode, activations from the non-semantic (letter) task were subtracted from those in the semantic task, and the patterns were compared across response mode. As in Cabeza *et al.* (1997), there was some shared activation across the three response modes. More striking, however, was that each response mode produced a unique pattern of activation such that 'different areas of the brain were recruited for semantic processing depending on how participants organized their response'. Indeed, analyses of the neural interaction between processing task and response mode showed that specific regions exhibiting *increased* activation for one response mode, often showed *decreased* activation for another response mode.

Jennings *et al.* (1997) justifiably used their data to impugn the additivity assumption underlying the widely employed subtraction technique in neuroimaging

† The Cabeza study would thus seem to satisfy one of the main criteria for postulation of separate memory systems, distinct neural implementation. It is worth noting that the two other main criteria—functional dissociation and different contents—also seem to have been met as it is widely known that recall and recognition can be dissociated as a function of frequency in the language; and the two tests appear to require memory for different kinds of information (recall requiring memory for a specific target event, recognition requiring memory for the context in which a target event occurred). Based on these criteria, then, recall and recognition would appear to be based on separate memory systems.

studies. However, given that this technique has apparently been successful in the identification of language and perceptual processes (e.g. Peterson *et al.* 1988), we suggest that Jennings *et al.*'s results may be essentially correct: there is no single locus for semantic memory in the brain. Rather, semantic memory is a psychological-level description of a class of *tasks* (or environmental challenges) that *interact* with the brain in different ways. No doubt these different ways have some things in common but, ontologically, there is no one core commonality that could be called 'the semantic memory system', and that corresponds in a one-to-one fashion with a particular system in the brain.

Our point in discussing these two studies is not to suggest that they are not useful. On the contrary, both are very interesting, well designed studies that tell us much about the neural systems underlying different kinds of memory performance. However, we question the ability of such studies to ever provide the kind of evidence that would prove the existence of memory systems. Indeed, we are unclear as to what form such evidence would take. The studies by Cabeza and Jennings may be important in telling us about the 'brain systems' associated with memory performance, but they do not, and could not, identify *memory* systems.

Lesion data have also been championed as providing direct support for a multiple systems view of memory. A full explication of the uses and inherent problems of inferring psychological function from lesion data is beyond the scope of this chapter. We restrict ourselves here to two points. First, there is little agreement on how best to characterize the deficits seen in amnesia and other neuropsychological syndromes. Thus, whether they show deficits in episodic memory, declarative memory, context memory, configural memory, or some other, as yet little understood, form of memory is a completely open question. We therefore think it premature to claim that patient data prove the existence of multiple memory systems.

The second point is simply to note the danger, described by both philosophers (e.g. Malcolm 1977) and neuropsychologists (e.g. Luria 1973), of treating psychological functions such as memory as isomorphic with brain structures. Psychology is not neurology. More specifically, psychological functions such as episodic memory are not isomorphic with neurological structures such as the hippocampus, just as the function of respiration is not isomorphic with the lungs but rather involves dynamic relations between the lungs, diaphragm, chest muscles, etc., as well as the gaseous environment in which respiration occurs.

Data from patients with brain damage, and neural activation studies, while certainly important for understanding the neurological substrates of memory, cannot adjudicate the multiple memory systems debate. In our view, understanding the psychological basis of memory is a prerequisite to understanding its neurological basis. The issue is one of levels of analysis (between brain and cognition/behaviour); and of what one means by the term 'memory'. If one views memory as equivalent to an underlying (neural) representation, then brain data do indeed become the Rosetta stone for understanding memory. If, in contrast, one views memory as a psychological phenomenon, something that reflects the interaction between a person with a prior history of experience and a task environment in which that history is relevant, then brain data, while interesting and important, cannot fully explain memory. To 'locate' memory in the brain is to miss the larger (functional) set of factors, external to the brain, by which memory is meaningfully defined.

A recent PET study by Schacter and colleagues (Schacter et al. 1996) illustrates this contrast. They were interested in the neuroanatomical correlates of illusory ('false') memories induced by asking people to recognize a visually presented word that was not studied, but which was semantically related to other, aurally presented study words (see Deese 1959; Roediger and McDermott 1995). Results showed increased blood flow in the left medial-temporal lobe for both true and false memories, but true memories exhibited additional activation in left temporoparietal cortex, a region that has been associated with phonological memory. Most relevant here is Schacter et al.'s account of their data; in particular, they state that their findings 'raise the possibility that illusory recollections of false targets seem authentic *because* they are accompanied by medial temporal lobe activity that is usually linked with veridical conscious recollection' (Schacter et al. 1996, p.271; emphasis added). The implication is that people assess veridicality by reference to which of their brain areas are currently activated. This is to be contrasted with explanations that appeal to the psychological properties of the false memory paradigm; for example, that non-presented words seem authentic because they are strong semantic associates to studied words. We don't question the fact that such-and-such brain areas were indeed activated by the various tasks, but wonder whether assigning causal efficacy to these areas provides a complete account of the false memory phenomenon. On our view, a complete account of false memory will have to make reference to the psychological properties of the initial event and the conditions under which it is later tested.†

Brain data are fascinating. There is no question that damage to the brain can cause specific memory impairments. It is also true that performance of different memory tasks activates different neural structures and pathways as measured by PET, fMRI, and other neurophysiological techniques. However, interpreting these findings as evidence for memory systems requires more than just the observation that performance of different memory tasks depends on, or differentially activates, distinct neural structures. The real question concerns how brain activity relates to memory as a psychological phenomenon, an issue that goes far beyond the multiple memory systems debate. As disappointing as it may be at the close of the decade of the brain, we still do not possess principled arguments necessary to equate brain stuff with the concepts of psychology, and psychology as an experi-

---

† Indeed, on further scrutiny the data presented by Schacter et al. (1996) raise troubling questions about the relationship between the neural activity and behavioural phenomenon, and thus may have deepened, rather than clarified, the false memory phenomenon. In particular, given that the brain responded differentially to true and false items, the data of Schacter et al. (1996) apparently demonstrate that the brain does not show false memory! If nothing else, this would seem to be a striking example of a reductionistic analysis losing the phenomenon it was attempting to explain.

mental science will suffer if it is dazzled by 'mind/brain' rhetoric and technology into thinking otherwise.

INTERIM SUMMARY

In the sections above, we have described some of the more difficult theoretical problems that face any multiple systems approach to memory. One of these problems is the fact that memory tasks are not pure with regard to the processes or systems they index. As shown by our discussion of Glisky *et al.* (1995), the process-impurity of memory tests can easily lead to the postulation of unnecessary memory systems. A second problem concerns the relation between memory and other aspects of cognition. Memory is not an isolated form of cognition, separate from other aspects of processing such as perception, reasoning, and action, but is rather embedded in those processes. Memory for prior events alters how we perceive, reason, and act; conversely, any instance of perception, reasoning, or action results in a modification of the brain (i.e. results in the creation of 'memory'), and there is good reason to believe that these modifications occur in the very same structures that mediate those other ('non-mnemonic') processes. The interrelation of memory and other aspects of processing undercuts the strategy of identifying 'separate' memory systems, and makes it impossible to ever truly evaluate the different-contents criterion.

A similar problem concerns the treatment of different forms of learning as distinct memory systems. Not only is learning in a different conceptual class from memory (i.e. by definition 'learning' is acquisition whereas 'memory' is storage and retrieval), but there is evidence that learning is a ubiquitous property of the brain. Many of the available neural activation studies also seem inconsistent with a multiple systems interpretation. Moreover, key terms in the neural implementation criterion, such as 'brain system' and 'neural mechanisms', are only vaguely defined; and when specific neural mechanisms are precisely identified (e.g. Hawkins and Kandel 1984), the evidence seems to support commonalities among forms of memory rather than differences.

In our view, all of these problems stem from a subtle, but fundamental, problem in the metatheory underlying the systems approach to memory. In particular, distinctions between memory systems are not based on a direct 'morphological' analysis of the structure of memory; rather, such distinctions are necessarily derived from a functional, task-based analysis. Tasks are specific environments which challenge the organism in a variety of different ways; memory systems are thus defined by their *function* within such environments. But this leads to a fundamental circularity in the explanation of memory: structures (memory systems) are inferred from functional (task-specific) uses of memory, but are then used to explain the very effects observed on those tasks. Moreover, in the absence of any hope of directly observing a psychological 'memory system', system theorists appeal to 'brain systems' as their explanation for memory phenomena.

Is there any way out of this circularity and wanton reductionism?

A neofunctional alternative to the question of memory

In describing an alternative to the multiple systems approach to memory, we ask readers to remind themselves of exactly what it is we are trying to explain. The central question faced by memory researchers is not 'how many memory systems are there' or even whether there are such things as memory systems. Rather, what needs to be explained, at least in the context of this debate, is the remarkable variety with which past experience influences subsequent thought and behaviour.

The multiple systems approach offers a dense theoretical armament for addressing this variety. Indeed, there is a sense in which the theoretical machinery of the multiple systems approach is as complex as the phenomena it is trying to explain; due, perhaps, to its tendency to enumerate a mixed list of tasks, paradigms, and phenomena. But even if it contains a descriptive kernel of truth, we believe that it is in many ways premature. It is certainly not uncontroversial and one may imagine an outside observer wondering whether the science of memory has reached the level of sophistication where so much of our time and effort is spent trying to establish the number and characteristics of hypothetical memory systems, or even debating their reality. That outside observer, having some basic training in the natural sciences, might also inquire into the goal of our theoretical debates: 'What are the fundamental empirical regularities of memory that your theories are trying to explain?'.

If you were to describe the most important principle discovered about memory in the last 100 years, what would it be? The question is a sobering one, for although one could point to numerous empirical generalizations—such as the level-of-processing effect, the Tulving–Weisman function, or the differential sensitivity of certain tests to prior perceptual or conceptual processing—few such generalizations have been shown to be invariant across situations. That is, for each empirical regularity that is announced, one can invariably devise a situation for which this regularity does not hold. In many ways, it is this non-uniformity, the lack of even one uncontroversial empirical law, that makes the study of memory less than a mature scientific endeavour.

Yet there is one principle that is relatively invariant, or at least general enough on which to base an empirical investigation of memory, namely, the principle of transfer-appropriate processing (Morris *et al.* 1977). Although this principle has been expressed in different ways by different authors—for example, as 'memory for operations' (Kolers 1976) or 'encoding specificity' (Tulving 1983)—each of these concepts expresses a central uniformity about memory: past events influence subsequent performance to the extent that cognitive activities occurring at retrieval are similar to those that occurred at encoding. In our view, this is one of the most important principles ever to be articulated about memory and thus we see it as the starting point for explaining the mnemonic variety that drives this debate. We also see it as a fundamentally *functional* principle as it embodies the notion that, whatever memory is (system, process, or, perhaps, disposition), it will have to be explained in terms of the relation or interaction between what a person was *doing* when an event was first experienced and what they are *doing* when that event subsequently exerts its influence.

The reference to activity in the preceding paragraph (i.e. memory as *doing*) is not unintentional. As described below, we view memory as an active process rather than a static representation. Nevertheless, we hesitate to rely too heavily on 'process' as the central theoretical construct in our account of memory because, in many ways, mnemonic processes are as metaphorical as the memory systems with which they are often contrasted. The label 'processing approach' is popular because of the success of the distinction between data-driven and conceptually driven processing in explaining dissociations among implicit and explicit tests (Jacoby 1983*a*; Roediger and Blaxton 1987); and because of evidence that the means of acquiring information (i.e. the specific operations performed) effectively define the memory acquired (Kolers 1976; Kolers and Roediger 1984). As shown by the popularity of these ideas, the process metaphor is certainly a useful one, and one that we rely on in our own research as well as in many of the passages below. But we believe that what most advocates of the 'processing view' have in mind when describing memory is more akin to the concept of *function* than it is to process.

To understand our point of view, consider the following basic definitions of function and process provided by Brent (1984): 'The concept of function focuses attention on changes in the relationship between a structure and its external context. The concept of process, on the other hand, focuses on changes in the internal relationships among the parts of the structure itself. A functional analysis thus views structural activity macroscopically, in terms of the broader context in which it is embedded. A process-oriented-analysis, on the other hand, views that same activity microscopically, as a causally integrated sequence of acts by the constituents of the structure' (Brent 1984, pp.18–19).

Thus, on Brent's definitions, the alternative to a multiple system approach is better captured by *function* than by process. A true process-based analysis would necessarily assume some underlying parts, such as mental representations, upon which the processes operate. Although beyond the scope of this chapter, we have reservations about the need to postulate mental representations to account for memory phenomena (see Van Gelder 1997; Verela *et al.* 1991).† Regardless, we believe that many of the theorists who use the process metaphor actually intend a concept more in line with function; namely, a macroscopic relationship between a holistic organism (e.g. a person) and its environment. Although 'memory process'

† Of course, another interesting interpretation of Brent's definitions is that to fully understand memory, the (microscopic) structures and processes that will need to be described are in fact neural. This may indeed be true but it would make an even stronger case for a *functional*, rather than structural, account of psychological abilities such as memory. That is, on this account, concepts of memory, perception, etc. would effectively refer to functional (macroscopic) relations between a person and their external context, with these functions (at least partially) realized by structural changes in internal (i.e. neural) relationships. But such a conceptualization even more strongly undermines the notion of memory systems *qua* psychological structures.

may serve a useful purpose in describing that relationship, like 'memory system' its explanatory role should be recognized as predominantly metaphorical and thus subsidiary to more concretely described functional relations. Indeed, even the data-driven/conceptually driven distinction can be viewed as drawing its explanatory power, not by reference to any specific 'process', but rather through the functional relations that obtain between particular test cues (e.g. a dictionary definition versus a briefly flashed word) and observed performance (e.g. the presence or absence of a levels-of-processing effect). It is for these reasons that we describe our alternative to multiple systems as functionalist (or 'neofunctionalist') rather than as a 'processing' approach.

Researchers who we would describe as functionalists tend to be rather eclectic, emphasizing similarities amongst diverse forms and tests of memory (e.g. Jacoby 1983*b*; Humphreys *et al.* 1989) while at the same time showing the striking variety with which a particular form of memory may subsequently influence thought and behaviour (e.g. Bransford *et al.* 1977; Jacoby 1988; Whittlesea 1993). Given this eclectic orientation, it is not as easy to group functional approaches (i.e. theorists or particular theoretical ideas) under a single banner as it is for multiple system approaches (Schacter and Tulving 1994*a*). Nevertheless, in the final sections of this chapter, we lay out what we see as the central tenets of a modern functional approach to memory. We believe that, taken together, these tenets provide a more promising and flexible approach to understanding of memory than does an approach based on the questionable doctrine of psychological structuralism.

Memory is an activity

'The fact that mental contents are evanescent and fleeting marks them off in an important way from the relatively permanent elements of anatomy. No matter how much we talk of the preservation of psychological dispositions, nor how many metaphors we may summon to characterize the storage of ideas in some hypothetical deposit chamber of memory, the obstinate fact remains that when we are not experiencing a sensation or idea it is, strictly speaking, non-existent' (Angell 1906, as quoted in Herrnstein and Boring 1965, p.502).

This quote, by a leader of the functionalist school, captures what was one of the central complaints against structural approaches to mind such as that advocated by Titchener, and also summarizes what we see as a major problem with present system-based approaches to memory. In particular, both are predicated on the notion that mental events, including memories, are to be treated as concrete entities instantiated in a mental or neural representation.

A very different orientation is to view memory as an activity. Here, memory is not a concrete thing (as is, for example, a brain structure) but is rather a transaction between a person and what we might call a retrieval environment. As Craik (1985) put it, 'the memory trace is perhaps not a specific structure located at some point (or even diffusely) within the central nervous system, but is rather an altered potential of the system to carry out certain mental activities provided that the context, task, goals, mental set, etc. present at the time of initial learning are also reinstated, either "driven" by external stimulation or reconstructed internally by the rememberer. By this account, remembering is essentially a form of perceiving.' Moreover, '[j]ust as it is not very sensible or meaningful to talk about the percept as a function of mental activity only (rather, it is by nature an interaction between stimulus information and specific "mental skills" of the perceiver), so it does not seem too useful to regard memory as a function of the mind alone' (Craik 1985, p.200).

The view of memory as activity has two major implications, outlined in the following two tenets.

Memory is not 'stored'

In structural (multiple systems) approaches, memory consists of concrete entities (representations) and the storage places (systems) in which they are kept. For the structuralist, then, memories exists (have ontological reality) when not in use. For the functionalist, in contrast, memory is a potential, disposition, or capacity for interacting with the environment in particular ways, or for achieving certain states of awareness that are similar to earlier states (see, for example, Ben-Zeev 1986).

Critically, to view memory as a potential or capacity, one necessarily gives up the metaphor of 'storing' memories. Memory is not something stored 'in' the person or even 'in' the brain, any more than music is stored in the radio, or walking stored in the legs. In each case (memory, music, and locomotion), the system under investigation has the potential to achieve certain states, or exhibit particular actions, when relevant conditions are met, but these states or actions do not reside in the system. Like walking, memory is a dynamic event that exists only in its operation. Extending the quote of Angell above, one could say that when we are not experiencing (e.g. recollecting) a prior event, or otherwise being ('implicitly') influenced by that event, memory is, 'strictly speaking, non-existent'.

Describing memory as an activity, and thus as something which is not stored, seems to befuddle many people. How can one speak of memory without first postulating the prior, independent existence of the thing remembered? Indeed, such questions arise even among those who grant that memory is an activity rather than a concrete entity. As noted by Malcolm (1977), even when trying to explain a 'memory-act' or 'memory-process', there follows a strong tendency to inquire about the *content* of this act or process: 'It is as if we thought of the memory-act or memory-process as being a *container* (something like a box); and then we ask, What is *in* this container? What are its contents?' (Malcolm 1977, p.35). We suggest that such questions stem from both ingrained folk psychology (see Roediger 1980) and the structuralist assumptions, embodied in system-based approaches, critiqued above. We also suggest that part of the solution to this problem involves the relocation of memory from something that exists 'in' the person or brain to something that obtains in the interaction between the person (and their brain) and the environment in which acts of memory occur.

Memory is an interaction between a person and a retrieval environment

A second major implication of the memory-as-activity view is that memory cannot be defined outside of the retrieval environment (i.e. the context) in which prior experience influences current performance. This definition of memory is similar to the definition of attentional automaticity put forth by Neumann (1984). Neumann argued that, rather than being an absolute property of a particular process, automaticity is better viewed as an emergent property of task performance, reflecting the coupling of input parameters (specified in the sensory array) with the skills of the performer. Similarly, mnemonic processes may best be defined in terms of how a current disposition, enabled by past experience, gets coupled to a retrieval environment such that prior experience becomes manifest.

When we say that memory reflects an interaction between a person and a retrieval environment, we mean quite literally that memory cannot be discussed in the abstract, outside of the context of retrieval cues and, as argued below, the goals of the rememberer. Recall our first two scenarios involving John's response to his wife's inquiry about the location of their car keys. In first scenario, John tells his wife to the look 'in the kitchen closet' to find the keys, while in the other he tells her to 'look on the nail'. In both cases, the initial event of John hanging the keys was the same, but his answer is different depending on how he (tacitly) interprets the question. In our example, this interpretation involved John's knowledge of his wife's prior experiences in their new house, whether they were of the kitchen closet or of the nail. There is no way we can describe John's memory outside of the context of the question he is asked. His memory does not exist as a fixed snapshot of the prior event that is later retrieved *in toto* and adapted to the current circumstance. Rather, the current circumstance determines how the prior event manifests itself in performance and, indeed, in subjective experience (see Kelley and Jacoby 1990; Whittlesea 1993). In this sense, then, the current circumstance is as much part of the memory as is the past event.

Memory is context specific

If memory reflects an interaction between the person and the retrieval environment, then one should expect to find a high degree of contextual specificity in the expression of memory. This contrasts with the structuralists' assumption, echoed in current multiple systems theories, that events can be represented abstractly, stripped of their episodic/contextual details.

What evidence is there for such contextual specificity? Some of the earliest evidence was uncovered in the initial research on what is now called 'implicit memory'. For example, studies of visual word identification (Jacoby and Dallas 1981; Kirsner and Smith 1974; Winnick and Daniel, 1970) showed that performance was highly dependent on the details of prior presentation, such as the modality in which words were initially presented. These results strongly contrasted with existing models of word recognition which suggested that word recognition was based on abstract representations that did not preserve the episodic details of initial processing. Evidence for contextual specificity led to changes in existing models of word recognition, including the postulation of modality-specific representations; and, more generally, to a revision and expansion of system-based explanations of priming. In particular, performance on word identification, instead of reflecting semantic memory as had previously been argued (Tulving 1983), was subsequently viewed as a form of procedural memory (Tulving and Schacter 1990). Even these adjustments, however, seem incapable of capturing the range of contextual effects shown, for example, in the sensitivity of word identification to changes in type font or case (e.g. Jacoby and Hayman 1987); in the sensitivity of re-reading to the original orientation of text (e.g. Kolers 1976); or the sensitivity of lexical decision to the conceptual biasing effects of preceding words (e.g. Masson and Freedman 1990).

As a further example of the degree to which memory can exhibit contextual specificity, consider experiments by Hayman and Tulving (1989) examining the 'hyperspecific' nature of priming on the implicit word fragment completion test. Subjects were first shown a list of study words (e.g. MOSQUITO) and then were given two successive fragment completion tests. Critically, the fragments presented on the two successive tests were either identical (e.g. –O–Q—TO on both tests) or were 'complementary' such that the two cues had little or no overlap (–O–Q—TO and M–S–UI–O). The critical results concerned the stochastic relations (degree of dependence) between performance on the two successive tests. In particular, when the same fragment was used, performance on the tests was found to be highly related (i.e. performance on one test predicted performance on the other). In contrast, when complementary fragments were employed, the two tests showed no significant relation (i.e. performance of the two tests was independent of one another). Witherspoon and Moscovitch (1989) also showed stochastic independence between successive measures of retention but their experiments employed demonstrably different tests (fragment completion and perceptual identification). Hayman and Tulving showed that such independence was also possible between different versions of the *same* test, and thus presumably tapping the same memory system.

Hayman and Tulving took their results to implicate the existence of a 'traceless QM (quasi-memory) system', a notion that was later incorporated into the word-form subsystem of the PRS (perceptual representation system). Such labels are fine, but what the reader should take away from these experiments is neither the labels nor the 'discovery' of a new system, but rather the phenomenon. That is, what is timely about Hayman and Tulving's elegant experiments is not the QM system (which was abandoned, or at best renamed, a year later), but the high degree of context specificity that can be elicited by subtle changes in retrieval cues.

Much of the research showing context-specific transfer has been limited to the perceptual domain. However, more recent research suggests that a similar level of specificity can be found on conceptual/semantic tests. Cabeza (1994), for example, has shown a double dissociation between two conceptual implicit tests (category–exemplar production and free association) as a function of the type of orienting task performed at encoding (categorical classification versus associative production). Similar results have been reported by other researchers (McDermott and Roediger 1996; Vaidya *et al*. 1997; Woltz 1996). We believe that such experiments are only the tip of the iceberg, and that further demonstrations in the semantic domain will eventually be as common as the forms of contextual specificity observed in recall and recognition (e.g. Morris *et al*. 1977; Tulving and Thompson 1973).

Although we view context specificity as a key assumption underlying functional approaches to memory, it is clear that memory is not completely context bound. To take again our example of John, although his 'memory' changes dramatically depending on the retrieval cues in which the prior (key-hanging) experience becomes manifest, there are a multitude of different questions he could be asked (or retrieval tests he could perform) that would all show memory for the keys' location. Given such generalization, how can one maintain that memory is context specific?

A detailed answer to this question is beyond the scope of this chapter but we hasten to add that, rather then being fundamentally problematic, the apparent lack of situational specificity becomes one of the most interesting, important, and difficult aspects of memory research, and leads to an emphasis on *transfer*, how activity in one situation is repeated, or acts as a source of influence in subsequent, but necessarily different situations. Critical here is appreciation of the fact that *no events ever truly recur*, so in fact all memory (transfer) is a case of generalization. Rather than abandoning the focus on context specificity, then, a functional approach recommends close examination of the activities performed during the initial event, as well as the retrieval demands made when that event exerts its influence (e.g. Whittlesea *et al*. 1994).

Memory is relative to (and thus defined by) task demands and goals

The context specificity of memory can be viewed as the primary factor underlying the observed variety with which prior events influence subsequent performance. It therefore leads to a program of research where, instead of the characteristics of hypothetical memory systems, the nature of retrieval environments (instructions, cues, task demands) become of central importance (e.g. Humphreys *et al*. 1989). In addition to an emphasis on the objective characteristics of retrieval environments, however, a functionalist approach also places a heavy emphasis on the goals of the subject in performing a task. This point can be appreciated by noting that dissociations arise even when a subject is given identical retrieval cues on two separate tests (e.g. Graf *et al*. 1982). The fact that such dissociations can be obtained suggests the need to consider not only the different retrieval environments in which prior experience may influence performance, but also how a subject conceptualizes that environment, and what they are trying to achieve within it. In the case of explicit and implicit memory, the determining goal appears to be whether the subject responds to test cues with or without reference to a specific prior event.

The findings of Morris *et al*. (1977) (see also Stein 1978) in the explicit domain can also be viewed as dependent on the goals of subjects. In particular, whether explicit memory-test performance was enhanced by semantic orientation at study (attention to meaning), or non-semantic orientation (attention to phonemic qualities), depended on the whether the subject's goal was to establish a meaningful (semantic-based) relationship between current and prior words, or whether the relationship to be established was phonemic (rhyme-based). These results and others are consistent with the claim that the goals of test performance can have a dramatic effect on whether a test stimulus acts as a conceptually driven or data-driven cue (see Toth and Reingold 1996).

Thus the approach we are suggesting is one in which both the prior event (the 'to-be-remembered' event) and the retrieval environment are analysed relative to the goals of the subject. This perspective is not unlike that advocated by Logan (1988) in his instance theory of automaticity: 'Each encounter with a stimulus is assumed to be represented as a processing episode, which consists of the goal the subject was trying to obtain, the stimulus encountered in pursuit of the goal, the interpretation given to the stimulus with respect to the goal, and the response made to the stimulus' (Logan 1988, p.495). This theory, which is supported by an impressive array of empirical findings, expresses our position that subject-determined goals and interpretations play a central role in determining what gets 'into' and 'out of' memory.

There is no principled distinction between memory and other aspects of cognition

Emphasis on the goals and purposes of processing leads, in our view, to a very different conceptualization of the relation between memory and other cognitive abilities than that implicated in the systems approach. As discussed earlier, memory permeates all cognitive activity, a claim borne out both in behavioural data and in the study of the brain. This leads to difficulties with views that postulate strong distinctions between memory and other cognitive activities such as perception, attention, reason, and action. Rather than analysing discrete stages in information processing, a functional orientation is more concerned with how these ostensibly separate abilities act in an integrated fashion to allow adaptive responding to environmental circumstances. Dewey's (1896) classic 'Reflex Arc' paper makes this point in his example of a child reaching for the flame of a candle. Dewey suggested that analysing the situation into sensation, perception, and motor action, either from a contents of consciousness view or from a stimulus–response view, obliterated the central psychological phenomenon of the relationship between the organism and its environment. The adaptive *coordination* of sensation, perception, and action is lost in an analysis of each of those faculties as discrete, separable stages.

A similar obliteration of phenomena occurs when isolated memory systems are charged with explaining mnemonic phenomena that are only slightly more complex than the typical isolated-word experiment. Consider a study of memory and problem solving by Adams *et al.* (1988). Subjects were exposed to acquisition sentences that could be used to solve word puzzles presented later in a test phase. An example of a test-phase problem is the following: 'Uriah Fuller, the famous Israeli superpsychic can tell you the score of any baseball game before it starts. What's his secret?'. The important manipulation involved the type of acquisition sentences subjects were exposed to at encoding. Some subjects were presented with *fact-based* sentences, such as 'Before it starts, the score of any game is 0 to 0'. A second group were given *problem-based* variants of these same facts: 'It is easy to predict the score of any game before it begins . . . the score is 0 to 0'. Despite the fact that both sentences-types communicated essentially the same information, problem-solving performance of these two groups was dramatically different: the problem-based group solved 56% of the test-phase problems, while the fact-based group solved only 36%. Similar results have been reported by Lockhart *et al.* (1988) who also showed that problem-solving performance in the fact-based group was no better than that of a control group not exposed to the acquisition sentences. Moreover, both studies presented strong evidence that the effects were not due to the induction of a general problem-solving set, but were specific to the sentences and problems to which subjects were exposed.

Consider these results in the context of the multiple systems approach. First, it is difficult to specify, in any principled way, the system or systems into which acquisition sentences are being encoded. Both types of sentences appear to have both episodic (autobiographical) and semantic (meaningful) characteristics but, in addition, the problem-based sentences exhibit a condition-action quality, thus implicating a procedural basis. Second, what memory systems would mediate performance when subjects later encounter the test problems? Subjects were not informed of the relationship between acquisition sentences and subsequent test problems, thus qualifying the problem-solving test as implicit. But the data show conclusively that performance is contextually (episodically) specific as to the particular problems presented. Moreover, the very nature of the problem-based sentences, and the nature of their transfer, suggests the operation of procedural (non-declarative) memory; this, despite the fact that the both the acquisition sentences and the test problems are obviously meaning-based (semantic/declarative). Perhaps at retrieval, then, the test puzzles are initially processed for meaning in the semantic system (after, of course, being perceptually processed by the PRS); simultaneously, episodic memories are (implicitly?) retrieved triggering condition-action (skill-based) representations for the problem-based sentences in procedural memory. These representations then interact with representations in semantic memory, allowing the subject to solve the problem.

Compare this tangled account with the more functional explanation provided within the framework of transfer appropriate processing: subjects presented with problem-based acquisition sentences engaged in a set of cognitive activities that overlapped substantially with the types of activities subsequently required to solve the test problems (substantial enough to produce a significant increase in problem-solving ability over control subjects). In contrast, subjects presented with fact-based sentences engaged in cognitive activities that overlapped very little, if at all, with those required by the test problems (as shown by the failure of fact-based subjects to solve problems above the level shown by control subjects). Exactly what these 'activities' are is currently underspecified, but a functional account at least gives some indication of what aspects of performance to focus on. In particular, the problem-based acquisition sentences involved the initial posing of a problem, followed by presentation of its solution, whereas the fact-based sentences presented a simple fact for verification. Moreover, one can infer that reading specific words had little affect on observed performance because fact- and problem-based sentences showed the same degree of overlap with the test problems.

Additional specification of the relevant activities is provided in a related problem-solving study by Needham and Begg (1991). In the first phase of their experiment, participants were asked to read a series of word problems, each of which contained a description of the relevant solution to the problem posed. One group was asked to examine the solutions and prepare to explain why they were correct, while another group was simply asked to memorize the problems and their solutions. Subsequent tests of the ability to solve analogous problems, or to remember the original problems and solutions, were then administered. Results showed that subjects who were originally instructed to solve the problems exhibited more transfer in solving analogous problems than did the memorization group; in contrast, the memorization group exhibited better memory for the original problems than did the problem-solving group. What is impressive about these results is that both groups were given exactly the same problems at acquisition. Thus, in addition to raising serious difficulties for system-based accounts of problem solving, the Needham and Begg (1991) study also adds further specification to a functional account of memory. It is not simply the posing of a problem-oriented question that determines transfer in problem solving, but whether the goals of initial processing were directed at future meaning-based explanation (i.e. problem solving) versus future reproduction (i.e. memory retrieval).

Experiments such those by Adams *et al.* (1988) and by Needham and Begg (1991) demonstrate the high degree of interdependence between memory and problem solving (reasoning), just as experiments on word or object recognition show the interdependence of memory and perception (e.g. Ratcliff and McKoon 1996). Indeed, the degree of interdependence is so extreme as to make distinctions among these faculties essentially arbitrary. These experiments also lend support to the 'memory for operations' view advocated by Kolers and colleagues (e.g. Kolers and Roediger 1984; Kolers and Perkins 1975). Rather than being a 'focal trace' existing in some static system, Kolers argued that memory is better conceptualized in terms of the mental operations or procedures used in initially interacting with an item or an event. That is, memory is not an abstracted copy or representation of some previous content but is simply the set of operations used in dealing with the event. There is nothing else. Note the parsimony and potential unifying quality of this proposal. Rather than stemming from differences in hypothetical memory systems, variety in the expression of memory arises naturally out the numerous skills or procedures that people have for interacting with their environment.

SUMMARY OF THE FUNCTIONALIST ORIENTATION TO MEMORY

In the sections above, we have tried to briefly identify some of the core assumptions of a functionalist approach to memory, and to give some flavour for that approach by choosing examples that illustrate major assumptions.† To briefly reiterate, we believe that memory is best viewed as a dynamic activity that is not stored in the person or brain, but rather emerges from interaction of the person (and their brain) with the surrounding environment. This view recommends against taking the concept of representation to mean an ontologically 'real' thing existing in either the mind or brain, because to see memory in a representation is to freeze in time and space what is in essence a fluid activity that is spread across both. It is to see rotation 'in' the wheel, or flight 'in' the wing, instead of seeing that rotation and flight are but one function that can be performed by wheels and wings.

By our account, memory is necessarily context specific and part of that context is made up by the goals of the rememberer. The ability of people to transcend context (i.e. generalize)—to remember out of context, or to act in opposition to prior habits—is a central theoretical issue and dovetails with concerns about the nature of similarity, as well as the appropriate interpretation of abstract knowledge. The context-sensitive, goal-directed nature of memory undermines the ability to separate memory into separate, independent memory systems, just as it undermines the ability to view perception, attention, memory, and action, as separate, independent stages of information (or neural) processing. Full appreciation of this latter point necessarily leads to a reconceptualization of the debate that sparked this book: the debate over memory systems is not one versus many, but zero versus any.

CONCLUSIONS

Multiple system structuralists see memory as something you can point to in the brain, or something located in that pernicious category of modern cognitive neuroscience, the 'mind/brain'. In doing so, they 'neuralize' what are, at their heart, psychological and behavioural events and thus participate in a form of neural Cartesianism (see Coulter 1997). For example, Mishkin and Appenzeller (1987, p.80) tell us that 'Ultimately, to be sure, memory is a series of molecular events'.

---

† Numerous aspects of our functional approach have been left out due to space limitations. These include the distinction between perceptual and conceptual processing, the concept of processing fluency and the general role of heuristics and attributions in memory, and the distinction between controlled and automatic uses of memory. Each of these concepts plays a central role in our view of memory and we hope to spell out their role in a future article. Also needed in a functionalist approach would be specification of the relation between memory as a psychological phenomenon and the operation of the brain (see footnote to p.255). Again, space limitations preclude us from extensive discussion except to note the correspondence between the functional approach recommended here and the 'neural context' approach to brain function advocated by McIntosh (1997).

Similarly, Norman and Schacter (1996, p.232) describe the 'raw material of memory' as 'changes in brain activity'. The problem with these statements is that they are referring to *the neural substrates of memory* not memory *per se*. Memory is something that obtains on laboratory tasks, or between people, or in the minds of the rememberer. No one remembers (or implicitly acts on) biomolecular events, and the raw material of memory is not brain activity but objects and events such as faces, cars, jokes, and baseball games.

In a similar vein, Squire (1994, p.204) states that 'declarative memory refers to a biologically meaningful category of memory dependent on a specific brain system . . .'. What does it mean to say that declarative memory is 'biologically meaningful'? Does this mean that facts and propositions are somehow used to carry out neurobiological functions? Of course not. If anything, declarative memory is a *psychologically* (and socially) meaningful category used to describe a particular kind of knowledge. It is molecular events and brain activity that are biologically meaningful.

Lest we be misunderstood, we believe there *are* important differences between the various forms of memory identified by researchers as constituting memory systems; it seems clear to us, for example, that sensory habituation differs from motor learning which, in turn, differs from memory for autobiographical events. Moreover, these different forms of learning and memory must, at some level, reflect the operation of different brain processes (at least on any monistic–materialist account of mind). Our concern is whether these different forms of learning and memory need to be considered as entirely separate, independent systems, both relative to each other, and relative to other aspects of cognitive processing. Stated differently, although the multiple system theorist's concern with task differences is certainly important to understanding memory, we believe that such differences should be balanced with a understanding of the similarities between tasks. Also, while a memory systems approach does a good job of cordoning off memory as a separate area of inquiry (both psychologically and neurologically), we believe there are important insights to be gained by asking how memory is integrated with other cognitive processes such as perception, attention, reasoning, and goal-directed action.

In their current forms, the structural/neurologically based multiple system approach and the functional/psychologically oriented process approach involve different domains of inquiry, different experimental approaches, and produce different kinds of theories. Which approach is most appropriate to understanding memory? We believe that both can be informative, but some researchers appear compelled to proclaim a rather different answer to this question: given the 'hard' nature of the brain, the backing of biology, and the high-tech armament of neuroscience, they think it is clear that 'a brain-systems view of multiple memories is more consistent with the biological and psychological facts than a processing view' (Squire 1994, p.215) and that '[t]he 'battle' over multiple systems is over, and the multiple-systems view has won' (Tulving, quoted in Roediger 1990, p.376). In the spirit of a lively debate, we close by suggesting that such claims are not only premature, but overly narrow, as they presuppose that by describing the structure of the brain one has explained the function of the mind. In contrast, we view mind and memory as adaptive mental functions that take place in a wider context of environmental demands and subject-determined goals; incorporation of these contextual factors will necessarily form a central part of any complete account of memory and mind. Moreover, proclamations of victory based on the 'brain systems view' incorrectly see the direction of influence in the study of memory as going from brain to mind. In actual fact, the direction of influence has almost always gone the other way. Every interesting 'multiple form of memory' was first identified, and subsequently elucidated, at the psychological/behavioural/functional level and only then were neuroscientists able to probe its neural underpinnings. And so it will always be. The structural/neurological investigators of memory need us functionalists much more than they realize.

ACKNOWLEDGEMENTS

We would like to thank Cheryl Logan, Jackson Marr, Randy Engle, John Dunlosky, and Rob Guttentag for illuminating discussions of the issues presented herein, and for incisive critiques of an earlier version of this chapter. We also express our appreciation to the editors of this volume, and to Kate Kilpatrick at Oxford University Press, for their encouragement and patience during the writing of this chapter.

REFERENCES

Adams, L. T., Kasserman, J. E., Yearwood, A. A., Perfetto, G. A., Bransford, J. D., and Franks, J. J. (1988). Memory access: the effects of fact-oriented versus problem-oriented acquisition. *Memory and Cognition*, **16**, 167–75.

Ben-Zeev, A. (1986). Two approaches to memory. *Philosophical Investigations*, **9**, 288–301.

Blaxton, T. A. (1989). Investigating dissociations among memory measures: support for a transfer appropriate processing framework. *Journal of Experimental Psychology: Learning, Memory, and Cognition*, **15**, 657–68.

Bransford, J. D., McCarrell, N. S., Franks, J. J., and Nitsch, K. E. (1977). Toward unexplaining memory. In *Perceiving, acting, and knowing: toward an ecological psychology*, (ed. R. Shaw and J. Bransford), pp. 431–66. Erlbaum, Hillsdale, NJ.

Brent, S. B. (1984). *Psychological and social structures*. Erlbaum, Hillsdale, NJ.

Buckner, R. L. and Tulving, E. (1995). Neuroimaging studies of memory: theory and recent PET results. In *Handbook of neuropsychology*, Vol. 10, (ed. F. Boller and J. Grafman), pp. 439–66. Elsevier, Amsterdam.

Cabeza, R. (1994). A dissociation between two implicit conceptual tests supports the distinction between types of conceptual processing. *Psychonomic Bulletin and Review*, **1**, 505–8.

Cabeza, R., Kapur, S., Craik, F. I. M., McIntosh, A. R., Houle, S., and Tulving, E. (1997). Functional neuroanatomy of recall and recognition: a PET study of episodic memory. *Journal of Cognitive Neuroscience*, **9**, 254–65.

Cohen, N. J. (1984).Preserved learning capacity in amnesia: evidence of multiple memory systems. In *Neuropsychology of memory*, (ed. L. R. Squire and N. Butters), pp.83–103. Guilford Press, New York.

Cohen, N. J. and Squire, L. R. (1980). Preserved learning and retention of pattern analyzing skill in amnesia:dissociation of knowing how and knowing that. *Science*, **210**, 207–9.

Collins, A.M. and Quillian,M.R.(1972).How to make a language user. In *Organization of memory*, (ed.E. Tulving and W. Donaldson),pp.309–51.Academic, New York.

Coulter, J. (1997).Neural Cartesianism.In *The future of the cognitive revolution*, (ed. D. M. Johnson and C. E.Erneling),pp.293–301.Oxford University Press, New York.

Craik, F. I.M.,Morris, L. W.,Morris, R. G.,and Loewen,E.R.(1990). Relations between source amnesia and frontal lobe functioning in older adults. *Psychology and Aging*, **5**, 148–51.

Criak, F. I.M. (1985). Paradigms in human memory research. In *Perspectives on learning and memory*, (ed.L.-G. Nilsson and T. Archer),pp.197–221.Erlbaum,Hillsdale, NJ.

Dawson, M. E. and Reardon, P. (1969). Effects of facilitory and inhibitory sets on GSR conditioning and extinction.*Journal of Experimental Psychology*, **82**, 462–6.

Deacon, T. W. (1989).Holism and associationism in neuropsychology:an anatomical synthesis. In *Integrating theory and practice in clinical neuropsychology*, (ed. E. Perecman), pp.1–47.Erlbaum,Hillsdale, NJ.

Deese, J. (1959).On the prediction of occurrence of particular intrusions in immediate recall. *Journal of Experimental Psychology*, **58**, 17–22.

Dennett, D. C. (1991). *Consciousness explained.* Little Brown,Boston,MA.

Dewey, J. (1986). The reflex arc concept in psychology, *Psychological Review*, **3**, 357–70.

Dunn, J. C. and Kirsner, K.(1989).Implicit memory:task or process? In *Implicit memory: theoretical issues.* (ed. S. Lewandowsky, J. C. Dunn,and K.Kirsner) pp.17–31.Erlbaum, Hillsdale, NJ.

Fodor, J. (1983). *Modularity of mind*. MIT Press, Cambridge, MA.

Gillund, G. and Shiffrin, R. M.(1984). A retrieval model for both recognition and recall. *Psychological Review*, **91**, 1–67.

Glisky, E.L., Polster, M.R.,and Routhieaux (1995).Double dissociation between item and source memory. *Neuropsychology*, **9**, 229–35.

Graf, P., Mandler, G.,and Haden, P. E. (1982). Simulating amnesic symptoms in normal subjects. *Science*, **218**, 1243–4.

Hamann, S. B. (1990). Level-of-processing effects in conceptually driven implicit tasks. *Journal of Experimental Psychology: Learning, Memory, and Cognition*, **16**, 970–7.

Hartman, M.,Knopman, D. S.,and Nissen, M. J. (1989).Implicit learning of new verbal associations. *Journal of Experimental Psychology: Learning, Memory, and Cognition*, **15**, 1070–82.

Hawkins, R. D. and Kandel, E. R. (1984). Is there a cell-biological alphabet for simple forms of learning? *Psychological Review*, **91**, 375–91.

Hayman, C. A. G. and Tulving, E. (1989). Is priming in fragment completion based on a 'traceless'memory system? *Journal of Experimental Psychology: Learning, Memory, and Cognition*, **14**, 941–56.

Herrnstein, R. J. and Boring, E. G. (1965). *A source book in the history of psychology*. Harvard University Press, Cambridge, MA.

Hilgard,E.R.and Humphreys, L. G. (1938). The effect of supporting and antagonistic voluntary instructions on conditional discrimination. *Journal of Experimental Psychology*, **22**, 291–304.

Hill, F. A.(1967).Effects of instructions and subjects'need for approval on the conditioned galvanic skin response. *Journal of Experimental Psychology*, **73**, 461–7.

Hintzman, D. L. (1990). Human learning and memory: connections and dissociations. *Annual Review of Psychology*, **41**, 109–39.

Humphreys, M. S.,Bain, J. D.,and Pike, R.(1989).Different ways to cue a unitary memory system:a theory for episodic, semantic and procedural tasks. *Psychological Review*, **96**, 208–33.

Jacoby, L.L.(1983*a*). Remembering the data:Analyzing interactive processes in reading. *Journal of verbal learning and Verbal Behavior*, **22**, 485–508

Jacoby, L.L.(1983*b*). Perceptual enhancement:Persistent effects of an experience. *Journal of Experimental Psychology:Learning, Memory, and Cognition*, **9**, 21–38.

Jacoby, L.L.(1984).Incidental versus intentional retrieval: remembering and awareness as separate issues. In *Neuropsychology of memory*, (ed.L.R.Squire and N. Butters),pp.145–56.Guilford Press, New York.

Jacoby, L. L.(1988).Memory observed and memory unobserved.In *Remembering reconsidered*, (ed. U. Neisser and E. Winograd),pp.145–77.Cambridge University Press, New York.

Jacoby, L. L.(1991).A process dissociation framework:separating automatic from intentional uses of memory. *Journal of Memory and Language*, **30**, 513–41.

Jacoby, L. L. and Brooks, L. R. (1984). Nonanalytic cognition: memory, perception and concept learning. In *The psychology of learning and motivation:advances in research and theory*, (ed. G. H.Bower),pp.1–47.Academic, New York.

Jacoby, L. L. and Dallas, M. (1981). On the relationship between autobiographical memory and perceptual learning. *Journal of Experimental Psychology: General*, **3**, 306–40.

Jacoby, L. L. and Hayman, G. A. (1987). Specific visual transfer in word identification. *Journal of Experimental Psychology:Learning, Memory, and Cognition*, **13**, 456–63.

Jacoby, L. L. and Witherspoon, D. (1982). Remembering without awareness. *Canadian Journal of Psychology*, **36**, 300–24.

Jacoby, L.L., Toth, J. P.,and Yonelinas, A. P. (1993).Separating conscious and unconscious influences of memory:measuring recollection. *Journal of Experimental Psychology: General*, **122**, 139–54.

Janowsky, J. S.,Shimamura, A. P.,and Squire, L.R. (1989).Source memory impairments in patients with frontal lobe lesions. *Neuropsychologia*, **27**, 1043–56.

Jennings, J. M.,McIntosh,A.R., Kapur, S., Tulving, E., and Houle, S. Cognitive subtractions may not add up:the interaction between semantic processing and response mode. *Neuroimage*, (In press.)

Johnson, M. K. (1983). A multiple-entry, modular memory system. In *The psychology of learning and motivation: advances in research theory*, Vol. 17, (ed. G. H. Bower), pp.81–123.Academic, New York.

Johnson, M. K. and Chalfonte, B. L. (1994). Binding complex memories: the role of reactivation and the hippocampus. In *Memory systems 1994*, (ed. D. L. Schacter and E. Tulving),pp.311–50.MIT Press, Cambridge, MA.

Johnson,M.K.and Hirst, W. (1993).MEM:memory subsystems as processes. In *Theories of memory*, (ed. A. Collins, M. Conway, S. Gathercole, and P. Morris), pp.241–86. Erlbaum,Hove.

Kelley, C. M.and Jacoby, L.L.(1990). The construction of subjective experience:memory attributions. *Mind and Language*, **5**, 49–68.

Kintsch, W. (1972).Notes on the structure of semantic memory. In *Organization of memory*, (ed.E. Tulving and W. Donaldson),pp.247–308.Academic, New York.

Kirsner, K. and Smith, M. C. (1974). Modality effects in word identification. *Memory and Cognition*, **2**, 637–40.
Kolers, P. A. (1976). Reading a year later. *Journal of Experimental Psychology: Human Learning and Memory*, **2**, 554–65.
Kolers, P. A. and Perkins, D. N. (1975). Spatial and ordinal components of form perception and literacy. *Cognitive Psychology*, **7**, 228–67.
Kolers, P. A. and Roediger, H. L. (1984). Procedures of mind. *Journal of Verbal Learning and Verbal Behavior*, **23**, 425–49.
Lockhart, R. S., Lamon, M., and Click, M. L. (1988). Conceptual transfer in simple insight problems. *Memory and Cognition*, **16**, 36–44.
Logan, G. D. (1988). Toward an instance theory of automatization. *Psychological Review*, **95**, 492–527.
Luria, A. R. (1973). *The working brain*. Basic Books, New York.
Lynch, G. and Granger, R. (1992). Variations in synaptic plasticity and types of memory in corticohippocampal networks. *Journal of Cognitive Neuroscience*, **4**, 189–99.
Malcolm, N. (1977). *Memory and mind*. Cornell University Press, Ithaca, NJ.
Masson, M. E. J. and Freedman, L. (1990). Fluent identification of repeated words. *Journal of Experimental Psychology: Learning, Memory, and Cognition*, **16**, 355–73.
McClelland, J. L. and Rumelhart, D. E. (1985). Distributed memory and the representation of general and specific information. *Journal of Experimental Psychology: General*, **114**, 159–88.
McDermott, K. A. and Roediger, H. L. (1986). Exact and conceptual repetition dissociate conceptual memory tests: Problems for transfer appropriate processing theory. *Canadian Journal of Experimental Psychology*, **50**, 57–71.
McIntosh, A. R. Understanding neural interactions in learning and memory using functional neuroimaging. *Annals of the New York Academy of Science*. (In press.)
McKoon, G., Ratcliff, R., and Dell, G. S. (1986). A critical evaluation of the semantic-episodic distinction. *Journal of Experimental Psychology: Learning, Memory, and Cognition*, **12**, 295–306.
Mesulam, M.-M. (1990). Large-scale neurocognitive networks and distributed processing for attention, language, and memory. *Annuals of Neurology*, **28**, 597–613.
Milner, D. A. and Goodale, M. A. (1995). *The visual brain in action*. Oxford University Press, New York.
Miskin, M. and Appenzeller, T. (1987). The anatomy of memory. *Scientific American*, **256**, 80–9.
Morris, C. D., Bransford, J. D., and Franks, J. J. (1977). Levels of processing versus transfer appropriate processing. *Journal of Verbal Learning and Verbal Behavior*, **16**, 519–33.
Moscovitch, M. (1989). Confabulation and the frontal systems: strategic versus associative retrieval in neuropsychological theories of memory. In *Varieties of memory and consciousness: essays in honour of Endel Tulving*, (ed. H. L. Roediger and F. I. M. Craik), pp. 133–56. Erlbaum, Hillsdale, NJ.
Moscovitch, M. (1992). A neuropsychological model of memory and consciousness. In *Neuropsychology of memory*, (ed. L. R. Squire and N. Butters), pp. 5–22. Guilford Press, New York.
Moscovitch, M. and Umilta, C. (1990). Modularity and neuropsychology. In *Modular deficits in dementia*, (ed. M. Schwartz), pp. 1–59. MIT Press, Cambridge, MA.
Moscovitch, M., Winocur, G., and McLachlan, D. R. (1986). Memory as accessed by recognition and reading time in normal and memory-impaired people with Alzheimer's disease and other neurological disorders. *Journal of Experimental Psychology: General*, **115**, 331–47.

Moscovitch, M., Vriezen,E., and Goshen-Gottstein, G. (1993). Implicit tests of memory in patients with focal lesions or degenerative brain disorders. In *Handbook of neuropsychology*, (ed. F. Boller and J. Grafman),pp.133–73.Elsevier, Amsterdam.

Musen, G. and Squire, L. R.(1993).On the implicit learning of novel associations by amnesic patients and normal subjects. *Neuropsychology*, 7, 119–35.

Nadel, L. (1992). Multiple memory systems: what and why. *Journal of Cognitive Neuroscience*, 4, 179–88.

Needham, D. R.and Begg, I.M.(1991).Problem-oriented training promotes spontaneous analogical transfer: memory-oriented training promotes memory for training. *Memory and Cognition*, 19, 543–57.

Neumann, O. (1984). Automatic processing: A review of recent findings and a plea for an old theory. In *Cognition and motor processes* (ed. W. Pring and A. F. Sanders), pp.255–93.Springer-Verlag, Berlin.

Nicholls, M. F. and Kimble, G. A.(1964).Effect of instructions upon eyelid conditioning. *Journal of Experimental Psychology*, 67, 400–2.

Norman, K. A. and Schacter, D. L. (1996). Implicit memory, explicit memory, and false recollection:a cognitive neuroscience perspective. In *Implicit memory and metacognition*, (ed.L.M. Reder),pp.229–59.Erlbaum,Hillsdale, NJ.

Petersen, S. E., Fox, P. T., Posner, M.I., Mintun, M.,and Raichle, M. E. (1988). Positron emission tomographic studies of the cortical anatomy of single word processing. *Science*, 240, 1627–31.

Petri,H.L.and Mishkin,M.(1994).Behaviorism,cognitivism and the neuropsychology of memory. *American Scientist*, 82, 30–7.

Phillips, L. W. (1958).Mediated verbal similarity as a determinant of the generalization of a conditioned GSR. *Journal of Experimental Psychology*, 55, 56–61.

Raskin, D. C. (1969).Semantic conditioning and generalization of autonomic responses. *Journal of Experimental Psychology*, 79, 69–76.

Ratcliff, R., and McKoon, G. (1996). Bias effects in implicit memory tasks. *Journal of Experimental Psychology:General*, 125, 403–21.

Razran, G. A.(1939).A quantitative study of meaning by a conditioned salivary technique (semantic conditioning). *Science*, 90, 89–90.

Riess, B. F. (1940). Semantic conditioning involving the galvanic skin reflex. *Journal of Experimental Psychology*, 26, 238–40.

Roediger, H.L. (1980). Memory metaphors in cognitive psychology. *Memory and Cognition*, 8, 231–46.

Roediger, H.L.(1990*a*).Implicit memory: retention with remembering. *American Psychologist*, 45, 1043–56.

Roediger, H. L. (1990*b*). Implicit memory: a commentary. *Bulletin of the Psychonomic Society*, 28, 373–80.

Roediger, H.L.and Blaxton, T. A.(1987). Retrieval modes produce dissociations in memory. In *Memory and cognitive processes: The Ebbinghaus centennial conference* (ed. D. S. Gorfein and R.R.Hoffman),pp. 349–79.LEA,Hillsdale, NJ.

Roediger, H.L.and McDermott,K. B. (1993).Implicit memory in normal human subjects. In *Handbook of neuropsychology*, (ed. H. Spinnler and F. Boller), pp.63–131. Elsevier, Amsterdam.

Roediger, H. I., and McDermott, K. B. (1995). Creating false memories: remembering words not presented in lists. *Journal of Experimental Psychology:Learning, Memory, and Cognition*, 21, 803–14.

Roediger, H.L., Weldon,M. S.,and Challis, B. H.(1989).Explaining dissociations between implicit and explicit measures of retention:a processing account.In *Varieties of memory*

and consciousness: essays in honour of Endel Tulving, (ed. H. L. Roediger and F. I. M. Craik),pp.3–41.Erlbaum,Hillsdale, NJ.
Rudy, J. W. and Sutherland, R. J. (1992). Configural and elemental associations and the memory coherence problem. *Journal of Cognitive Neuroscience*, **4**, 208–16.
Rumelhart, D. E., Lindsay, P. H., and Norman, D. A. (1972). A process model for long-term memory. In *Organization of memory*, (ed. E. Tulving and W. Donaldson),pp.197–246.Academic, New York.
Schacter, D. L. (1987). Implicit memory: history and current status. *Journal of Experimental Psychology:Learning, Memory, and Cognition*, **13**, 501–18.
Schacter, D. L.(1989).On the relation between memory and consciousness:dissociable interactions and conscious experience. In *Varieties of memory and cognition: Essays in honor of Endel Tulving*, (ed. H. L. Roediger and F. I. M. Craik), pp.355–89. Erlbaum, Hillsdale, NJ.
Schacter, D. L. and Tulving, E.(1994a). *Memory systems 1994*. MIT Press, Cambridge, MA.
Schacter, D. L.and Tulving, E.(1994b). What are the memory systems of 1994? In *Memory systems 1994*, (ed. D. L.Schacter and E. Tulving),pp.1–38.MIT Press, Cambridge, MA.
Schacter, D. L., Harbluck, J. L., and McLachlan, D. R. (1984). Retrieval without awareness:An experimental analysis of source amnesia.*Journal of Verbal Learning and Verbal Behavior*, **23**, 593–611.
Schacter, D. L.,Bowers, J.,and Booker, J. (1989). Intention, awareness, and implicit memory: The retrieval intentionality criteria.In *Implicit memory*, (ed. S. Lewandowsky, J. C. Dunn,and K.Kirsner),pp.47–65.Erlbaum,Hillsdale, NJ.
Schacter, D. L., Reiman, E., Curran, T., Yun, L. S., Bandy, D., McDermott, K. B., and Roediger, H.L.(1996).Neuroanatomical correlates of veridical and illusory recognition memory: evidence from positron emission tomography. *Neuron*, **17**, 267–74.
Shallice, T. (1988). *From neuropsychology to mental structure*. Cambridge University Press
Sherry, D. F. and Schacter, D. L. (1987). The evolution of multiple memory systems. *Psychological Review*, **94**, 439–54.
Squire, L. (1994). Declarative and nondeclarative memory: multiple brain systems supporting learning and memory. In *Memory systems 1994*, (ed. D. L. Schacter and E. Tulving),pp.203–31.MIT Press, Cambridge, MA.
Squire, L.R.(1987). *Memory and brain*. Oxford University Press, New York.
Stein, B. S. (1978). Depth of processing reexamined: the effects of precision of encoding and test appropriateness. *Journal of Verbal Learning and Verbal Behavior*, **17**, 165–74.
Titchener, E. B. (1898). The postulates of a structural psychology. *The Philosophical Review*, **7**, 449–65.
Toth, J. P. and Reingold,E.M.(1996).Beyond perception:conceptual contributions to unconscious influences of memory. In *Implicit cognition*, (ed. G. Underwood), pp.41–84. Oxford University Press, New York.
Toth, J. P., Reingold, E. M., and Jacoby, L. L. (1994). Toward a redefinition of implicit memory: process dissociations following elaborative processing and self-generation. *Journal of Experimental Psychology:Learning, Memory, and Cognition*, **20**, 290–343.
Tulving, E. (1972). Episodic and semantic memory. In *Organization of memory*, (ed. E. Tulving and W. Donaldson).Academic, New York.
Tulving, E.(1983). *Elements of episodic memory*. Oxford University Press, New York.
Tulving, E. (1984). Précis of *Elements of episodic memory*. *The Behavioral and Brain Sciences*, **7**, 223–68.
Tulving, E. (1985a). How many memory systems are there? *American Psychologist*, **40**, 385–98.

Tulving, E. (1985b). On the classification problem in learning and memory. In L.-G. In *Perspectives on learning and memory*, (ed. L.-G. Nilsson and T. Archer), pp.67–94. Erlbaum,Hillsadale, NJ.

Tulving, E. (1986). What kind of a hypothesis is the distinction between episodic and semantic memory? *Journal of Experimental Psychology: Learning, Memory, and Cognition*, **12**, 307–11.

Tulving, E.and Schacter, D. L.(1990).Priming and human memory systems. *Science*, **247**, 301–5.

Tulving, E. and Thompson, D. M.(1973). Encoding specificity and retrieval processes in episodic memory *Psychological Review*, **80**, 352–73.

Vaidya, C. J., Gabrielli, J. D. E., Keane, M. M., Monti, L. A., Gutierrez-Rivas, H., and Zarella,M.M.(1997).Evidence for multiple mechanisms of conceptual priming on implicit memory tests. *Journal of Experimental Psychology:Learning, Memory, and Cognition*, **23**, 1324–43.

Van Gelder, T. (1997). The dynamical alternative. In *The future of the cognitive revolution* (ed. D. U. Johnson and C. E.Erneling).pp. 227–44.OUP, New York.

Varela, F. J., Thompson, E., and Rosch, E. (1991). *The embodied mind*. MIT Press, Cambridge, MA.

Watkins, M. J. (1990). Mediationism and the obfuscation of memory. *American Psychologist*, **45**, 328–35.

Whittlesea, B. W. A.(1993). Illusions of familiarity. *Journal of Experimental Psychology: Learning, Memory, and Cognition*, **19**, 1235–53.

Whittlesea, B. W. A.,Brooks, L.R.,and Westcott, C. (1994).After the learning is over: factors controlling the selective application of general and specific knowledge. *Journal of Experimental Psychology:Learning, Memory, and Cognition*, **20**, 259–74.

Winnick, W. A.and Daniel, S. A.(1970). Two kinds of response priming in tachistoscopic word recognition. *Journal of Experimental Psychology*, **84**, 74–81.

Witherspoon, D. and Moscovitch, M. (1989). Stochastic independence between two implicit memory tasks. *Journal ofExperimental Psychology:Learning, Memory, and Cognition*, **15**, 22–30.

Woltz, D. J. (1996). Perceptual and conceptual priming in a semantic reprocessing task. *Memory & cognition*, **24**, 429–40.

10
Component processes versus systems: is there really an important difference?

ALAN J. PARKIN

Reading the brief introduction by Foster and Jelicic one learns that each chapter of this book 'concentrates upon the central theoretical question of how long-term memory can best be conceptualized' (p.1). Looking down the author list one will also spot two key names, Roediger and Tulving, and perhaps know that these authors represent the poles of the debate implied in the title of this book. Or do they? Roediger addresses the brief by making a substantive, and by now familiar, attack on the systems approach and, in its place, he advocates the component processing approach. Tulving, however, does not appear to even recognize the debate Roediger refers to. True, he includes a section on process-oriented versus system-oriented accounts of memory but the issues discussed here, centring on a dichotomy between cognitive and neurocognitive approaches to memory, bear no resemblance to the issues raised by those arguing for a process-oriented viewpoint. From then on the idea of multiple systems is, for Tulving, an inescapable conclusion whose progress has simply been hampered by irrational bias against new ideas.

Among the other process-oriented chapters Weldon and Toth and Hunt both make lively, if at times overstated, claims for rejecting the systems approach. Like Roediger these authors base much of their critique around difficulties in deriving sustainable operational definitions of what constitutes a 'system'. In particular much is made of the four criteria devised by Sherry and Schacter (1987) as the basis for defining a memory system. It is therefore a pity that only one contributor purportedly in the structural camp, Mayes, takes on the issues raised by the criteria. As noted above, Tulving pays no attention to these issues and this is also true of McDonald, Ergis, and Winocur in their straightforward localizationist account of memory abilities. Indeed the debate between process and system seems so irrelevant to McDonald *et al.* that they use terminology relating to the two positions interchangeably throughout their contribution. For example, they state 'The concept of multiple memory *systems* in the mammalian brain represents an important advance' (p.67, emphasis added) yet, in the next paragraph, 'we focus on five brain regions . . . that have been reliably identified with learning and memory *processes* (p.67, emphasis added). Later, in their conclusion, 'memory is not a unitary process but one that consists of multiple *components*' (p.94, emphasis added).

Mayes does tackle the issues raised by the process theorists in relation to the Sherry and Schacter criteria but his conclusions seem equivocal and one could not describe him as someone writing from an ardent systems position. Indeed one can make a plausible case that Mayes attempts perhaps the most detailed explication of a component process view of memory! Only Gabrieli takes on the process theorists in their own territory and argues for memory systems. In particular, he highlights how the process-based account fails to explain patterns of dissociated performance in human amnesia. The contribution by Blaxton, ostensibly a process theorist, does not enter into the debate at all because, by her own admission, she believes that research has transcended concerns raised by the systems versus process argument.

Part of my brief was to try and come to some conclusion about the 'debate' represented in this book. The reader will see an obvious limitation in that there is not a great deal of overlap between what the two camps have written about. The major thread of commonality was provided by the issues raised by Roediger *et al.*, Weldon, and Toth and Hunt (from now on the 'process camp') in relation to the operational criteria devised by Sherry and Schacter. I have therefore decided to summarize the principal aspects of their arguments along these lines and, where appropriate, look for counter arguments both from the 'systems' camp (Tulving, MacDonald *et al.*, Gabrieli, and Mayes). Where appropriate, I have also chipped in with my own views.

CRITIQUES OF THE SYSTEMS APPROACH

Sherry and Schacter outlined four criteria which must be met if something is to be defined as a memory system:

Functional independence: This refers to the observation that an independent variable has a certain effect on a task assumed to tap one memory system and either no effect or a different effect on a task presumed to tap a different system.

Stochastic independence: The demonstration that performances on two tasks, each assumed to represent processing in a different memory system, are uncorrelated.

Different neural substrates: Different memory systems must have different neural substrates as revealed by localizing techniques.

Functional incompatibility: Memory systems are specialized to the extent that the function carried out by one system cannot be carried out by any of the others.

Functional independence

Perhaps the biggest problem for functional independence is the 'process-purity problem' and all the process camp emphasize this difficulty. In a typical experiment, two tasks, A and B, are devised around the assumption that they tap different processes and that these processes, in turn, represent fundamental differences in the way in which these assumed systems operate. However, while the *prima facie* demands of tasks may meet the criteria of the hypothesized memory systems, it may be a different matter when one considers what subjects might actually be doing. This problem has been illustrated many times in studies which examine the relation between implicit and explicit memory. In a typical experiment, one is assuming (more like hoping) that completion of the implicit task occurs in the absence of explicit recollection of the learning event—otherwise what one concludes about the operation of the implicit system is contaminated by the contribution made by explicit recollection. However, attempts to devise procedures to avoid this, such as the retrieval intentionality criterion (e.g. Schacter *et al.* 1989), have not met with great success. Thus, despite the massive amount of research on implicit memory, there is no sure-fire way of measuring implicit memory performance unambiguously. Gabrieli gives a particularly clear account of this problem in the interpretation of amnesic performance in implicit and explicit tests.

Toth and Hunt, in particular, develop the process-purity issue further by citing various lines of evidence that even procedural memory—defined as memory for information not accessible to consciousness—cannot be measured in a pure form. Even conditioning, they argue, can be mediated by higher-level explicit processes such as intentionality and type of verbal instruction. There is also the thorny issue of episodic and semantic memory. As Toth and Hunt point out, the two forms of memory are intimately related because semantic memory underpins the interpretation of episodic memory. Increasingly complex complication does not stop there, however, as both Weldon and Toth and Hunt stress the difficulty of studying any memory process independently of other cognitive, and even motivational, factors.

Weldon raises the additional issue that functional dissociations can be observed within what is considered a system. She highlights several studies showing, in animals, that lesions can lead to the selective disruption of one form of conditioning—thus, within systems logic, we have several conditioning systems rather than one. This is problematic for taxonomies such as Squire's in which, for convenience, 'conditioning' is considered a subsystem of procedural memory. More problematic, perhaps, are functional dissociations within higher-level memory systems. It is well known that a number of variables dissociate recall and recognition and that memory-impaired patients equated with controls on recognition performance still show impaired recall. As Roediger points out, these data provide a strong case for a memory system but no one has ever proposed separate recall and recognition systems. This is because the basis for specifying systems is one of shifting ground with systems being defined in varying ways such as content (e.g. facts, events), processing characteristics (top-down, bottom-up), form of access (conscious, unconscious), and memory phenomenon (skills, priming). In the case of episodic memory, recall and recognition are both classed as episodic because they address consciously accessible events even though they dissociate at another level. If the systems approach is characterized as the implementation of criteria specified at one level which can then be abandoned at another level if necessary, it is a theoretically sterile activity.

Stochastic independence

Early studies of the relation between implicit and explicit memory laid considerable emphasis on the lack of correlation between implicit and explicit tasks (e.g. Tulving *et al*. 1982). However, there have been a number of criticisms of stochastic independence as a source of evidence (e.g. Hintzman and Hartry 1990). These authors argued that so many other factors influence performance on implicit measures that it is largely impossible to detect a contribution fron explicit memory. Testing for stochastic independence, they argue, 'is like trying to measure the weight of a man bearing an unknown amount of lead in his pockets and holding the tether of a helium balloon' (p.345). Others have also criticised stochastic independence along similar lines (e.g. Ostergaard 1992, 1995), and there have been rebuttals of these arguments (Tulving and Hayman 1993; Hayman and Tulving 1995). Recently Poldrack (1996) has, via computer simulation methods, argued that the sample sizes used in studies have typically been insufficient for finding moderate amounts of dependence between measures of memory. Poldrack (1996) concludes that searching for stochastic independence is a 'perilous technique'. Thus, while this debate may rumble on it would seem an unlikely basis for providing strong arguments in favour of systems. Moreover, even if one puts aside concerns about power, stochastic independence can be observed within a task assumed to tap into a single memory system (Hayman and Tulving 1989) (see Roediger, and Toth and Hunt in this volume).

Differing neural substrates

The third criterion is that different memory systems must be seen to be reliant on different neural substrates. Roediger makes a nice point when he argues that any two tasks showing functional double dissociation must, by definition, make use of different neural substrates. As a result, any functional dissociation indicates separable memory systems. This, he argues, leads to an almost infinite expansion of memory systems and rejection of the systems account as non-parsimonious.

The structural camp respond differently to this *reductio ad absurdum* argument. In Chapter 8, Gabrieli is clear, 'I propose that if two expressions of memory are psychologically and neurally dissociable, they ought to be interpreted as reflecting the operations of two different memory systems of the brain . . . . This applies equally to dissociations between classes of memory (e.g. declarative and procedural) as to dissociations within classes of memory (e.g. two kinds of motor skill learning or two kinds of conceptual priming)' (p.222). Taken to its logical extreme one might, to use Mayes' example, find evidence for a dissociation between tulip and daffodil memory—the argument being that memory for these two forms of knowledge occupies different clusters of neurons. Mayes is more conservative and argues that the case for different memory systems can only be made if one can show that different processes are in operation when those two types of information are being encoded, stored, or retrieved. This additional constraint somewhat undermines Roediger's point but, nonetheless, in Chapter 6 Mayes concedes that adopting the Sherry and Schacter criteria cannot avoid a massive expansion of memory subsystems.

Functional neuroimaging has, of course, figured greatly in arguments about memory systems. Weldon gives considerable space to outlining short-comings of this approach. She highlights difficulties underlying subtractive logic and the choice of an appropriate control task. In the case of subtractive logic it is the case that only those brain regions differentially activated in experimental and control tasks come to be identified as critical components of the hypothesized memory system. Thus, structures that are critically implicated in both tasks are not implicated. Weldon draws attention to a particularly good example of this: failure to implicate the hippocampus in encoding and retrieval tasks. Lesion studies show beyond doubt that the hippocampus is critical for memory. Its non-appearance in these functional neuroimaging studies may thus be an artefact of its ubiquitous involvement in memory. The control task is also relevant here. Dolan and Fletcher (1997) have recently shown hippocampal activation during learning related specifically to the appreciation of novelty. It appears that previous failures to show hippocampal activation may have occurred because the control task contained novel elements which excited the hippocampus to the same extent as the experimental task. Weldon also outlines other concerns. She notes that trivial differences in tasks can often give rise to very different patterns of activation and that there is often gross inconsistency in the patterns of activation observed in different studies measuring operation of the same putative memory system—a point I have recently emphasized in relation to proposals concerning an executive component to working memory (Parkin, in press).

Toth and Hunt also make a concerted assault on functional neuroimaging studies. They note two studies emphasizing the problem in establishing clear regions associated with putative episodic and semantic memory systems. In the first, marked differences are found in the activation patterns underlying recall and recognition—a finding perhaps reflecting the functional dissociations observed between these two measures. As noted above, no one has ever argued for separable recall and recognition systems, yet, applying the systems criteria, one would have to concede this as being the case. Worse still, they cite a study by Jennings *et al.* (in press) in which subjects answered identical general knowledge questions but varied what the response mode was. Different patterns of activation were found depending on how subjects responded. Again this study emphasizes the limitations of neuroimaging as an underpinning for specifying systems quite possibly because the subtractive logic method fails to emphasize the common brain region involved.

Toth and Hunt in Chapter 9 are clearly aware of the false reductionism offered by functional neuroimaging. Detecting patterns of activation in PET in no way explains how memory occurs at a psychological level. However, the example they use to illustrate this is just plain wrong. They cite a study by Schacter *et al.* (1996) in which false recollections were associated with a different pattern of brain activity to that associated with true recollections. Schacter *et al.* concluded that these findings 'raise the possibility that illusory recollections of false targets seem authentic because they are accompanied by medial temporal lobe activity that is usually linked to veridical conscious recollection' (Schacter *et al.* 1996, p.271). Toth and Hunt choose to interpret this as an implication 'that people assess veridicality by reference to which of their brain areas are currently activated' (p.252). Anyone familiar with this research knows that there is no such naiveté of interpretation, and that the results in this study were attributed to real memories being distinguished from false ones by their association with perceptual attributes—a purely psychological level of explanation.

Only Weldon considers the issue of lesion data in any detail. She outlines a number of familiar problems. First, the appearance of deficit because a particular brain structure is damaged does not mean that the structure is the memory system—it may just be a small component. Another problem is the assumption that those aspects of mental ability that survive a lesion are carried out in a normal fashion. There have been repeated concerns that patients with lesions can obtain normal performance using abnormal strategies—this causes problems in assuming a pure deficit in one area and normal function in another. If one uses lesion data as a basis for ascribing neural substrates to specific cognitive systems there is a major constraint in that there is no *a priori* reason to suppose that anatomical boundaries map on to functional boundaries. Weldon emphasizes this point by describing a study in which the localization of language is shown to be diffuse and not showing a 'hot spot(s)'. However, given that this book is about memory, it would have been more instructive if Weldon had taken her example from the memory literature. Here, the position is very different, with the consistent identification of certain structures with certain memory functions—a point repeatedly shown in the contribution of MacDonald *et al.* (Chapter 4).

Functional Incompatibility

The fourth criterion, functional incompatibility, is problematic as a basis for specifying memory systems as Roediger, Weldon, and Toth and Hunt all point out. Functional incompatibility works well when considering highly specific domains such as song learning and foraging in birds but less so in the complex world of human beings. In the case of birds, the two domains in question can be argued, on an *a priori* basis, to require different representational formats. This is less so with humans. In the proposed distinction between episodic and semantic memory, it is not obvious that essentially incompatible representational systems are involved— indeed one persuasive view of episodic memory is that it is simply a record of the activation of semantic memory at a particular point in time. In representational terms, episodic memory therefore involves the same elements as semantic memory.

However, I would not reject the functional incompatibility argument absolutely. On intuitive grounds it seems perfectly reasonable that the representational format used to represent specific motor patterns might have complete incompatibility with, say, representations mediating a conditioned response.

Mayes devotes considerable space to the distinction between episodic and semantic memory. He reiterates the point that different systems must represent the differential processing of information not just differences in the information stored. One line of evidence suggesting that this might be the case is the finding that retrieval in episodic tasks involves right pre-frontal activation whereas retrieval of semantic information involves left pre-frontal activation. This might provide *prima facie* evidence for different search processes operating. However, a further study by Wiggs *et al.* (1996) showed that when episodic and semantic tasks are equated for difficulty a different pattern emerges with retrieval of semantic information now producing larger amounts of right frontal activation than the episodic task. Thus this seems another example of apparently non-essential changes in task characteristics producing major changes in the pattern of functional neuroimaging, and thus a gross undermining of this form of data as a means of specifying systems.

TULVING'S ACCOUNT

As noted at the outset, Tulving's contribution fails to acknowledge any of the issues raised by the contributions of the process camp because, for him, this is a misconception of the debate. However, when one examines his arguments it is clear that the issues raised by the process camp are relevant and should have been addressed. In his section 'Conversion of a unitarian' Tulving describes four 'critical incidents' which led him to a multiple systems view of memory. The first was discovery of stochastic independence between fragment completion and recognition. As we have seen, not everyone is as convinced as Tulving about the value of stochastic independence as a statistical measure and therefore a means of bolstering the idea of systems. Indeed, even if one puts aside statistical concerns, stochastic independence can equally be used to make the claim that components of processing are dissociable.

The second incident is Tulving's investigations of KC, a man who had lost the ability to remember any personally experienced events, although in most other respects he is quite normal; can read and write and solve problems, 'he knows mathematics, geometry, history, and how to play chess and the organ . . . [But] regardless of how precisely or specifically he is prompted and reminded of happenings in the past, and regardless of how hard he tries, he cannot remember, that is, consciously bring to mind, any events, single or repeated, from any period of his life . . . The striking *dissociation* between KC's totally dysfunctional episodic memory and his relatively functional semantic memory, suggests a separation of the corresponding processes at the neural level' (p. 24, emphasis added).

At a phenomenal level Tulving's argument seems compelling, but it bears greater scrutiny. First KC does *not* represent a genuine dissociation between episodic and semantic memory. By definition, a dissociation is only demonstrated when two separate forms of impairment combine, via the logic of double dissociation, to illustrate the existence of separable mental abilities. Thus to be sure that KC has a dissociated impairment we must also have access to at least one individual who shows the reverse—normal episodic memory and impaired semantic memory. So-called 'semantic dementia' had been considered an example of this, but recent investigations suggest that these patients have impairments in both fact and event memory (Graham and Hodges 1997) (see also Mayes, Chapter 6 this volume). In my own view the search for the reverse dissociation is a hopeless one on logical grounds. Experience is based on our interpretation of the world which, at a conscious level, I take to be the operation of semantic memory. Episodic memory represents the record of this experience. Logically, therefore, if one did not have a semantic memory one could not, *ipso facto*, have an episodic memory. This also makes the idea of different neural substrates more difficult to accept.

With this in mind, KC's episodic deficit might reflect one of task sensitivity. One obvious possibility relates to the idea that the representation of a given piece of information in memory might vary in its redundancy. Memory for a specific event might have a sparse representation, whereas facts about the world may be represented in many places. Consider two questions: 'Tell me about an event involving you and an elephant' and 'Tell me about elephants'. In the former question a response is only possible if a specific event can be isolated, but the latter can be answered from a variety of sources. It follows, therefore, that a brain lesion which randomly destroys part of memory would have a more devastating effect on episode-based remembering than general knowledge-based remembering.

A final point on the episodic–semantic debate is hinted at in Tulving's observation that KC's semantic memory was 'relatively functional'. It has now become clear that semantic memory is far more affected in amnesia than was originally thought in earlier reviews (e.g. Parkin 1982). Most strikingly, Butters and Cermak showed, via their study of PZ (e.g. Butters 1984), that an amnesic professor's memory for factual information was as impaired as his autobiographic recall and showed the same temporally graded loss. Other studies of amnesics have confirmed this position (e.g. Verfaellie and Roth 1996), and it should also be noted that most tests used to demonstrate retrograde amnesia actually measure semantic and not episodic memory. While one or two challenging findings exist (e.g. Kapur 1994), the overwhelming position is that retrograde amnesia does not dissociate across the episodic–semantic divide. It is often argued that normal IQ represents a pointed example of preserved semantic memory in amnesics. This is also a shaky claim. Tests such as WAIS-R measure intellectual abilities assumed to be attained by early adult life. We know that early memories are usually preserved in amnesics, so normal IQ is not surprising. Further, as we have seen in the case of PZ, when knowledge acquired later in life is assessed amnesics show deficits.

The third and fourth Tulving incidents both relate to functional neuroimaging findings, the first of which was the early demonstration that performance on episodic and semantic tasks led to gross differences in brain activation along the anterior–posterior dimension. The second concerns the discovery of an asymmetry between encoding and retrieval operations in the frontal cortex. These findings, he concludes, 'have added powerful support to the biological reality of separate memory systems' (p. 26). At this point one can ask 'why call these systems and not processes associated with different patterns of brain activation?'. Tulving seems clear on this point in that processes and systems are complementary 'we cannot have one without the other . . . on logical and rational grounds there is no conflict between them' (p. 26). Here Tulving seems to be side-stepping the whole point of the process camp's argument. If you are going to call a group of processes a system, you must be attributing some additional property to that collection of processes. It is exactly those additional properties, specified most clearly in the Sherry and Schacter criteria, that Tulving has failed to acknowledge.

ALTERNATIVES TO THE SYSTEMS APPROACH

This book offers four alternatives to the systems approach, three from the process camp itself and a fourth from one of the structural camp. I will begin with Toth and Hunt as their account provides the most radical alternative. They put forward a view of 'memory as an activity' which is based on the principle of transfer appropriate processing (e.g. Morris *et al.* 1977). Within this framework, the concept of a discrete memory trace for an event is replaced by the idea that the act of memory corresponds to an interaction between the configuration of the nervous system encoded at time point 1 and the extent to which the activities that initiated this encoding are reinstated as a retrieval context at time point 2. This is, of course, a familiar argument which can be traced back to Richard Semon and has had various more recent manifestations, most notably encoding specificity (see Schacter 1982).

Toth and Hunt's spin on this argument is, however, quite extreme. Their view, if I understand it correctly, is that memory traces do not exist. Memories are states of activation that arise as a consequence of an interaction between 'a current disposition, enabled by past experience' and a retrieval environment. Thus 'memory is best viewed as a dynamic activity that is not stored in the person or brain, but rather emerges from an interaction of the person (and their brain) with the surrounding environment' (p. 264). While I would not profess expertise in the history of memory research, I think it is fair to say that others who have pursued this functional line, including Semon himself, felt the need to postulate representations of memories. It is not clear to me how Toth and Hunt think they can get away with a traceless notion of memory. What, for example, is the difference between a memory trace and 'a current disposition enabled by past experience'? None, in my opinion, except that a memory trace has typically been conceived of as atomistic whereas Toth and Hunt are arguing for memory traces as distributed representation.

At the heart of Toth and Hunt's proposal is the vast array of data concerning contextual influences on memory—an essential adjunct to their interactionist view. I have no quibble with these data but what they omit to say is how small many effects of context are. However, even when one looks at substantial effects it is clear that more than context is needed. In a classic study, Light and Carter-Sobell (1970) showed that recognition of a target word 'jam' was greatly reduced if studied in the intrinsic context 'traffic' and tested in the changed context 'strawberry'. Nonetheless, examination of the data indicates that around 44% of the effects obtained relate to factors other than context. Another problem is that retrieval environment factors interact with context. Godden and Baddeley (1975, 1980) showed that learning environment (underwater versus dry land) greatly influenced free recall but had no effect on recognition (similar effects are also found with drugs, see Eich (1980)). This is a difficult result for the interactionist, who is forced to conclude that the provision of copy cues provides all the context that is needed to optimize recognition but, if recognition were affected, then copy cues would be held insufficient. Thus, in general terms, they are forced to conclude that, in a situation where a manipulation of context influences performance, there is an interaction between context and environment. However, when a contextual manipulation fails, they must argue that there were no critical retrieval environment differences. This is a familiar circularity, which arises because Toth and Hunt are no more able to specify independently the potential for person–context interaction at retrieval than systems theorists are able to unambiguously relate task to process. Another related difficulty is inflexibility. Does it really make adaptive sense to have a memory system that is retrieval context-dependent in the sense argued by Toth and Hunt? It seems more logical that an organism would be more efficient if it could retrieve information independent of context.

Roediger *et al.* in Chapter 3 put forward the 'components of processing' view of memory. A view of this nature is also alluded to by Weldon, although her account of an alternative to systems is very brief. Essentially, the component-processing view can be seen as the converse of the systems approach in that it emphasizes similarities in performance factors across tasks rather than the differences emphasized by the systems-oriented approach. Much of their argument is based on a series of functional neuroimaging experiments examining the neural correlates of unprimed stem completion, primed stem completion, and stem cued recall. The essential findings were that the two completion tasks had largely similar patterns of activation (visual cortex, motor regions, and left prefrontal cortex), and that the stem cued recall tasks shared these same patterns but, in addition, showed involvement of other areas, namely the anterior frontal cortex and the precuneus. While data such as these could be seen as evidence for systems, Roediger *et al.* argue that they are much more readily accommodated by a components approach; thus, the common patterns of activation represent components of processing shared by the tasks, whereas the differences represent processes unique to each task.

The criticisms put forward by Roediger *et al.* strike at the heart of the systems debate because functional independence no longer serves as a basis for specifying a system. Instead this independence serves to indicate different components to a system. This point is illustrated in their discussion of evidence supporting declarative versus non-declarative memory. Levels of processing is known to enhance stem cued recall but not stem completion priming, thus suggesting a functional independence between the two forms of memory. However, levels of processing does influence other types of implicit memory, such as generating category instances. Roediger *et al.* thus suggest that a more plausible approach is to suggest that implicit memory tasks do not engage the same system but engage different components depending on task demands. They foresee the study of memory as one in which more general questions could be asked, for example the extent to which a range of tasks share common features, and in which specific components and their relation to particular brain structures could be examined.

It is also of interest that one of the structural accounts, that of Mayes, puts forward a view of memory that seems very similar to the component process view. These processes are memory representations, enhanced fluency, attributions and active search. As example of this approach, Mayes argues that episodic and semantic memory do not depend on a different system to that mediating what he terms 'item-specific implicit memory'. He develops his argument by stating that 'all forms of explicit memory (episodic and semantic) depend on enhanced fluency and a memory attribution process, but not necessarily an active search process' (p. 147). This implies that implicit and explicit memory are differentiated by more involvement of active search in the latter.

As readers will know, there are four opponents of the systems approach represented in this book but, so far, I have not mentioned the contribution by Teresa Blaxton. In her chapter, she describes a series of studies involving both 'disruption' and 'activation' techniques as a means of mapping conceptual and perceptual memory processes onto specific brain regions. Essentially, she identifies two brain regions, the occipital cortex and the superior temporal gyrus, as the neuroanatomical substrates of perceptual memory processes, and three regions, inferior frontal gyrus, medial temporal gyrus, and inferior temporal gyrus, as being involved in conceptual memory process. Given all the above concerns about brain mapping techniques as a means of establishing neural substrates of memory, Blaxton's contribution rests uneasily with the contributions of Weldon, and Toth and Hunt. This point is not missed by Blaxton who notes 'to those readers who count themselves in the systems camp . . ., it is admittedly ironic that a process theorist would be so concerned with questions of brain structures subserving memory. You might ask whether this is suspiciously close to a systems account'. Yes you may indeed. By providing evidence of different neural substrates mapping on to functional dissociations between tasks, Blaxton is providing data which would warm the heart of a systems theorist. However, Blaxton is having none of this, and argues instead that the process versus systems argument is 'just not relevant to the debate any more'. However, I am unclear as to what 'the debate' is if we transcend the systems versus process argument, and equally baffled as to what the 'bigger questions' we have moved on to are. An alternative account of Blaxton's work is that mapping techniques can identify brain regions associated with particular types of process, which in turn represent the properties of different memory systems, with the perceptual system appearing remarkably like the much vilified perceptual representation system (Schacter and Tulving 1994).

It is appropriate at this point to consider Gabrieli's critique of the process approach, because this is very much fired by Blaxton's demonstration of a component-processing approach, in which a distinction is made between conceptual and perceptual processes. Early studies of amnesia indicated that patients showed normal or near normal performance on a range of implicit memory tests such as repetition priming, stem completion, and fragment completion. This contrasted with their extensive impairments on explicit tasks such as recall and recognition. Blaxton (1992) pointed out that this functional independence might just as readily be explained as a distinction between perceptual and conceptual processing. In a series of experiments Blaxton (1992) found that manipulations of conceptual processing had similar effects on conceptually based tests of both implicit and explicit memory and that manipulations of perceptual processing had parallel influences on perceptually based tests of implicit and explicit memory. This led her to suggest that memory-impaired people have a fundamental deficit in conceptual as opposed to perceptual processing.

I have always felt that amnesia is the Achilles' heel of the process theorists, and Gabrieli shows this clearly to be the case. If one first considers implicit tasks involving conceptual processing, there is ample evidence that amnesic patients show normal performance alongside poor performance on conceptually based explicit tasks. Keane *et al.* (1997), for example, required amnesics and controls to study lists of category exemplars under either semantic or non-semantic incidental learning instructions. They were then asked to generate as many exemplars as possible to a category cue (implicit task) or to generate exemplars that had been in the prior study list (explicit memory). Priming was normal in the amnesic patients, as was the level of processing effect on priming. Explicit memory performance was, however, impaired. Thus in this study, as in many others, it is the recollective demands of the task (explicit/implicit) that predict amnesic deficits, not processing demands. Conceptually based implicit tests can, however, show deficits in amnesia.

Perhaps the most counter-intuitive prediction from the process theory is the possibility that amnesic patients should perform normally on perceptually based tests of explicit memory. This prediction was disconfirmed in a study by Vaidya *et al.* (1995), who showed that amnesic patients were impaired on both a conceptually based explicit task, word-associate cued recall, and a perceptually based task, word fragment cued recall. In contrast, the amnesic patients showed normal performance in conceptual and perceptual implicit tasks based on the same retrieval cues as the explicit tasks. Again, it is the recollective demands that predict amnesic performance rather than the type of processing evoked by the tasks.

CONCLUSION

From what I have read in this book, there does appear to be a major problem with the idea of memory systems—at least when one examines the evidence in terms of the criteria laid down by Sherry and Schacter. The best alternative, to my mind, is the component process view put forward by Roediger *et al.* in which tasks are dissected into components which, in turn, can be mapped on to brain structures. The emphasis on ascertaining the similarities and differences between tasks is a useful one, but I do have some problems. At the centre of the problem is this. If we find a task component, for example graphemic processing, which can be isolated via manipulations of functional independence, and is therefore by definition functionally incompatible with other components (e.g. semantic processing), and (if one accepts the vicissitudes of neuroimaging and lesion data) associated with specific brain structures, why not refer to it as a memory system? The goals of the component-processing approach thus seem rather similar, except that the outcome is components rather than systems. In other words, the component-processing approach does not necessarily buy you out of the systems concept. If, for example, one finds two clusters of components which seem mutually exclusive, would it not make sense to think of these clusters as systems?

There is also the proliferation problem. Much is made of the potential for infinite expansion within the systems approach, but is the componential approach likely to be more parsimonious? There is a danger that the term 'component' predisposes us towards even more complex expositions of memory than that yielded by systems. What seems lacking is any account of how the component process approach will be managed so as to avoid exactly the same problem they accuse the system theorists of creating.

I also have some difficulty in understanding how the component process theory can explain amnesia. There are a number of demonstrations that a conceptual manipulation allows good implicit memory performance, but poor explicit performance. If the same objectively defined component has a different impact as a function of retrieval demands, something in addition to that component must be specified. Process theorists appear silent on this issue. One could of course argue that there is a component concerned with establishing the basis for conscious recollection, but how this would be distinguished from the idea of an episodic system I have no idea. In a similar vein, I would also like to know how process theorists explain dissociations between implicit and explicit memory performance that are pharmacologically mediated.

At the end of the day, I am not convinced that component process and system theorists are really saying anything radically different, although this is ultimately for the reader to judge. Rather it seems a case of emphasis. System theorists emphasize differences in the processing undertaken across tasks whereas process theorists also emphasize similarities as well as differences—as a result process theorists are not embarrassed by functional independence within alleged systems. However, both approaches seem to seek the same criteria for establishing their existence by testing for functional independence at a task level and looking for neural substrates—Blaxton's contribution being a clear example of process theory combined with the search for neural substrates. I also think that use of the term 'system' will survive even if only to define a group of tasks that hang together in some intuitive sense. I was struck that, in writing this chapter, how one so often had to evoke the term system in constructing and discussing an argument. It may be that the real value of the systems concept is generic, in that it enables us to talk efficiently about a range of abilities that have some underlying commonality. The level at which this commonality is expressed may be variable, unsystematic, and ultimately non-scientific. But if it is one everyone understands at some intuitive level, its use will survive. Thus, if a colleague were to ring me up and say 'I have a patient with an episodic memory problem' I would not, despite having read all the arguments espoused by process theorists here, have any doubt as to what he or she was talking about.

REFERENCES

Blaxton, T. A. (1992). Dissociations among memory measures in memory-impaired subjects: evidence for a processing account of memory. *Memory and Cognition*, **20**, 549–62.

Butters, N. (1984). Alcoholic Korsakoff's syndrome: an update. *Seminars in Neurology*, **4**, 229–47.

Dolan, R. J. and Fletcher, P. C. (1997). Dissociating prefrontal and hippocampal function in episodic memory encoding. *Nature*, **388**, 582–6.

Eich, J. E. (1980). The cue-dependent nature of state dependent retrieval. *Memory and Cognition*, **8**, 157–73.

Godden, D. and Baddeley, A. D. (1975). Context dependent memory in two natural environments: on land and underwater. *British Journal of Psychology*, **66**, 325–31.

Godden, D. and Baddeley, A. D. (1980). When does context influence recognition memory. *British Journal of Psychology*, **71**, 90–104.

Graham, K. S. and Hodges, J. R. (1997). Differentiating the roles of the hippocampal complex and the neocortex in long-term memory storage: evidence from the study of semantic dementia. *Neuropsychology*, **11**, 77–89.

Hayman, C. A. G. and Tulving, E. (1989). Is priming in fragment completion based on a 'traceless' memory system? *Journal of Experimental Psychology: Learning, Memory, and Cognition*, **15**, 941–56.

Hayman, C. A. G. and Tulving, E. (1995). On the measurement of priming: what is the correct baseline? *European Journal of Cognitive Psychology*, **7**, 13–18.

Hintzman, D. L. and Hartry, A. L. (1990). Item effects in recognition and fragment completion: contingency relations vary for different subsets of words. *Journal of Experimental Psychology: Learning, Memory, and Cognition*, **16**, 955–69.

Jennings, J. M., McIntosh, A. R., Kapur, S., Tulving, E., and Houle, S. Cognitive subtractions may not add up: the interaction between semantic processing and response mode. *Neuroimage*. (In press.)

Kapur, N. (1994). Remembering Norman Schwarzkopf: evidence of two distinct long-term fact learning mechanisms. *Cognitive Neuropsychology*, **11**, 661–70.

Keane, M. M., Gabrieli, J. D. E., Monti, L. A., Fleischman, D. A., Cantor, J. M., and Noland, J. S. (1997). Intact and impaired conceptual memory processing in amnesia. *Neuropsychology*, **11**, 59–69.

Light, L. L. and Carter-Sobell, L. (1970). Effects of changed semantic context on recognition memory. *Journal of Verbal Learning and Verbal Behaviour*, **9**, 1–11.

Morris, C. D., Bransford, J. D., and Franks, J. J. (1977) Levels of processing versus transfer appropriate processing. *Journal of Verbal Learning and Verbal Behaviour*, **16**, 519–33.

Ostergaard, A. (1992) A method for judging methods of stochastic independence. Further comments on the current controversey. *Journal of Experimental Psychology: Learning, Memory, and Cognition*, **18**, 413–20.

Ostergaard, A. (1995) Who is mistaken about priming in 'recognition/identification' experiments? A reply to Tulving and Hayman. *European Journal of Cognitive Psychology*, **7**, 1–12.

Parkin, A. J. (1982). Residual learning capability in organic amnesia. *Cortex*, **18**, 417–10.

Parkin, A. J. The central executive does not exist. *Journal of the International Neuropsychological Society*. (In press.)

Poldrack, R. A. (1996) On testing for stochastic dissociations. *Psychonomic Bulletin and Review*, **4**, 434–448.

Schacter D. L. and Tulving, E. (1982). Amnesia and memory research. In *Human memory and amnesia* (ed. L. S. Cermale). Lawrence Erlbaum, Hilldale, NJ.

Schacter, D. L. and Tulving, E. (1994). What are the memory systems of 1994? In *Memory systems 1994*, (ed. D. L. Schacter and E. Tulving), pp.1–38. MIT Press, Cambridge, MA.

Schacter, D. L., Bowers, J., and Booker, J. (1989). Intention, awareness and implicit memory: the retrieval intentionality criteria. In *Implicit Memory*, (ed. S. Lewandowsky, J. C. Dunn, and K. Kirstner), pp.47–65. Erlbaum, Hillsdale, NJ.

Schacter, D. L., Reiman, E., Curran, T., Yun, L. S., Bandy, D., McDermott, K. B., and Roediger, H. L. (1996). Neuroanatomical correlates of veridical and illusory recognition memory: evidence from positron emission tomography. *Neuron*, **17**, 267–74.

Sherry, D. F. and Schacter, D. L. (1987). The evolution of multiple memory systems. *Psychological Review*, **94**, 439–54.

Tulving, E. and Hayman, C. A. G. (1993). Stochastic independence in the recognition/identification paradigm. *European Journal of Cognitive Psychology*, **5**, 353–73.

Tulving, E., Schacter, D. L., and Starke, H. (1982). Priming effects in word-fragment completion are independent of recognition memory. *Journal of Experimental Psychology: Learning, Memory, and Cognition*, **8**, 336–42.

Vaidya, C. J., Gabrieli, J. D. E., Keane, M. M., and Monti, L. A. (1995). Perceptual and conceptual memory processes in global amnesia. *Neuropsychology*, **9**, 580–91.

Verfaellie, M. and Roth, H. L. (1995). Knowledge of English vocabulary in amnesia: an examination of premorbidly acquired semantic memory. *Journal of the International Neuropsychological Society*, **1**, 443–53

Wiggs, C. L., Weisberg, J., Garber, S., and Martin, A. (1996). Brain regions associated with semantic and episodic memory. *Neuroimage*, **3**, 568.

Index

acquisition sentences 262–3
act psychologists 32
action, artificial separation of 242–5
activation and disruption techniques, combining 104–25
active retrieval search, and long-term memory 146, 149
Adams, L. T. 261–2
algorithmic
　level 132–3, 168
　processes, and working memory 143
Alzheimer's disease 219–21
　basal ganglia 87–8
　lesions 109
amnesia 131–2, 206–11, 213–14, 238, 280
　basal ganglia 88
　and conceptual processing capabilities 214–17
　and episodic memory 21, 24–5
　global 215
　implicit memory 21
　lesions 109
　and long-term memory 3, 4, 151, 152, 154–6
　and perceptual processing capabilities 217–19
　retrograde 79, 82
　thalamus 79
amygdala 72–7, 93
　aggressive, defensive, and fearful behaviour 73
　amygdalectomy 73
　auditory system 75
　behavioural abnormalities 72–3
　conditioned fear response 74–6
　emotional responses 73–5
　face recognition 74
　hippocampus 76
　second-order conditioning 77
　Urbach–Wiethe disease 74
　violent tendencies 73
anterolateral lesions, long-term memory 150
Ardila, R., multiple memory systems 17
associations, storage of 153
associative learning 241
auditory
　recognition paradigm
　　PET 117–19

　system, and the amygdala 75
　verbal memory 142
　　brain imaging *187*
Bartlett, F.
　history of memory research 2
　processing theorists 42
basal ganglia 86–92
　Alzheimer's disease 87–8
　amnesia 88
　caudate nucleus 86, 87
　　lesions 90
　conditional associative learning 92
　dopaminergic neurotransmitter system 87
　frontal lobe tests 87
　Huntington's disease 87–9
　lesions 89
　　caudate nucleus 90, 91, 94
　　fornix 91
　Morris water maze 90–1
　Parkinson's disease 86–9
　radial arm maze 90, 91
　stimulus-response learning 90–2, 94
　striatal damage 89
　Tower of Hanoi 87
　Wisconsin card sorting test 87
B-cell memory 41
Bechara, A., amygdala 77
behavioural abnormalities, and the amygdala 72–3
biology of memory 39–41
　B-cell memory 41
　episodic and semantic 39
　female reproductive system 41
　　labour 41
　immune system 40–1
　immunologists 40
　long-term potentiation 40
　neurobiologists 40
　priming 40–1
　T-cell memory 41
Blaxton, T. A. 214, 283–4
　memory systems and memory processes 47–8
　processing theorists 7
blood oxygen level dependent echoplanar imaging technique 120

box and arrow model 166–9, 173
  information processing model *166*
brain 249, 253, 252
brain imaging 25–6, 185–92
  activation levels 188–9
  areas of auditory–verbal long-term memory *187*
  blood oxygenation level-dependent 185
  category cued recall 185
  cerebral blood flow 25
  control task 185–6
  critical system properties 191
  electroencephalography 185, 190
  episodic memory 185–6
  event related potentials 186
  face identification task 187
  functional magnetic resonance imaging 185, 190, 192
  hemispheric encoding/retrieval asymmetry 25
  hot spot approach 183–4
  measurement of metabolic activity 190
  neurons, functional role of 190–1
  paired image subtraction 185, 191
  positron emission tomography 26, 185, 190
  regional cerebral blood flow 185, 188, 191
  semantic and episodic retrieval 25–6
  spatial and temporal resolution 189–90
  structural equation modelling 191–2
  subtractive logic 185–6
  weak distributed activity 191
Brown–Peterson test, thalamus 78
Buckner, R., processing theorists 7
Bucy, P. C., amygdala 72–3
Bunge, M., multiple memory systems 17

Cabeza, R. 250
caudate nucleus 86, 87
  lesions 90
cerebellar lesions
  cognition 175
  long-term memory 156
cerebral blood flow, brain imaging 25
Chiras, D. D., biology of memory 40–1
classification problem 246
cognition vs properties of the brain, models of 166–7
cognitive
  activities 261
  dissociations 163
  domain specificity 170
  impenetrability 170
  information encapsulation 170
  neural hard-wiring 170
  and neurocognitive approaches to studying memory 12–15, *13*
    embeddedness and complementarity 14–15

neuroscience approach 163
psychologists, and long-term memory 4
psychology 165, 166–8
system 169, 170
tasks, process purity of 175–6
  cerebellar lesions 175
  dissociations 175
Cohen, N. J., memory systems research, history of 207
complex
  fact memory 147
  interactions, localization of 181–2
component processes
  vs systems 273–86
computational level 168
conceptual
  memory tasks
    PET 119
  and perceptual distinctions 219–21
  priming 219–20, 214–15
  processes 221–2
    and amnesia 214–17
    mapping 104–25
    neural basis of 123–4
  representation system 219–21
  retrieval
    PET 116–17
  tests 58
    implicit 259–60
  see also perceptual
conditional associative learning, basal ganglia 92
conditioned fear response, amygdala 74–6
consciousness 236
context specificity 260
converging
  measures, importance of 106–8
  operations, localization of 181–2
Craik, F. I. M. 256
cued recall test 50, 210
  brain imaging 185
  long-term memory 146
  perceptual 218

damaged brain, study of 180–4
declarative knowledge 34, 58, 131, 140–5, 207, 209–10, 220, 222, 233, 236, 241, 243, 265
  long-term memory 156
defensive behaviour 73
Dennett, D. C. 244
Descartes
  defining 168, 170–2
  history of memory research 2
  memory systems 165
Dewey 261
disruption
  and activation techniques, combining 104–25
  paradigms 108–15

dissected mind 194–6
dissociations 136, 218–19, 222, 238–41, 280
    cognition 175
dopaminergic neurotransmitter system, basal ganglia 87
dorsomedial thalamus 93
double dissociation 259–60
    long-term memory 154
dual memory theories, and the hippocampus 68

Ebbinghaus, H.
    cognitive and neurocognitive approaches to studying 12–15
    history of memory research 2
electrical cortical stimulation 107, 112–15
    epilepsy 115
    intracarotid sodium amobarbitol testing 112
    intractable partial seizures 112
    language mapping 113
    limitations of 115
    priming 113
    semantic cued recall 113–15
electrical stimulation mapping *184*
electroencephalography 185, 190
emotional responses, amygdala 73–5
encoding
    encoding deficit hypotheses, thalamus 79
    and retrieval processes 139
    specificity 254–5
epilepsy
    electrical cortical stimulation 115
    lesions 108
    repetitive transcranial magnetic stimulation 110
episodic memory 20, 24–5, 33–4, 39, 47–8, 140, 193, 207, 232, 233, 236, 241, 242–3, 249, 262, 275, 278–9, 280
    amnesia 21, 24–5
    biology of 39
    brain imaging 185–6
    imaging 25–6
    vs implicit 21–2
    and long-term memory 146
    retrieval 57, 134
        and semantic retrieval 25–6
    tests 45
Ergis, A.-M., systems theorists 5–6
event related potentials, brain imaging 186
evolved brain, consideration of 192–4
explicit memory 208, 210, 214, 244, 275
    conceptual 111
    long-term memory 147, 148, 149
    repetitive transcranial magnetic stimulation 111
    test 53
eyeblink conditioning 209

face recognition 117

amygdala 74
    brain imaging 187
fact-based sentences 262–3
factlearning, long-term memory 152
familiarity 218–19
fearful behaviour 73
female reproductive system 41
    labour 41
Fodor, J. A., memory systems 170–1
forgetting curves 143
fornix lesions, long-term memory 153
free recall 50
    long-term memory 146
frontal lobe tests, basal ganglia 87
function
    impaired 182–3
    localization of 181–2
    recovery of 182–3
functional
    and structural approaches 31–3
        act psychologists 32
        Gestalt psychologists 32
    brain mapping *107*
    disassociation 136
        of brain regions in learning and memory 66–94
        and the process-pure problem 238–41
    incompatibility 38–9, 135, 193, 278–9
        writing systems 38–9
    independence 35–6
functional magnetic resonance imaging (fMRI) 54, 107, 120–3, 185, 190, 192, 205
    blood oxygen level dependent echoplanar imaging technique 120
    conceptual and perceptual conditions 120
    definition of 120
    haemoglobin 120
    limitations of 121–2, 122–3
        head coil designs 212
        peak detection approach 122
        statistics 122
    long-term memory 146, 155
    semantic repetition effects 120
    visually based perceptual memory tasks 121
functionalist approach 153–64, 256, 260

Gabrieli, J. D. E. 275, 276, 284
    systems theorists 6–7
general knowledge 216–17, *217*
Gestalt psychologists 32
Glisky, E. L. 239
graphemic cued recall 48, 248

habit memory 140
haemoglobin, functional magnetic resonance imaging 120
Hayman, C. A. G. 259
    stochastic independence 37

hemispheric
  damage, to the right 70
  encoding/retrieval asymmetry model 25, 57
hierarchical model of the brain function 166–7
hierarchy of memory systems 131
hippocampus 67–72, 81, 93, 133, 138, 175, 193
  amygdala 76
  circuitry 197
  dual memory theories 68
  lesions 71, 84–5, 181
    perirhinal 71
  locale system 68
  long-term memory 150–3, 155–6
  medial temporal lobe amnesic syndrome 68–71
  paired associate learning 67
  retrograde amnesia 70
  right hemisphere damage 70
  spatial memory 69–70
  taxon system 68
  visually guided complex maze learning 67
Hirsh, R., hippocampus 68–9
history of 1–2
  Bartlett, Frederick 2
  Descartes 2
  Ebbinghaus, Hermann 2
  Lashley, Karl 2
  Plato 1
hot spot approach 183–5
  brain topography 183–4
  electrical stimulation mapping *184*
  language 183
  localized functions 184
Hunt, R. R. 275, 277, 278–9, 281–2, 283
  processing theorists 8–9
Huntington's disease 212
  basal ganglia 87–9

image memory 198
immune system 40–1
implementational level 132–3, 168
implicit memory 154, 193, 197, 208–10, 213–14, 244, 258, 275
  amnesia 21
  conceptual 111
  vs episodic memory 21–2
  long-term memory 154, 156
  repetitive transcranial magnetic stimulation 111
  tasks 283
  test 53
integrated imagery instruction 51
intent 236
intentional remembering 195
interactive imagery 51
intracarotid sodium amobarbitol testing 112
introspection 247

ISIM, long-term memory 147, 148, 149, 155, 156
isolated imagery instruction 51
item memory 239–40
item context associations, long-term memory 149, 154

Jacobsen, R., prefrontal cortex 82
Jennings, J. M. 250–1
Johnson, M. K. 186

Kinsbourne, M., memory systems research, history of 207
Kluver, H., amygdala 72–3
Kolers, P., processing theorists 43
Korsakoff's syndrome, thalamus 78–9

language
  hot spot approach 183
  mapping, and electrical cortical stimulation 113
Lashley, K.
  history of memory research 2
  learning and memory 66–7, 68
  structural and functional approaches 32
learning 253
  functional disassociation 66–94
  habituation 245
  and lesions 66
  lower forms of 245–6
  perceptual priming 245
  sensitization 245
  simple associative learning 245
left temporal lesions 108–9
lesion
  Alzheimer's disease 109
  amnesia 109
  anterolateral 150
  basal ganglia 89
  behavioural studies 108–10
  caudate nucleus 90, 91, 94
  cerebellar 156
  conceptual transfer 109
  data interpretation 181, 251
  epilepsy 108
  fornix 91, 153
  hippocampal 71, 150, 155–6, 181
  and learning and memory 66
  left temporal 108–9
  limitations of research in 110
  long-term memory 150
  medial temporal lobe 156
  occipital 109–10
  perirhinal 71
  right temporal 109
  thalamus 81
lexical decision task 34
locale system 68

localization
  of function, converging operations and complex interactions 181–2
  of systems, ability to 177
Logan, G. D. 261
logic, subtractive 182
long-term memory 33, 236
  active retrieval search 146, 149
  amnesia 3, 4, 151, 152, 154–6
  associations, storage of 153
  attribution 146, 149
  auditory verbal 142
  aware memories 156
  cognitive psychologists 4
  component processes of 145–9
  cued recall 146
  declarative and non-declarative memory 156
  double dissociations 154
  enhanced fluency 145–6, 149
  and episodic memory 146
  explicit memory 147, 148, 149
    and implicit memory 154, 156
  fact learning 152
  free recall 146
  functional magnetic resonance imaging 146, 155
  hippocampus 151, 155
    system damage 152–3
  implications of the framework 149–57
  ISIM 147, 148, 149, 155, 156
  item–context associations 149, 154
  item recognition 152–3
  lesions 150
    anterolateral 150
    cerebellar 156
    fornix 153
    hippocampal 150, 155–6
    medial temporal lobe 156
  memory representations 145
  perirhinal cortex 152–3
  prefrontal association cortex 150
  recall 154
  recognition 154
    tests 154
  recollection and complex fact memory 147
  redundancy view 147
  semantic
    dementia 151
    episodic memory 146
    judgements 146
    memory 149–57
  and short-term memory, difference between 140–5
  stochastic independence 36
  subliminal priming 149
  systems-orientated neuropsychologists 4
  systems vs processes 3–4

thalamus 78, 80
unaware memories 156
long-term potentiation 40, 138, 198

macroscopic level, storage at 138–9
mapping 284
  across levels of description 172–5
  conceptual processes 104–25
  memory systems 196–7
  of visual areas and their connectivity 49
Marr, D. 168, 172
Mayes, A. R. 276–7, 279, 283
  systems theorists 6
maze learning
  Olton's radial arm maze 69
  visually guided complex maze learning 67
McDermott, K., processing theorists 7
McDonald, R. J.
  amygdala 76–7
  systems theorists 5–6
medial temporal lobe
  lesions, right 218
  long-term memory lesions 156
medial temporal lobe amnesic syndrome 68–71
Melton, A., unitary memory systems 16
memory
  as an activity 256–7
  artificial separation of 242–5
  biology of 39–41
  cognitive and neurocognitive approaches to studying 12–15
  and conceptual processes, mapping 104–25
  connections with other processes 195
  context specific 258
  interaction between person and retrieval environment 258
  is not stored 257
  neofunctional alternative to 254–6
  and other aspects of cognition 261–3
  problems and the prefrontal cortex 82–3
  task demands and goals 260
  traces 281
  see also declarative, episodic, explicit, implicit, non-declaritive, procedural, processes, semantic, systems
Mesulam's model 173, *174*
metabolic activity, measurement of 190
mind–body relation 165
mirror tracing 206
models
  box and arrow 166–9
modularity-of-mind hypothesis 243
monohierarchical concept 242
Morris water maze
  basal ganglia 90–1
  thalamus 81
Moscovitch 52–3, 134, 177
  memory systems 171–2

Moscovitch (cont.)
  and processing 58
  word stem completion 57
motor responses 173
motor skills 131
multiple brain sites 173
multiple memory system 11–30, 136–58, 162–200, 205–23, 211–12
  brain/mind system 17
  critical analysis 237–53
  debate 232–66
  declarative memory 212
  Huntington's disease 212
  evidence for 66–94
  identity hypothesis 17
  vs short-term memory 15–22
    memory test 18–19
    remembered events and acquired knowledge 17–20
  structuralism in 235–6
multiplexity 167–8

Nadel, L. 244
  hippocampus 68–9
necessity vs sufficiency 176
Neisser, processing theorists 42
neural
  activity 250
  basis of conceptual and perceptual processing 123–4, *124*
  connectivity 192
  hard-wiring, cognition 170
  mechanism 249, 253
  networks
    integrated properties of 198
    and working memory 141
  pathways 37–8
  substrates, differing 276–8
  systems 134
neurobiologists 40
neurocognitive approaches to studying memory 12–15, *13*
  embeddedness and complementarity 14–15
neuroimaging 277
neurological model of the brain 167
neurons 137–8
  functional role of 190–1
    excitatory and inhibitory 190
  neurotransmitter 190
neuropsychological dissociations 136
  double 142
neurotransmitter 190
non-associative memory 140
non-declarative memory 34, 140–5, 156, 222, 242
  long-term memory 156
  tests 58
non-verbal memory 140

occipital lesions 109–10
  right 220
O'Keefe, J., hippocampus 68–9
Olton's radial arm maze 69
ordering tasks, and prefrontal cortex 84

paired associate learning, and the hippocampus 67
paired image subtraction 185, 191
parallel distributed processing 169
Parkin, A. 9
Parkinson's disease, basal ganglia 86–9
partial least squares analysis 192
perception 261
  artificial separation of 242–5
perceptual
  and conceptual distinctions 219–21
  and conceptual memory tasks 119
  and conceptual processes 120, 123–4, 221–2
  memory tasks 119, 197
  priming 218–20
    learning 245
  processing 104, 117
    and amnesia 217–19
  representation system 20, 48, 220, 259
  skills 131
perirhinal cortex 94
  lesions 71
  long-term memory 152–3
picture naming, PET 119
Plato, history of memory research 1
positron emission tomography (PET) 26, 54, 56, 107, 116–20, 185, 190, 197, 205, 252
  auditory recognition paradigm 117–19
  conceptual and perceptual memory tasks 119
  conceptual retrieval 116–17
  definition of 116
  limitations of 119–20
  memory for unfamiliar faces 117
  perceptual processing 117
  picture naming 119
  regional cerebral blood flow 116, 117
  semantic cued recall 118–19
  semantic word association 118–19
prefrontal
  activation 279
  association cortex
    long-term memory 150
prefrontal cortex 82–6, 93
  hippocampal damage 84–5
  memory problems 82–3
  ordering tasks 84
  working-with-memory concept 83, 93
premorbid memory, and the thalamus 82
primed perceptual identification 105
priming 40–1, 219–21, 237
  conceptual 219–20
  electrical cortical stimulation 113

perceptual 218–20
working memory 140
problem solving 263
  thalamus 79
procedural memory 131, 207, 233, 236–7, 241, 275
procedural/non-declarative knowledge 243
process-impurity, wider implications of 241–2
process-purity problem 274–5
  and functional dissociations 238–41
process theory 106
processes 1–9
  dissociation procedure 218–19
  encoding and retrieval 139
  and systems 3–4, 11–30, 46–52, 136–58, 212–20, 273–86
    contrast between 136–58
processing
  approach 255
  category cued recall 46
  category instance generation 46
  components of 31–59
  conceptual 44, 104–25
    tests 44–6
  data-driven 44
  dissociations 43
  explicit tests 45
  framework 42, 52
  free recall 46
  implicit tests 45
  perceptual 104
  perceptual tests 44–6
  Santayana 31
  and systems debate 31, 212–20
  theorists 7–9, 42–6
  transfer appropriate processing 43, 45

quasi-memory system 259

radial arm maze
  basal ganglia 90, 91
  thalamus 81
reason 261
  artificial separation of 242–5
recall 199
  long-term memory 154
recognition 199
  familiarity 218–19
  long-term memory 154
  memory 105
  test 50, 105
redundancy view, and long-term memory 147
regional cerebral blood flow 116, 117, 185, 188, 191
repetition priming 208
repetitive transcranial magnetic stimulation 11–12, 107
  epilepsy 110

implicit and explicit conceptual memory 111
limitations of 112
  potential risks 112
  seizures 112
retrieval 208
  and encoding processes 139
  environment factors 282
  episodic memory 57, 134
  and semantic retrieval 25–6
retrograde amnesia, and the hippocampus 70
right hemisphere damage 70
right temporal lesions 109
Roediger, H. L. 35, 275, 278–9, 282
  biology of memory 41
  processing and systems debate 212–13
  processing theorists 7
Ryle, Gilbert 34

Schacter, D. L. 35, 134, 177, 243–4, 248, 252
  the evolved brain 192, 193–4
  functional incompatibility 38–9
  memory systems research, history of 207
  stochastic independence 37
second-order conditioning, and the amygdala 77
seizures 112
  repetitive transcranial magnetic stimulation 112
semantic cued recall 248
  electrical cortical stimulation 113–15
  PET 118–19
semantic dementia 280
  long-term memory 151
semantic memory 20, 21, 33–4, 39, 47–8, 140, 193, 207, 236, 239, 240, 242–3, 249, 250–1, 262, 275, 278–9
  biology of 39
  category specific functional architecture *169*
  and episodic memory 25–6
  long-term memory 146, 149–57
semantic repetition effects, fMRA 120
semantic word association 118–19
Semon, R. 281–2
sensation 261
separate memory systems 136–58
Sherry, D. F. 35, 243–4, 248
  the evolved brain 192
  functional incompatibility 38–9
short-term forgetting 143
short-term memory 11–30, 33, 140–5
  history of 2
  and long-term memory, difference between 140–5
  vs multiple memory system 15–22
    remembered events and acquired knowledge 17–20
    test 18–19
  phonological 141, 142, 144

short-term memory (*cont.*)
  stochastic independence 36
  thalamus 78
  visuospatial 141
simple associative learning 245
simple classical conditioning, and working memory 140
single
  dissociations, and working memory 144
  semantic task 250
skill and habit memory 140
source memory 239–40
spatial
  attention 173
  memory and the hippocampus 69–70
  and temporal resolution 189–90
Squire, L. R. 177
  declarative memory 34
  memory systems research, history of 207
  priming 237
  working memory 140
stem cued recall 56–7, 282
stimulus–response theories 66–7, 68
  basal ganglia 90–2, 94
stochastic independence 23–4, 36–7, 135, 278, 279
  memory test 23–4, 36
  short- and long-term memory 36
storage places 257
striatal damage, and basal ganglia 89
structural and functional approaches 31–3
  act psychologists 32
  Gestalt psychologists 32
  structure/processing debate 32
structural description system 48
structural equation modelling, and brain imaging 191–2
structural psychologists 31–2
structuralism 234
  and multiple systems theory 235–6
structure/processing debate 32
study-phase responses 216
subliminal priming, and long-term memory 149
subtractive logic and task performance 182
sufficiency vs necessity 176
synapses
  changes in 137–8
  plasticity 139
systems 33–9, 53
  alternatives to 281–5
  amnesia 206–11
  characterizing 163–80
    demarcation and localization of *164–5*
  vs component processes 273–86
  critiques of 274–9
    functional independence 274–6
  cued retrieval tasks 210
  declarative knowledge 209–10

  definitions of *170–1*
  dichotomies of 207–10
  dissociations 222
  eyeblink conditioning 209
  future 221–3
    perceptual and conceptual processes 221–2
  history of 206–12
  mirror tracing 206
  models of *178–9*
  logic 275
  long-term memory
    amnesia 4
    cognitive psychologists 4
  perceptual representation system 20
  and processes, debate on 3–4, 11–30, 46–52, 136–58, 212–20
    cued recall tests 50
    free recall 50
    graphemic cued recall 48
    interactive imagery 51
    long-term memory 3–4
    map of visual areas and their connectivity *49*
    neuropsychologists 50
    perceptual representation system 48
    recognition tests 50
    structural description system 48
    testing systems 50
    word fragment completion 47–8
    word frequency 51
    word stem 47–8
  repetition priming 208
  retrieval processes 208
  search for 162–200
  single-deficit interpretation 210
  theorists 5–7
  working 20
systems-orientated neuropsychologists 4

tachistoscopic presentations 34
task performance 247
  and subtractive logic 182
task selection, bias in 194
taxon system 68
T-cell memory 41
thalamus 78–82
  amnesia 79
    retrograde 79, 82
  Brown–Peterson test 78
  encoding deficit hypotheses 79
  hippocampus 81
  Korsakoff's syndrome 78–9
  lesions 81
  long-term memory 78
    test of 80
  Morris water maze 81
  premorbid memory 82
  problem-solving abilities 79

radial arm maze 81
  short-term memory 78
Titchener, E. B. 247
  structuralism 235
Toth, J. P. 275, 277, 278–9, 281–2, 283
  processing theorists 8–9
Tower of Hanoi, and basal ganglia 87
transfer appropriate processing 43, 254–5
Tulving, E. 134, 177, 242–3, 246, 259, 279–81
  episodic and semantic memory 34
  the evolved brain 192, 193–4
  memory systems
    history of 207
    and memory processes 47–8, 50
  multiple memory systems 17
  stochastic independence 36, 37
  systems theorists 5

unitery systems 162–200
Urbach Wiethe disease
  amygdala 74

verbal and non-verbal memory 140
violent tendencies, and the amygdala 73
visual perception 198
  fMRA 121

Wechsler Adult Intelligence Scale 215
Wechsler Memory Scale 215
Weldon, M. S. 275, 277, 278–9, 283
  processing theorists 8
White, N. M., amygdala 76–7
Wickelgren, W. A., forgetting curves 143
Winocur, G., systems theorists 5–6
Wisconsin card sorting test, and basal ganglia 87

word fragment completion 47–8, 135
word frequency 51
word recognition 258–9
word retrieval 34
word stem 47–8
  completion task 53–8, 197
    cued recall 56–7
    variants of 55
working memory 20, 140–5
  algorithmic processes 143
  declarative and non-declarative memory 140–5
  episodic memory 140
  forgetting curves 143
  long-term memory
    auditory verbal 142
    and short-term memory, difference between 140–5
  neural networks 141
  neuropsychological double dissociations 142
  non-associative memory 140
  priming 140
  semantic memory 140
  short-term forgetting 143
  short-term memory 140–5
    phonological 141, 142, 144
    visuospatial 141
  simple classical conditioning 140
  single dissociations 144
  skill and habit memory 140
  verbal and non-verbal memory 140
working-with-memory concept, prefrontal cortex 83, 93
writing systems, and functional incompatibility 38–9